# WILLIAM RONAN, S.J.
# 1825 - 1907

### War Chaplain, Missioner,
### Founder of Mungret College

By

Thomas J. Morrissey S.J.

**WILLIAM RONAN, S.J.**
**1825 - 1907**

# CONTENTS

# Preface

William Ronan was not a major public figure, yet he played a not unimportant role in Ireland of his time, and his influence across the English-speaking world was greater than that of most people. His life is of interest for a number of reasons. He was chaplain to the Irish Sisters of Mercy in the grim hospitals of the Crimea during the first war vividly reported by war correspondents, and his account of the person and work of Florence Nightingale in the hospitals differs from the almost saintly image painted by her supporters. Subsequently, Ronan became one of the best-known missioners and retreat directors in Ireland, and this part of his life reflects aspects of the celebrated Irish devotional revolution/evolution, which became marked from the 1850s. During his years as a preacher in different parts of the country, he came across many young men who would have wished to become priests but lacked education and funds. This led him to contact bishops in America, Australia, South Africa, even India, all of whom were short of priests, that they might sponsor the education of suitable candidates who would then go on to serve in their dioceses. The result was the establishment of Mungret College Apostolic School, whence hundreds of young men went forth to serve in the English-speaking world overseas and, in the process, contributed greatly to the respective countries both spiritually and materially. Ronan returned to the college he founded in his final years, and died there alert to the end.

This work has been in progress, on and off, over many years. In that time I owe a great deal to the support and assistance of successive religious superiors and colleagues. I would wish to link my thanks to them to my appreciation of the assistance received from the gracious archivists at Farm Street and Southwark, in London, and from David Sheehy of the Dublin Diocesan Archives. In a special way I wish to thank Sr. M. Patrick Quinlan, archivist at the historic convent of the Srs. of Mercy, Kinsale, for her most generous assistance, and her on-going interest in this book.

Once again, I am indebted to Fr. Brendan Woods of the Miltown Park Library for his backing and practical support, and to my generous readers and advisers, Professor V. A. McClelland and Dr. Fergus O'Donoghue, S.J., who are not responsible for any deficiencies remaining in the text. In conclusion, a word of special appreciation to Alan McGuckian, S.J. and the staff of Messenger Publications for their keen interest and efficient publication.

Thomas J. Morrissey, S.J.

# Chapter 1

# *From Newry to Maynooth:*
# *The Early Years, 1825-1848*

Even at the time of his ordination no one could have expected that William Ronan would before long be involved in an international war, and thereafter become known throughout Ireland as a spiritual guide and missioner and be destined to influence the development of the Catholic Church across the English-speaking world. The little that is known of his early life suggests nothing out of the ordinary.

### What is known is easily summarised

William Ronan was born in the town land of Kinghill, Cabra, in the parish of Clonduff, not far from the town of Newry, Co. Down, on 13 July 1825. His father, Patrick, had married a girl whose family name was Rooney, from the town land of Goward,[1] but her Christian name is now not known. Of the children of the marriage all that is recorded is that William had a brother, whose son, also called William, became in his turn a priest of the Dromore diocese, and was present at his uncle's funeral at Mungret College, Limerick, in December 1907.[2]

The parish of Clonduff, which is situated in the barony of Upper Iveagh, County Down, comprises a portion of mountain and bog, and a larger area of good arable and pasture land, through which the river Bann flows.[3] The Catholic population in the 1830s were largely cottiers and labourers very much dependent on their landlord. The main landlord in the area was the marquis of Downshire, who was noted for his hostility to the Catholic Church.[4] The Ronans, however, lived in a part of the parish owned by 'a fervent Catholic', Alexander Mac Mullen of Castlewellan.[5] They appear to have been farmers and comfortably off to judge from the fact that when William went to St. Coleman's diocesan college at Violet Hill in Newry his fees were paid in advance.[6]

The diocesan college provided an intermediate education for boys, but had primarily in mind preparing young men for the priesthood by providing a grounding in Latin and Greek. It seems fair to assume that Ronan went to the college with a view to the priesthood. It represented a position of status which would be welcome to his family, but what precisely influenced Ronan himself is not clear. He was frequently in later life described as a pious and zealous priest and this suggests that his decision was mainly motivated by zeal, influenced perhaps by the faith of his parents, or by the parish priest, John McLeigh, a former teacher at the college, who was a Greek scholar, had a well stocked library, and was 'popular among all classes',[7] or, again, by the very fact that the diocese of Dromore, under its ascetic, reforming bishop, Michael Blake, was noted for high standards among its clergy and for the active involvement of the laity in confraternities and in teaching catechism,[8] or by an amalgam of some or all of these.

Of Ronan's two years at the college, however, nothing has been recorded. His time there coincided with increased tension in the local community. Daniel O'Connell had commenced his campaign to repeal the Act of Union and this gave rise to angry displays of opposition by the unionist population. In January 1841, as William started at Violet Hill school, large crowds gathered in the district of Dromore and Hillsborough and burned O'Connell in effigy.[9] Again, there is no information how such demonstrations affected William and his family, or the school, or, indeed, the bishop, who was a strong supporter of O'Connell. All that is recorded is that on 1 February 1843, having graduated from St. Coleman's college, Newry, he entered the Humanities class in Maynooth College to study for the priesthood.

### The Years at Maynooth

Being a zealous Catholic priest in the first half of the nineteenth century was a daunting task. There was a 51% increase in the Catholic population between 1800 and 1840, from 4,320,000 to 6,540,000, which meant a large increase in the number of parishioners to each priest.[10] In Ronan's small diocese of Dromore, there had been a 62% increase in the number of priests between 1800 and 1840, from twenty-one to thirty-four priests, yet in 1840 there were 2,934 parishioners per priest. As the growth in the parishioners occurred mainly among the poor, the livelihood of the priest was likely to be precarious in many areas, and family support was necessary. This, in addition to the cost, for example, of a Maynooth training, meant that Ronan's fellow students were in the main the sons of comfortable farmers, or of businessmen, shopkeepers, or well-to-do trades men in the cities and towns.[11]

Ronan's years at Maynooth, 1843 to 1848, covered a period of historic and tragic significance for the country, a period when O'Connell's repeal movement rose to a crescendo and then faded, and when large sections of the country were ravaged by the Great Famine. Yet no record remains of Ronan's personal impressions or of his yearly performance at college. All the biographer can do is place him in the physical and academic setting that was meant to form him and relate it to some of the major external events likely to impinge on the life of the institution.

The physical conditions, even for the time, were spartan. The college was lit by oil lamps and flickering candles, and there was no heat in the students' rooms,[12] which was not unusual, but the recently arrived Lord Lieutenant, Lord Clarendon, following a visit to the college in 1847, also observed that 'the single-bedded rooms' were 'not much larger than those in Pentonville prison', while the rooms with three or four beds in them were 'wretched, comfortless, and ill-ventilated, such as no one in England would ask a servant to sleep in for a night.'[13]

The round of student life, too, made no concession to comfort and relaxation. Little had changed from the early days of the college. 'From six o'clock in the morning (five o'clock after Easter) to ten at night the days were spent in a round of duties, interspersed with brief periods of recreation, everything regulated by the bell.'[14] Most students, nevertheless, coped with the system. Statistics supplied by the college president, Laurence Renehan, for the decade 1844-53, indicated that of the 920 students who entered the college some 701, or 76.2 per cent, were ordained.[15]

The formation provided during Ronan's time at Maynooth was focused on intellectual and spiritual training. Little seems to have been provided of a social or a cultural character, apart from the informal schooling acquired by living under a disciplined regime in a very large community. For entry to the college some competence in Latin, and to a lesser extent in Greek, was required. There was no entrance examination, however, in English grammar or composition, and such examination as existed for History was nominal.[16] While at Maynooth, students were required to attend lectures in such subjects as French, ecclesiastical History, ancient and modern History, Logic or Rational Philosophy, and experimental Physics - or Natural Philosophy, and Algebra and Geometry. The Irish language was available, especially for students from Irish-speaking dioceses. Core subjects, however, were Moral and Dogmatic Theology. The emphasis on these resulted in Scripture Studies receiving relatively little attention, while such practical requirements as preparation for preaching, and training in catechetics were deficient or non-existent.[17] Criticisms of the studies programmes spoke of too many students, too few staff, and too many subjects in the time available.[18]

The student body was composed of mainly young men of eighteen or nineteen years, destined to be ordained at twenty-four or twenty-five years of age. Their spiritual formation was entrusted to the college deans. In the first few years, the senior dean regularly addressed his charges on Wednesday and Saturday mornings, and on the greater festivals, on 'how to make mental prayer and how to observe the rule'. Instruction for the more senior students was more intermittent. Morning and night prayer were prescribed by rule; the rosary was recited publicly during Lent, and at other times usually in private. Students went to confession once a fortnight. They chose their confessor at the beginning of the year, but were free to change him. The Saturday evenings, 6.0 p.m. - 8.0 p.m., were set aside for confessions. Communion, as a general practice, was received weekly, but many did so twice a week on the advice of their confessor.[19] There was also an annual retreat for all. Little appears to have been done to introduce the students to a deeper contemplative prayer which would nourish their busy lives as curates and enable them to guide others in prayer.

During Ronan's later years at Maynooth, news of the failure of the potato crop, and of the subsequent harrowing scenes as people starved to death or died from famine fever, necessarily impinged on the body of students. They, and their professors, were removed from the terrible scenes, but news from the different distressed areas were relayed by some of the many priests who had been educated at Maynooth. Indeed by April 1846, Ronan was likely to have heard that his own bishop and the priests of the cathedral feared that some five hundred people, in the relatively favoured area of Newry and its surroundings, could no longer survive without relief, and that Bishop Blake had announced at a public meeting that there had already been one death from starvation.[20] Many of the professors at Maynooth responded to the multiple cries with 'large alms, both publicly and privately, to relieve the distress'.[21] By 22 August 1846, the impact of the failure of the potato crop in certain regions throughout the country was reflected in three columns in *The Nation* news-paper, and by 9th September there was a public letter from William Smith O'Brien addressed to the prime minister, Lord John Russell, which called attention to the seriousness of the problem and questioned the government's grasp and its readiness to cope with it. 'Never more than at the present moment', he exclaimed, 'has Ireland had reason to deplore the loss of its legislature ...'[22]

The reference to 'its legislature' indicated how alive the longing for repeal remained. The *Nation* at this stage, indeed, devoted far more space to repeal than the reports of the famine. The embodiment of the repeal longing came personally to Maynooth during Ronan's penultimate year. On 12 January 1847, a weak and faltering O'Connell visited the college. Some of the professorial staff were less than enthusiastic about the visit. They had come to view O'Connell with the critical eyes of the Young Ireland leaders.[23] The students, however, provided a resounding welcome. O'Connell addressed the senior and the junior students, and then all together, on which occasion some seniors delivered addresses of thanks for all his work and expressed their love of him and confidence in him.[24] His death four months later came as an immense shock. It was only with his passing, and the responses it provoked in Europe, Britain, and North America, that the extent of his achievements and his international stature were fully appreciated. Even the hostile *Morning Chronicle* acknowledged that:

Mr. O'Connell supplied the place of a government in Ireland. The confidence which the law and institutions of the country never called forth was given him and his various societies. He was, in fact, *the first in modern times who ruled the people with their own consent.*[25]

Although Ronan left no record of his political views, it may be assumed that he, like the general body of students, took pride in O'Connell's past achievements, especially as his bishop had been a close friend of the Liberator and had hosted one of his public meetings in the grounds of the cathedral in October 1834.[26]

Meantime, as a further part of the *mise en scène* to Ronan's concluding period in Maynooth, the Irish newspapers continued to carry news from different counties, north and south and west, of fever, hunger, helpless destitution, and death, and also of the flight from Ireland of thousands of its young people.

In 1848 William Ronan was ordained to the diaconate at Maynooth. He was due to be ordained at the college in June 1849,[27] but he was called home by his bishop, Michael Blake, before the completion of his course, and he was ordained to the priesthood in Newry, Co. Down, on 27 July 1848.[28]

# Chapter 2

# *First Years as Priest and Jesuit, 1848-1854*
# *Participating in the Devotional Revival*

Following ordination, William Ronan served as a curate in the bishop's parish in Newry, 1848 - 1849, and from there moved to the parish of Clanallen, which has Warrenpoint as the nearest post town, where he was curate from 1849 to 1850.[1]

At this period the diocese had but seventeen parishes and some forty priests,[2] but the state of religion was 'flourishing', in the estimation of the *Catholic Directory* for 1846, and it added that 'several elegant churches' were 'built during the present administration'.[3]

Within two years of ordination, nevertheless, Ronan decided to turn from the life of a diocesan priest to that of a member of a religious order. He applied to the Society of Jesus, and was accepted. Again, there is no record of the reason for his change, or why he chose the Jesuits rather than some other religious order or congregation. The decision to enter a religious body is often linked to a desire to live a more structured life, with more time for prayer, and with a detachment from material goods reflected in a vow of poverty, in addition to the promises of celibacy and obedience made by secular priests. The emphasis in his subsequent career on retreat and mission work, joined to much activity and achievement, suggests that the Jesuits' accent on both contemplation and external action may have had a special appeal. In addition, his future life would also provide evidence of two contrasting features: that he could be strongly self-willed and stubborn, and that he deeply valued the virtue of obedience. The Jesuit stress on obedience may have had, as a result, a particular appeal for him. His choice, moreover, may have been influenced by his years in Maynooth, where the memory of a former Jesuit vice-president, Peter Kenney, was held in reverence. Kenney's spiritual notes still circulated among professors and may have made their way to individual students.[4] That the order was favourably regarded at the college was further indicated by the entry to the Jesuits of one of Maynooth's most distinguished professors, Edmund O'Reilly, who joined the year after Ronan, and by his being followed three years later by two particularly able students, William Delany, future president of University College Dublin, and Matthew Russell, nephew of Dr. Charles Russell, president of the college. There was the further consideration that Ronan's bishop, Michael Blake, was well disposed to the order. He had been a close friend of Peter Kenney, with whom, together with Archbishop Daniel Murray of Dublin, he had received his early education from the former Jesuit, Fr. Thomas Betagh. Whatever the weight of such factors, William Ronan entered a Jesuit novitiate on 9 November, 1850.[5] He was described at this period in his life as a strong, cheerful, clean shaven young man.[6]

### First Years as a Jesuit

In the absence of a novitiate in Ireland, Ronan commenced his Jesuit noviceship at St. Acheul, on the outskirts of Amiens, in the French Jesuit province of Francia.[7]

At St. Acheul, Ronan may have completed only one year's noviceship, instead of the customary two, because he was already a priest. It is noted that he stayed on to study there, before going on to complete his theological studies, 1852-53,[8] but no further information is provided. He was back in Ireland by the late summer, or early autumn of 1853.

On his return he was appointed to the busy Jesuit church of St. Francis Xavier, Gardiner Street, Dublin. There he participated in the work of the church and also became a member of the Jesuit mission team, which was led by the rector of the Gardiner Street Jesuit community, Fr. Robert Haly. This was one of the pioneering groups engaged in the popular parish missions, which played such an important part in the countrywide religious revival in the years before and the decades after the famine. In various forms these parish missions and retreats were to engage Ronan for much of his life as a priest. He contributed to the religious revival.

## The Expansion of Devotion

There was a vast upsurge of popular devotion during the 1850s under the inspiration of Archbishop Cullen of Dublin, as Professor Emmet Larkin of Chicago University demonstrated as far back as 1972;[9] but well before Cullen there was evidence of a religious renewal in the south and east of Leinster and in the sea port cities of Munster. From the 1830s a major factor in the expanding renewal was the gradual introduction of parish missions in almost every parish in the country. 'These missions' which 'began about the year 1835 or 1836' were, according to Archbishop Cullen, in his evidence before the Royal Commission of Inquiry, Primary Education Ireland (the Powis Commission), in 1869, 'the cause of the greatest improvement in the morals of the country, and consequently of the utmost benefit to society'.[10] In those years the two religious bodies most associated with these missions were the Vincentian Fathers and the Jesuits. Both, indeed, were singled out for recommendation by the bishops at the Synod of Thurles, 1850.[11] Subsequently other religious orders, most notably the Redemptorists, became prominent in the work.

The Jesuits in the 1850s, apart from some missions in the midlands, were largely associated with the parishes of the west, south, and north of Ireland. At that time, under the leadership of Fr. Robert Haly, the Jesuit missioners were particularly prominent in the diocese of Killaloe. Hence, it is not surprising that William Ronan made his acquaintance with mission work in County Clare. The general mode of procedure where the missioners were concerned was largely as follows. The preachers, on the invitation of a parish priest or a bishop, travelled to a parish, remained there for a number of weeks, preaching each evening, offering Mass each morning, and encouraging people to acknowledge their sins, go to confession, and renew their lives. By day, the missioners visited the sick of the parish, in their homes or hospitals, chatted and prayed with them, and called into the schools to explain what the mission was about and to encourage children to pray for the success of the mission, to remind their parents of it, and to encourage them to come themselves to the special children's services.

## On the Mission Team

Ronan's first experience of a popular mission was at Ennis in November 1853. He was the new recruit in the more seasoned team of Haly, John Dwyer, and John Gaffney.[12] That he was chosen indicated that he had already shown himself a competent preacher at Gardiner Street, with a voice capable of filling a church.

*The Munster News* on 22 November, 1853, remarked on the large crowds 'hastening to the chapel even before day break every morning, and up to ten and eleven o'clock at night'. 'A sermon was delivered every morning and every evening by the zealous Divines', the paper's correspondent continued, 'during which even our spacious chapel was thronged to excess, and, among the thousands who assembled, I was happy to see on some occasions, Mr. Henry Keane, and other persons, notorious contributors to the "souper" operations in this town. They may have come to scoff, but if God has pity on them they went home to pray.' The reference to Henry Keane had a double-edged significance. It evoked the name of his brother, Marcus Keane, the harsh unrelenting land agent of the absentee landlord Mr Edward Westby, and the anti-Catholic proselytism associated with the Keanes and their followers.

At Ennis Henry Keane went out of his way to involve the Jesuits and the mission in public controversy. The missioners refused to be drawn. Haly made it clear that they had not come to Ennis 'to enter into controversy with Protestants' but 'to instruct' the members of their own faith 'in their several duties and to render them better Christians and better men'.[13]

A special feature of the missions was a public procession. The first one to be reported in the newspapers was during the Ennis mission.[14] Public processions had been part of the public missions on the continent. In Ireland, however, such public manifestations were prohibited by law. Even the Act of Catholic Emancipation excluded the public exercise of Catholic rites and ceremonies. Because of the law, processions took place within the church grounds,[15] and, as if in defiance of the discriminatory law, large numbers attended.

At Ennis, in keeping with the fervour displayed by the people, the procession was considered 'one of the most impressive ceremonies ever witnessed'. Haly noted that the newspapers estimated that there were up to four thousand people present.[16] There were many young girls and boys, dressed in white, whose singing earned praise from reporters. The parish clergy and the missioners, and many people who attended from the rural parishes, joined in the singing. Four local ladies carried the draped canopy.[17]

In their missions in the 1850s, the missioners concentrated on a three-point plan to meet the needs of a people who had suffered from the twin tragedies of the Penal Laws and the Great Famine, and from a deficiency in instruction because of the poor ratio of priests to the population. They sought: to provide religious instruction, giving special attention to the children; to encourage a return to the sacraments by those who had neglected them; and to form a church-going people by means of sound preaching and devotional practices. With respect to these aims, Haly and the missioners were conscious that the enthusiasm of a mission could be a transitory affair. Hence, Haly at Ennis began a process, which became a frequent occurrence at the end of a Jesuit mission. He convened a meeting to discuss ways and means of preserving the good effects of the previous weeks. Among the results of such endeavour were the formation of confraternities, and sodalities, which were scheduled to meet regularly. At Ennis a significant result was the decision to invite the Irish Christian Brothers and the Sisters of Mercy to found communities in the town. Previously the Brothers had attempted a foundation, but had to leave because of administrative and financial difficulties. A number of foundations of nuns had also been of short duration. Ennis, indeed, was described by the historian of the diocese, Ignatius Murphy, as 'a graveyard of religious communities between 1830 and 1850'.[18] In 1854, however, the Brothers returned, and some time later the Sisters of Mercy took up the invitation. Their foundations were still active almost 150 years later.

As a further means of solidifying the effect of the mission, a mission cross was erected, especially after the first mission in a parish. This was a widespread practice in seventeenth century Europe.[19] It was a constant reminder to the people to be faithful to the resolutions they had made. Haly, or one other of the mission band, usually returned to the parish some months later for what he termed 'a refresher', at which time he would address the people, remind them of their resolutions, and, perhaps, bless the mission cross which served as the permanent memorial of the missioners and their teaching. The cross erected near the side-door of the church at Ennis stands almost eleven feet in height and bears the names of the bishop, the parochial clergy, and the missioners. Among the latter names is that of William Ronan. It marks his first experience of the intense work, emotional involvement, and sense of fulfilment experienced by the preachers in these early days of the domestic mission movement in Ireland. That he fitted in well with the rest of the mission team was indicated by an invitation from Haly to take part in another mission in the diocese of Killaloe. This was six months after the Ennis mission and at Kilrush, Co. Clare.

Once again, four of the team were from the Gardiner Street community, William Fortescue, John Dwyer, Ronan, and Haly. The mission opened on Sunday, 7 May 1854, with the bishop of Killaloe, Daniel Vaughan, present to impart his blessing.[20] The *Munster News* of 17 May praised the quality of the sermons and of the music rendered by 'an excellent and well-trained vocal choir'. Once more the fervour of the people was intense. 'From early dawn to a late hour at night', the paper observed, people 'could be seen thronging the streets and roads in all directions from the surrounding parishes eager to be present ...' They came not just to hear the preachers, but also to 'obtain pardon of their sins in the sacred tribunal of penance'. Despite the 'super human efforts of the Jesuits', *The Munster News* added, and 'the zeal and perseverance' of the diocesan clergy in making themselves available for penitents, 'hundreds were obliged to leave each evening disappointed but hopeful of being more successful the next morning,'[21]

Many Protestants attended the Jesuits' lectures, and the mission, as a result, did not pass without some negative reaction. At the close of the first day of the mission, Haly dedicated the entire parish of Kilrush to the Blessed Virgin. This occasioned adverse criticism from the Evangelical rector, J. F. Robins, who, in a letter to *The Munster News* of 31 May, expressed his concern lest Catholics by turning to Mary would turn away from Christ, and he made it clear that he was utterly opposed to the presence of the Jesuits in Kilrush. He had a collection of handbills printed and distributed, which charged the Catholics with adoration of the Virgin Mary. This evoked replies from correspondents in the *Munster News* but not from the missioners.

At the end of the mission there was the usual elaborate procession to the place where a cross was erected, blessed and incensed. The devotion of the people to these crosses as a sign of the Redemption, and as a reminder of the graces received during the missions, was remarkable, Haly observed. 'Every day in the year they are seen kneeling and praying most fervently before them in spite of rain and storm and mud. No fury of the elements is capable of interfering with their devotion.'[22] It was all a stirring baptism for the still young and relatively inexperienced William Ronan.

As he returned to Dublin, however, one of the vivid impressions which remained with him were the large number of idealistic young men who seemed very suitable for the priesthood but who would never have the opportunity to follow such a calling because they had not the means of pursuing the required seminary education. The thought remained germinal. It was pushed aside for a while, however, by the more immediate demands of the first major war in forty years. The declaration of war against Russia was greeted with enthusiasm in Britain and Ireland, and young men rushed to join up with an almost unseemly haste.[23] Ronan served as chaplain and spiritual adviser to the Sisters of Mercy in the war hospitals by the Bosphorus, where he experienced the stresses and raw horror of the conflict as he sought to bring peace alike to over-stretched nurses and to mainly Irish soldiers dying in great pain. It was an experience that was to leave an indelible impression on him and to age and mature him.

# Chapter 3

# *In the War Hospitals of the Crimea: Florence Nightingale and Religious And National Differences*

Ronan arrived in the war hospitals of Turkey when the conflict was several months old, the fatalities already heavy, the wounded numerous. His time there was to be short but intense. To gain some appreciation of his experiences during that time, it is necessary to view them in the overall context.

The Crimean War between the allied governments of England and France and the emperor of Russia was declared on 27 March 1854. Russia's proposals for the partition of Turkey, and its claims to be protector of Christians within the Ottoman empire, occasioned fresh fears of Russia as a land and sea power in the Mediterranean. Popular opinion in support of the war in Britain and France bordered on hysteria. Quick and glorious victories were expected. Time was to show, particularly on the British side, that the military commanders were elderly and rigid, the war department lethargic and incompetent, effective transport, communications, and general readiness for war largely absent, and medical care for the army deplorably inadequate. This last was to determine Ronan's role.

Shortly after the landing of allied troops in the Crimea in September 1854, the successful battle of Alma was fought. The outcome was greeted with jubilation in Britain. But soon the troops faced the rigours of October and encroaching winter weather without warm clothes and with cholera rampant in their ranks. At the British expeditionary force headquarters at Scutari, a small town on the Asiatic shore of the Bosphorus facing Constantinople, there was constant disruption. The medical headquarters occupied an enormous artillery barracks known as the Barracks Hospital, and a half-mile away there was a further building known as the General Hospital.

The Barracks Hospital was damp and dirty, built over sewers, and had no kitchen to prepare food. Surgical and medical appliances were in short supply, straw sacks on the floor served for beds, and for nurses there were elderly male orderlies and pensioners.[1] The General Hospital was not much different. Nearer the front, in the field hospitals of the Crimea, the situation was even more desperate. Although the temperature stands at 17 degrees fahrenheit, 'the poor men are still in the same miserable state', the English Jesuit chaplain, Fr. John Butt of the 88th Regiment, Light Division, informed Lady Georgina Fullerton on 8 January 1855, 'lying on the bare ground in tents which suffer the snow to drift in to the depth of two or three inches, with perhaps but one torn blanket doing the duty of both mattress and coverlid, and complaining that it is now the second or even the third day since they got a warm drink.'[2]

Letters sent home complaining of such conditions were published in the public press in Britain and Ireland. They confirmed the graphic reports in *The Times* by William Howard Russell, who was the first 'special correspondent' to accompany an army into battle and to write without censorship. Although the troops had been six months in the country, Russell announced on 12 October 1854, there were 'no preparations for the commonest surgical operations'. Men were sometimes left for a week 'without the hand of a medical man coming near their wounds'. The following day he described 'the worn-out pensioners, who were brought as an ambulance corps' as 'totally useless', and he contrasted British medical arrangements with those of the French, which he judged 'extremely good'. Their surgeons, he remarked, are 'more numerous, and they also have the help of the Sisters of Charity who have accompanied the expedition in incredible numbers. These devoted women made excellent nurses.'[3]

Such searing criticisms changed the mood of the nation. On 14 October a letter in *The Times* asked the question, 'Why have we no Sisters of Charity?' Seeing an opportunity to counter the intense contemporary campaign against nuns and Catholicism, Bishop Thomas Grant, of Southwark, approached the Sisters of Mercy at Bermondsey, London, for volunteers. The response was immediate. Four volunteered, under the leadership of Mother Mary Clare Moore, and were joined by six other sisters, not nurses, of the Congregation of the Faithful Virgin, Norwood. All became part of an expedition led by Miss Florence Nightingale, who had been part of an influential group interested in the reform of nursing. The group included the Secretary of State for War, Sidney Herbert, and his wife, Elizabeth, and Mary Stanley, daughter of the Bishop of Norwich.[4] Nightingale was designated 'Superintendent of the Female Nursing Establishment of the English General Hospitals in Turkey'; having under her control everything relating to the distribution of nurses, their hours of duty, their selection and allotment, subject to the sanction and approval of the chief medical officer of the army. The expedition also included a number of lay nurses, poorly trained, and fourteen Protestant religious - of whom eight were Protestant sisters of Mercy, known as Sellonite Sisters after their foundress a Miss Sellon. A Mr and Mrs Bracebridge, staunch supporters of Miss Nightingale, brought the number of the party to forty. On 27 October the entire party sailed for Constantinople.[5]

Before leaving, Miss Nightingale required all to sign an agreement placing themselves under her authority. No allowance was made for the religious sisters as regards community life, prayer together or separate accommodation. All were to experience Nightingale's single-minded, controlling zeal, which would provoke opposition from medical officers, and induce her to make representations and misrepresentations to the War Office to achieve her ends, assured, as one biographer observed, that she had 'both the ear and confidence of ministers and the interest and sympathy of the court'.[6] The possibility of differences between the Bermondsey sisters and the nursing superintendent was eased by Mother Moore's compliant nature and her empathy with Florence Nightingale.[7] It was to be quite different with the Irish contingent of Mercy sisters with whom Ronan was associated.

## Different Arrangements for the Irish Sisters

In England, before long, newspaper reports on casualties underlined the need for more nurses. Sidney Herbert, despite a written agreement with Florence Nightingale that no new nurses were to be sent except at her request, took it on himself at the beginning of December 1854, to arrange for a second party of volunteer nurses for Scutari. These were placed under Mary Stanley, a friend of Nightingale and one of the nursing reform group. The Irish Sisters of Mercy were among the volunteers. There was a growing awareness in the War Office of the concern in Ireland for the ten thousand or so Catholic soldiers, mainly Irish, almost devoid of spiritual support and of nursing care. As well as Irish nurses, there was a demand for chaplains. After prolonged negotiation with the War Office, conducted mainly by Bishop Grant, seven Catholic chaplains were permitted, a handful for so many troops. Among these were three Irishmen, Michael Cuffe, Thomas Moloney, and Michael Canty, who had arrived in the Near East in October 1854.[8] Cuffe and Moloney came to see themselves as the senior chaplains, the experienced fore-runners, and took on airs and responsibilities that were soon resented by fellow chaplains and by Mother Mary Francis Bridgman, the leader of the Irish Mercy Sisters.

There were fifteen Mercy sisters, drawn from various communities in Ireland and England: women of diverse talents, including the resourceful Mary Joseph Croke, who, like Bridgeman, kept a diary of her Crimean experiences, and was a sister of the formidable Thomas Croke, Archbishop of Cashel, and Mary Joseph Lynch, an assertive individualist destined to initiate many foundations in North America (See Appendix). All worked harmoniously under Mary F. Bridgeman, who had been superior of the Mercy convent in Kinsale, Co. Cork, where she had nursed people through the Famine fever, and subsequently through a cholera epidemic, and had also devised schemes of employment for young women in the region, and initiated foundations in England and North America. She was seen as the best qualified person to lead such a diverse group and was instructed to keep the group together and not to relinquish her role as superior to anyone,[9] while yet serving under Miss Nightingale in all that pertained to nursing. Related to the great Irish leader, Daniel O'Connell,[10] she would show herself, in distressing circumstances, a strong and persistent personality.

Certain rules were agreed upon between the War Office and the bishops with regard to the Irish sisters. In addition to their nursing, it was agreed that they might attend 'to the spiritual and material needs of the Catholic soldiers in the hospitals, but to the material needs only of the non-Catholics'. They were not to discuss religious topics with those outside the Catholic Church, but if a desire for knowledge of Catholic doctrine was evinced they might inform the hospital chaplain. They were to obey their religious superior with regard to 'external and spiritual matters, and the daily distribution of time', but within the wards they were under the medical officers and the superintendent of nurses. Even within the wards, however, except where direct communication might be necessary at a bedside, the superintendent was to communicate with the sisters only through their own superior. Moreover, there was always to be a priest to provide for the spiritual care of the sisters, and the sisters were to form a separate community under their own superior, in a house of their own or in a distinct quarter of a large building.[11]

One issue delayed the departure, the appointment of the special chaplain who would travel with them. Bridgeman and another sister called on Sidney Herbert to discuss the matter. After a long discussion they eventually accepted that the priest who would accompany them would not be their special chaplain but a priest charged with their care who would also be a hospital chaplain. Herbert subsequently, under pressure from Anglicans, withdrew his assurance that the priest would travel with them. This occasioned disquiet and distrust in Bridgeman and her sisters, and their former trust was further undermined when Herbert went back on the agreement to the extent of requiring them to sign a document of complete subordination to Miss Nightingale. Angry, Bridgeman saw this as an undermining of her entrusted and acknowledged position and refused to sign or to permit any of the sisters to sign. The only document she would put her name to was the one previously agreed between her ecclesiastical authorities and the War Office. She held out and won. Dr. Edward Henry Manning, the future cardinal, who was involved in the negotiations, witnessing this first test of her mettle, remarked to Mary Stanley that she was 'an ardent high-tempered and, at first, somewhat difficult person - but truly good, devoted and trustworthy'. She was a woman of humility, prepared 'to yield everything but principle'.[12] Bridgeman at this stage was a vigorous, attractive woman of forty-one years, with a more than ordinary experience of nursing and of hardship.

## The Chaplain Appointed

The priest, or spiritual director, to accompany the sisters was sought from the Dublin archdiocese, but none was forth-coming. The Jesuit provincial was approached, and William Ronan was nominated and appointed in November 1854. He went to meet Manning, who was sufficiently taken by him to assure Mary Stanley, who was to lead the second nursing expedition and had a fear of 'Jesuitry', that she would 'like and trust Mr. Ronan'.[13] Ronan assured Manning that he would not be travelling with the sisters on 2 December, but would follow later.[14] He was present, however, as the sisters made their departure, and made a very positive impression on at least one member of the party. She noted almost in passing that he was 'a fine, strong young priest, very cheerful and good. He gave us his blessing, after which he knelt to Reverend Mother for her blessing, saying he was her child and on the ground claimed it.'[15] Clearly, Ronan had experienced an immediate rapport with Francis Mary Bridgeman, but that a military chaplain in the heyday of male dominance would kneel down before a woman for her blessing was unusual. One certainly could not visualise the hard-bitten Frs. Cuffe and Moloney doing so. It suggested openness towards women, and a degree of sensitivity likely to make life particularly difficult for him amid the filth and carnage of the war hospitals. Such sensitivity was also likely to leave him little in common with his two fellow Irishmen, Cuffe and Moloney, who were of a rougher, less vulnerable mettle, and found support in each other's company.

Long before dawn on 2 December 1854, the sisters left the convent in which they were staying for the London Bridge station. They were 'most enthusiastically received as they passed through England', and at Bologna 'crowds came to greet them'.[16] But their reception on arrival at Scutari was very different. It set the scene that would greet Ronan on his arrival.

## Reception at Scutari

Florence Nightingale only heard of the new nursing contingent when the expedition was underway. Her nerves stretched to the limit by overwork and tension, by administrative chaos and undisciplined often drunken nurses, she turned on Sidney Herbert in passionate anger accusing him of sacrificing her and his own written word to a popular cry, and making it impossible for her to continue as Lady Superintendent.[17] When the party arrived on 17 September she had Bracebridge inform them that they were not needed. Bridgeman and her sisters spent Christmas at the school of the French Sisters of Charity in Galata, across the bay of the Golden Horn. Nightingale contemplated sending the entire expedition home, but following representations from the British ambassador, Lord Stratford de Redcliffe, she relented. She insisted, however, in sending home at short notice some religious sisters from the earlier group: some of the Sellonite and the Norwood sisters. She then offered Bridgeman places for five of her sisters in the hospital at Scutari, under Mother Moore as their religious superior.[18] The remaining ten could not be accommodated. Bridgeman pointed out that she was under instruction to keep the party together and not to surrender her position as superior. After negotiation and an unfriendly reception, she eventually agreed to have five of her sisters work in the hospital provided she was one of the group. She sought to counter Nightingale's declaration that there was no room for the other ten in the hospital by proposing that they work in the hospital each day while living outside. Nightingale refused, and made a comment which was later used against her, namely, that as regards the ten sisters, other than the five she wished to choose for the Scutari hospital, she had 'no power to dispose of them; they had not been consigned to her'.[19]

On Christmas Day, 1854, Nightingale wrote two letters from the Barracks Hospital, Scutari, to Sidney Herbert, which showed her mind with respect to Bridgeman and the new nuns. She was aware that she had met a formidable, self-assured woman from whom she could not expect blind obedience. She endeavoured to dismiss her as someone who 'obviously came out with a religious view - not to serve the sick but to found a convent'. The sisters she spoke of as 'assistant or female ecclesiastics', a description she was to use more than once. She believed they would try to 'worm their way in and intrigue with the priests afterwards'.[20] In the second letter she resorted, as was her wont with adversaries, to caricature, belittling her opponent by means of an unbecoming nickname. She spoke and wrote of Bridgeman as 'the Reverend Brickbat'.[21] Not surprisingly, Bridgeman had come away from her meeting with the Lady Superintendent of Nursing with the belief that she was dealing with 'an ambitious woman ... on whom she could not possibly rely'. Future dealings, she resolved, would be by letter.[22]

It was a tragic division, which might possibly have been overcome by more flexibility and empathy on both sides. If Bridgeman could have put aside the negative impact of their discourteous and manipulative reception, and made allowances for Nightingale's personality and pressures, and if, more to the point, Mrs. Moore had acted as a go-between and explained Nightingale to Bridgeman, perhaps better relations might have ensued. As against that, there was Nightingale's ineluctable neglect of the sensibilities of others, which alienated senior medical personnel, led to bitter criticism from some of the Sellonite Sisters, and made her nurses' lives miserable. She was unable to handle authority, was incapable of seeing the propriety and value of explaining her difficulties to those who worked with her, and the importance of a kind word. When Miss Jones, the superintendent of a house for the nurses, suggested that these women, with all their failings, needed encouragement, the Superintendent of Nursing responded with dismissive arrogance that she had no time to attend to such trivial matters, and expected others to be too busy so to indulge themselves.[23] There is evidence, however, that with the passage of time she took the remonstrance to heart where her nurses were concerned.[24]

On 5 January 1855, she sent Mother Clare Moore across the Bosphorus with a partial concession. Bridgeman could be one of the five sisters employed at Scutari, but they were not needed to nurse the sick, 'for as there had been no general engagement lately, the wounded were either dead or convalescent'. 'Most of those then in hospital', Moore continued, 'were only suffering from scurvy, dysentery and enteric fever, and therefore needed no nursing.[25] The sisters would have to be satisfied with employment in either the stores or kitchens. Bridgeman accepted the ultimatum and promised in writing, on 8 January 1855, to act while in Scutari 'in such a manner as to give no one reason to complain or to cause the least inconvenience or division'.[26] She was appalled, however, by Nightingale's restricted view that only the wounded and surgical cases needed nursing, and that medical cases such as dysentery and cholera did not. She also perceived before long that the Nursing Superintendent did not believe in contagion, and was prepared to place operation cases in fever wards, even in beds vacated by dead fever patients.[27]

At Scutari two sisters were put to work in the kitchen, two put sorting linen, while Bridgeman, pointedly, in an exercise of petty control, was given nothing to do. Her perceptive eye, however, took in the disorder, the lack of hygiene, the paucity of nursing; and she experienced the agony of passing through corridors 'filled with sick and dying', hearing their moans and seeing their crying necessities, knowing 'that fifty to ninety were dying daily' and being 'debarred by Miss Nightingale from rendering them any of the services we had left our convents to render them'.[28] The feeling of being unused, and split up despite earlier agreements, was reinforced by the sense of hostility emanating from Miss Nightingale, the Bracebridges, the Protestant chaplains, and many of the nurses.

New hope dawned, however, at the start of 1855 when the commander-in-chief, Lord Raglan, required nurses for the General Hospital at Balaclava, which had opened in September 1854, and Lord Stratford de Redcliffe also decided to open an extra hospital on the Bosphorus. These provided openings for Miss Stanley's party. Lord Stratford's hospital was a converted barracks at Koulali. It was opened on 27 January 1855. Nightingale had a nominal superintendence over the Koulali hospital, but as she never visited it the hospital was placed under the authority of Lady Stratford, and she, with the approval of her husband, and of Lord Paulet, and with the sanction of the medical officers, appointed Mary Stanley as superintendent of nursing.

Meantime, in the third week of January, Mother Bridgeman received a letter from Sidney Herbert, which informed her that he had made a mistake in sending the second party of nurses without Miss Nightingale's approval, and that she was now empowered to choose whom she wanted to keep and to send the rest home. He added a postscript, however, which stated that he had learned 'that your kind services may very possibly be required in Galata, which, if it relieve you from your present difficulties, I should be glad to hear had been the case.' This reference to the new hospital at Koulali, in Galata, Bridgeman saw as permitting her to obtain employment for the ten sisters languishing in Therapia, whom Nightingale had declared she had 'no power to dispose of' as 'they had not been consigned to her'. She also saw it as a means of liberating herself from her own futile position in Scutari Barracks Hospital.[29] She discovered, however, that it was not easy to effect an escape from Miss Nightingale's passion for control. In the circumstances, Ronan's arrival prior to 20 January 1855, proved important. He was the necessary catalyst to bring about change.

## *Ronan's Arrival and Impact*

'I had great pleasure in making acquaintance with Father Ronan who is every way fit for the position to which he is going', Manning confided in his letter to Cullen on 4 January 1855. Ronan was now half way there, he hoped.[30] A week after Ronan's arrival, Fr. Cuffe, at this stage quite critical of the Superintendent of Nursing, informed his archbishop that he had given Ronan full particulars 'of the past and present state of things' and 'of the character of Miss Nightingale'. He emphasised 'the great necessity of firmness in his demands of that lady respecting the nuns' and he urged him 'to draw up his demands in the form of propositions' so that 'a clear yes or no might be the answer'. As 'a fellow priest' he commented to him in confidence on 'the precipitance of Mrs Bridgeman' in moving into the Barracks Hospital and dividing her party of nuns. Ronan, he added, did not preserve that confidence.[31]

Ronan, in fact, had acted decisively soon after his arrival. Having acquainted himself with the situation, he went to visit the bishop of Constantinople, and also consulted the French Sisters of Charity and other religious, and found that all were critical of the position the sisters were in and advocated change along the lines of the agreed pre-arrangements. Thereafter, Ronan regularly sought the counsel of the bishop of Constantinople.[32] Following his various consultations, he sought and obtained a meeting with Miss Nightingale.

From Scutari on 22 January 1855, he sent an account of the overall situation and the steps he had taken in a letter to

Archbishop Cullen for his approval.[33] He sent it care of the Irish Jesuit provincial, Fr. John Curtis. When he arrived, he declared, he found the sisters 'in a disagreeable position'. To understand the situation it was important, he added, to realise 'that there are three great hospitals here. The first and most important is the Barracks. It contains 3,000 sick. The second is the General Hospital, which is half-a-mile distant from the Barracks. The third is near a little village called Koulali about seven miles from Constantinople. The last two hospitals have each about 1,000 invalids.' When he arrived he found five of the recently arrived nuns in the Barracks hospital with the five who had come earlier with Mrs Moore, who acted as superior of all. The remaining ten religious were left 'living in a private house without any employment'. From an interview with Mrs Moore he learned that these could not be accommodated either in the Barracks or the General Hospital 'because their number far exceeded Miss Nightingale's demands and expectations'. Mrs Bridgeman informed him, Ronan told the archbishop, in apparent contradiction to what he had just written, that Miss Nightingale had requested that five sisters be under the direction of Mrs Moore and that she, Bridgeman, had refused 'on the ground that she had been appointed their superior and would not transfer her authority to anyone'. There was also the consideration 'that the convents from which the late Irish nuns were taken' had 'not confidence in Mrs Moore and refused to allow their subjects to pass to her authority'. 'I must say', Ronan observed, 'that my impressions of Mrs Moore are not favourable.' He had learned from the chaplains that the nuns in the hospital gave no instruction 'to the poor sick', and he found on investigation that such was 'the real state of things'.

'I then called on Miss Nightingale', Ronan continued, 'to know what were her intentions with respect to the ten nuns at Therepia. She could give no security for their employment. I told her that by my position as chaplain and guardian of the nuns I had full powers to direct their movements and take them home if not required or if they could not have the essentials of the religious state.' Having thus asserted his position by claiming powers, which it was not at all clear that he possessed, he 'proposed to her conditions which were necessary if she wished to have a satisfactory arrangement with reference to the Sisters of Mercy'. He outlined the conditions for the archbishop.

'1. That the fifteen sisters last arrived be placed under the discretion of Mother Bridgeman, for she is their duly appointed superior and cannot transfer her authority to any other.

2. That ten of these fifteen sisters be sent to Koulali Hospital (there was no other place they could go) and the remaining five to the General Hospital, there being accommodation for no greater number, or if it be thought better to keep these five in the Barracks Hospital they shall form a distinct community under the direction of Mother Bridgeman.

3. That all the sisters, those from Bermondsey as those lately arrived, besides their accommodation as nurses, have, wherever placed, or however distributed, an oratory to which they can retire for the performance of their religious exercises.

4. That as the Order of Mercy requires its members to attend to the spiritual instruction of the Roman Catholics, as well as to the relief of all the sick, the sisters shall have full liberty throughout their respective hospitals to instruct Roman Catholics, particularly when requested to do so by the patients themselves, or by the R. C. chaplain in attendance. The Sisters of Mercy, on their part, pledge themselves not to interfere in the religious concerns of Protestants. They also engage to give undistinguishing relief according to their ability to the corporal sufferings of all and to promote amongst all respect for the hospital authorities.'

Ronan assured the archbishop that he had discussed the foregoing with all the chaplains and others and that 'all unanimously approved of them'.

He observed that 'Miss Nightingale too agreed to them, but refused to sign them'. Things, therefore, he continued, 'begin to look better'. 'Five nuns will go to the General Hospital in the course of the week. There is a priest there, Rev Mr Moloney, who will say Mass for them everyday. The five in the Barracks Hospital also have daily Mass in their oratory. The ten who go to Koulali shall have the divine sacrifice like the others.' 'This last hospital', he went on 'is not under Miss Nightingale but Miss Stanley, a lady who is in perfect understanding with Mrs Bridgeman. So the greater number of the nuns will remain in this hospital. I intend to live there and do the duties of hospital chaplain also, then I will come here (Scutari) once a week to hear the other nuns' confessions.' Ronan continued:

> Miss Nightingale is easily dealt with if she had not evil advisers. Mrs Moore is one of these. She opposes having an oratory with all her might. She is the adviser of Miss Nightingale and tells her everything. She is encouraged by a priest, Rev. Mr Bagshaw, but he is going away soon, and it would be very much for the glory of God if she were sent to England.

'I have mentioned this whole matter to Dr. Manning', Ronan added, 'and begged him to explain it to Dr. Grant.' He requested Fr. Curtis, the Jesuit provincial, to do the same office for him with Archbishop Cullen. He would have written directly to his Grace, he explained revealingly, 'but I am so unsettled that I could scarcely make my meditation. I require all the spiritual assistance you can give me.'[34]

This last suggests that already the pressure of the work and the anti-Catholic hostility were upsetting him both physically and spiritually.

In fairness to the Rev. Bagshaw and Mrs. Moore some balancing comments are necessary. Bagshaw came from a background and attitude of mind at variance with that of the Irish priests. His tradition was to work quietly, and not draw down the criticism of the government or that of the hostile majority. The inflammatory speeches of Sir John Russell and the public riots at the establishment of the English Catholic hierarchy were a very recent memory. He conveyed to Grant, on 21 January 1855, the day previous to Ronan's letter, his quite different view of the situation in the hospitals. The Bermondsey nuns, he reported, 'work very hard and are well trusted and liked by the authorities' whereas the Irish nuns 'came out with the wrong ideas' and seemed to forget that the government sent them out 'as nurses for the sick and not as missionaries'. 'Fr. Ronan', he continued, 'professes to have no end of authority' over the Irish sisters, though he had no document from Bishop Grant to support his claim, and was 'inclined to come it rather strong'. 'Mr. Cuffe and his colleagues', he continued, 'however estimable as clergymen' were 'in a social point of view the most detestable set of snobs' he had ever come across in his life. He hoped that Cuffe would not be placed in authority over the chaplains. He added that Ronan and the other Irish chaplains were 'inclined to snub our English nuns, and they for their part 'did not wish to have them as confessors'.[35] The snobbery, presumably, reflected the sense of spiritual superiority which seems to have been not infrequent among Irish churchmen after the achievement of Catholic eman-cipation and the survival of Catholic belief in the face of penal legislation, and which found expression in an assertiveness regarding their beliefs quite at variance with the guarded, let-us-not-disturb-the-authorities mentality of most English Catholic laity and clergy.

The reference to the snobbery, or projected superiority, of the Irish chaplains may be relevant also to Mrs Moore's situation. Cuffe, and Moloney, as well as Ronan, had complained about her to Archbishop Cullen; and Moloney, and Cuffe subsequently complained to Bishop Grant that Mrs Moore's 'influence over Miss Nightingale was so injurious' to the interests of the Irish sisters that she should be recalled.[36] Cuffe, at this stage, was not an unbiased witness against Mrs Moore, nor was Moloney, it seems, and Ronan's views, it might be argued, were coloured by his having his services as chaplain and protector to the Bermondsey sisters turned down as 'interference'.[37] The views of the English Jesuit chaplain, Sidney Woollett, however, cannot be easily discounted. He was a very independent personality, without any alleged Irish spiritual superiority, or other grounds for prejudice, yet he judged the Bermondsey sisters very severely in his diary with respect to their time in the near east. They had lost sight, he thought, of the general good of religion. 'They rather conducted themselves as ordinary nurses than as religious, and hence they seldom gave instruction to the soldiers and were quite subservient to Miss Nightingale.' 'They were not respected by the common nurses', he added, and 'even the soldiers spoke to them sometimes in a very disrespectful way', something which never happened with Mother Bridgeman's nuns. She 'always insisted on the station and respect due to her religious'.[38]

It must be said, however, that such negative images of the Bermondsey Sisters, and especially of their superior, Mother Clare Moore, do not cohere with other estimations of Mrs Moore's character as a woman of high principle and deep spirituality who had worked with the foundress of the Mercy Sisters, Catherine McAuley, and subsequently in England had been an influence for much good. She evoked the gratitude and affection of Florence Nightingale and met a deep spiritual need in that complex personality.[39] She sensed, it seems, beneath the egotistical drive for power and the neurotic refusal to recognise limitations, the lonely inner person, cloaking insecurity by endless work and a drive for tangible results and recognition. 'I am here', Nightingale had written to Manning from her hospital in Harley Street on 21 August 1853, 'without a single creature to help me. Others have priests and sisters and superiors. I have no one. I am wholly unfit to be a superior myself.'[40]

With respect to Ronan's meetings with Miss Nightingale, it is noted in the Bridgeman diary that Mary Stanley was present at most of them and 'quite admired' Ronan's 'quiet, respectable, *firm, gentlemanly* manner of treating with her'. Nightingale and Stanley received a copy of the conditions.[41]

Thereafter, matters worked more smoothly. Bridgeman appointed one of the five sisters, now moved to the General Hospital, Scutari, as acting superior of the community there, while she and the others went happily to Koulali to work under Miss Stanley. There, the number of sick and wounded soon led to the establishment of a second hospital, which Stanley handed over to Bridgeman's nursing care. The sisters at Koulali, after a brief period of suspicion from the medical staff, soon overcame internal opposition by their competence, hard work, and general caring and nursing skills. The doctors became their strongest supporters, and contrasted their quiet, ready service with the fussy and demanding style of the Lady Superintendent of Nursing. The patron, Lady Stratford de Redcliffe, who disliked the Lady Superintendent of Nursing, was flattered by the good condition and growing reputation of Koulali under the nuns' influence, but she had a fear of Romanism and responded to the rumours and charges of proselytism being levelled against the Irish sisters and the Jesuit Ronan by the Protestant chaplains and some of Nightingale's supporters, which the Lady Superintendent did nothing to dispel. Indeed, she was receptive to the accusations.[42]

Part of the criticism was occasioned by the very success of the sisters with the doctors and the patients. The sick and wounded Irish soldiers blossomed under the nursing and spiritual care of the sisters, and this excited the interest of patients who were not Catholic. At least fifty of these, in Bridgeman's recollection, became Catholic without it coming to the knowledge of any authority. 'Most of them, on recovery, went to Fr. Ronan's room without even intimating their intention to the sisters who had charge of them, probably fearing to get any of them into any difficulty.'[43] The sisters appear to have made no attempt to influence Protestant patients to change their religion, but their presence, attitude and work spoke eloquently. Ronan was later to observe - 'Everyone received by me into the church at Koulali attributed his conversion under God to the Sisters of Mercy.'[44]

Ronan and Bridgeman, after a while, decided they could not afford to allow innuendoes and accusations go unchallenged. Hence, among many other challenges,[45] Lady Stratford was confronted by Mrs Bridgeman when she called on her and announced confidentially 'that she had been informed that Father Ronan ... had presented to Miss Nightingale a document from Cardinal Wiseman which intimated that the Irish sisters had come 'not to nurse but to teach'. Bridgeman pointed out that there had been no contact with Cardinal Wiseman and that their actions at Koulali were proof enough they came to nurse. Not convinced, Lady Stratford went to Mary Stanley and told her that the senior Protestant chaplain, Rev. W. Sabin, was her source. Stanley investigated. Nightingale stated that she had never heard of such a document. Sabin became evasive and said Lady Stratford must have been mistaken. She denied this indignantly. The sisters believed, Bridgeman noted, that Sabin was the author of the lie, and that Lady Stratford, and Lord William Paulet, in charge of the Scutari hospitals, were 'his dupes'.[46] She added, not mincing her words, that Lady Stratford 'was a weak-minded, silly bigot, who was at the mercy of every knave, believed every tale without question, and so kept herself and us in *perpetual agitation.'[47]* The pursuit and exposure of many such innuendoes, and more explicit accusations, proved exhausting and dispiriting. The general climate of opinion was so negative, so ready to believe almost any canard involving Catholic nuns and Jesuits, that Lord Paulet and others were persuaded to complain to the War Office of proselytism by the sisters.[48] Not surprisingly, with such pressures adding to the stench and dirt and daily horrors of hospital life, the sisters and Ronan were heard from time to time longing for the peace of home or that of the Greek islands.

### Criticisms by Father Cuffe

Fr. Cuffe reported adversely on such comments, treating them as signs that the person was unsuited for life as chaplain or nurse in the military hospitals.[49] He was a zealous but difficult man who had earlier clashed with Lord William Paulet, Florence Nightingale, and most of his colleagues, and whose recall had been requested by the War Office and approved by Bishop Grant. He was allowed to stay because of shortage of chaplains. He had not a good word to say about any of the priests or religious except his friend, Fr. Moloney.[50] The fact that Ronan was a Jesuit was an added ground for criticism. Appealing to the climate of suspicion and hostility, he sought to impress on Archbishop Cullen on 28 January and again on 2 May that, despite his Grace's instruction, it was not reasonable to have 'a permanent chaplain for the nuns, especially a Jesuit. 'The Jesuit and his nuns': how formidable they sound in the Protestant ear!' They had been made to ring in Lord Paulet's ear. Hence, when the latter proposed to send Ronan 'to the camp', he 'did not give much opposition.'[51]

The criticism of the sisters, usually in conjunction with Ronan or another Jesuit, seems to have followed their refusal to take Cuffe's and Moloney's advice not to work in the General Hospital at Scutari, and there is probably also a link to Bridgeman's firm refusal, prior to Ronan's arrival, of Moloney's ministrations, perceiving him as endeavouring to establish himself as superior and spiritual director of the community.[52] Cuffe's asserted belief that changing Ronan's quarters would 'do no injury to religion',[53] and the formal, insensitive manner in which he informed Ronan of his change to the camp, - something also experienced by others at his hands[54] - left Ronan with the problem of making special representation to Lord Paulet and with a possible charge of insubordination. Deeply angry with Cuffe, Ronan wrote to Archbishop Cullen on 6 May 1855.

Paulet, in the past, Ronan stated, had tried to prevent the sisters from instructing Catholics, and he had had to clarify matters for him. Now, Paulet sought to send him to the Crimea and he, Ronan, had to write assuring him of his readiness to obey his commands 'in everything consistent with obligation and duty', but that his position at the hospitals was of a peculiar nature. He had then outlined for the commandant the arrangements between the bishops and the War Office by which the sisters were to have 'a protector and spiritual guardian' during their stay in the Near East, and he enclosed a copy of a letter from Dr. Manning announcing the agreement with the War Office in which he was named specifically as the guardian and protector of the sisters and was to stay at Scutari. Circumstances, which were 'foreign to the object of this letter', he concluded, brought the sisters to Koulali, and he with them, with his lordship's approval.

'I am convinced your Grace', Ronan continued, 'that the commandant will give me no further trouble with regard to this affair, but shall he, I intend to resist respectfully but firmly to the end.' He was also persuaded, he added, that Paulet would be 'much more cautious in giving orders and consequently trouble us less if Mr. Cuffe did not so easily lend his co-operation'. The instruction to go to the Crimea, he explained, had come to him through Mr. Cuffe in the baldest terms. He then quoted Cuffe's letter.

> Dear Sir,
> I am directed by Lord W. Paulet, the commander of Her Majesty's forces in the Bosphorous, to request that you will with as little delay as possible proceed to the Crimea to join the forces there as Catholic chaplain.
>
> (Signed) Michl. Cuffe.

He had confronted Cuffe on the matter, Ronan went on, and reminded him that he was aware of his, Ronan's, special position, and that by his actions he was acting against your Grace's wishes. He told him, moreover, that he would mention the whole business to your Grace. 'It seems to me', Ronan observed moderately, 'that he did not see the consequences of his letter and therefore that he is not to be blamed for it. I hope he will communicate no more disagreeable messages. All that we have received from the commandant came through him. I mention this to your Grace', he reiterated, 'because I believe Mr. Cuffe lends himself too easily to promulgate Lord Paulet's orders. I think too,' he added, 'that he and Mr. Moloney are submissive to the authorities to a degree which does injury to religion.'

Knowing that this was a serious allegation, he proceeded to justify it in strong terms. Father Moloney had charge of the General Hospital. When a dying Presbyterian, wishing to become a Catholic, sent for a priest, Moloney had not gone to him because the senior Protestant chaplain, who was a friend of Lord Paulet, had decreed that no man should change his religion at the hour of death. 'The man died crying in vain for a priest.' Asked by Cuffe, in the presence of Moloney, about the case, Ronan had declared bluntly that nothing could justify such conduct, and that if he were similarly called he would go though the whole British army opposed him. This, it should be noted, was at a period when it was widely held by Catholic theologians that outside the Catholic Church there was no salvation. Ronan's northern Irish plain-speaking was likely to add to the sense of guilt in his two 'prudent' Dublin colleagues, and to increase their hostility towards him. 'On another occasion', he continued accusingly, 'a Protestant presented himself to Mr Cuffe and asked to be admitted into the Catholic Church. He was told in answer that before he could change his religion he should have permission of Lord Paulet. 'This last case', Ronan explained, 'rests on Mr Cuffe's own testimony.'

He mentioned these cases, he went on, to show his Grace 'the necessity of appointing and sending out a chief chaplain without delay.' With him should be sent another priest as his assistant. It was important, he added pointedly, to have superior men, as the church was being judged by 'the appearance and manner of its ministers' and now, if ever, was the time 'to take a firm footing in the army'. 'I write thus warmly', he concluded, 'because I am convinced that the salvation of thousands of our brave soldiers depends upon the position which religion is about to take.'[55]

All, however, was not harassment and discouragement. Ronan opened his letter with a grateful reference to a letter from Cullen to Mrs Bridgeman. The archbishop had written from Rome on 18 April saying that he had sent her long and interesting letter to the Pope who sent his blessings and good wishes. Cullen then added:

> I am sorry to hear you have so many trials to meet. Bear everything patiently. Do not let your enemies frighten you away. Hold your ground until you shall be sent away by force, or recalled by your spiritual superiors. I think you are quite right in not putting your own little community under any authority except your own.[56]

Ronan, in his letter of 6 May, thanked the archbishop for the news of the papal blessing and for the encouragement provided by his letter, and, in response, included in his letter one of the few accounts of his own work.

They had been very busy, he explained, from the end of January up to a few weeks ago when the number of invalids had greatly decreased. He administered the sacrament to about seven dying men each day. Most of the sick had intermittent fever which rendered them quite stupid and almost senseless. 'Take into account' he declared, 'the necessity of instructing these men from the beginning, and preparing them for death in the hospital wards, where the beds are placed so close together that one could scarcely go between them, and you will understand the difficulty of this consoling labour. I have spent from six to ten hours dayly (sic) in this work of mercy. The nuns' assistance to me was invaluable. They instructed, suggested sentiments to and prayed with the dying so perseveringly and so well that they gained for religion universal respect and reverence.'

Another 'most consoling duty', Ronan continued, was to prepare healthy soldiers for the sacraments. These were men on guard and hospital duty who were changing constantly. Some forty of them came to communion weekly, a hundred on Easter Sunday. The great bulk of these men never received the sacraments before and had to be instructed. Not half of them, he insisted, 'would have come to me but for the sisters'. 'Another delightful work' was to instruct and receive Protestants into the Catholic Church, and to instruct and receive back lapsed Catholics. In all, he had received more than forty without the Protestant ministers knowing of even one conversion. A large share in this work, too, was due to the nuns, he emphasised, who, although they were prevented from speaking of religion to Protestant soldiers, yet spoke powerfully by their example. The Protestant ministers were quick-sighted enough to fear the nuns' example, 'hence they calumniated them, and left no means untried to have them sent away'. It was they who persuaded Lord Paulet to try to prevent the sisters from instructing Catholic soldiers.[57] As against that, there were Protestant doctors and ministers who came forward to defend the sisters and witness to 'the universal love they showed to all'.[58]

On 18 June Mrs Bridgeman sent the archbishop further good news. She outlined the nature and impact of their work at Koulali, their good relations with the doctors and patients, the special support they received from the purveyor and from the nursing superintendent, Miss Emily Hutton, who sought *more* sisters for the hospital.[59] In contrast, Fr. Cuffe sent scarcely any news of his own work but continued to provide much that was critical of others, especially of Ronan and the sisters.

Towards the end of June matters began to come to a head for Ronan. On 28 June Cuffe wrote dismissively of Ronan speaking longingly of visiting the isles of Greece, to which he, Cuffe, had replied - 'God help me, I am about eight years a priest and I never had three days vacation'.[60] Ronan's talk probably reflected not just a momentary longing for peace and beauty but a decline in physical health that required a temporary vacation. Bridgeman noted in her diary that although he, in dealing with Nightingale and the authorities, presented himself as the protector, guardian and spokesman for the sisters, yet when he wrote home, explaining the problems that arose and requested authority to act resolutely as circumstances might demand, he was refused and forbidden to take any important step without first writing home for direction, a process which would last at least a month, and even two or three months. Bridgeman, moreover, had written to Dublin asking to have Ronan appointed their ecclesiastical superior, but was told it could not be done, that she was 'the spiritual and temporal head of the little band'.[61] 'This restriction' on him, Bridgeman added, 'quite broke down the health and spirit of the devoted Father Ronan, who daily witnessed the *need* we had of *prompt, vigorous* resolves and measures, while he *dared not even advise* what his judgement and feeling suggested.'[62]

The situation had to be particularly galling for Ronan in that he suspected that a combination of forces had unwittingly cohered to undermine him - letters of Nightingale to the War Office with complaints of proselytism and Jesuit intrigue, letters of Mother Moore on the need for more prudence on his part and on the part of the Irish sisters, letters of Lord Paulet and the Protestant chaplains with complaints of proselytism and Jesuitism, and most upsetting of all the letters of his fellow priests, Cuffe and Moloney, which added to the weight of accusation. Cuffe, indeed, seems to have played a direct part in Ronan's final collapse.

In an attempt to obtain a change of scene, Ronan was prepared to go even to the immediate war zone. Although he had previously argued successfully with Lord Paulet against being sent thither, he now was persuaded by his English Jesuit colleague, Sidney Woollett, who was at Balaclava, and who had been a doctor, to exchange places with him for a few weeks for the sake of his health.[63] He applied and obtained permission from headquarters to go to the camp in an exchange with Woollett. Cuffe wrote to Cullen on 2 July that Paulet was mystified by this change on Ronan's part, and asked Cuffe for his opinion. He recommended 'that Father Ronan should not be allowed to leave Koulali', but concealed his main concern, namely, his serious doubts about the suitability of Fr. Woollett. He suggested to Paulet that because of the recent spread of cholera he should inform Lord Raglan that he had been ordered by the Secretary of War to detain Fr. Ronan in Koulali. 'His Lordship was much pleased with that opinion and said he would act upon it that very evening.' On returning from his meeting with Lord Paulet, on 29 June, Cuffe had written to Ronan. He enclosed the letter for his Grace.

That letter said nothing about his recommendation to Paulet, but instead asked Ronan to 'break up' the arrangement with Fr. Woollett because 'a Protestant nun or lady nurse' at the General Hospital, who travelled out on the same boat as

Woollett, complained to Fr. Moloney that he behaved in an unpriestly manner, exhibiting 'an over lively gaiety', 'great familiarity with all the females on board', and in 'eating meat on Good Friday in the presence of them all'. 'Everything she saw in him' made her surprised that he could really be a priest. This fitted in, Cuffe added, with his own recollection of the week Woollett spent at Koulali, 'the great anxiety which he manifested to visit again and again three female fellow travellers of his who resided at Koulali', and of 'his boasting' to Cuffe 'what a great favourite he was with them'. All of which indicated that it would be better if Fr. Woollett stayed at the camp rather than come to Koulali.[64]

'Father Ronan', Cuffe informed the archbishop on 2 July, 'has answered my letter by saying that Father Curtis in Dublin wished him for the good of his health a change of air, and the doctors so recommended him too, *therefore* he applied to Mr. Woollett to suffer him to go up to the camp and for him to come down.' To which, instead of reflecting that Ronan must be in a bad way if he sought relief at the front, Cuffe remarked:

> All I say, my Lord, to this is that Mr. Ronan is the first out of all the thousands who came out on this operation who wished to do duty in the camp for the sake of its good air!!

'He is not, my Lord, by any means in delicate health', he added. 'A doctor's certificate maybe had by a priest (or indeed anyone) for a *mere how do you do.*'

Cuffe concluded his letter by stating that he and Moloney had gone to visit his Grace, Mgr. Hassan (Bishop of Constantinople), on 29 June, and Moloney had told his Grace all he had heard about Mr. Woollett and of the intended exchange between Woollett and Ronan. 'His Grace seemed horrified and advised to have it, if we can, prevented.' In a postscript he observed that 'Father Woollett is a young man not I believe thirty years of age'.[65]

The glaring omission in this climate of resentment, charge and counter-charge, is the seeming inability to sit down together to acknowledge and discuss problems, to find out what the sisters really needed and wanted, to see where each party stood. Instead, and especially, it seems, on the part of Cuffe and Moloney, there was a rush to judgement. The real state of Ronan's health could have been easily checked out with a little empathy and good will. It was evident to another chaplain, Father McSweeney, on 20 August, that 'the Rev. Father Ronan' was 'very poorly'.[66] Similarly, a brief enquiry would have resulted in a different estimation of Father Sidney Woollett.

### The Enigmatic but Zealous Fr. Woollett

Woollett, despite his youthful appearance and boundless energy, was not as young as Cuffe thought. He was a qualified doctor and had been married. His wife had died, and he had abandoned his medical practice once he entered on his studies for the priesthood. He was twenty-nine when he entered the English Jesuit noviciate in 1847.[67] He had a bouncy, somewhat challenging and irreverent manner that did not change very much with his religious avocation. In the words of a fellow English Jesuit - Francis Charles Devas, DSO, OBE - he was 'frank, outspoken, clear-minded, sure of himself, and of his divine mission, as fearless as he was humorous'.[68] He had at times, it would seem, an almost undergraduate tendency to say outrageous things, a practice which he indulged, one suspects, in the presence of the more formal and serious minded Frs. Cuffe and Moloney. Thus, his visits to the 'three female fellow travellers' while he was at Koulali were explainable by the fact that they had expressed an interest in learning more about Catholicism. One of these was the lady nurse, Fanny Taylor, whose religious doubts he was able to allay. She went on to become not only a Catholic but also the founder of a religious congregation. She, and other Protestant women, would readily have been able to explain, if asked, how Woollett would cheerfully claim that he was 'a great favourite with the women' and how he could be perceived by one Protestant lady as exhibiting 'great familiarity with all the females on board'.

Fanny Taylor related, in fact, how on one occasion at Koulali, when she was talking over her difficulties with Woollett, a group of eight or nine Protestant ladies burst upon her in chorus: 'Oh do let Father Woollett dine with us! He is our guardian angel; we could not have got through without him!' He stayed 'and kept the whole party in roars of laughter'. It emerged that on the journey out many of the women were sick, and the captain appealed to Woollett to use his former medical training to assist them. He did so, curing them physically and raising their spirits. Taylor, indeed, saw a very different side to Woollett than that depicted by Cuffe and Moloney. She saw 'his unselfishness, his readiness to be all things to all men, his burning zeal for God's glory'. 'He was devoted to his work' and 'reckless of his life in the service of the army'. In her view 'there could not be a better type of the soldier of Christ than dear Father Sidney Woollett'. 'The Rev. Mother of the nuns', she added, 'one of the noblest souls I have ever met with, held him in high esteem.'[69]

From Cuffe's and Moloney's more cautious, and less well-disposed point of view, Woollett's words and manner were open to misconstruction and liable to offend the authorities. Woollett, in fact, seemed to have little fear of the authorities. At times, he openly coped with oppression by means of laughter and ridicule, a trait that endeared him to the sisters and to a number of the high church women. Fanny Taylor, speaking revealingly of 'the reign of terror' under which they had lived at Koulali in case they be accused of proselytism by the ever watchful Protestant pastors, recalled how Woollett disapproved of their fear and declared they should 'take the bull by the horns'. He 'used to keep us in alternate fits of terror and laughter, as he would "brave the British Lion" *our* bugbear.'[70]

It is interesting to note that Woollett's independent attitude towards authority did not prevent good relations with officers or soldiers. His open genial spirit, far removed from the siege mentality of many Catholics, led to an invitation to dinner from senior officers shortly after his arrival at Balaclava in April 1855. 'To win their confidence' he accepted the invitation, and was treated 'with marked kindness and courtesy' by General Sir R. England, Colonel Edwards, Major Kennedy and others. 'For over two hours they enquired all about Jesuits and thanked him for enlightening them', as all they knew previously was 'the grossest misrepresentation'.[71] Edwards and Kennedy before long became concerned for his health when they found that he was for a time the only priest looking after four divisions, the other chaplains being ill. They threatened, in jest, to place a sentinel over him to prevent him working so hard.[72] Woollett's standing with the military authorities enabled him to obtain leave to relieve Ronan, and also probably to assist Ronan's quest for permission. From his first contacts with Ronan and the Irish sisters he had been impressed by 'the zeal and courage' they displayed 'under trying circumstances',[73] and it was now evident to him that Ronan was 'disabled by illness'.[74]

Ronan did not get his leave of absence, Cuffe happily informed Cullen on 5 July 1855.[75] His health declined to the point where he could not continue. He sought a replacement without success. On 5 September 1855, Monsignor Robert Whitty, vicar general, and a future Jesuit, wrote from London to Archbishop Cullen that he had had a letter from Ronan 'in which, after telling me he was about to sail for home in a few days, he says that Revd Mother, Mrs Bridgeman, feels extremely the loss of their chaplain and thinks she will be compelled to return home with her little community unless some spiritual provision be made for them'. 'They have asked for the English Jesuit, Mr Woollett', Whitty continued, but the provincial thought it a pity to remove him from the camp while he was 'doing so much for the extreme spiritual wants of the poor soldiers' there. Whitty petitioned Cullen for a suitable priest.[76]

Woollett, meanwhile, was placed in the ironical position of catering for Cuffe, who, as a result of complaints against him, was himself sent to the camp. On arriving in Balaclava on 5 August, Cuffe was directed by the officers to consult Woollett, and at the latter's suggestion he was appointed to the Light Division.[77] Cuffe was not deterred, however, from firing a final broadside at Ronan and Jesuits generally. 'I have not consulted with Fr. Ronan as you recommended me', he informed Bishop Grant on 14 August 1855, 'for I know his opinions already. Long since he has got tired of this mission for it was not the fields of glory which he expected. There may be some priests who for the grand and educated may be found zealous and attentive but regardless of the poor - Jesuits are such. Believe me my Lord I know it all too well.'[78] The negativity reflected a trait noted by Bagshaw in a letter to Grant the following March. A number of chaplains were 'at daggers drawn' with Miss Nightingale, he reported, and Mr. Cuffe was so 'generally with everybody (a good many at least)'.[79]

Towards the end of August, Woollett came up with a proposal, which, as he put it, would supply for 'Fr. Ronan's place, who in consequence of illness had been induced to return by his superior, Fr. Curtis'.[80] He discussed it with Mother Bridgeman and gained her full approval. The proposal was to move the sisters' hospital work to the Crimea, as work at Scutari and Koulali had greatly declined. Only convalescent patients were now being sent down from the Crimea. Woollett forthwith obtained leave to go to Koulali to replace Ronan. He arrived on 2 September. Ronan left the following day.[81] On his state of health, Mother Bridgeman observed:

> Fr. Ronan's ill health obliged him to return home - he remained with us longer than prudence or self-preservation should have suggested, hoping from day to day his place might be supplied. He had written to London and Dublin repeatedly stating the impossibility of his remaining, and begging a priest might be sent to take charge of us. All seemed deaf or heedless and at length our devoted Father was forced to leave us to our fate on the 2nd September, but not before we had reason to fear his health was finally broken down.[82]

The nature of Ronan's illness was not defined. It would appear to have been a form of nervous breakdown, which, perhaps, interfered with his sleep and left him permanently exhausted and over-tense so that he could no longer work effectively or, as indicated earlier, even meditate.

### Concluding the Nuns' Story

In subsequent days, Woollett called on the bishop at Constantinople[83] and contacted the chief medical officer, Dr. John Hall, regarding the move of the sisters to Balaclava. Hall was delighted and wrote to Miss Nightingale to relinquish any claims she might have to control nursing at Balaclava.[84] Nightingale, whose formal control was for Turkey and did not extend to the Crimea, consented. Mother Bridgeman, instructed by the chief purveyor of the hospitals to get ready to come to the Crimea,[85] wrote to Nightingale to inform her that she was withdrawing her sisters and bringing them to the Crimea where the need was greater, and that she had the approval of Dr. Hall. The tension between them flared up again. Nightingale, sensing, it seems, a snub to her authority, insisted they could not go without *her* consent'. Two government officials and one or two priests also opposed the decision. Bridgeman, 'notwithstanding ..., determined with firmness either to take all the nuns to Balaclava or else return to Ireland'.[86] Nightingale wrote strongly to the War Office in criticism of Bridgeman and demanding the extension of her own nursing control to the hospitals of the Crimea. She also requested a meeting with Woollett to win him over to her side.

The interview took place affably on 7 October 1855. During it she read documents to him which, she claimed, conferred powers on her as a result of which Dr. Hall and Mother Bridgeman might be seen to have exceeded their powers and 'the passage of the nuns might be countermanded'. Woollett agreed, 'that it would seem that some authority was conferred on her but the extent of that authority was not clearly defined'. He remarked in his diary, that he perceived a great change in Miss Nightingale from when he knew her previously - 'especially in (her) marked love of command', adding, 'what with the imperious manner of the ambassadress, the love of authority of Miss N., and the opposition to both on the part of the lady nurses' there was 'not a little discord and ill will' in the nursing area.[87] Woollett's diary entry three days later, 10 October, observed significantly that he escorted the Irish Mercy Sisters to the hospital in Balaclava 'in order to prevent Miss N. taking any measures in favour of her own views and against the nuns'.[88] Thereafter, he tried to combine his work among the troops with the needs of the sisters.

At the General Hospital Balaclava the sisters found conditions almost as bad as they had been initially at Scutari. Again they worked to clean and humanise the large buildings, and once again they established a strong rapport with doctors and patients. Before long, however, they lost two of their number, Sr M. Winifred and Sr Mary E. Butler, both from Liverpool, who were buried with full honours and deep affection. News that the first of them, the much loved Sr. M. Winifred was dying of cholera was sent by telegram to Woollett by Miss Nightingale, and at the nun's bedside 'while reciting the prayers Miss N. knelt down and joined in'.[89] Fr. Cuffe, who had advised against Mother Bridgeman and her sisters leaving 'their comfortable station' at Scutari and Koulali, declared predictably - Fr. Woollett is much to be blamed for advising and encouraging (them) to come up to the Crimea.'[90] The remark reflected not just a continuing dislike and distrust of Woollett, but also a protective, patriarchal attitude to nuns, which was calculated to infuriate Bridgeman and other independent spirits. His outlook was best indicated perhaps in a letter to Grant on 5 October 1856, when he complained that Fr. Bagshaw, now chaplain at Koulali hospital, had 'the nuns singing psalms and hymns' while 'exposed to the full gaze of the soldiers'. He did 'not approve of the nuns singing'.[91]

On 16 March, 1856, coinciding with news of a cease-fire, it was announced to the army, as part of general orders, that the supervision of nursing at the General Hospital, Balaclava was entrusted to Miss Nightingale. Dr. Hall protested to no avail.[92] About the same time it came to Mother Bridgeman's attention that Miss Nightingale, in reporting on nursing to the War Office, had made criticism of her and the Irish sisters to the effect that - they had withdrawn from her authority, that they felt it their duty to convert Protestants, that they were extravagant, and that the number of sisters were too many for the number of patients. Bridgeman firmly rejected the criticisms in a letter to Dr. Hall on 21 March 1856.[93]

On 25 March, Nightingale, to her surprise, was informed by Dr. Hall that it was 'for Mrs. Bridgeman to decide' whether the sisters would continue under the new arrangement, adding that they had given him 'the most perfect satisfaction by the quiet and efficient manner' in which they had performed their duty since they had been employed in the hospital.[94] Nightingale, in conciliatory mood, went out of her way to assure Bridgeman that she would 'not interfere or make any change so long as Dr. Hall was satisfied', but Bridgeman's experience had exhausted trust. 'I came out to work with you', she responded, but 'you yourself dissolved the connection. Now that I am disconnected with you, as before I left home, and no exigency at all existing now, since the war is over, I do not see the necessity of renewing our connection.'[95] Nightingale refused to accept this as final, saying she would call again the following evening.

Bridgeman took counsel with four chaplains who called after Nightingale had left. They and Dr. Hall and David Fitzgerald, the deputy-purveyor, did not trust Nightingale's assurances and encouraged her to resign. That way the decision was the sisters. Otherwise, they would be in Nightingale's power and might be sent home in disgrace like the Norwood nuns. The second visit of the Lady Superintendent appears to have been less than ladylike. She arrived accompanied by General Codrington, and, allegedly, sought admission to the sisters' quarters 'by kicking at the door'. She asked Bridgeman's decision. The latter referred her to Dr. Hall, with whom their arrangements had been made. On 28 March, Hall informed Bridgeman that it rested entirely with her whether she wished 'to remain subordinate to Miss Nightingale or not'. On the same day, Bridgeman tendered her letter of resignation directly, and pointedly, to Dr. Hall. Her resignation coincided with the signing of the Peace of Paris on 28 March 1856.[96]

### Aftermath and Review

The 'Annual Letters of the English Jesuit Province' for 1856 noted, with perceptible partisanship, that 'early in April', Woollett, following an illness, was ordered back to England and 'requested at the same time to escort home the Irish Sisters of Mercy who preferred to return to Ireland rather than, according to a recent order from the War Office, be placed at the disposal of Miss Nightingale (this blessed virgin of the Protestants). It would have been better if the English Sisters of Mercy had done the same.'[97] Sr. M. Joseph Croke, recounted in her journal that at 5.0 p.m. on Saturday, 12 April 1856, they left the harbour of Balaclava 'amid the blessings and good wishes of all'.[98] She expressed her feelings and those of her companions in the exclamation 'Every heart beats light - Going home! Alive after such scenes! And going home, *alive*![99]

Before long, however, disquieting news came from the Vincentian chaplain in the General Hospital, Fr. Michael Gleeson. Writing from there on 21 April, 1856, he informed Bridgeman that her friends were defending her system of nursing and organisation against all efforts 'that are daily made to bring disrepute on everything done by you. Miss N's only object at present appears to be to try and reflect upon everything done by you. She finds fault with this for feigned reasons'.[100] Subsequently, before a Royal Commission, Miss Nightingale made further charges against the sisters to the effect that there had been 'a horrible neglect of the patients', that their hospital in Balaclava had been dirty and disorderly, that they had deserted their post, and had been generally disobedient and troublesome. The deputy-purveyor, David Fitzgerald, sent a report to the War Office contradicting Nightingale's accusations, and Fr. Gleeson, from Dublin on 14 April 1858, did so on the grounds of his own personal experience of the working of the hospitals.

On 20 March 1858, in a letter to Sidney Herbert, Dr. John Hall added his protestations at the inaccuracy of Miss Nightingale's statements.[101] Other medical staff also spoke up for the sisters, as did Emily Hutton, the superintendent at Koulali, Fanny Taylor, and Mary Stanley; and many others paid tribute to their work and dedication. Miss Nightingale's accusations, however, prevailed and became the accepted 'truth'. The contribution of the Irish Sisters of Mercy was relegated to the shadow-lands of history.

Mother Bridgeman and her sisters made no public statement. In her diary, however, Bridgeman gave vent to trenchant, frustrated, even caustic comment about the Lady Superintendent. 'The title of the Goddess of Humbug had been conferred on Miss N. in the Crimea',[102] Bridgeman wrote. She took credit and notice for the work of others, and was prepared to use lies and insinuations and her influential contacts to preserve control and reputation irrespective of the good of the patients. Indeed, Bridgeman went on, in Miss N.'s report 'on the nursing establishment', made to the War Office in November 1855, she proved 'her disregard for truth, for in it she not only states falsehood, but makes statements which her very own letters ... are sufficient to prove unequivocally false'.[103]

In a war zone, with its horrors and pressures, and far removed from home, and with two strong principled people such as Nightingale and Bridgeman, it was inevitable that a clash of personalities would come. That it came so early in the relationship was reprehensible and regrettable. A recent biographical work by a North American historian, Dr. Mary C. Sullivan, on *The*

*Friendship of Florence Nightingale and Mary Clare Moore*
concluded, after an effort to view the conflict objectively from
both points of view, that although 'there were in varying degrees
failures of judgement and conciliation on both sides of the complex dispute, ... in the end one must say that, as Superintendent
of Nursing, Florence Nightingale bore greater, though not complete responsibility for the unfortunate outcome: the Irish sisters
increasing disaffection from her, their finding work where they
could, and their eventual resignation and departure from
Balaclava in April 1856.'[104]

Mixed in the dispute, as has been seen, were tensions between
the medical officers and Florence Nightingale, and Irish-English
and Catholic-Protestant assumptions, prejudices and fears. To
which may be added the tensions, divisions, and prejudices
between Protestants, and between Catholics themselves. This last
found expression not only between some of the secular clergy
and some of the Jesuits, but also between such as Frs. Cuffe and
Moloney and the Irish Mercy Sisters, and between the Irish
sisters and those from Bermondsey. The intensity of the disagreement between Catholics, and the Irish-English dimension
in the dispute, was mirrored in the action of one Jesuit chaplain
and the reaction it provoked. Fr. Patrick Duffy, was a man who
thought in military terms, cherished the obedience and courage
of the Light Brigade, and could be fiercely partisan in support
of causes or people he cherished. On instruction, or on his own
volition, he decided to refuse confession and communion to
some of the Bermondsey sisters who, according to Nighingale,
he called, 'among other epithets ... a disgrace to the Church'
because he identified them with the opponents of the Irish sisters
and their work:[105] an action which evoked from her the dismissive comment - 'None so coarse as an Irish R.C. priest'.[106] The
use of 'Irish' in this way was not just a passing irritation. It
reflected the kind of assumption and prejudice conveyed in her
friend Sidney Herbert's confidential comment to her, following
her letters to him critical of Bridgeman and the Irish nuns:

> The real mistake we made in the selection of these ladies
> (between ourselves) is that they are Irish. You cannot make
> their lax minds understand the weight of an obligation.[107]

Needless to say, Bridgeman and her Irish sisters, Ronan, Duffy and others sensed the condescension, and reacted against it; even as Bagshaw, and perhaps Mary Clare Moore, sensed the spiritual condescension of the Irish chaplains and reacted against it.

## Home Again

On 17 July 1886, Bridgeman wrote from Kinsale to each of the members of her former band, 'the more I am resting the more tired I am feeling and the more I feel my strength and energy exhausted ... I feel I have had in two years and a half the experience of more than a long, long life under ordinary circumstances ...'[108]

The words she used about exhaustion and experience conveyed, it may be assumed, something of Ronan's experience also. Although he had been in the hospitals for a much shorter period, and had returned home ingloriously, he had been exposed to persistent pressure and criticism and had not, at that stage, it would seem, her remarkable energy. All her life Bridgeman remained grateful to him for the support he provided in human and practical terms while chaplain, and for his work as a priest in giving talks each week on their 'Holy Rule', for his exhortations, the provision of Mass and the sacraments, and for his personal example, all of which combined to keep their spirits up and to deepen their capacity to find God in others, especially in those they nursed, and in the events of life.[109]

Looking back on his time in the hospitals of Scutari and Koulali, Ronan had many memories to cherish, which countered any sense of failure at having had to retire from the scene. At the very end of his life he recounted to Lieutenant General Sir William Butler:

'During my time in the hospitals at least twelve hundred soldiers must have received at my hands the last rites of the Church. Some of these poor fellows were strangers to prayer. All that I could do for them was to ask them to repeat after me an invocation to God, an ejaculatory prayer for His mercy ere they passed away. Others had time for longer preparation, and others again had been taught the prayers and precepts of the Church, but, of each and all alike, I have never doubted for an instant that they went straight to heaven, and when I die,' he added, smiling, remembering perhaps the dying men's dependence on him, 'I believe they will come to meet me at the gates; they will elect me their colonel, and I shall stand at their head...'[110]

In addition, he had received more than forty soldier converts. Mary Stanley, moreover, had reason to remember Manning's advice that she 'would like and trust Fr. Ronan'. She had been impressed, as Bridgeman noted, by his 'quiet, firm and gentle-manly manner' in treating with Nightingale, and also by the example of the Mercy Sisters and by the faith and courage of the Catholic patients. She decided, following consultation with Ronan, to enter the Catholic Church but to do so secretly for the present. She made her first communion and was received into the church by Ronan in March 1855.[111] She was received formally in England a year later. He also received Fanny Taylor into the Catholic Church: this time formally. Mary Stanley subsequently devoted her life to assisting the poor and the sick. Fanny Taylor, who claimed to owe her vocation above all to the faith and cheer-fulness of the Irish Catholic soldiers, and to the example of the Irish sisters, and the frankness and optimism of Fr. Sidney Woollett, went on to found the religious congregation of The Poor Servants of the Mother of God. She kept in touch with Ronan for many years, as did the nuns of Kinsale. He was to conduct the annual retreat at their convent in 1857, 1860, 1861, 1874, 1875, 1876, 1879, 1883, he visited there in 1886, and was present as Mother Bridgeman was dying in February 1888.[112] In short, in his brief experience of the horrors of war, of religious division, and of physical and psychological pressure in the hospitals of Turkey, he fulfilled a long time. It deepened him personally, sharpened his awareness of the consolation religion can bring to the very sick and the dying, and left him with memories of courage, faith, endurance and patience, as well as the damage done by prejudice and rash judgement, on which he could draw for his own instruction and that of others.

During the Crimean campaign, most of the chaplains suffered ill-health at some stage. Seven priests and two nuns died.[113] With regard to the other prominent chaplains during Ronan's time in the east, the irrepressible Sidney Woollett spent the last thirty-two years of his very active and dedicated life as a missioner in Jamaica, dying at the age of eighty;[114] and Revs. Cuffe and Moloney, apart from a short space after the war, continued as chaplains to the forces, Cuffe from 1859 to 1884, Moloney from 1859 to 1879. In the interval after the war, when there was a need for military chaplains in India, they both volunteered and were favourably described by Archbishop Cullen as experienced and zealous men.[115] Florence Nightingale, of course, lived on to become the honoured reformer of nursing in Britain, raising the status of the profession. She continued to drive herself beyond the limits of exhaustion, and to view obstacles in her path as deliberately placed to frustrate her mission.[116] She lived, nevertheless, to the age of ninety, dying in 1910, having fulfilled her life's dream. She outlived Ronan by three years, who also fulfilled his dream, which in his case, however, only crystallised well after the Crimean campaign.

*Florence Nightingale*

*The wounded at Balaclava*

*Improved hospital conditions at Scutari*

# Chapter 4

# *Missioner and Retreat Director*
# *1856 - 1871*

On his return from Turkey, Ronan spent some time recuperating. How long is not clear. It is possible that he was back on light church work for Christmas, and perhaps by Easter giving retreats to religious sisters, or preaching to the large crowds attending Lenten ceremonies at Gardiner Street church. The first definite indication of a full return to health, however, was his participation in the Jesuit mission in Killaloe, Co. Clare, from 21 September to 12 October 1856. Parish missions and retreats were to occupy a great deal of his time and energy over the next fifteen years. Something of what this involved has been indicated in an earlier chapter. A fuller account of the work in the 1850s and 1860s chronicles the growth in Ronan's reputation and evokes the intensity of the 'devotional revolution'.

Many years later, in a letter to Archbishop William J. Walsh of Dublin, he provided an informative account of the various types of missions conducted by Jesuits, and of the aims and content of their preaching. 'In the cities, and in large centres', he observed, 'missions of three weeks, conducted by four missioners, seem necessary at intervals of time to reach the absentees from the sacraments, and to regulate such parishes ... Missions in smaller parishes, and parochial retreats, can be satisfactorily given in a fortnight by two Fathers, who preach night and morning, and hear confessions for six hours daily.'

On the content of their missions and retreats, using a two-week model, Ronan explained: 'The Spiritual Exercises of St. Ignatius (of Loyola) are the subjects of our lectures at all the missions and retreats.'[1] This meant that the early part of the mission was devoted to considering the greatness and goodness of God, the evil of sin and God's compassion for sinners - considerations meant to induce people to come to confession. Thereafter, the preaching focused on the life of Jesus Christ, his invitation to follow him, and his continuing presence with his people through his grace, the sacraments and the gift of the Holy Spirit.

The overall programme, however, was presented in a manner appropriate to the congregation. To counter the influence of proselytism and superstition, the missioners gave much attention to clear, basic instruction on the ten commandments, the articles of the Creed, and the nature and aim of the sacraments - especially the sacraments of penance, confirmation, matrimony, and the sacrament of the sick then envisaged as extreme unction or the last rites. In certain areas family feuds and bitterness over land required emphasis; and drunkenness, unchastity, and dishonesty were failings frequently addressed.[2]

The Killaloe mission from 21 September to 12 October, which marked Ronan's return to mission work, was declared by *The Limerick Reporter* and *Tipperary Vindicator* of the 30 September to be 'working wondrous results'. The missioners were Robert Haly, William Fortescue, William Ronan, and Alexander Kyan, and they were assisted for confessions by 'about twenty priests from the immediate parish and the neighbouring parishes'. Haly opened the mission, and at the high Mass the bishop, Right Rev. Dr. Daniel Vaughan, preached and conducted Benediction. *The Limerick Reporter* indicated the daily timetable:

> Mass is celebrated at six o'clock each morning; confessions commence at seven o'clock, the community mass at eight o'clock and a sermon by Dr. Haly. Confessions are heard again until half-past twelve o'clock when a sermon is preached by Fr. Ronan and confessions are resumed until half-past four o'clock p.m. Rosary is said at seven o'clock and a sermon by Fr. Fortescue. At eight o'clock there is Benediction of the Blessed Sacrament.

The paper remarked on 7 October, 'The Fathers are most indefatigable'. It was clear that much was also being done to involve the children. Two hundred girls dressed in white, with chaplets of roses on their heads and baskets of roses in their hands, walked in the processions, while 'the litanies and hymns were well chanted by the boys in surplices and red soutanes, under the management of Mr. Ronan, S.J.'. *The Reporter* on 14 October observed that on the Friday of the final week of the mission there was 'an important and impressive ceremonial', namely, the consecration of the cross of the mission. 'The passion sermon', the paper remarked, 'was most powerfully preached on the occasion by Father Ronan, S.J.'. The final day, Sunday, 'was fine, and thousands wended their way to the parish church to witness the close of the mission'. At the high Mass the choir, composed of amateur voices, accompanied by a harmonium, sang one of Mozart's masses 'in finished style'. At the end of the Mass, the report continued, Haly 'delivered a most powerful sermon' in which he recapitulated all the principal subjects preached on during the previous three weeks, and urged the people to persevere with the resolutions and good fruits of the mission. There was a final large procession, in which the choir of boys was again led by Ronan, while the responses were sung by the choir from the church at Nenagh who had come especially to sing at the concluding Mass.

After Benediction, 'the bishop, clergy and people resolved themselves into a public meeting in the church for the purpose of perpetuating the memory of the mission by instituting suitable school houses, male and female, for the children of the parish'. On the motion of Haly, seconded by Ronan, the bishop, Dr. Vaughan, 'was called to the chair' and then Fr. Andrew Connellan, a curate at Killaloe, was requested to act as secretary. The parish priest spoke and offered his contribution of ten shillings, wishing it was more, and encouraged others to contribute, including their Protestant neighbours who had played an important part in the building of the parish church. Haly, in turn, spoke briefly and announced his modest contribution of five shillings. A practical and lasting fruit of the mission had been inaugurated and promoted.[3]

On 17 October *The Limerick Reporter* noted that Haly left Killaloe 'amid the prayers and blessing of the entire population' and that the following Sunday he and the Jesuit Fathers were to open a mission in Ennistymon.

On Saturday, 1 November 1856, *The Munster News* and *Provincial Advertiser* was moved to high-flown comment on the attendance at the Ennistymon mission. 'From an early hour', the report commenced, 'the country round about appeared to be astir, swallowed up, as it were, within the vortex of religious enthusiasm, while the crowds might be seen flocking into town from all quarters to see and hear those holy missionaries.' The reporter was cheered to see 'such vast masses come together at the call of religion, after years of famine, of extermination; after the ravages of the clearance system and crowbar brigade had done their best, leaving traces of desolation over the fair fields of Clare.'

Although there are relatively few references to Ronan during 1857, those that have survived indicate that it was a busy and important year for him in terms of retreats and missions. A retreat commencing on 6 August 1857, at the Mercy convent, Kinsale, provided the opportunity for a moving and memorable reunion with Mother Bridgeman and her community. As noted in an earlier chapter, it was the first of many retreats to that community, where he remained a favourite and was always welcome over many years.[4] Later in August 1857, Ronan commenced another long lasting relationship when he gave their annual retreat to the Discalced Carmelite Sisters at St. Joseph's Monastery, Loughrea, Co. Galway. He was to be their retreat director each year, with few exceptions, until 1892. A note in the archives of the convent indicates the high esteem in which he was held and, indirectly, the depth and sensitivity of his spirituality. 'God, who in his divine providence sent him to us', the account states, 'destined him to be the spiritual father and greatest friend of this community ... from that day forward ... and to his intercession with God for us we attribute the many blessings that have since attended us.' He was also 'many years extraordinary confessor to the community' and 'was Mother Catherine's greatest friend, and her spiritual director in all her supernatural favours. God revealed to her many events regarding his future career' and after her death 'he related how everything occurred exactly as she predicted'.[5] How accurately this last represents what Ronan actually said is difficult to determine. His provincial, as will appear, saw him as a pious man, but as well informed on theological and religious topics and deliberate in his judgement.

Ronan was building in 1857 that reputation as the conductor of retreats for religious that made him sought after throughout the country. The retreats, usually of eight days duration, in which silence was preserved throughout by the retreatants, were "preached retreats", that is, the priest conducting the retreat usually gave three or four sermons or addresses, each normally of thirty to forty-five minutes duration, as well as a homily at Mass. He was also available for confession and consultation each day, and frequently conducted Benediction of the Blessed Sacrament in the evening. Each retreat, as a result, required special preparation, and though the material for one retreat sometimes might be adapted without too much effort for the next one, the retreat director had to be careful to keep the material fresh to convey his own conviction, and also to ensure that on returning to a place he did not repeat what he had given the previous year. Frequently, it was satisfying, if tiring work for the retreat giver.

The most noteworthy event for him during 1857 was probably the formal establishment of a permanent Jesuit retreat staff. These were named as Robert Haly, William Fortescue, William Ronan, and a John Dwyer who never seems to have functioned thereafter as a missioner and subsequently left the order. His place was taken by different people as the need arose. The choice of Ronan reflected his growing reputation as a preacher and, presumably, the close working-relationship that had developed between Haly and himself.[6]

The new team, who, in fact, were already used to working together, appeared in a mission in Ballinasloe from 5 to 26 April 1857. Dwyer's place was taken by Alexander Kyan. *The Western Star*, clearly not a Catholic paper, announced on 25 April that the four ecclesiastics had been engaged in the town 'in the services peculiar to their order', and then focused its attention on 'the Rev. Mr. Fortescue (we are informed a seceder from Protestantism)' whose sermon on Friday evening drew a large attendance. He preached on the text, 'the man who perseveres to the end will be saved', and evidently made a keen impression on his audience. The paper's account of the sermon was in line with the description of Fortescue's preaching by a Jesuit contemporary. He 'thundered at the people on the great truths of religion and stirred them to terror and to repentance by his fiery zeal, which was also combined with a gift of racy humour ... When Father Fortescue set to work to rouse his congregation, sometimes their exclamations and groans almost drowned his own stentorian voice.'[7]

In contrast to this revivalist type of preaching, Haly spoke gently but movingly 'of the love of God and of his mercy for even the greatest sinners',[8] while Ronan also took a more reasoned, calm approach, displaying a considerable capacity to convey even abstruse matters in a clear manner, so that he was frequently given the task of explaining the truths of religion to both adolescents and adults. He evidently related easily to the younger members of the congregation.

Not long after Ballinasloe, Haly, Fortescue, Ronan, and the eloquent Alexander Kyan, moved to Navan to open a four-week mission on 10 May.[9] Before that was fully completed, Ronan and Kyan moved to Castleconnell, Co. Limerick, to commence a mission there. Haly later joined Ronan, Kyan, and a Fr. Charles Young at Castleconnell. *The Limerick Reporter* and *Tipperary Vindicator* of 2 June 1857, observed that the mission had opened the previous Sunday with a high Mass in the presence of the bishop and many clergy, followed by an effective sermon from Fr. Kyan on the aims of the mission. At the Mass and during the sermon, the paper continued, the pressure of the crowds was such that the windows of the church 'were removed in order to enable those who were obliged to remain outside ... to see and hear'. 'In the evening', the report added, 'the duties of the mission were resumed at seven o'clock, when the church was again thronged in every part, and when an admirable discourse was preached by Rev. Father Ronan and Benediction of the Blessed Sacrament was given.'

The next record of Ronan's involvement in a mission concerned a three-week commitment in Roscommon from the end of September to 18 October. The *Roscommon Messenger* of 3 October told of large crowds and 'strong men in tears', and on 11 October it reported that 'not less than 10,000 persons' had attended the previous Sunday - 'Weary, footsore and poor, they thronged the approaches to the chapel at early dawn, many from a far distance'. The crowds provided a moment of drama. At 'the high mass for the dead on Friday morning', the *Messenger* explained, there was an alarm 'that the galleries were falling' and public panic was only averted by the parish priest hurrying from the altar to oppose the rush for the door.

Six months later, the bishop, George J. P. Browne, wrote to Haly to arrange a retreat in Roscommon for the priests of the diocese, and to book another popular mission for the autumn. 'Thank God', he declared, 'the fruits of the mission have survived the winter here. It is incredible how much good has been done to all the country around - God bless the good Fathers for it.' 'The people are so much up for missions', he added, 'that in future we will be forced to give them at least one each year.'[10] That autumn, Haly, Fortescue, and Ronan, gave at least one other mission in the west of Ireland. *The Galway Vindicator* of 24 November 1858 reported their arrival in Claregalway, and the immense crowds that gathered to hear them. Galway, indeed, was to become a focus point for the mission staff.

The bishop of Galway, John Mac Evilly, who attended the opening of the Claregalway mission, had approached the Jesuit provincial concerning the establishment of a Jesuit intermediate college in Galway. The bishop offered his own residence as a place for a temporary school while a college and Jesuit church were being financed and built. On 15 February 1858, the provincial and his consultors, decided to fulfil two objectives in one. They envisaged the new premises at Galway as being the centre of the mission staff, with Haly, as rector, able to use his extensive contacts as a source of funding for the new enterprise. Frs. Ronan and Peter Foley were to be attached to the house. The changeover was to commence with a mission in Galway in June.[11]

Matters did not quite go as planned during 1858. The following year, however, the Jesuits returned to Galway, where they had been before their suppression, with Haly as superior, and Ronan as minister. Haly did not prove an unqualified success as a fund-raiser. He spent much time away from the house, but more at missions and retreats than at collecting funds.[12] The daily work of organisation and supervision was left to Ronan as minister of the house and church, or second-in-charge; but he also found time to involve himself in fund-raising, to assist in some missions, to give a number of retreats, and some charity sermons. The Presentation Sisters availed of the *Galway Vindicator* on 26 March 1859, to thank him publicly 'for his successful and impressive appeal on Sunday, the 13th instance, on behalf of the poor children of the convent schools'. Such appeals were one of the few sources of income to support poorer children in the Catholic schools. In St. Patrick's church, which the Jesuits were administering, Ronan said Mass, heard confession, and assisted people with difficulties.

Earlier in March, the mission team had conducted a mission in the city. On the penultimate Sunday Ronan delivered what the *Vindicator* described as 'an eloquent discourse' at the church of St. Nicholas, which produced a larger collection than usual. The boys of the Model School took part in the mission procession and were praised highly by Ronan. Moreover, he 'visited the school and spoke in high terms of the progress of the pupils and the system of education pursued'[13] - an unusual step, given the opposition of many of the hierarchy, including the bishop of Galway, to the state sponsored model schools. The following August, the assembled bishops were to adopt a resolution condemnatory of the national board in charge of these schools.[14] During Holy Week, 1859, the Jesuits conducted the ceremonies in their church of St. Patrick, and it was noted that the chanting of the office by the choir on Good Friday 'was conducted by the Rev. Mr. Ronan'.[15] In March of the following year, Ronan learned with regret of the death of his former bishop, Michael Blake of Dromore. Protestants as well as Catholics attended the large funeral at Newry.[16]

From 1860 to 1862, while the fund raising continued in Galway and the building of the new Jesuit school, church, and community residence was planned and being undertaken, Ronan continued his work of conducting retreats and missions. Only a few of these appear to have been chronicled. References are extant of a retreat at the Mercy Convent, Kinsale, on 6 August 1860, and of a mission in Kilrush in December 1860,[17] of a further annual retreat at Kinsale in August 1861, a mission in Athlone from 16 February, 1862,[18] and of a short mission in Galway - one week to 'young men and old', and a further week for women when the church was said to have been 'daily crowded with the beauty and fashion of Galway'. 'The discourses of the Rev. Father Ronan', were described in local journalese as 'admirable and peculiarly suited to his auditory'.[19] In May 1862, Haly and Ronan from Galway, and Kyan from Dublin, gave a mission in Scariff, Co. Clare, attended by 'thousands', and they moved from there to Cooreclare, Co. Clare.[20]

In 1863 there was rejoicing at the opening of the new school and church at Sea Road, Galway. That year also, however, Ronan found himself drawn into an unsavoury conflict between the bishop, John Mac Evilly, and the parish priest of Rahoon, near Galway city, Peter Daly. In January, Mac Evilly, in accordance with the agreement of all the hierarchy, except Archbishop Mac Hale, set about having all Catholic children withdrawn from the model schools. His task was rendered more difficult by the fact that his predecessor had tacitly approved of the schools. Peter Daly did not approve the bishops' stance, and when their lordships' pastoral against the schools came out he 'flung it aside publicly on the altar'. Reporting all this to Archbishop Cullen, on 23 August 1863, Mac Evilly expressed his belief that Daly was abetted by Mac Hale. Previously he had had reason to suspend Daly, but in April 1862, the suspension had been lifted.[21] He was restored subject to certain conditions. These included not attending or supporting the Mechanics Institute, which Mac Evilly subsequently described as 'the focus of all mischief in Galway'.[22] Ronan had been involved in having Daly restored, and he was present when Daly agreed to the bishop's conditions. During 1863 Daly showed signs of support for the Mechanics Institute and was determined to attend its meetings,[23] and, moreover, he had apparently informed Mac Hale that he had not made any promises in April 1862. The bishop, having Daly's signature to the agreement, made in Ronan's presence, he requested Ronan to confirm the fact of Daly's promises in a letter to Archbishop Mac Hale.

Hence, on 30 August 1863, Ronan assured his Grace that Fr. Haly and himself had brought to the bishop of Galway 'a paper written by Rev. Mr. Daly containing the conditions the bishop required of him to sign before his restoration'. 'I certify', Ronan continued, 'that I have seen on this day in the hand of the bishop of Galway the paper alluded to ... That paper was written by Rev. Mr. Daly in Father Haly's presence and signed by him. As one of the parties concerned in Mr. Daly's restoration, it is my duty truthfully to state the facts.'[24] Peter Daly died five years later, 'leaving vast property', according to Bishop Mac Evilly, 'and an unsatisfactory will'. Most of his wealth went to his friends![25]

Meanwhile, Ronan's standing within the Society of Jesus in Ireland seems to have received a boost. The note book of the consultors of the Irish vice-province shows that in June 1864 his name came second in the terna (three names) put forward for superior of the Gardiner Street church and residence, and he was named third for superior at Galway and at Limerick. Then, in October, an unusual step was taken. He was raised to the status of professed father of the order, those members who take a special vow of obedience to the Pope, are especially at his disposal, and normally achieve that status following high academic results in theology - success in a special *ad gradum* examination, and a proved reputation for solid spirituality and sound judgement. Only professed fathers were eligible to be superiors of certain houses. Ronan's theological standing did not qualify him for the status, but in 1864 he was raised to the position in recognition of his work as a preacher, an unusual step at that period. The consultors' notebook for 6 October 1864 carries the entry:

> Should Fr. Ronan, who has not succeeded in his *examen ad gradum*, be recommended for profession on account of excellence in preaching. The consultors unanimously answered that he ought to be so recommended.[26]

The following year when an invitation came to the Irish provincial from Dr. Goold, bishop of Melbourne, to send men to Australia, the consultors, on 6 January, 1865, suggested that Frs. John Gaffney and Ronan be sent to investigate. It was a time of new openings and some confusion. The invitation to Australia coincided with one to Killarney, in the diocese of Kerry. Killarney was turned down because the only possible viable opening appeared to be a novitiate, but that need was already being met at Miltown Park, Dublin. On 17 January, the provincial, Fr. John Curtis, proposed the closure of Belvedere College, Dublin, but the consultors disagreed with him; and then on 25 January 1865 it was decided to send two men to Australia without any further investigation. The two chosen were outstanding figures, Victor Lentaigne, a former provincial and the current rector and master of novices at Miltown Park, and William Kelly an able theologian. Ronan's name was one of those proposed to replace

Lentaigne as rector and master of novices. Following such prominent mention in terms of appointments in 1864 and 1865, there was no mention at all in 1866 and 1867. It may be that the question did not arise because there were no positions to be filled, but one wonders if a complaint made against him to Cardinal Cullen in 1866 may not have had an influence. It was a complaint, based it seems on a misrepresentation, which caused him much upset.

A letter from Cardinal Cullen to the Jesuit provincial, Edmund J. O'Reilly, in October 1866, conveyed complaints from two Carmelite convents and a Poor Clares' convent that Ronan encouraged them to renege on their commitments in works of education and charity because these were foreign to their vocation as contemplative congregations. O'Reilly consulted Fr. Curtis, superior of the Gardiner Street community, where Ronan was now stationed, and gave Cullen's letter to Curtis for Ronan to read and comment. The latter's reply addressed to the provincial conveyed his sense of shock and barely concealed anger, and he asked the provincial to convey his reply to his Eminence. He apologised for writing in haste, but he was clearly anxious to respond straightway.

'I certainly gave retreats this year', he declared, 'to the Carmelite nuns of Warrenmount and Lakelands and to the Poor Clares of Harold's Cross. But I deny ever having said those things that have been brought as an accusation against me. I hope that God will preserve me from ever saying anything that could tend in any way to make religious violate their holy engagements. I certainly never said anything with that intention.' 'For the last twelve or thirteen years', he continued, 'I have given retreats throughout Ireland to all classes of men, women, and children - and as my superior you will be able to say to his Eminence whether I have ever before upset a religious community or preached what would lead to such fearful consequences as the violation of vows.' Dealing with the actual accusations contained in the cardinal's letter, he insisted:

> I have merely to say in all truthfulness that I never spoke against the schools, orphanages or any other works of charity or mercy that have been undertaken by the Carmelites or Poor Clares. What I did say to these

communities on the community life was in substance that they were contemplative religious, that the peculiar position of this country had obliged them, like the ancient hermits in time of persecution, to leave their retirement and to take up some of the duties of the mixed life; that they were bound to discharge these duties with great perfection as long as the Church in her wisdom thought fit to impose them, but still that these religious should cultivate the contemplative spirit and should observe their rule as far as they could consistently with their active duties.

'This is the substance of what I have said to these religious', he asserted, 'on the subject of (the) accusations which is brought against me.' It was for his Eminence to say 'whether these statements are incorrect, or imprudent, or calculated in any way to upset the minds of religious.' Then, turning the accusations back on his accusers, he explained: 'The truth is that the minds of these religious were upset long before I went to give them their retreats. The nuns in Warrenmount have been long anxious to give up their schools. They have been in correspondence with the Presentation nuns of George's Hill to give up their house and schools at Warrenmount to the Presentation nuns. This correspondence was going on before I gave the retreat or ever set foot in Warrenmount. The Carmelites at Warrenmount were anxious to go to some place where they might have no schools. Again, the Carmelites of Warrenmount have asked for a visitation long before I ever knew them. I did my best to introduce peace, and I think it very hard to be blamed by his Eminence for disturbances that existed long before I gave my retreat at all. What I say of the Carmelites of Warrenmount is equally true of the nuns of Lakelands and of Harold's Cross. I found in all these places a desire, which was very general and of long standing, to give up their schools and their other active duties; and if matters are examined closely I will venture to say that the religious who wish for the primitive rule are not the least perfect of these communities. But be that as it may, I can say with a safe conscience that I have encouraged all to the best of my power to keep their vows, to discharge faithfully their active duties, and to observe their rules as far as they could consistently with their active duties.' He concluded with the assurance - 'Of course I shall obey strictly the orders of his Eminence,' adding unctuously, 'Pray for me that I may bear patiently this heavy cross.'[27]

Every lecturer is aware how easy it is to be misconstrued by one's listeners, but perhaps what gave pause to Cullen was that the complaint came not from one source but from three. He appears to have accepted, however, Ronan's explanation, especially when it was backed up strongly by Cullen's own former assistant in Rome and his theologian at the Synod of Thurles, Edmund J. O'Reilly, now Jesuit provincial. The latter enclosed Ronan's response in his reply to Cardinal Cullen, a reply that was noticeably relaxed and gave his own comment as part of a letter including other issues. His comment on Ronan, however, was informative and significant. Ronan's letter, he observed carefully, was 'written evidently in haste and under a certain amount of excitement natural in such cases, which will account for any strength of expression observable in it. I am a little not myself at times, as you had occasion to know formerly; so I don't condemn such things'. 'To come to the matter in hand', he went on, 'I must say, in the first place, that Fr. Ronan is an exceedingly good, conscientious, pious man; that he is well informed in theological and religious subjects, that he is deliberate and thoughtful in his mode of proceeding and not precipitate. He has generally speaking given great satisfaction by his retreats to nuns. He was likewise considered - besides being a good preacher - a good catechist on missions, in the way of clear expositions of doctrine. If he be withdrawn from all direction of nuns in this diocese, it will be a loss to various convents and will involve an imputation on him, not serviceable to his character, which has hitherto been excellent.' After this clear, characteristically succinct comment, O'Reilly took the occasion to ask for a number of authorizations.[28]

The Cullen papers a year later contain a letter from Edmond J. O'Reilly, obviously in response to a query from a convent for a satisfactory retreat giver. The letter was the essence of brevity. 'Dear Rev. Mother, the father I suggest is Father Ronan'.[29] That it survives in the diocesan archives suggests that O'Reilly, or the nun recipient, sent a copy to the cardinal. No further questioning of Ronan's orthodoxy seems to have arisen during his career.

In May and October 1868, Ronan was mentioned in the consultors' notes as one who had not yet governed.[30] Two years later, however, his name occurs once more in *terna* for government, second choice for Galway.[31] It was not until 1872 that he was a first choice. On 26 July 1872, the consultors noted that he was first choice for the rector of the college and church community at the Crescent, Limerick.[32] It was a turning point. Henceforth, for a number of years, his name was to be mentioned in connection with different appointments. In Limerick, moreover, he was to fulfil what he would perceive as the main purpose and achievement of his life, a foundation that would influence the lives of thousands across the English-speaking world for almost one hundred years.

# Chapter 5

# *Rector in Limerick, 1872-1882*
# *New Beginnings*

The school and church over which Ronan presided from 1872-1882 instanced the accelerated Catholic educational and ecclesial expansion taking place from the close of the 1850s. The Jesuits in Ireland were a relatively small body. Prior to the 1860s they had in Dublin an intermediate school, Belvedere College, a novitiate, house of studies and residence at Miltown Park, and a large church at Gardiner Street; an intermediate boarding school, Clongowes Wood College, in Co. Kildare; and a small preparatory boarding school and local church at Tullabeg, near Tullamore, in the midlands. Then in 1859-1860 came foundations in Limerick and Galway, and later in the 1860s the opening of an Australian mission, and early in the 1870s the expansion of the Tullabeg school, under the visionary energy of William Delany, into a thriving intermediate college entering its students for the matriculation examinations of London University, and then developing an university wing for the same university. Subsequently, in the 1880s, there was to be added University College Dublin. It was all an immense drain on relatively few men, but fortunately there was a large percentage of able people in the overall number. The Limerick college and church during Ronan's term benefited from the ministrations of a number of such people.[1]

Ronan came to a college and church which were in debt, and which also were not in favour with the local clergy. He managed to clear the debt and even expand the church by questing, for which he had a flair, and he also won the favour of the bishop and of the large body of the clergy.

The background to the Limerick foundation necessarily influenced Ronan as rector. The college, which had commenced in 1859, was known as St. Munchin's College and had started at no. 1 Hartstonge Street at the corner of the semicircle of buildings known as the Crescent. Initially, it functioned partly as a diocesan college: a school for lay pupils from whom the bishop, Dr. John Ryan, hoped to recruit some of his future clergy. In the late autumn of 1861, however, Richard Russell, J.P., put on the market his rather splendid residence and garden, known as Richmond House, in the middle of the Crescent, and in January 1862, the Jesuits purchased the property in trust. On 9 September the school was moved to the new premises, and with this permanent location the Society of Jesus returned definitively to Limerick, the cradle of the order in Ireland. The first Jesuit school had been opened in Limerick in the 1560s, within a decade of the death of the founder, St. Ignatius Loyola, and, despite interruptions because of persecution, there was still a school and oratory in the city (in Castle Lane off Athlunkard Street) in 1773, when the order was suppressed by Pope Clement XIV.[2]

The school to which Ronan came as rector outlined its aims shortly after its foundation. The prospectus for the academic year 1862-3 announced that it catered for 'young gentlemen' who sought preparation for 'the university and ecclesial colleges; for the learned professions; for the public service - civil and military; and for the departments of mercantile and commercial life';[3] and it was also careful to mention that the pupils 'were instructed in the doctrines of the Catholic faith and trained with great care to piety and virtue'.[4] The number of pupils in the school during its first twenty years never exceeded ninety.

The Jesuit church, adjoining the college, was built in the large garden of the former Richmond House. It was finished in red brick to match the other buildings on the Crescent, and was opened with great ceremony in January 1869, and named the Church of the Sacred Heart, the first in Ireland to be so dedicated. In the view of the *Limerick Reporter*, it was built 'in the graceful style of Grecian architecture' and 'furnished not only comfortably but elegantly'.[5] Ronan's inclination to build and develop was first manifested at the Crescent. During his rectorship a western apse dedicated to St. Joseph was added to the church, balancing, as it were, an eastern apse dedicated to Our Lady of Lourdes, both representing particular devotions of the rector. A new high altar composed of 22 varieties of marble was constructed, and matched by smaller equally elegant altars in the side-chapels in the apses. All three were consecrated by the bishops of Ross, Cloyne, and Limerick on Sunday, 16 January 1876.[6]

Ronan preached in various places collecting for the church. The archives of the Sisters of Mercy, Kinsale, record for 21 November 1875 that he arrived in the town collecting 'for his new church of the Sacred Heart, Limerick'.[7] He would later indicate to his provincial that he spent many of his early years as rector so engaged.[8] Henceforth, his life was to be marked by begging ventures to pay for building projects and plant improvements. As well as preaching and collecting, however, he continued at this period to conduct retreats in various convents, especially throughout Munster, and sometimes preached special sermons in support of their work. The Mercy archives, Kinsale, 1874, record a retreat by him to the Industrial School children and his preaching the annual charity sermon in the parish church, and in October of the following year it is noted that he delivered 'the annual charity sermon in aid of our poor'.[9] Despite his frequent absences from Limerick as a retreat director, preacher, and fundraiser, the school of which he was rector became widely known for its educational achievements.

A few years before his arrival the school had suffered a decline. In 1867 the new bishop of Limerick, Dr. George Butler, decided to establish a separate seminary for the diocese. He called it St. Munchin's College. There were now two colleges called after Limerick's patron saint, and the Jesuit college lost some of its pupils. This was accentuated in 1868 when the Jesuits roused the hostility of many of the diocesan clergy and laity by not voting in a bitterly contested political election. One of Ronan's actions after his arrival was to change the title of his school to Sacred Heart College, thereby removing the anomaly of two St. Munchin's Colleges. A few years later circumstances enabled the college achieve national prominence. The introduction of the Intermediate Education Act in 1876 provided state subsidies based on examination results. This offered an opportunity for Catholic schools, which, unlike their Protestant counterparts, received no form of state subsidy. It was generally felt, of course, that the subsidised schools, because of their resources and tradition, would win the top places and prizes in the new examination system. In the event, the overall winner in terms of places and prizes was the college of the Holy Ghost Fathers at Blackrock, Co. Dublin, and the next most successful was the Jesuit college at Tullabeg. The overall individual winner in that first year, junior grade, however, was a boy from Ronan's school. The results, published in September 1879, were hailed in the press and provided a powerful morale boost to the Catholic institutions. Telegrams and letters of congratulation were addressed to Ronan as rector, including one from the chairman of the recently formed Catholic Headmasters' Association, William J. Walsh, president of Maynooth College.

The successful Crescent student was Charles Doyle, whose achievement generated intense enthusiasm amongst his fellow pupils.[10] In succeeding years he obtained first place in the middle and senior grades. Two other Crescent boys won distinctions in the junior grade, and two passed in the first division of the matriculation of London University.[11] All combined to make the Crescent's name known throughout Ireland.

Despite his capacity for relating easily to young people, there is no record of any involvement on Ronan's part in the concerts and dramatics that were a regular feature in the life of the college, nor of any interest in tennis, cricket, rowing, sailing and swimming, which seem to have been the favoured sports among the pupils.[12]

As the rector of the Crescent, educating the sons of many of the prominent citizens, he could not but be aware, however, of the commercial and political developments in the city. Among the strong merchant class one figure stood out, the Scots Presbyterian, Peter Tait, who had come to Limerick as a youth, and in 1850 had exploited the possibilities of the newly-invented sewing machine to set up the first ready-made clothing factory in the world. His name may have been known already to Ronan before he came to Limerick, as Tait had secured contracts during the Crimean war for immense quantities of uniforms. He became the official supplier of the whole British army, and employed some 1,000 people, mainly women.[13]

Another figure whose name was likely to have been familiar to Ronan before he arrived in the city was that of Isaac Butt, often described as 'the father of Home Rule', who was a member of parliament for Limerick. His Home Rule meetings at O'Connell's monument in front of the Jesuit residence were to be a familiar sight during Ronan's years as rector.[14] He resigned from politics in 1879. In County Limerick, meantime, one of the two members of parliament, William Monsell, was elevated to cabinet rank as post-master general in 1871. He was to play an important part in Ronan's plans. One of three distinguished Co. Limerick converts to Catholicism during the Oxford Movement, the others being Lord Dunraven and Aubrey de Vere, Monsell became Lord Emly in 1874.

While such events were proceeding, Ronan's reputation as a spiritual director of religious communities of both sexes, and of clergy in very many dioceses, became even more fully established. 'His zeal, his spirit of prayer, and his extraordinary devotion to the Sacred Heart' were said to have brought blessing on his work. He was also noted, as suggested earlier, for his confidence in and devotion to Our Lady of Lourdes and St. Joseph.[15] His religious zeal had urged him for some years to give substance to an old ideal, the establishment of an 'Apostolic School'. His efforts to pursue it were to bring humiliation and frustration before eventual acceptance and support.[16]

## Towards an Apostolic School

On 12 August 1880, Ronan wrote from the Mercy convent, Loughrea, where he was giving a retreat, to the new provincial, Fr. James Tuite, to explain the genesis and development of his ideas for an Apostolic School. After much difficulty the school was due to open the next month, and he wished to have more support from Fr. Tuite than he had experienced from his predecessors. He felt more at ease with Tuite, who had been a member of his community at the Crescent in 1872-3.[17]

In the more than twenty years he had spent on the home missions, Ronan explained, 'I became more and more convinced that we have in the youth of our virtuous poor ... inexhaustible materials for priests and religious'. 'The most promising boys at our various missions I have tried to form into sodalities for serving mass and have placed under the care of the local clergy.

I constantly meet with some of these sodalists who have become good priests. The great mass of them, however, were lost to the Church on account of the poverty of their parents. I have thus been led to think what a grand thing it would be for the church if institutions could be established where promising boys could be educated and formed gratuitously to the apostolic life.'

'When I heard of the apostolic schools being formed by our fathers in France', Ronan continued, 'I thought that some effort might be made in that direction in this country if we only had the means. So I spoke to a friend of mine, Miss Martin, now deceased. She promised me £1,000 to begin the work and she would, I believe, have given me twice that sum. But on making efforts to interest the rectors of our colleges I could not get one to take up the work or accept the money. So all the money went to another charity.'

Following this patent lack of co-operation from the established Jesuit schools in educating his prospective candidates, Ronan appears to have put aside his project for some years. He had other pressing demands on his time. 'For the first years of my stay in Limerick', he informed Tuite, 'there was so much to be done in begging for the church and trying to clear off the debts that I could think of nothing else.' In more recent times, however, it seemed to him that he should speak to the provincial, Fr. Nicholas Walsh, about it. The latter gave him encouragement and, hence, Ronan, in the course of his annual letter as rector to the Jesuit Father General, Pieter Becks, told of his hopes and plans. 'His Paternity', Ronan observed, 'seemed to me in his reply to be so much in favour of the project that I concluded that I would be allowed to make a trial if I could secure the means to begin.' He went to a Mr. Devereux of Wexford whom he thought would be interested. Devereux came to Limerick and, in Ronan's words, 'heard all I had to say and went away without doing anything, but evidently much pleased with the plan'. Subsequently, to Ronan's disappointment and perhaps righteous anger, he heard from the provincial, Fr. Walsh, 'that Mr. Devereux had given £1,000 for the apostolic school, but that the project had been condemned by the consultors of the province as being impractical. The money had been given to Clongowes!' 'I took this decision as final', Ronan declared, 'and never said anything to any superior afterwards.' His comment marks the first clear indication of a distrust of province authorities that was to become prominent in later years.

In 1879, however, during the provincialate of Aloysius Sturzo, new hope was generated. Fr. Alfred Weld, the English assistant to the General, wrote to Ronan that the General 'had always been in favour of the apostolic school and was determined to have it started'. A letter to that effect was sent to Sturzo, and 'soon after', as Ronan related, 'I had a letter from Fr. Sturzo asking me for my plan, and in the course of a little time he told me that I had leave to try what support I could get for the institution'. 'It was a very bad year to begin', Ronan observed. The agricultural depression had been intensified by crop failure. In June, Parnell had advised tenant farmers in danger of eviction to hold on to their home-steads, and, in October, the National Land League had been formed. Nevertheless, in December, he decided to go ahead, 'not knowing what might happen a year hence' and also thinking 'that the Lord may have chosen that time to show, if it succeeded, that it was his work'. Accordingly, on 8 December, he began by sending circulars, explaining his plans and asking support, to all the bishops and the religious houses of priests in Ireland. The following day, a reluctant and anxious Sturzo, conscious of how stretched were the resources of the province, sent a circular letter to the Irish Jesuit superiors announcing that 'to comply with an express wish and I might say an order of our Very Rev. Father General we are about to try and see if we can open an 'Apostolic School', as our Fathers have already done in France, Belgium and even Italy'. Because the work was a difficult one it was important 'to ask help from heaven in a special manner' and hence he wished 'that each community in the province should make a novena for that purpose to the Sacred Heart of Our Divine Lord'.

'Fifteen of the bishops', Ronan informed Tuite, had in reply given him 'encouragement and promises of assistance' and 'about thirty superiors of religious houses and as many secular clergy promised annual donations of from one to five pounds.' Fr. Weld promised to pay for two places in the new school, and Fr. Sturzo promised the same. Moreover, eight priests promised annual collections in their parishes for the school. The response to the circular was considered 'very good', but Ronan was not satisfied. He felt that he could achieve much more by explaining the project directly to the clergy who, he believed, had 'a strong sympathy for foreign missions, particularly those where the poor Irish had found a home'. He started with a request to the Archbishop of Cashel, Dr. Thomas Croke. 'He invited me to his (diocesan) conference,' Ronan declared, 'and spoke most kindly in favour of my project and allowed me to address his clergy. The result was that nearly all the clergy promised me annual donations, the parish priests £2 and the other clergy £1.' 'I have gone to the conferences of Cloyne, Limerick, Killaloe, and Waterford', he added, 'with the same result.' From each diocese there was an annual commitment - 'Cashel (archbishop £20) £120; Limerick (bishop £5) £150; Cloyne (bishop £5) £127; Killaloe £90 (two conferences not yet visited); Kerry about £100; Waterford £100.'[18] Everywhere, Ronan reported, he was treated with 'extreme kindness ' by the bishops. They kept him at their houses, brought him to the various conferences, 'spoke most warmly of the project ... and complimented the Society in the highest terms'. 'The clergy also took the thing up at once.'

In one diocese, however, he was severely tested. At the conference in Waterford he experienced 'open hostility'. There were three conferences within the diocese. At Clonmel and Dungarvan he had been well received. Each conference promised £50 a year. But in Waterford city his project was seen as a threat to the diocesan college. 'The president, Fr. (Pierse) Power, made a long statement of the good his college was doing even in the missionary way and how this project would interfere with its success.' Anything the priests had to give, he asserted, should be given to their own college. One of the professors at the college, Fr. Joseph A. Phelan, spoke next and, in Ronan's words, 'showed a good deal of hostility to my project but little argument against it'. Ronan asked the bishop's leave 'to offer a few remarks to their statements'. He was glad, he said, to have objections raised so that he might answer them. The project, he then explained, 'could not possibly interfere with the distinguished institution of which Fr. Power was president'. The boys entering that institution had to pay pensions (fees), but the boys he (Ronan) was looking for had no hope of entering Waterford College, as they 'came from a class below the average student', could not pay pensions, and 'required special training in accent, good manners etc.' which was not necessary in other institutions. The bishop, Dr. John Power, took up the case, and declared that the arguments and reasons were all on Ronan's side.

At this point, Fr. Phelan requested Ronan to kindly withdraw so that the conference would be freer to discuss the question. Ronan walked up and down outside for nearly half an hour before the conference broke up. The bishop, who was pained by the whole proceeding, brought him to his house and told him that the two gentlemen, Power and Phelan, 'had organised a general system of hostility to the Apostolic School' and that 'the final decision of the conference was put off to their next meeting'. He, as bishop, had told them that they might refuse to contribute, but that their opposition 'did not rest on any fair reason'. Ronan, having thanked the bishop, left himself in his hands either to go to the next conference or to write to remind him of the promise of the conference to decide at their next what they should do.

Concluding his letter to the provincial, Ronan remarked that Pierse Power, before the conference, had requested a Jesuit to conduct a retreat for his students in September. 'It is of great importance', he emphasised, 'that some Father should be sent who would be certain to give great satisfaction.' The Waterford experience, he assured Tuite, was 'the only unpleasant thing' he encountered. 'Indeed', he added, 'there is no accounting for the wonderful success of my mission except ... that it is the work of God and that his good priests have recognised it as such and taken it up.' He closed with an apology for giving Tuite the trouble of reading 'such a long document', yet added carefully that it was necessary to put him in full possession 'of the whole thing', as he, Ronan, wished in all things to be guided by God through his superiors!

The then efficient postal service ensured that he had a 'very kind note' from Tuite by return next day. Hence, on 13 August, the day after his long letter, he sent a further explanatory letter. At the conferences, he explained, he had indicated clearly the kind of boys that were required so that the clergy would be on the look out for them, and he also endeavoured to establish structures to ensure that the promised funds were forthcoming. At each conference he got one priest, named by the bishop, usually the secretary of the conference, to collect the annual subscriptions and to be a link person. Already he had received and lodged £543. He went on to indicate his arrangements for the selection of suitable students. He gave to each conference which contributed £25 a year one free place in the Apostolic School, and left it to the vicar of the conference to choose the most worthy of the students nominated by the clergy, and to this end he was translating certain 'informations' or outlines of questions used by the French Jesuits to assist in choosing candidates. 'I mentioned to the clergy', he added, 'that when we found any boy unsuitable I would give notice to the vicar and ask for another. In this way I have tried to make the arrangements self-acting and permanent.' He followed up such indications of practical management skills by informing Tuite that the priests were very much impressed by his announcement that the Society intended to give to the project a free house, furnished, while supporting the priest who was to be spiritual director. He 'also brought out the point', he stated, 'that this is not an experiment but an organised system of education and formation which is working in France and Belgium under the care of the Society for nearly twenty years with great success.'[19]

In this connection, Ronan explained in the *Mungret Annual* of January 1904, that it was his practice to inform the assembled priests that he would be following the lead of the French apostolic schools with regard to the requirements they sought in the candidates who applied to them: - *They should be the children of virtuous parents and mostly of old Catholic families. They should be over fourteen years of age. They should have a good constitution and an agreeable appearance. Their talent should be above the average. They should be well grounded in English and Science (such boys as are selected in schools as monitors). They should have a good vocation to the priesthood. They should all go on foreign missions. They could become regular or secular priests; if they chose to become regulars, they could select any order or congregation approved by the Church that had members on foreign missions. Their parents should contribute to their support according to their means; but no one, who was otherwise eligible, would be rejected for want of means.*

Frs. Weld and Sturzo had thought it right, Ronan explained to Fr. Tuite in his letter of 13 August, that he visit some of those apostolic schools of France and Belgium to see how their system worked. He visited the schools of Boulogne, Amiens, and Tourhout in the north of Belgium. He found that the heads of the schools met together from time to time and that all followed the same system of rules and discipline. It all looked 'marvellous', but in practice he could not see it being applied completely in Ireland. He was taken, however, by the method used in France of starting a new school. They sent a certain number of the best of the students from a functioning school to help commence the new one. The French provincial allowed him to take 'four of the best of the apostolic scholars of Amiens and Boulogne, all Irish, to make a beginning' in Ireland. The great remaining difficulty was to get a spiritual director who both knew the apostolic school system and spoke English. The French provincial was eager to help but had no one to spare. There was also no one available in Belgium.

In keeping with his trust in devotion to the Sacred Heart, Ronan went to Paray-le-Monial, where the devotion had received renewed impetus from the visions of the seventeenth century religious sister of the Visitation Congregation, Blessed Margaret Mary (since canonised), and the active promotion of the Society of Jesus. He prayed at the shrine, asking the assistance of Margaret Mary and of the Sacred Heart. Afterwards he returned to the Jesuit house in the town and there, to his delight, found a young French Jesuit priest, Jean Baptiste René, who had studied at the English Jesuit theologate at St. Bueno's, in Wales, spoke English fluently, and the previous year had been for a time in charge of the Apostolic School at Poitiers. René was completing his tertianship, or final year of Jesuit spiritual formation, at Paray-le-Monial, and his tertian-instructor assured Ronan that he was the man he wanted. René expressed his readiness to come to Ireland if his provincial, Fr. Champellan, approved. The latter, who had himself been superior of an apostolic school, agreed that he could go for a year to organise the Irish foundation. René, in fact, was to stay for seven years. 'He and his four scholars', Ronan assured Fr. Tuite on 13 August, 'will be with us, please God, by the end of the month.' Ronan, meantime, had managed to rent a house at the Crescent, adjoining the community house and college, and had obtained it rent-free from the proprietor who, it appears, was as impressed as most of the clergy had been by Ronan's enthusiasm and zeal.

The school opened on 24 September 1880, with eight boys. They attended classes at the Crescent College. Ronan acted as rector of the community, the college, and the new school. René was the spiritual director of the apostolic students. He had very definite standards. Between April and June 1882 he dismissed four students. Two others left of their own accord. The numbers, notwithstanding, rose rapidly. By the end of the second year numbers had risen to twenty-eight, of whom, according to the diary of the Apostolic School for 1881-'82, twenty-six sat the public examinations in December 1881, sixteen in junior grade, four in middle grade, and five for the matriculation examination of the Royal University. By the end of the second year of the project, therefore, its success pointed to the need for larger premises. The solution proved complex. Different interests and priorities were implicated.

# Chapter 6

# *Moving to Mungret College*

The large premises that Ronan sought proved to be Mungret College some three or four miles west of Limerick city. It was only gradually, as a result of a combination of circumstances, that he came to envisage possessing such a property. The combined circumstances which paved the way involoved the bishop of Limerick and his diocesan college, and the history of Mungret College and the obligations of its trustees.

The decision of Bishop Butler to reopen a separate seminary college in 1867 had been influenced by the desire of one of his priests, Joseph Burke, to start a college at number 1 Hartstonge Street at the corner of the Crescent and to invest his own capital in the venture. Bourke had an ambitious programme. The school he opened was far from confined to educating seminarians. He announced that his college would 'prepare young men for business, for the civil service, or for any of the professions'.[1] Success came quickly, hastened by the circumstances of the bitter parliamentary election of 1868: the Jesuits' decision to abstain from voting leading to a large number of pupils being withdrawn from their school and sent to the diocesan college. In 1869, therefore, Bourke found himself with a full complement of students. The success continued, and after twelve years he planned an ambitious expansion. He decided to lease Mungret Agricultural College.

That institution resulted from a bill passed in parliament in 1852, which vested some buildings and seventy acres of land in five trustees with a view to establishing a model farm and a college teaching agricultural science. In 1853 the trustees leased the property to the National Board of Education to set up the college. Their venture never prospered and was closed in September 1878. The trustees were bound under the terms of the act of parliament to run a college or get someone to do so. A purely agricultural college was not likely to attract leaseholders. Some flexibility, however, was afforded the trustees by a further act of parliament which enabled the Lord Lieutenant to decide to whom the property might be entrusted and to approve its purpose. The five trustees, under the leadership of Lord Emly, sought new tenants. The other trustees were: Sir David Roche, Sir Stephen de Vere, E. W. O'Brien Esq., and James Greene Barry Esq. who was also secretary. They were disposed towards St. Munchin's College by the personal friendship which existed between Bishop Butler and Lord Emly, and by the presence on the teaching staff of the diocesan college of Mons. L'Abbé L'Heritier, chaplain to Lord Emly's French wife. On 11 August, 1880, the college and lands were leased to Joseph Bourke at an annual rent of £79.[2]

The college opened its doors, as part of the St. Munchin's college still functioning at Hartstonge Street on the corner of the Crescent, on 23 September, 1880. The teaching staff at the city side of the college were also expected to travel to Mungret to teach there. The venture opened with optimism. Despite a brave start, it was evident by the end of the first academic year that from both an educational and financial point of view the project could not continue. In the summer of 1881 Bourke was obliged to terminate the venture and to return to No.1 Hartstonge Street. To pay off his debts, he contemplated selling the school at No. 1 Hartstonge Street. This led to criticism from some priests of the diocese, led by his former friend Edward Thomas O'Dwyer, the future bishop of Limerick. Bourke emphasised that the college was not the property of the diocese. In the end he sold the furniture to cover his debts, and the college at Hartstonge Street continued, but under the presidency of Fr. O'Dwyer.[3] O'Dwyer continued to manage the school at Hartstonge Street into the following year, but Bishop Butler was not happy with the situation.

The trustees, meanwhile, were left with another failure at Mungret. Lord Emly turned to the Holy Ghost Fathers who had made such a success of their colleges, Blackrock, in Co. Dublin, and Rockwell, near Cashel, Co. Tipperary. The conditions governing the Mungret property, however, proved unacceptable to the Holy Ghost negotiators, Fr. Huvetys, superior of the Holy Ghost Congregation in Ireland, and Fr. Francis X. Libermann. They balked at the requirement that the school and land be governed by a board of five trustees, two Protestant and three

Catholic, who would have overall authority over the school and its policy. Emly's assurances that the conditions were more theoretical than practical, and that the non-Catholic members of the board were his friends and would do as he suggested, were not sufficient.[4]

The disappointment of the trustees rendered them even more pliable about conditions with respect to the next candidate. It proved to be William Ronan. In a letter to his provincial, Fr. James Tuite, on 29 December, 1881, he explained that on a Christmas visit to Bishop Butler the latter expressed a wish 'that we should get Mungret College and should educate there our apostolics and his diocesan students'. He also advised that Ronan write to Emly to learn the conditions required to obtain possession of the college, and then submit the conditions to the provincial. 'Last night', Ronan stated, 'I wrote to Lord Emly as the bishop desired. I mentioned to him that I had no authority to treat of the matter but merely asked him for the conditions that I might submit them to our provincial.' Meantime, he said, he was writing to Tuite 'as a *friend* and in *private*' so that he might know what was being done. It seemed providential to obtain 'a grand place like Mungret for the training of the apostolics and also the training of the future priests of the diocese'. Fr. René, he continued enthusiastically, could take charge of studies and spiritual formation, and acquire, besides, 'two or three first rate professors and a couple of lay brothers' from France, which would mean that the apostolic school would not want more than one man from the provincial. 'Once the thing was fairly started', Ronan went on, referring to his term as rector, 'I could give you my *nunc dimittis*, and surely I am not asking too much at the end of ten long years to be released.' He concluded, as if in passing, with two weighted remarks, namely, that the Father General's assistant, Fr. Alfred Weld, when in Ireland 'expressed a great desire to get Mungret for the Apostolic School', and that Bishop Butler 'had no idea we would take up Mungret, otherwise he would not have consented to Lord Emly's request to invite the Fathers of the Holy Ghost'.[5]

Three days after Ronan wrote to him, Emly replied from Paris that his letter was 'the best new year gift' he had received. He had long wished Ronan to have Mungret but thought it impossible with his college already in Limerick. As with Frs. Huvetys and Libermann, he assured Ronan that the conditions were 'merely nominal' and would have 'no practical effect'. He suggested that Ronan get his provincial's approval and then have Fr. René write to him 'offering to take Mungret on the same conditions as Fr. Bourke had it, making no allusion to ecclesiastical students'. It would be well, he added, 'to enclose a letter from Fr. Bourke consenting to hand over to Fr. René'. The sooner René started operations the better. He would give every help he could.[6]

Through January there was an interchange of letters between Ronan and the provincial. The latter raised a variety of objections made by his consultors, Ronan pressed the advantages of the acquisition and sought to answer the problems posed. From Athlone, at the start of the month, where he was preaching and collecting money for the apostolic school, he wrote that Bishop Butler was determined to acquire Mungret and invite a religious order to run it as a diocesan seminary. This would have serious consequences for their school at the Crescent, he warned. Given that 'Fr. O'Dwyer has taken from us nearly thirty of our day scholars, what would be the case if we had to contend with such men as the Fathers of the Holy Ghost?' To the objection that having apostolic and diocesan students mingling would create difficulties, he explained that Fr. René intended to keep them quite separate. In a letter two days later he sweepingly assured the provincial that Mungret College had 'been too long lying idle for the government to trouble itself with it' and that the government and the trustees would be 'only too happy to have the place utilised as an Intermediate school'. To the objection that if day boys shared the school with apostolics they would look down on them, he replied that this did not happen at the Crescent. On the contrary, the apostolics were respected by the day boys, and the masters found them 'a great advantage' as they studied better and were 'better conducted than the day scholars'. On 4 January he sent on Fr. Bourke's leases which he had received from the bishop, who repeated to him what Emly said, that the conditions were a matter of form.

The conditions were examined in detail by Tuite and his consultors. Ronan doggedly sent letters with information and responses to questions and objections on 5, 9, 11, 12, 13, 15

January, and then on 24 January the provincial announced - 'All the consultors of the province unanimously agree that we cannot accept the college under such conditions.'[7] Ronan refused to give up hope. With typical persistence, he replied on 3 February that as it was the time of year for him to write his annual letter as a superior to the General of the Society he would explain the situation to him. He then mentioned the enthusiasm of two bishops he had met recently, Drs. Thomas Nulty of Meath and Laurence Gillooly of Elphin, when he explained to them the nature of the training in the apostolic school. 'Think', he exclaimed, 'what would be the effect if the students of Limerick were trained on the same lines, and how it would change the discipline of the seminaries of the whole country and increase the confidence of the bishops and clergy in the Society.' His arguments and patent zeal caused Tuite to waver. Ronan pressed home the advantage. On 10 February he informed his provincial that he had sent to the General an abstract of the lease, the agreement with Fr. Bourke, and the scheme of studies, and had explained at length to him 'the whole case' so that he 'would be ignorant of nothing'. 'Then', he continued, 'to make everything quite satisfactory I sent the documents in a registered letter to Fr. Weld, and I asked him to talk to Lord Emly over the matter.' Weld, as the Assistant for England and Ireland, was the normal channel of approach to the General. 'Nothing remains to be done', Ronan concluded, 'but to pray that God's will may be done in this and in all other things.' It was to be done as he hoped.

On 16 January, 1882, the General, Pieter Beckx, sent the crucial reply to the provincial.

> I understand from the letter your Reverence sent me on 4 February that having heard the consultors about accepting Mungret College, you first judged that the college should not be accepted with the conditions which were proposed, but that afterwards, having considered what was said on the other side, you were in doubt. Because the matter seemed to me to be of the greatest importance, I sought fuller and more accurate information. Having considered this, and what the Father Assistant had to say, *I judge that the college should be accepted*.

Your Reverence will therefore let Fr. Ronan know as quickly as possible so that he can enter into the necessary arrangements with the trustees of the college and the matter can be quickly brought to a safe conclusion. From it I hope and believe your province will derive the greatest benefit ....[8]

Following on this decision, Ronan negotiated with the bishop and Lord Emly for concessions and for the fulfilment of requirements laid down by Fr. George Porter, Assistant to the General. He also impressed on the harassed provincial the need for an efficient academic staff to make the college a success. From Cloyne on 6 March he assured Fr. Tuite, who was worried about the financial implications of the new undertaking, that God would never see them short. When he arrived at the Crescent, he stated pointedly, he found 'nearly £5,000 of debt on the place - a sum which all the concerns would scarcely realise if put up at the time for auction', and 'the province gave us little encouragement and no assistance in paying off that debt'. 'Yet all that debt is paid', he stated, 'except £300, and nearly £4,000 of alms were expended on the church. A good library was purchased and anything required for the carrying on of our work was procured. Surely we ought to be grateful to the Sacred Heart for all these blessings.'[9]

The provincial informed him that he 'could not hope for an efficient staff from the province'.[10] As the venture was evidently dear to the General, Ronan requested the new Assistant, Fr. George Porter, to look out for men from other provinces. France was the most likely place. In March 1880 an anti-clerical government had ordered the Society of Jesus to evacuate all its houses and colleges. The emphasis on assistance from France occasioned concern to the Irish provincial and his consultors. Ronan, on 19 March, sent a long informative and carefully crafted letter from the Crescent to the provincial. He agreed that 'of course Mungret should be essentially an Irish seminary', though the French presence supplied 'order, system, perseverance', but it was essential that the college have a good staff and 'the foundation of a good system of studies'. If he had Fr. Tom Finlay as prefect of studies, minister, and master of a senior class, Fr. Thomas Head, a former secular priest 'much esteemed by the bishop and clergy', to teach classics, and a good master to teach mathematics, he would 'not require to have any Frenchman except Fr. René and Lord Emly's chaplain'. With this staff, and the teaching assistance of the senior apostolics, it would be possible to manage, and the staff, besides, would be as thoroughly Irish as Fr. Tuite desired. Two Jesuit brothers could manage the farm and the cooking, and he intended, much to the delight of the bishop, 'to make the seminary boys keep their part of the house clean etc. like the apostolics'.

He went on to speak revealingly about his work and himself. Because it was coming up to Easter when the clergy collected their dues, he thought it only right to give up his 'parochial begging' for a little time. He had 'established annual collections in ten or twelve parishes', he stated, and had got over £500, of which about two-thirds was promised him annually. He experienced great kindness from the clergy and the goodness of the people to him was marvellous. He continued:

> Begging I have always found a terrible ordeal. Besides the repugnance I have to it, there is the terrible labour and fatigue. I used to awake at night with cramps and I was often overpowered with exhaustion. And yet I have constantly blessed God for giving me an opportunity of seeing through the begging the goodness of people ... I have the consolation of knowing that my absence has done no harm to the house. I have asked no one to do any work for me except to preach on the Sunday when my turn came and I was absent.

On 26 March Ronan informed the provincial that the trustees had given him all he asked. It would be necessary, however, to follow the programme of the Royal University to suit 'the bishop's scholars', rather than the Intermediate. Lord Emly was presenting the new scheme of studies to the Lord Lieutenant for his approval. On 31 March he relayed that Lord Emly had called and informed him that he had found that 'he and the other trustees can give the lease and the agreement without reference to the Lord Lieutenant', and that as the application for the substitution of the Royal University programme for that of the Intermediate would entail considerable delays he had written to the other trustees 'to dispense with the application to the Lord

Lieutenant' and 'go on with the programme'. The decisions were precipitous and would create problems at a later date.

On 12 April, Ronan announced that the lease was signed that day.[11] It was for 500 years. Fr. Bourke, who still retained possession of the farm and the house, was to be written to by the attorney of the trustees offering to forgive the rent of two years if he handed over possession at once. Finally, Ronan informed the provincial that the bishop had readily approved the conditions sent by Fr. Porter governing the acceptance of the seminarians in Mungret College.

### Beginning a New College as the First Rector

Towards the close of the month, Ronan pressed the provincial to have a rector of Mungret appointed as soon as possible. Two days later, 1 May 1882, the General wrote to Fr. Tuite that the business of Mungret College had advanced enough to think about a superior who could straightway set about the work of preparing the college. 'Having considered and weighed up all that has been done so far', Fr. Beckx declared, 'it seems equitable and convenient that Fr. Ronan should be rector of the new college.' This meant that a replacement was needed for the rector of the Crescent College, and he asked the provincial to forward a terna to him. The fact that no terna was asked for rector of Mungret caused concern to the provincial and his consultors. Fr. Beckx felt it necessary to write again on 1 June: 'Having consulted with the Fathers Assistant and considered your Reverence's and your consultors' judgements, I decree in the Lord that Father William Ronan is to be constituted rector of Mungret College.'[12]

The General's concern for the success of the new school was reflected in the number of letters he sent to the provincial during 1882. One thing remains to be said of Mungret College, he wrote on 17 May, namely, that it was not of the same kind as the other colleges of the order, and needed a method of teaching and of governing proper to itself; hence those deputed to undertake duty there needed to be selected with much care and consideration. The result of this prompting was reflected in his letter to Fr. Tuite almost two months later. On 11 July he thanked him for his letter of 3 July, adding briefly, 'as the selection of those Fathers destined for Mungret College is pleasing to you and to Fr.

Ronan, it also satisfies me.' He remained unimpressed, however, with the general attitude of the provincial and his consultors.

On 23 July he commented on a letter from Tuite dated 7 July and on 'subsequent ones from various quarters'. St. Ignatius held it of great import, he reminded the provincial, that wherever we work we should highly esteem the prelates of the church and endeavour to carry out their wishes. Consequently, as the Bishop of Limerick wanted the Society to undertake its work at Mungret as soon as possible, it was 'our duty to find out how best and most expeditiously this can be done'. 'If there appear to be difficulties', he continued, 'and some have already been mentioned, we ought to consider that God rewards not so much those works that men esteem and consider most important but rather those that are done with generous promptitude in a humble and generous way for the glory of God, and it is not always what is easy or popular or impressive that is best and most useful.' In the same hortatory vein he pointed out that the need for Catholic education was greatest among 'those young people who for lack of home education and care are in most danger, namely, the children of the poor', and if this involved, he added, 'some deflection from our accustomed way of acting ... that certainly is not something unworthy of us who are disciples of him who said "Suffer little children to come unto me and forbid them not".'

Before these trenchant sentiments reached Ireland, Fr. Beckx felt it necessary to address further objections. It was represented that higher class families might object to the indiscriminate mixing of boys, and that there could be objections on the grounds of cleanliness and urbanity. To the first he responded on 26 July, that if such a difficulty really existed, it could be met by segregating the boys of different schools in times of recreation and by having different exit and entry doors or at any rate different times. As far as cleanliness and urbanity were concerned, 'nothing needs to be said', he commented, 'other than that this depends on the vigilance and care of those who have charge of the boys. If there are any at the beginning who are failing in cleanliness or courtesy, they can, as in other places, be gradually changed by patience and wise discipline; should there appear to be no hope of improvement they could and should be sent away from the school.'[13]

The diary of the Apostolic School, 1881-'82, kept by the apostolic prefect, Michael Mahony, noted that on 1 July, 1882, Fr. Ronan took possession of Mungret College, and that on the following day he and all the apostolics visited the house, and he blessed it. Also present were Lord Emly's chaplain, Pere L'Heritier, and a young French Jesuit scholastic, Joseph de Maistre. The latter was to play a prominent part in the early years of the college, and his father, Count de Maistre, was to prove a generous benefactor. The apostolics played cricket in the grounds after the ceremony. In subsequent days the apostolics became accustomed to their new location by visiting, cleaning the house and putting things in order, playing cricket, and going to Tervoe, Lord Emly's nearby estate on the Shannon, to swim. On 20 July the diarist observed: 'Final settlement of affairs respecting Mungret'.

Thereafter, furniture was moved each day until 18 August when all the apostolics finally left the Crescent and assembled for dinner at Mungret. Eight days later the boats of the apostolic school were brought from Limerick and drawn up on the bank at Tervoe. On 5 September, Ronan and the greater part of the Mungret staff came to stay, and on 13 September came the final arrivals, the seminarists, who arrived before dinner and went for a walk afterwards with the apostolics.[14]

On 14 September Ronan arranged for Bishop Butler to say Mass in the presence of staff and students and to dedicate the college to the Sacred Heart. He obtained permission for the dedication from the General, even though the Intermediate college at the Crescent was already Sacred Heart College. A further possible occasion of confusion was reflected in a misleading advertisement he ran in *The Munster News* from August to 16 September which invited applications from lay students paying a pension of £32 a year. The advertisement also informed the public that the course of studies would 'embrace agricultural training and all the subjects prescribed for the three grades of the Intermediate Education as well as for the subjects required for the matriculation examination of the Royal University'. It added that 'The superiors ... believe that, if successful, this college will be fruitful of advantages to youth by preparing young men for the different professions and by helping to promote and maintain a high educational standard among the influential men of the country'.[15] There was no mention of apostolics or seminarists. Sending a copy of the prospectus to all the clergy of the diocese, Ronan added an explanatory note. 'I enclose a prospectus of Mungret College. By the express desire of our Venerable Bishop I have made no allusion to the diocesan seminary, in order to save the trustees from all embarrassment. However I am instructed by His Lordship to inform your Reverence that the candidates for the secular priesthood of the diocese must spend at least one year in Mungret College.'

The first Mungret community, after all the negotiation, consisted of seven priests, one scholastic, and two brothers. Involved also in the work of the school was a drill master and a band master, and the senior apostolics who taught a number of classes and fulfilled other important offices during the first six years. The names and offices of the first community were: William Ronan, rector; Jean Baptist René, director of the apostolic school and of the seminarians, professor of philosophy, and prefect of discipline; Charles McKenna, minister, prefect of the church, of health, and of the reading at meals; William Sutton, prefect of spirituality and studies; Maurice Wolfe, teacher of middle school and of mathematics; Patrick Hughes, an elderly man, acted as bursar; Thomas Head, taught the members of lower school and had responsibility for them, and was also librarian. The scholastic, Joseph de Maistre, was assistant to Fr. René for the apostolic school. Brother Daniel Hickey was cook, and Brother James O'Grady, plant supervisor.[16]

The early weeks were hectic and somewhat chaotic. On 11 November the bishop reminded Ronan that no one from the college had attended the diocesan conference the previous Friday. His excuse that all were 'so busy' that he could not spare any one, was not well received. It was clear that the mistake must not be repeated. There was also confusion in those early months about lines of authority, a questioning by Irish members, perhaps, of the authority of the foreigner amongst them. Word reached the General who, with his now familiar concern for the new venture, sent an instruction to the provincial on 22 November, 1882. 'So that there might be no further room for doubt', he announced, 'I again declare: Fr. René has full authority and power over the students in all things which concern their discipline and regimen, so that in the care and direction of the alumni Fr. René is subject to no one except the rector of the college. I ask your Reverence to make this known to the superiors of Mungret College without delay.'[17]

A further factor inducing some confusion was shortage of accommodation. From the college's diary for 1881-'82, and the Marks Book, it appears that in the first year at Mungret there were thirty-two apostolics and thirty-one seminarians of whom fifteen were lay students. And these numbers, together with the Jesuits, meant that seventy-three people had to be accommodated. This could not be done satisfactorily. For the first two years, indeed, the apostolics' dormitory also served as their study hall.[18] An expansion of the premises was needed. This was further underlined by the action of Bishop Butler and Lord Emly as trustees for the estate of Lord Dunraven, which had left £2,000 for Catholic purposes. They presented the money to Ronan to build a chapel, on condition that he could find an equal sum for other buildings. He arranged for a chapel to be built some distance from the residential building and for another building to join the two. Plans were entrusted to the well-known Dublin architect, William Hague, whose name was to be associated with the design of Letterkenny cathedral, Miltown Park chapel, and the new residence-cum-library for William Walsh, Archbishop of Dublin. Before any building could begin, however, more money had to be collected. Hence, once life at the new college began to settle down, Ronan set off again on a roving commission of retreats, short missions, and public addresses aimed at raising funds .

During his journeying he kept in touch with René by letter. Extant correspondence during 1883-84 came from Kenmare, Dublin, Newry, Dromore, Bruff, Bagnalstown, Monastereven, Killarney, Kenmare again, Loughrea, Mallow, Kinsale.[19] From the title of some of his letters such as 'Bishop's Palace, Killarney', or 'Chapel House, Newry', it is not unlikely that in a number of locations he conducted missions. An undated note in his handwriting, but clearly from the early years at Mungret because of reference to Frs. Sutton and René, tells of a three week mission in Newry during Lent, and of four parochial missions at places not mentioned.[20] From the various venues he mentioned to René the amounts received or promised, and also requests from certain clergy with regard to prospective apostolics. His notebooks for the overall years 1880-1884, indicate that approximately 948 priests from 22 of the 27 dioceses contributed about £1,651 in that period. The non-contributing dioceses, judging by the same source, were Galway, Killala, Down and Connor, Raphoe, and Ossory.[21]

His letters to René were also concerned with affairs at Mungret, with lines of policy, or with regard to certain details about which René had enquired. The latter seemed to need encouragement and the assurance of Ronan's support, again, perhaps, because of some questioning among members of staff. 'There is no danger of misunderstanding between us', Ronan assured him from St. Clare's convent, Kenmare, on 2 August, 1883. 'When any difficulty arises we discuss it and we come generally to an understanding about it. I am always most anxious that you should have every facility to carry out your views regarding the discipline and spiritual training of all the scholars. Your training of the apostolics leaves nothing to be desired. You know it thoroughly and have experience of it. But the seminarists are a new element and their training should be on apostolic lines. This is the desire of our V. Rev. Fr. General and this is what we have promised our bishop. If you knew the want of the apostolic spirit among the clergy you would see that it is necessary for the seminarists as for the apostolics.'

Despite the support of the General, Ronan, under constant pressure to collect money, felt increasingly on the margins of Jesuit work and interest in Ireland. Few shared his dream or had the commitment he expected. In his preoccupation he failed for the moment to realise that the province itself was preoccupied with various demands, especially the need to fund and supply men of high academic calibre to ensure success at University College Dublin, which had recently been entrusted to the province by the Irish Catholic hierarchy. He expressed his sense of isolation and neglect in a letter to René on 25 July, 1884, as the latter was setting out for France. He requested him to seek further aid from his French provincial, Fr. Chambellan. Tell him, Ronan insisted, 'how grateful I am to him and how in our present circumstances we have no one but himself to whom we can appeal'. 'We have a great work here', he continued, 'which God has wonderfully blessed with success and with the cross. We are merely tolerated in this province. Our Fathers don't seem to understand our work, and we have not found in those of them who were sent to us that devotedness which is essential for the development of our work.' The new provincial, Fr. Thomas Browne, he acknowledged, was kindly disposed, and, as he had not suitable men available, he had given him leave 'to take good masters from good Fr. Chambellan, a mathematician and a father to teach French and music and to look after the discipline of the house. These men, as you know', Ronan concluded, 'would in a couple of years be able to form our scholars into efficient masters'. Training the senior apostolics to teach was being seen as an essential prop to the college's survival and success.

René's quest proved successful. In September, Fr. Eugene Carré, and two scholastics, Felix Perrin and Sylvanus Allenou, came as teachers. They belonged to the Paris Jesuit province and had been on the point of setting out for the Chinese mission but, due to war conditions, their vessel was delayed for a year. In 1885 there was a further influx: Fr. Joseph Rousseau, who stayed for a year, the scholastic Marcus Barthelemy for two years, Fr. John Aubier from 1885-88, and Fr. Joseph de Benaze, 1885-7. Finally, in 1886, Fr. James Daniel came for two years.[22] All these, together with M. l'Abbé L'Heritier, constituted a formidable and effective French contribution to the academic life of the college. A number of them, moreover, especially René and the scholastics, shared in much of the social life of the students. They joined in many of the apostolics' boat outings. A trip to Foynes with the outgoing tide, some twenty miles down river, was not infrequent. During the fortnight's vacation at Easter the apostolics did not go home for the first five or six years, except for special reasons in individual cases. At this time, and again on the free day each week, outings to various locations were regular features and nearly always some members of the community shared the hardships and joys with the students.

Meantime, during 1883-84, Ronan was finding fundraising a slow process. He informed the General of his problems, and he conveyed the latter's response almost casually in his letter to

René of 25 July. In a post script he remarked: 'You will have full charge of the house next year. *V. Rev. Fr. General has ordered me to go to America to beg for the apostolic school.*'[23] Six weeks later, on 2 September, he wrote from Kinsale, after a summer of retreats and preaching, 'I am very tired and unfit for my long journey'. Still, he had promised the Rev. Mother of the Reparation Convent, Limerick, to give a retreat to her community and felt it would be wrong to refuse her. During it, he hoped to make a short retreat of his own to prepare himself for his mission.

On the eve of his departure, he was moved by the lengthy entertainment and concert which the apostolics put on for him. On 21 September, on board the 'Oregon' at Queenstown, he wrote to thank them and to offer 'a few parting words'. The first virtue in perfection he wished them to cultivate, he declared, was 'holy obedience'. 'Fr. René holds my place', he continued, 'he is my representative in all things. Carry out his instructions even to the smallest details as God's representative in your regard.' He asked prayers for himself and the success of his mission, and observed that he was setting out with great confidence because he went out of holy obedience and hence the task was God's will for him.[24] In this spirit of mission he was to travel 20,000 miles, traversing the United States from east to west and north to south, and venturing into Canada, with a driving energy and optimism which belied his fifty-nine years.

# Chapter 7

# *Letters from America:*
# *Funding the Apostolic School*

The first few days of the 'Oregon's' voyage were stormy and many became sick. Ronan, however, claimed to have enjoyed the sea journey. It enabled him, he informed René on 27 September, to shake off 'all the fatigue of many months of great labour'.[1] It also gave him ample opportunity to prepare his presentation of the apostolic school for his American listeners. The school, he would have explained, was designed to serve the needs of the church in the English-speaking world, and especially in the United States,[2] by providing candidates for the priesthood who had been educated up to university degree level, followed by two years philosophy, and whose moral rectitude and reliability were assured. Theology was not provided by the school but could be obtained in an Irish theologate, or elsewhere according to the wishes of the diocese for which the young man was destined. What was required to obtain apostolics for a diocese was to pay so much a year for the training of a student. Contributions for the general work of the apostolic school were also welcome.

Ronan planned to approach bishops first, then parish clergy, especially those with Irish names or links, wealthy laity, and, of course, American Jesuits; and his message was not just mendicant, rather did he place emphasis on the benefit he and his school were bringing to the American church.

On 28 September 1884, he arrived in New York, and went to St. Francis Xavier's College, West 15th Street, where he was warmly greeted by the provincial, Robert Fulton. Writing of his arrival to Fr. Rene, to whom he wrote regularly, sometimes daily, he told how Fulton wrote a letter for him addressed to all the superiors of the province ordering them to let him preach and collect in all the churches and to help on his mission by every means in their power. The high expectations raised by this welcome were brought sharply to earth the following day when he called on John McCloskey, the cardinal archbishop of New York, to ask his leave to preach and collect throughout the diocese. The cardinal was too infirm to meet people. Business was transacted through his coadjutor archbishop, Michael A. Corrigan, who treated Ronan to a general denunciation of all beggars and particularly of Irish beggar priests. Ronan then pointed out that he had come not to look for anything for himself but to help the bishops and the Catholic people of the United States by providing apostolic men for them. Corrigan admitted his claim but said that in his diocese there were more candidates for the priesthood than were wanted. Ronan observed that it was so in Ireland also, but yet the bishops allowed him to preach and collect in their different dioceses. He handed the archbishop letters of recommendation from the Irish bishops and asked him to show them to the cardinal. Next day, the archbishop announced that his Eminence refused to look at the letters or have them read to him, and that, therefore, Ronan might not preach and collect publicly in the diocese. He would not be interfered with, however, in begging aid from a few friends, and he might, if the superiors approved, preach and collect in the Jesuit church.[3]

A few days later prospects looked a little brighter. He met two prominent lawyers from Limerick, the Liddy brothers, one of whom had been at the Crescent. Their law firm employed four or five hundred clerks. They told him there were many wealthy men from Limerick in New York who would be sure to help him. On 3 October he informed René that the rector had asked him to write out a notice of his mission and of his sermon for Sunday week, so that he might get it printed and circulate it the next Sunday. Promising to send René a copy, Ronan remarked apologetically that he would see by it that he was 'getting into the big ideas of this country. *Now we are henceforth the Apostolic College*, going to renew the mission of the Irish saints in the golden age of our history'. By means of the English language and the Irish race Christianity was to be spread, as it was first spread over the world 'by means of the Greek language and the Roman people'.[4]

By 15 October, however, he was dispirited and experiencing the loneliness of the exile. 'Here I am in the middle of the third week since my arrival', he complained, 'most anxious to know the result of the examination of the prefects and of those who were to matriculate' but *'I have not got one line from you or from anyone else in the college'*. He had one item of good news, nevertheless. His sermons the previous Sunday resulted in the largest collection for years.[5] On 19 October, he was back on a plangent note. In trying to obtain the names of rich people likely to be interested in his mission he had received no help from other Jesuits. 'All refused on one pretext or another.' Writing of this to René, with an eye to the apostolics, he added 'our young missioners for whom I write these facts must not depend too much on men'. 'I am learning', he continued, 'to take all opposition in the spirit of faith. God permits these little crosses to come for my sanctification ... I remind him that he has sent me here to do his work and that when one door is shut against me he must open another.'

The other door was opened by James Liddy, the former pupil of the Crescent, who made out 'a splendid list' for him, one much better than could have been made out by all the Jesuits together. Yet another door was opened by a visit to an old friend, Fr. Henry O'Loughlin, a parish priest, who at first did not recognise him. Ronan in explanation made reference for the first time to his wearing a beard, 'by order of the doctor'. O'Loughlin was a relative of John Loughlin, Bishop of Brooklyn, and, as a result, Ronan was given permission to collect and preach throughout the diocese. On 26 October he reported joyfully to René that he had preached that day at the church of St Mary Star of the Sea, Brooklyn, at all Masses and prepared the people for his visit to their houses during the week. On 4 November he recounted the successful outcome of these visits, especially because of the generosity of many Irish people. He found the process too exhausting and time consuming, however, and decided that for the future he would concentrate on preaching and collecting in the churches.

He wrote that letter from Baltimore. He had gone there single-mindedly to avail of the opportunity of meeting all the bishops of the United States who had gathered there in plenary council. He hoped to obtain leave to preach and collect in their dioceses, and also to induce their lordships to take apostolics from Mungret and pay for free places. There were eighty bishops. On his way to Baltimore, he obtained, he said, his first view of the American countryside. He was impressed by the signs of material prosperity, but was also moved to reflect on the signs of spiritual growth. 'I think', he remarked, 'of eighty bishops where there was only one bishop within the memory of some who are still living'. The respect of people for religion, and their readiness to learn everything about the Church led him to believe that there was 'a great future for the Catholic Church' in the country.[6]

This optimistic picture was strengthened by his experiences at Baltimore. Writing on 30 November to his 'young friends', the apostolics, he told of a fortnight filled by visits to the bishops of the council. He was not permitted to address the prelates assembled, but he managed to meet most of them at the seminary of St. Sulpice, where they dined each day and where he was introduced by an old friend, Fr. Hogan, superior of the Sulpitian seminary, Boston. Some of the bishops stayed outside the city, however, and these he could only see at night. Often he had to call again and again before meeting them, and then, frequently, they were tired after the day's work. Nevertheless, they received him with kindness and, he observed, 'all heartily approved and blessed my mission. Many invited me to preach and collect in their dioceses, and a certain number engaged to take subjects from Mungret College'.

Furthermore, the presence in Baltimore of the provincials and the superiors of the Jesuit missions in the United States was important. They welcomed him and promised to give him sermons and collections in all their churches and to help in every way they could. The superior of the Rocky Mountain mission, moreover, Fr. Cataldo, had six gifted Indian boys whom he considered good material for the priesthood and proposed the experiment of sending them to Mungret College. 'And so', Ronan declared optimistically, 'we shall have the privilege of educating for the priesthood the first Indians of the Rocky Mountains'. 'Altogether', he added, '*I have applications for about 30 subjects* from the bishops and our superiors. Another advantage of my visit to the council is that I know now where I am to go and I can make out the programme of my journey.'

The programme of his journey, based on the promises of many bishops, bespoke an irregular itinerary, with turnings off east and west from the main routes, and it was to include much retracing of steps when his arrival in a diocese coincided with someone else's begging campaign, or when a bishop insisted that he postpone his visit to a more convenient time. There were further disappointments, too, when prelates who promised support at Baltimore proved quite uncooperative when he arrived in their territory. An indication of the distances traversed and of the criss-cross nature of his journeying may be gathered from the map provided. To endeavour to recount his journey and experiences in detail would be tedious. What follows, therefore, is a selective presentation, which seeks to capture the flavour of his experiences and to note something of the impact of the country and of his intensive questing on himself.

By 30 November he was able to feel that much had already been accomplished. He sent René a short and sanguine note.

> As we are pretty secure now for five years to come with thirty students who shall be paid for by the bishops and our Fathers, I dare say that the best use to put the money I shall collect is in building the new house. As soon as you finish the chapel you should I think begin the new building.[8]

On 6 December he wrote again. As Christmas approached, thoughts about aspects of life in Mungret kept coming to the forefront of his mind. On this occasion he expressed concern lest some of the more gifted apostolics fail to obtain first class exhibitions because their studies were interrupted by time spent teaching. He also expressed concern at news from René of delays in building the college chapel. He pressed him to urge Hague, the architect, and the contractor to get on with the project. Shortly after Christmas, still concerned about the building, he warned that 'the building fund' was to be kept distinct from the current account. He had informed Rev. de Maistre of this before he left Limerick, he continued, and also that the account should be in both their names. He hoped René had no objection to that arrangement. He also referred to a financial arrangement with a Mr. Bruton and feared that the financial arrangement the latter made of Clongowes paying the debt they owed him to Mungret instead, might not occur because of Clongowes' poor financial situation. He urged René to go to Dublin to visit Bruton. If questioned as to what he was doing in Dublin, Ronan remarked disingenuously, - 'You could make an excuse ... Say for instance that I asked you to go to see the *provincial* and tell him how sorry I am at his illness particularly as *I did not part in such friendship with him as I wished*. Say that I asked you to ask pardon for me and to assure him that I would not willingly give him any offence or cause of trouble.'[9]

He went on to respond to comments of René signifying that misgivings and prejudices had been expressed concerning his proposal to accommodate six Indian students in Mungret. 'They are not savages', he protested, adding that Fr. Cataldo, who was on his way to Fiesole, the location of the Jesuit generalate following the order's expulsion from Rome by the Piedmontese in 1873, would call to Mungret and assure René that there was no more risk in taking these boys than in receiving any others. 'Tell Lord Emly', he concluded pointedly, 'that they are not *black* nor *deformed*. They are quite a handsome race but red. If they turn out to be material for priests the advantages to the tribes not yet civilised would be immense.'[10]

The following day he sent another letter to René. Again, he was concerned about money matters. The expenditure of £220 a month, he remarked, 'seems far beyond our expenditure of last year'. His attitude conveyed a lack of confidence in René's competence in managing financial matters. And to add further umbrage, he mentioned that he had written to Lord Emly about bringing the students to the forefront in Royal University examinations, with little sensitivity, it seems, as to how this might be viewed by René as the director of studies.[11]

Ronan spent Christmas in New York and in January, despite advice that he was wasting his time going south, he set off for Florida. On 18 January 1885, he sent a long letter from the Episcopal Residence, St. Augustine, Florida, to his 'young friends' at Mungret. He described the journey from New York to Washington and thence to Charleston, and from there along the coast to Savannah, the capital of Georgia, conveying his impression of immense districts of rice fields and corn fields where only coloured people were employed as the white man could not live in that hot moist terrain, and so to Jacksonville and his present location, where he was made welcome by the bishop of St. Augustine, John Moore, who invited him to stay with him and took him on a tour of the town.

'The city is unlike anything I have seen in the United States', Ronan continued. 'It is an old Spanish town' that 'has one of the oldest cathedrals of America, which was built nearly 100 years ago by a certain Fr. O'Reilly from Cavan.' With respect to Mungret, he judged Florida the most promising state of the union. *'This diocese'*, he enthused, *'is considerably larger than Ireland, yet the bishop has only eleven priests*, and is very anxious to have their numbers increased. It is perhaps the finest climate in the world; spring and summer are always in Florida - no winter - even in summer the heat is not great.' Next day, Ronan added, he was returning to Jacksonville where he had promised Fr. Kenny, the parish priest, he would give a parochial retreat in his church.*12*

On 2 February he moved on to New Orleans, and from there two days later wrote to thank René and de Maistre for 'the extremely gratifying details of expenses and receipts' they had sent him. 'I bless God that your temporal affairs are in a condition that leaves nothing to be desired', he told René, and continued contritely and soothingly: 'I see that my letter on this subject must have given you pain and I ask your pardon. I have the greatest confidence in you, and *I have not got a single report of you since I left which was not most favourable.*' He then went on to give a detailed account of his own financial state. This included some unusual items.

I have nearly a thousand pounds in the bank. I have another three thousand pounds promised which I hope soon to receive. I have got a thousand acres of land of the first quality in a good part of Florida, which is worth £2000, but the gentleman who gave it advises me to keep it for a year until the country it is in is opened up by the railway and then it will be worth double that sum. This gentleman wishes to have one free place for the diocese of St. Augustine in Florida and another for the Zambesi mission and the *remainder to help us in our new buildings.*

Another gentleman, Ronan continued, anxious to procure a free place for his parish in the diocese of St. Augustine, had given 'a lot of valuable land for an orange grove valued £100 which he intends to raffle as soon as possible'. 'So much for Florida', he announced triumphantly, 'where I was told before going that nothing could be got but sand and pine trees and flowers and oranges'.[13]

Ronan spent three weeks in Florida with New Orleans as his base. From there, his immediate plan was to continue eastward to Houston, Texas, and thence to Galveston on the coast before heading north to St Louis via Little Rock. From Galveston he wrote to the apostolics on 6 March. As always his letter to them was descriptive, positive, and hortatory. He had been in New Orleans 'for the Grand Exhibition and the gayeties (sic) of the carnival' and was greatly impressed by the extent and variety of the products and industries from the entire United States and from Mexico that were on display. 'On the day of my visit', he continued, 'I was fortunate to hear many speeches'. He had often heard of men 'stumping the country' but was not prepared for the Exhibition speeches. It appeared to him 'that no man in this country' was 'of any account until he could make a speech on the shortest notice'. Indeed, from what he had seen, he added playfully, his young friends 'must do a good deal of 'stumping' if they are to take the place which I have assigned them in America'. He had heartening news for them of former apostolics, those who had been trained at the school in the Crescent, Limerick. They had won 'the highest esteem' for the apostolic school, and they took the greatest interest in Mungret. 'If you keep up the character I am giving you', he added persuasively, 'and I know you will, priests from Mungret will be at a premium with the bishops and religious of the United States.'

On his arrival at St Louis, Ronan found two African missionaries conducting a begging campaign in the city so he decided to embark on the long journey north eastward to Detroit. He stayed at the Jesuit College, 353 Jefferson Avenue, and writing from there to the apostolics on 29 March he demonstrated how America's diversity of peoples and varieties of endeavour had expanded his vision beyond what would be considered practicable at home. He envisaged, he announced, sending some young men of German stock, and perhaps some Bohemians, Poles, Italians, and Spaniards to the Mungret Apostolic School because, being a missionary college, it 'should have representatives of different races even civilised Indians'. As the Germans were scattered over every city and province a knowledge of their language was essential to a priest in some places and useful everywhere. He urged them to learn German, as well as being able to speak and write French. He added self-consciously - 'You see how big one's notions become in this country'!

He went on to speak more directly of his own mission. Everywhere in the southern states he found a great scarcity of priests and an almost total lack of vocations to the priesthood. There was not one ecclesiastical seminary. The bishops and priests depended entirely on external help for their priests, and they were most anxious to make Mungret College their seminary. They had asked him for 26 students and 'they would be glad to have double that number if they could pay for them and we could supply them'. 'Another thing', he confided, 'the bishops of the south are most anxious that all their students in Mungret College should make their theology with us and should take their degrees in the Catholic University of Ireland', and he saw a great many advantages in following their suggestions.

It was an unwise floating of an idea to the apostolics, which was likely to cause embarrassment to Fr. René and the trustees and to be quite unwelcome to the authorities of an over-stretched province. Even the reference to 'degrees in the Catholic University' was unreal as the Catholic University had never conferred degrees, and University College Dublin, which formerly housed Newman's Catholic University, received its degrees from the Royal University of Ireland.

Following this raising of unreal expectations, he returned to the actuality of his immediate work. He had two aims in the United States, he explained: to collect what could be a permanent endowment for Mungret College, and to place young missioners from it 'in the most advantageous positions for the advancement of the glory of God'. In the south of the United States, he rhapsodised, he found a healthy and enjoyable climate; and in its cities there was 'a large number of most excellent Catholics nearly all Irish who would do anything for a priest'; hence, the south was to be their *'principal field of apostolic labour'*. This did not mean, however, that Mungret's missioners would be confined to the south. He had already made commitments in other areas and, he acknowledged, 'I dare say when I go to the west I shall find work for our apostolics'.[14]

His journey westward, however, was to be of the most circuitous kind. He moved west to Kansas City and St. Joseph Missouri, and then went south again to Little Rock Arkansas and thence east to Nashville Tennessee. 'All these places are said to be in the neighbourhood of St. Louis', he remarked, but 'the journey is upwards of a thousand miles'. Returning to St. Louis, he travelled north from there to Baltimore, and thence to Canada, before eventually going westward again through Nebraska and Colorado to California.

Kansas City he found of particular interest. It 'sprang up in the last eighteen years and now has a hundred thousand inhabitants'. Sixteen railways made it their centre. The place was full of noise all day long. He had what he termed 'a profitable week' there. He indicated what this meant in an earlier letter to René on 3 May: the bishop, John J. Hogan, from Bruff, Co. Limerick, had been very good to him; six gentlemen of the diocese had each promised to adopt an apostolic student and pay for his support; and he had collected, besides, a few hundred dollars. On his way south from Kansas City to Little Rock, he found a further item of special interest at Fort Smith, on the border of Indian territory. The pastor there, a Fr. Smith, had visited Ireland and had brought some of it back with him! He brought home a quantity of shamrocks that took root in his parish, and a blackbird and a thrush, both of which survived and, as Ronan observed, 'sing and whistle enough to satisfy most people'. He had a couple of very pleasant days at Fort Smith before undertaking the full day's journey to Little Rock. The bishop of that city, Edward Fitzgerald, was also a Limerick man. He had built a large cathedral, which he declared no preacher could fill. 'I preached three times in it in one day', Ronan, the experienced missioner, observed, 'and I was I believe very well heard.'

He came back from Arkansas to St. Louis through Memphis, Tennessee.[15] On 20 May he wrote from St. Louis to René to thank him for his letter and to express his disappointment at the slow progress of the building. He reminded the harassed René not to forget 'about the provision for theology for next September'.[16] After a month at St. Louis, he moved northward to Baltimore. Thence, after a visit to Washington, he planned to journey to Montreal.[17] He had little success in Canada, and on 15 July he was back in Washington and arranging to go west and to defer further intensive work in the eastern states until after the summer heat.

By 6 September, Ronan was writing from the Jesuit run Creighton College, Omaha, Nebraska, as he made his way rapidly to the extreme west. A week later he was able to report that the bishop of Omaha, James O'Connor, had promised to support two students for his diocese. Ronan's main hopes, however, as he informed René on 13 September, were centred on Denver, Colorado. The bishop, Joseph P. Machebeuf, had assured him at the Council of Baltimore he would be welcome to preach and collect in his diocese. When he called on the bishop in Denver, however, his lordship refused to allow him to preach or collect in any church of the diocesan clergy. Fortunately, the Jesuits came to his relief, allowing him preach and collect at all Masses in their church.

Refusing to be deterred, Ronan travelled from Denver to San Francisco. His enchantment with the journey was conveyed in a letter to the apostolic students dated 16 September. 'We have passed through the state of Wyoming where the miners are,' he wrote, 'and we saw the troops encamped at Rock Springs to prevent the miners from killing any more Chinese. The poor Chinese are flying in numbers back to their own country. We have several of them on the train. A family of them are opposite me and are as noisy as if they were Christians'! 'Our way through Wyoming', he continued, 'was through mountains and deserts'. For the highest point, Mt. Sherman, 8250 feet, two engines were required. Thence to Ogden the descent was continuous. 'Coming into Utah', he exclaimed, 'the mountain scenery is inexpressibly grand and unlike anything I have seen. We seemed to be in another planet. The mountains arose above us to an enormous height and are quite red.'

Having given this account, he moved to a matter which concerned him very deeply, namely, the news of his replacement as rector by Fr. René. He presented it in a positive light. 'I have to congratulate you', he stated, 'on the new rector whom God has sent you ... I got him at Paray le Monial through the intercession of B. Margaret Mary to do work that was quite beyond my power. I have helped him in my poor way to the best of my power. *I shall do all I can whilst I am in this country to procure means to establish permanently the apostolic college ...* Continue your prayers for my success.' He signed himself in an almost valedictory way, 'Your Affectionate Friend and Old Father in Christ'.*18*

It is not clear how he heard of his removal from office. Fr. René's letter regarding the change did not reach him till later. Certainly he seemed to have had no inkling of the impending removal, which presumably had to be sanctioned by the Jesuit General. On 15 July he had written to René regarding the official visitation of the provincial to Mungret, a time when changes were likely to be indicated, with the very ordinary comment: 'I hope you have got the visitation satisfactorily over and received clear permissions for all you purpose to do next year.'

Despite his upset, he made no reference to the change in his next letter to René. On 21 September he told of his unfavourable reception at San Francisco by the archbishop, Patrick W. Riordan, who forbade him to preach or collect in the churches of the diocesan clergy. The Jesuits, fearing his Grace's displeasure, were reluctant to have him preach and collect in their churches, so, disappointed, he decided to leave California and revisit Kansas City, 'a journey of four days', on his way to Chicago. En route, on 27 September, he sent a brief note about a possible applicant for the apostolic school. It was not until the following day, when he had arrived at St. Mary's College, Kansas, that 'a kind note' from René, dated 7 August, caught up with him. It enabled him to express a sense of grievance, tinged with restrained self-pity. He put his own interpretation on the change.

So Almighty God has arranged through his representatives, our superiors, that I should be done with begging on return. I am very glad. That is the meaning of your appointment. *There was such a cry all over the province that I was injuring the Society by begging that the provincial was obliged to put a stop to that work.* All along begging was most painful to me. I undertook it because I was asked by the General and I continued to do it as in duty bound never minding what anyone said of me ... I am glad to be free from responsibility and I am delighted at your appointment. I am rejoiced that at my return I shall have no more begging.

That meant in effect, he added deprecatorily, that he would be of no further use in Mungret. 'I could not teach. I am not able to be a procurator ... I have no talent in that way ... During the remainder of my life I hope to be employed in some humble missionary work which is all I am fit for.' René would be freer to act if he, Ronan, were away. 'I have always seen', he explained, 'that a new superior is embarrassed by the presence of his predecessor.' Turning to René himself, he advised: 'Leave matters in God's hands. He will help you in your charge.' He, Ronan, took the silence of the provincial for consent to carry on his programme and to visit the principal cities and towns in the eastern states. 'I hope before I leave this country', he concluded, 'to put your college on a good financial basis.' [19]

The precise reason for the change remains unclear. Given that the General encouraged Ronan to go to the United States to collect money, it seems unlikely that he would sanction his removal for begging. Again, if begging was the problem why was he not recalled and his collecting terminated? One wonders, then, if there was not a combination of factors. Perhaps complaints about his collecting from some American bishops and Jesuits joined to concern at home at the promises he was making to bishops and priests on his travels, had brought about a demand for his removal by Lord Emly and some members of the Mungret community. After all, there must have been considerable concern at the college, and among the province consultors, at his assurance to a number of American bishops that theology would be available at Mungret, and at the prospect of a struggling school having to face an influx of Indians and other nationalities, not to mention the strain his promises and requests were making on a college director already over-extended with building programmes on top of teaching, administration, letter writing, and endeavouring to keep reasonably happy bishops, clergy, staff, students and parents, not to mention his board of trustees.

In any event, Ronan's American odyssey continued. On 10 October, he wrote from St. Ignatius College, Chicago, to René whom he henceforth tended to address as 'My dear Rev. Father'. In Kansas and St. Louis he had visited those benefactors who had previously promised contributions. Having received these, he journeyed on to Chicago, where he was most kindly received. Archbishop Feehan and the clergy whom he visited were, he declared, 'all very favourably disposed towards us and I think I shall with God's blessing do well here for a few weeks.' On his own situation *vis-à-vis* Mungret, he put on a positive face assuring René that he was happy with the change. Providence had arranged it in good time, because by the time he was finished in the United States he would not be able for much more work. 'It is not easy to understand', he declared, 'what a hard life I have had since I left you. When I have carried out my programme I will give up begging as a thing that I am no longer able for during the rest of my life.'[20]

In November he moved east to Baltimore, and from Loyola College on 13 November he informed René that he had arranged with the bishops who were pledged to take the students that they 'would make four years of theology with us'. A somewhat disjointed letter referred again to his collecting alms at the wish of the Father General, an activity which incurred 'the odium of the whole province and the disapproval of my superiors'. As long as he remained at Mungret the antagonism against him would be directed against the college, hence he would request the provincial to move him elsewhere. 'Don't imagine that I feel hurt at the change. I am delighted with it', he insisted. 'I always disliked superiority, and I often begged to be freed from it.' For all his protestations that he was happy with the change, he returned on 1 December to the theme of begging and giving it up on his return, and meanwhile continued to work at it through a severe winter. Three days later, from Troy, New Jersey, he sent a letter containing a cheque for £514.13.4. On the back of the letter was written in Ronan's handwriting: 'Oct. £1,225. Dec. £1,224.10.4; Jan. £514.13.4 ' total £2,964.3.4.

For Christmas he returned to the College of St. Francis Xavier, New York, where he had received support from the start. The rector of the college acted as his treasurer. On Christmas day he responded to a senior apostolic, who had written on behalf of number of fellow students. As with his letters to apostolics it contained far more on his work and spirituality than in his letters to René. He told of mixed fortunes in Cincinnati, Washington, Philadelphia, and of the depressing opposition of the pastors in Irish parishes in Buffalo. Just when things looked darkest, however, and he had come to the conclusion that he could do nothing but write letters and visit the falls of Niagra, he had received a letter from the rector of the Jesuit college in Baltimore announcing the pleasing news that '*a good Irishman of that city had given 2,500 dollars*' to found a free place in Mungret College. 'It is in this way', Ronan explained, 'that the Sacred Heart has done to me ever since I left you.'[21] From Holy Cross College, Worcester, Massachusett, where he made his retreat, he sent further instances of disappointments proving the forerunners of good news.[22]

Having finished his retreat, he responded to a request from the provincial, sent to him by René, for information on the results of his mission. 'Here it is in a few words', he declared:

1. £500 in cash. The rectors of New York and Detroit having £3200 in their safe keeping for you.
2. Fifteen burses promised, only one of which is paid for.
3. Fifty-two students adopted and their first year paid for.
4. Twenty-six other students adopted in a doubtful kind of way (He explained this in some detail).
5. I put the thousand acres of land for two burses, which is much below its value. Besides, I have got donations of property to the value of 2,200 dollars and I have asked all these to be turned into money before Easter.

'Now it is just a year since I began regularly to beg', he observed, 'and taking into account the state of this country I look upon all these results as almost miraculous and as the effect of all the prayers that are constantly offered for my success.' Every parish was building schools or churches or was in debt. He concluded his letter to René by informing him that he had sent a full account of himself to the provincial, 'asking for nothing and refusing nothing' but ready to do whatever his Reverence wished for the rest of his life.[23]

By 20 January 1886, he was in Philadelphia. A letter to René on that date contained a postscript which suggested that his time in the United States, and his solitary driven-work, had temporarily affected his practical judgement, particularly with reference to the Irish Jesuit province. ' *I have written more fully to our Fr. Vicar-General and Fr. Keller (Assistant to the General) on the necessity of teaching theology to those of our apostolic students who are to become secular priests*, and after giving them full time to deliberate *I took their silence for consent and promised the bishops to that effect*. It is about a year since I heard from Fr. Keller and I did not get a line from V. Rev. Fr. Vicar²⁴ since I came to this country. Still I wrote every three months while I was rector. Now, however, I am, thank God, released from all obligations of writing, and I don't intend to write any more letters to Fiesole. It is your business now to insist on that agreement which I have made with the bishops being carried out.'

His preoccupation with his mission, which he constantly attributed to the wishes of the Father General (who was now incapacitated and his work being undertaken by Fr. Anton Anderledy as vicar-general), seemed to have blinded him to, or made him wilfully ignore, the need of working harmoniously with the leaders of the Irish province. The apostolic school had been started only on the insistence of the General. It was not a priority in a province already stretched in a variety of educational endeavours. It was most unlikely that the General would insist that the province theologate be moved from Dublin to Limerick, and the provincial could argue that there were not suitable men available to start a second theologate and that it was not advisable to become dependent on French or other foreign Jesuits. To René the position was clear, and the call that he insist on a theologate to fulfil promises made by Ronan without permission must have seemed quite unreasonable. Ronan, having overcome all sorts of obstacles in the past, presumably saw this as but another hurdle to be cleared for a greater good, and yet, one suspects, he must have had misgivings about his own presumed permission in the face of silence from the Generalate.

## *Death of an Influential Friend as the Mission Concludes*

Whatever strain may have arisen between Ronan and René, following his unreasonable insistence, soon faded with the news of the death of Bishop George Butler and the fear of what this might mean for the future of Mungret, especially if the successor was Edward Thomas O'Dwyer. Ronan responded to Rene on 20 March 1886, from Portland, Maine. 'In the spirit of faith I believe with you', he stated, 'that God's representative in the diocese will not injure God's work. The only thing that a future bishop could do against us would be to take away the diocesan seminarists or to shorten their course which we would not I think agree to. Now Fr. Dwyer (sic) knows from his own experience the difficulties of working a seminary with secular priests and he would I think be the last man to do it. He was glad that we got Mungret, but he was hurt because Dr. Butler told him nothing of the transfer of the seminary to us until it was accomplished.' 'Besides', Ronan continued, 'a contract with all the conditions clearly laid down has been made regarding the diocesan students between Dr. Butler and Fr. General and is signed by both. There are two copies. One is in our safe, the other must be among the bishop's papers. Now, as long as we keep to the conditions of the contract it will not be easy to break it up.' 'But should things come to the worst', he added unrealistically, 'we could utilise the whole building and make it a great apostolic college and a grand school of theology for the province.

A month later, he confided to Rene that he considered O'Dwyer 'the best man to be bishop' and that he had 'written him a letter of congratulation on the choice of the great majority of the clergy and the public demonstration of the people of Limerick.'[25] The appointment of Dr. O'Dwyer was to lead, in fact, to the withdrawal of the seminarians from Mungret, and to protracted disagreements, marked by faults on both sides, which finally ended with an appeal to Rome which went against the bishop.[26]

Meantime, Ronan's main preoccupation was with expanding and securing his American mission. In his letter of 20 March he once more complained to René of the latter's failure to write to benefactors of the college, and he enclosed a letter to be shown to the apostolics concerning one of their number, a Mr. Kenny, whose 'insubordination' had obliged René to send him away. Kenny had been a very able student. Ronan's cautionary letter emphasised the importance of humility and obedience and warned of the number of very talented men who had left the priesthood for lack of those virtues. Despite this firm line, a month later, having learned, perhaps, that Kenny planned to join the American Jesuits, he privately appealed to René to take Kenny back and even re-instate him in his position as prefect. It was important to be, and to be seen to be, men of mercy, he counselled, and it was important that Kenny, who hoped to join the American Jesuits, not leave under a cloud and with a sense of grievance. He judged that Kenny would become one of the foremost men in the mission of New Orleans. It was a case of magnanimity not seldom being the best policy. Whether or not René followed Ronan's advice, Michael Kenny left Mungret in 1886 with no prejudice against the college. He was one of the first Jesuit novices in the New Orleans province, then known as the southern province. Later he became professor of philosophy, of jurisprudence, of sociology, regent of Loyola Law School and associate editor of *America*, as well as the author of four books. He contributed to the *Mungret Annual* in 1897, 1900, and 1901.[27]

In the same letter of 20 April, written from Newburgh, New Jersey, Ronan announced that he had arranged for two good students to be sent next September to the Colorado and New Mexican mission, and he wished two outstanding men to be sent to Fr. Fulton of New York, the Jesuit province that had done most for him. He got 'no positive help elsewhere', he claimed, 'except in New Orleans'. He also had two provided for New Orleans. 'So', he concluded, 'there are six provided for and if you have twice that number to give I shall have them provided for.'

Relations between him and René remained good. The latter, knowing his wholehearted zeal, made allowances. 'It is very good of you', Ronan continued, 'to take in such a nice way the remarks I ventured to make on the correspondence. Of course you know my object. I have not left one thing undone to secure perfect success for my mission.' It was clear, however, that his energy was beginning to flag as he faced the final stages of his fund-raising. 'I intended going to Mexico', he added, 'but I was dissuaded by the provincial of the place. I also thought to finish by visiting New Brunswick and Newfoundland, but after taking counsel I decided that a visit would be only a useless expenditure of money. The same might be said about going back to any of the places which I have visited.' He would do what was to be done by correspondence. 'Yesterday', he announced, 'I wrote fourteen letters. Oh what a life I have had and what would I give for a little rest.' Eight days later, back in New York, he announced that he had engaged his place on 'The Alaska', which would leave New York on 18 May.

### Reviewing the Achievement and the Cost

There is no definitive statement as to how much money Ronan collected during his almost twenty months in the United States. As he is credited with paying for the new wing to the college, and this cost £12,000, it is likely that he raised about £13,000.[28] His driving energy, strong faith, seemingly guileless charm, and single-minded zeal enabled him to achieve so much at a time when the American church was itself struggling to finance new schools and churches.

His single-minded zeal, however, evoked opposition in the Irish Jesuit province, as has been seen, and, it appears, among some of the American bishops, and it also led him, at times, into extravagant promises, misjudgements, insensitivity, and even deviousness. It will be remembered that in his zeal he went over the heads of the provincial and his consultors to the General, as he had a right to do, when they opposed the establishment of an apostolic school, and thereafter he was appointed rector of the new school by the General without the usual consultation with the provincial and his consultors. It was not a combination of events likely to endear him or his new school to the leaders of the province. Again, in his belief in the justice of his cause, he had a confrontation with the provincial, Fr. Browne, with the result that, as he informed Fr. René, he did not part with him in such friendship as he wished and sought his pardon; also the persistent zeal which he exhibited in raising money for the apostolic school appears to have embarrassed a number of his fellow Jesuits and lessened their good will towards the school.

The extravagant promises and misjudgements relate especially to his efforts to have theology taught at Mungret. Although he received no reply from the Vicar-General or the Assistant to the General to his request to set up a theologate, and had made no approach, it seems, to his own provincial, he assumed permission and promised a number of bishops that theology at Mungret would be available to their charges. That he must have known that this was doubtful, even devious behaviour, is indicated by his admission that he kept writing for permission as rector, and again by his attempt to obligate René, as rector, to continue to press for a theologate - which René probably did not want and the Irish province certainly did not envisage. This insensitivity towards René was further manifested in his promise to take six Indian students, and in his talk of accepting students from different nationalities, without consulting him as director of studies, or considering the views of fellow Irish Jesuits or those of the trustees; and there were promises of apostolics, such as were made to Fr. Pantanella in Colorado, which René was not in a position to supply. Another oddity was that in his letters he protested that he hated begging and would never undertake it again once his American mission was over, yet on his return he recommenced it and eventually the provincial found it necessary to tell him to stop.[29]

There were two other incidents, prior to his American venture, which bespoke deviousness to some of Ronan's fellow Jesuits. The first concerned Mr. William Bruton of Aughrim Street, Dublin, mentioned earlier, who was owed £432 by the Jesuit college at Tullabeg and £869 by Clongowes. After a persuasive conversation with Ronan about the needs of the apostolic school, Bruton transferred the two debts to the apostolic school. There was no dispute about the Tullabeg debt, nor about the capital sum of the Clongowes debt (which, however, was not paid for many years), but there was about a demand for interest on the capital sum due from Clongowes. The Clongowes authorities believed that Ronan had persuaded Bruton to transfer the debt and to state, in the transfer document, that the principal was to be paid within a reasonable time and that there would be 3% interest. They had *a prima facie* case for this belief, because the transfer document was in Ronan's handwriting! He claimed repeatedly, however, that Bruton made the transfer without being asked and that 'when I discovered that Clongowes was unwilling to pay either principal or interest I begged Mr. Bruton to give us some other investment'.[30] Duplicity or simplicity on Ronan's part? It is difficult to know. In the event, the dispute between Clongowes and Mungret continued for years, and was eventually solved in 1917 by the General deciding that Clongowes pay half the interest due, up to the time of the payment of the capital!

The other incident, also involved money and interest on behalf of the apostolic school. A Mr. Harris of Hartstonge Street, Limerick, according to a rather obscure entry in the apostolic school journal, gave houses in the Crescent to the apostolic school, interest payable at 5%. The houses seem to have been valued at £500 and came to be occupied by the Jesuit community at the Crescent, presumably after the apostolics moved to Mungret. Annoyance was aroused in the Crescent community when, in 1884, Ronan demanded the capital value and the interest. On 1 August, 1884, he wrote to the provincial: 'The Crescent House, Limerick, owes the Apostolic School upwards of £500, a gift from Mr. Harris for a perpetual free place in the Apostolic School. I have given notice to Fr. O'Connell, the rector of the Crescent House, I should require of him 5% interest and the principal when convenient.' Fr. Philip O'Connell asked if he had any documents to prove that Mr. Harris made the donation to the apostolic school. Ronan went to Harris and asked him to put in writing the substance of the interview between them when he made the donation. Ronan included Harris's document in his letter to the provincial. The problem dragged on for more than two years. A letter from the socius (or assistant) to the provincial, on 23 February 1887, stated: 'The appeal of the procurator of Mungret concerning the Limerick houses is decided adversely'. The money was not paid. There was no doubt, as Redmond Roche, the chronicler of the apostolic school, observed, 'that Fr. Ronan aroused opposition'.[31]

Ronan's persistent zeal, immoderate at time, his stubborn tenacity, even disingenuousness, when he felt a principle was at issue or a religious development was in jeopardy, inevitably aroused opposition; yet his very zeal and tenacity contributed immensely to the establishment and success of the apostolic school. There was also within him, it would seem, a sense of distance from his province or, at least, from his provincial superiors, whom he felt did not trust him; an experience which made the practice of obedience, which he highly valued, particularly difficult for him. With all that, he was undoubtedly a man of prayer and strong faith, a person of disarming simplicity, friendliness, and charm, and hence was liked and reverenced by the apostolics, and was one of the most sought after spiritual directors in the country by religious of both sexes and by the secular clergy. Even his critics found it difficult to harbour ill feeling towards him.

## The Homecoming

On his return to Mungret on 26 May, 1886, Ronan was met at the gates of the college by the community and all the students, and greeted with cheers, band music, and a triumphal arch.[32] He was put in charge of the apostolic school under René, and for the next year happily combined that work with his customary round of retreat direction.

On 24 August, the rector and Ronan accompanied seven of the senior apostolics to Queenstown (Cobh) as they sailed for the United States. Two others entered the noviceship of the Redemptorists at Bishop-Eton for the Australian mission. In September, six of the seminarist students went on to Maynooth College, and on 15 October three apostolic students set out for the American College, Rome, to begin their theology. They were destined for the diocese of St. Augustine, Florida. It was a confirmation for Ronan of the fruits of his American tour, and a fulfilment of his dream of a missionary college.

In his final year at Mungret, his interest in his apostolics, whom he termed his 'spiritual children', won over those who previously had not met him. His youthful enthusiasm, which had enabled him to adapt readily to American ways, led him to introduce baseball to Mungret. Doubtless he saw it as an introduction to American life for his future missioners. As there were some American students in the college at the time, the game enjoyed temporary popularity.[33] A more lasting contribution was noted in the college magazine, *Kostka*, in its Easter number, 1887: 'Owing to the energy and taste of Rev. Fr. Ronan, groves have sprung up in all directions. A most beautiful gravel walk, between two rows of trees, runs from the garden gate along the boundary wall and meets the front avenue at the lodge. The walk, together with the avenue, has been found to measure one mile.'[34]

In the summer the news came that Ronan was to leave the college for Miltown Park, Dublin. When he left in September, it was recorded in the diary of the Apostolic School for 8 September that a seance, or special entertainment, was given in his honour after supper. A senior apostolic student, M. Gallagher, delivered a declamation in praise of Ronan and promised, in the name of all the students, that they would do their best to put into practice the principles he had been inculcating so long. Ronan answered in his usual simple style, remarking that 'he would still be attached to the work as if he were living in the house', and stating 'that if they wanted to please him they could do so most easily by making themselves worthy of their vocation.'[35]

### The Aftermath: 'Untold Good ... to the End of the Earth'

In the years immediately after Ronan's departure three major developments threatened the college he had founded. The most serious was the recall to France of Fr. René and the other French members of the community in the summer of 1888, which almost coincided with an announcement from Bishop Edward Thomas O'Dwyer that he intended to withdraw his seminarians. To make up for this last blow, the college authorities expanded the school for lay pupils, which operated largely separate from the apostolics. The third development was the arrival in Limerick in 1887 of a government commission to investigate educational endowments, which in Mungret's case involved an examination of the original concessions made by the trustees to the Jesuits. This development involved Ronan in much correspondence, in an appearance before the commissioners, and in a printed submission claiming that the Jesuits had faithfully fulfilled the 'essential conditions' laid down by the trustees. Despite a number of submissions in support of the original agreement it was found that the trustees were at fault, and that the effective promotion of agricultural science required by the lease was not carried out. The commissioners decided that the college authorities should pay £2,500 in order to hold the college as independent property, in fee-simple, without further trusts or liabilities. This was agreed, and the money was to be devoted to agricultural and technical education in Limerick. Some years later the Technical Institute in George's Street (subsequently O'Connell Avenue) was established from these funds. Ronan was greatly upset. He had thought that his intense labour had made sufficient provision for both the college and the apostolic school. Some £12,000 had been spent on the property, and he had also collected over £11,000 in burses. That another £2,500 had to be found was a bitter disappointment.[36]

In addition to the anxiety and problems occasioned by these difficulties, and the prolonged tension arising from disagreement with the volatile Bishop O'Dwyer, there was also down the years, within the Irish Jesuit Province, recurring instances of the earlier ambivalence towards the Mungret Apostolic School. The training of priests for overseas missions had been an important part of the work of the Society of Jesus from its earliest years. Mungret Apostolic School was in that tradition. But the Irish Jesuit Province had its own missionary venture in Australia which demanded men of quality for work in schools and churches, and in addition, as has been seen, there were the demands on its limited numbers from University College Dublin, the schools of Clongowes, Belvedere, Crescent and Galway, from the churches in Dublin, Limerick and Galway, and from the home mission staff. Mungret Apostolic School, therefore, found itself in frequent competition for quality Jesuit teachers. This was especially the case after the setting up of the National University of Ireland and the withdrawal from Mungret of its university classes. Even within Mungret itself, rivalry developed between the lay school and the apostolic school, and provincials did not always show preference for the Apostolic School.

Nevertheless, despite these various obstacles and problems, the school survived and more than fulfilled Ronan's prophecy in his letter to the provincial, Fr. Tuite, on 19 March 1882, that they were 'starting a work which is capable of producing untold good in the future not to this diocese alone but to the ends of the earth'.[37] Already in 1895 a printed 'Report of the Apostolic School Mungret' told of students who finished the previous year and were destined for the United States of America or Australia, and of past students studying in Rome, Aix, Montreal, Cincinnati, Emmetsburg, Carlow, and All Hallows College, Dublin; and during 1907, the college's jubilee year, letters came from past alumni in the United States, South America, the Philippine Islands, China, India, South Africa, and Australia. Though not included in the early years, England, Scotland and Wales, became subsequently an important destination.

From the Apostolic School's inception to its close in 1967, there went forth seven hundred and one students who became priests, three who became religious brothers, and fifty others who died while preparing for the priesthood.[38] The greater number served in the United States, but, as indicated, there were representatives on all five continents. In various issues, moreover, the *Mungret Annual* celebrated those past students who became bishops and archbishops and returned to visit the school. These included: Bishop E. Green, Port Elizabeth, South Africa; Bishop John Norton of Bathurst, and Archbishops Andrew Killian of Adelade and P. M. O'Donnell of Brisbane, Australia; and in North America - Bishop Michael J. Gallagher, Detroit, William Turner, Buffalo, Thomas M. O'Leary, Springfield, Mass., and Archbishops Michael J. Curley, Baltimore, and his successor, Patrick Barry, formerly of St. Augustine, and Timothy Manning, Cardinal Archbishop of Los Angeles.[39] Ronan's foundation had reached almost literally 'to the end of the earth'.

Above: **Mungret College**

Below: **William Ronan, S.J. with some students in 1902**

*Lord Emly*

# Chapter 8

## *Drawing to a Close 1887 - 1907:*
## *- through Scandal and Turmoil to Serenity*

In 1887, with the security that came from seeing obedience to superiors as being acceptance of God's will for him, Ronan moved readily to Milltown Park, Dublin, to undertake a responsible and congenial task. The Jesuit home missions seem to have suffered a partial decline with the illnesses of Robert Haly, which resulted in his death in 1882. Ronan was placed in charge of a newly formed mission staff. This involved much letter writing: acting as liaison with bishops, offering the services of the mission staff for long and short missions. He was also the person contacted by religious congregations requiring retreats run by a Jesuit. He continued with his own retreat work and participated in missions, though no record of these activities appears to have survived. One event relating to a retreat, however, has been carefully preserved, his visit to Kinsale in February 1888, to the deathbed of his old friend from the Crimean years, Mother M. Francis Bridgeman.

For many years before her death, Francis Bridgeman suffered from what has been described as 'a most distressing infirmity'. She managed, nevertheless, to observe the common life of the community. Her final days were heralded when, after breaking her arm, she underwent 'a severe attack of bilious fever from which for a while there seemed little chance of recovery'. She rallied, and then caught a bronchial infection, which brought on her final decline. It was decided to write to Fr. Ronan to ask his prayers. A reply from him on Thursday, 9 February, stated that he was coming that day to Limerick, and was to commence a retreat on Friday evening. Mother Bridgeman 'joyfully assented' to a proposal that Ronan be invited to visit her before he returned to Dublin. Some of the sisters decided that he should be asked to call before the retreat, and sent him a telegram. His immediate reply informed them that he would arrive in Cork at 8 p.m. and would expect a telegram with further instructions. He was met by a messenger with a letter saying there seemed no immediate danger and that he could come by early train next morning, but if he wished to come immediately there was a car waiting. He took the latter course, and arrived at the Mercy convent at about midnight.

Next morning, he spoke to his grateful friend, and then said Mass and gave her viaticum. He felt at that stage that she might recover. After breakfast he went to see her once more, heard her confession, encouraged her, and came away with a revised opinion. He remarked to the sisters that there was not a hair between her and the Lord, which they subsequently related to the patient, who quietly replied - 'Thanks be to God, I hope not'. That evening, or next morning, Saturday, Mother Bridgeman suffered a stroke. She kept praying until she relapsed into a coma, and her body became much distressed. She died that Saturday afternoon at 3.25 p.m. Among the many letters of condolence were some from Ronan. A few sentences were preserved in the Kinsale archives from his many letters of sympathy:

> Thank God that our dear mother has gone to her eternal rest. Of course we shall do all that grateful hearts will inspire to follow her with our prayers, though we believe that she has finished her purgatory with her mortal life. She will be a great power for us all in heaven. So cheer up. It would be mere selfishness to wish her back again.

Tributes came also from some other Irish chaplains who worked with her in the Crimea, from Michael Gleeson, C. M., and Patrick Duffy, S.J.[1]

### Gardiner Street Community and Church

Five years later, on 15 August 1893, Ronan was appointed to the Gardiner Street community, while continuing as superior of the mission staff. It was a time of large crowds in Gardiner Street church at Masses, sodalities, novenas, and sermons for special occasions by sought-after preachers such as William Delany,

Francis Bannon, Robert Kane, and William Butler. Ronan, though not an intellectual, was liked and respected by the educationalist, William Delany, and was likely to have had much to discuss with Bannon, who had also been a war chaplain, but in the American Civil War. Two years after his arrival at Gardiner Street, on 31 July 1895, Ronan was appointed superior of the community and church. In the 'Brief Chronological Notes of the Irish Province, 1803-1914', put together to mark the centenary of the restoration of the Society of Jesus, it was remarked of Ronan's appointment: 'He brought great experience to the guidance of the affairs of this residence; he had been minister here and had been a long time on the missions.'[2]

He was to have only two years in the position before he was obliged to retire, yet in that time he made a remarkable number of changes, which were testimony to his energy, and determination. They raise the question, however, whether he tried to do too much in a short time and created opposition to himself from some members of the community and their friends. In the 'Brief Chronological Notes' it was explicitly mentioned that 'Father Ronan made several changes both in the church and in the house - Litanies to be recited immediately after recreation; telephones were put into the various rooms'. Indirectly, there was mention of many more. In 1895 a sodality for the metropolitan police was put on a permanent footing, and a retreat for the police was revived after a lapse of many years ; a new staircase was completed connecting the top corridor of the house with the middle corridor; and then, and in the following year, Ronan's strong social conscience was expressed in a number of ways. On the first Sunday of Advent, 1895, Fr. Robert Kane commenced a series of well-attended sermons on 'The Church and this Age - Progress; Profit; Pleasure; Power.' For the Lenten devotions, it was noted that 'a new departure was made by Father Ronan: admission free to every part of the church' and 'no collection except on Sundays and Holy days'. He moved a step further in July, 1896, when 'the two penny place in the church was abolished and the space for the poor enlarged'.

In 1896 there were other developments. During Lent special lectures were introduced on Sunday afternoons at 4 p.m. They were given by Ronan's friend, William Delany, on 'The Re-union of Christians', and drew a good attendance. Afterwards they were published by Browne and Nolan, Dublin. On the material side, 'the hydraulic blower for the large organ in the church was completed' in March, which made it possible to manage without 'the services of several men'. On 20 August 'the work of decorating the church was commenced. The installation of electric light was started ... a generating plant was also erected so that the church could be independent of the Corporation'. The beatification of Bernardine Realino, S.J., was celebrated, 22 to 24 November with a triduum which included a high mass and a sermon each day. A special transparency over the high altar representing a scene near the close of Blessed Bernardine's life was installed and greatly admired. Then, on 31 December, heralding the new year, 'the church was filled to overflowing at the *Te Deum*', giving thanks to God for the year past, and 'the electric light was first used' to dramatic effect.

Finally, it was perhaps because of Ronan's contacts with many bishops that when Dr. Patrick Duggan, Bishop of Clonfert, died at Jervis Street Hospital on 15 August, 1896, his remains were moved that evening to the Ignatian chapel in the Gardiner Street church, and on 18 August, his Grace, William Walsh, Archbishop of Dublin, sang the Requiem Mass, the cardinal, Michael Logue, presiding. Some three hundred priests attended.[3]

The following year was significant for the church and community in different ways. On 26 March it was announced that William Delany was reappointed to the rectorship of University College Dublin. It left a gap in the working staff of the church, which was not easy to fill, and also deprived Ronan of a strong supporter. Ronan's final material addition to the church was a reliquary altar of Sicilian and Carrara marble, which was erected in the Ignatian chapel during September.

On 24 October 1897, he was replaced by the more conservative Fr. John Conmee, who was nominated vice-superior. The grounds for the change were said to be for reasons of health, but the main cause was the prospect of scandal occasioned by charges made against him of having an intimate friendship with a wealthy widow, a Mrs Doyle, a benefactor of the Society.

## *Four Years of Anxiety and Scrutiny*

The accusations led to four harrowing years, during which he felt that his own reputation and that of the woman were being unjustly undermined, and that his provincial superior and the General of the Society were not sufficiently supportive. As in the past, however, he refused to be cowed by criticism and opposition and, with characteristic stubbornness, continued to assert his innocence and to visit Mrs Doyle.[4]

Ronan related easily to women, as was noted during his time in the Crimea. He was valued throughout Ireland by religious women who felt at ease with him and trusted his sure spiritual direction. With some he established close friendships. His friendship with Mother Bridgeman lasted to the end of her life. The annals of the discalced Carmelite nuns, at St. Joseph's monastery, Loughrea, Co. Galway, tell not only of Ronan giving the community retreat in 1857, and every year thereafter until 1892, but they add, as noted earlier: 'God, who in his Divine Providence sent him to us, destined him to be the spiritual father and greatest friend of this community ... and to his intercession with God for us we attribute the many blessings that have since attended us. He was Mother Catherine's greatest friend, and her spiritual director in all her supernatural favours.[5]

There was never any suggestion in Ronan's long career of anything untoward in his relations with women until 1897, when he was seventy-three years of age! There seems, indeed, to have been a particular innocence and assurance in his way of communicating. This made the charges against him all the harder to bear. The provincial, Fr. Thomas Keating, however, considered these to be sufficiently serious and damaging to the reputation of the order for him to inform the General, Fr. Luis Martin, and to forbid Ronan visiting the lady. Annoyed at the restrictions placed upon him as a result of what he considered malicious criticism, Ronan complained to the General.

On 18 June 1897, Fr. Martin, writing to Keating, conveyed Ronan's words to him. Ronan's judgement, it was clear, clashed with that of his provincial. The latter's action seemed to him yet another example of province superiors being wrong, as they had been about the apostolic school, and again treating him unfairly. He had written:

I think it extremely hard that I, superior as I am of this house, and have been in superiority of one kind or another for nearly forty years, and am now an old man of 73 years of age, should have such a restriction placed upon me for the first time in my life. I regard the prohibition as most unconstitutional: however for the sake of peace and good order I submitted, until I should appeal to your Paternity for the protection of my character.

'If I am not left free to act according to my own prudence in visiting and receiving visits', Ronan continued, 'I am not fit to be superior, and the sooner I am removed from office the better.' He went on to outline the grounds on which the restrictions were imposed.

All this (the restriction, etc.) comes from the evil tongues of a few women, five or six in all, whom I very unwillingly and of necessity offended, in my efforts to remedy the abuses I found in the house and church, when I came into office. These talking women have made accusations against the good lady and myself, beginning with the most absurd things and ending with the most wicked: they have planned together, and have gone round to the different confessionals in the church, pouring out those calumnies as scruples of conscience ... Nearly all the Fathers rejected their insinuations and calumnies as insane accusations; but a few were impressed by them.

'These talking women', Ronan added, 'are striving to drive me from office, and are already boasting that I shall soon cease to be superior.' 'One of two things, I believe, must be done', he concluded, 'either my liberty of action in visiting and paying visits of duty must be restored, or I must resign my office.'[6]

Allegations of sexual misconduct were a sure way of gaining the attention of bishops and of major religious superiors in the Irish Church. False charges were not unknown, but all had to be taken seriously. The Jesuits were even more sensitive to such accusations. Their founder had expressed the desire that where chastity was concerned his followers should be like angels! Fr. Martin, depending largely on his provincial's advice, agreed with him that Ronan should be quietly removed from office, and 'sent to the island of Jersey for the sake of his health'. Fr. Martin also wrote to Ronan that while he had no definite judgement on this 'most vexatious matter', it seemed clear that it was being used to slander the Society and, hence, the provincial had been obliged to intervene.[7]

By 20 December 1897, news concerning Ronan was occasioning much concern to the General. He was said to be almost out of his mind at the way he had been dealt with over what he asserted were unfounded accusations, and he was threatening to throw up his vocation. Martin reminded the provincial that Ronan merited well of the province and should be shown the greatest consideration. Keating should write to him 'with much kindness, consoling and calming him to ensure that this good old man not descend into extreme desperation'.[8]

In January 1898 Ronan moved from Jersey to Cannes. The following month, Keating was requested by the General to find out if Ronan was meeting with the Irish woman there, and what his relations were with her. He was also asked to consult the Jesuit superior at Cannes as to whether Ronan visited lay people in the area and if he called on Irish priests and received financial assistance from them. The superior was also to be asked to keep Ronan under scrutiny and to report on any of these occurrences and especially if, when, and where he visited the Irish woman, and if he made any 'excursions' with her.[9] A further instruction to report on his actions was sent in April.[10]

By June 1898, Fr. Martin was sufficiently disturbed by the reports from France to require Fr. Keating to write to Ronan in a kindly way inviting him back to Ireland. It was important, he emphasised, to get him away 'from the company of that woman'.[11] The provincial's letter had little effect. Ronan declined to return home, but declared that 'in the mountains of Madura' he 'could find a genial climate and a little work' which he 'could have the heart to undertake'. The General approved his request, and instructed Keating to request the provincial of the Toulouse province 'to receive Ronan for a year or two in Madura where he could minister to English speakers. It would keep him from Mrs Doyle, and at the end of it he might be ready to go home.'[12] Two months later, on 15 December, the General was pressing again for Ronan's return to Ireland or to England. He suggested that the English Jesuit, Fr. Peter Gallwey, a life-long friend of Ronan, be enlisted to encourage him to return.[13] At this stage, Fr. Martin does not seem to have been concerned about scandal in Ireland following Ronan's arrival.

The sorry saga continued for a further two years. Ronan's state of body and mind appears to have seriously declined. He sent the General a doctor's certificate, without any covering letter, stating that it would be dangerous for him to leave the Mediterranean costal area or to apply himself to any serious mental work.[14] This removed the pressure for his return for a year. On 28 July 1900, however, Martin was moved to remark exasperatedly that Ronan 'had given scandal in his own province' and that 'now that he is staying in France he has taken greater freedom to himself and is giving as much or more scandal there than he did at home, to the wonder and embarrassment of Jesuits and others.'[15]

By December 1900 there was a new Irish provincial, Fr. James F. Murphy, and Ronan, significantly, expressed his readiness to return to Ireland. The General once more displayed compassion for him. Deal gently with him about his return, he told Murphy. 'That old man has served the province well as rector and missionary, and deserves consideration.' Now that Ronan was ready to return, however, the Irish provincial, and presumably his Jesuit advisers, became worried about having him back and wrote of the danger of scandal erupting on his return. The General gave them short shrift.

'In your letter of 15 December', he wrote on 9 January, 1901, you talk of the most serious dangers and numerous obstacles presented by Fr. Ronan's return, and suggest he should be kept in Lyons or some other province to obviate the danger of scandal. It would be unjust to impose on another province this burden which you want to shuffle off yourselves, especially as he is causing difficulties and dangers for the Lyon's province greater even than he did at home, and he is creating a major vexation there by his intimate friendship (*familiaritas*) with that Irish woman.

'I've already written to Fr. Ronan', Martin continued, 'that on his return to Ireland he is to break off all dealings with the woman for good. He is living a useless life in France, performing no ministry, and a nuisance to his superiors by his way of living (which he claims is totally innocent). Among his own people in Ireland he could do some work and the dangers you fear are less than in France.' Ronan had asked to stay on in France until May, Martin added. This he granted willingly. Murphy should acquaint Ronan of this, but also insist that he had to return in May.[16]

Murphy, nevertheless, sought ways of preventing the return to Ireland. Ronan's reputation for an independence bordering on insubordination evidently remained a live issue with the province's authorities. Murphy proposed that he be sent to the province's mission in Australia. Fr. Martin was not impressed. 'I am astonished' at your suggestion, he wrote on 1 April 1901, of 'obliging a man of such advanced years, who was stubborn and difficult, to go to a far-off region as though into exile. You will have to put up with him in your province, but on this condition, as I have explained to him, that he break off for good all dealings with that woman, and all occasions of scandal. I want you to get his consent and promise on this, but prudently and with gentleness so that it may not lead to any of the outcomes you fear. It would be terribly sad if such an old man, who formerly served the province so well, were to leave the Society.'[17]

Worn out at seventy-seven years, Ronan acquiesced and was received back in Ireland, though far from Dublin. His appointment, however, was to a place where his memory was held in deep regard and where he was sure of a welcome, namely, Mungret College. There, as in a haven, his strength returned, and his final years passed peacefully.

Some months after his return, Fr. Murphy informed the General of important information that Ronan had provided regarding the challenge posed by the bishop of Limerick, Dr. E.T. O'Dwyer, to Mungret having lay students. Ronan reported that Bishop Butler had given him written permission to accept lay students in Mungret and that he had given the document to Bishop O'Dwyer. 'If I had known that when I was dealing with Propaganda', Martin commented, 'I would have made good use of it, as it would have strengthened our case considerably. The first chance I get, I'll mention it to the Secretary of Propaganda'.[18] So, the 'useless' old man still had his wider uses. Moreover, he fitted smoothly into the life of his school and became a cherished member of the community.

Reflecting on the four painful years, one observes again a clash with authority not dissimilar to earlier years, when Ronan was establishing Mungret Apostolic School. Then, feeling he was doing what was right, he appealed to the General and obtained his support. On this occasion, his appeal to Rome was not supported, though Fr. Martin consistently sought to temper the more demanding and punitive responses of the Irish provincials. In an era when submissive obedience was the practice, Ronan's independence was again seen as an occasion of scandal and disorder; and that it was exercised in the name of truth and fair play made it no more palatable, particularly in the context of allegations of improper relations with a wealthy widow. His persistence in his contacts with the woman, in France as well as in Ireland, and his continued assertion of the innocence of their relationship, smacked of imprudence and defiant disobedience to his religious superiors, while to him it was an expressive assertion of the justice of their cause. He persisted in this assertion with a stubborn courage that was almost his hallmark. It was typical of official Church reaction, at the time, that the response of the order's authorities was not to thoroughly investigate the charges but rather to run from scandal by moving the subject of the allegations from the scene, irrespective of the damage to his reputation and with scant regard for that of the woman.

## Celebration and Culmination at Mungret

On his return to the college he had founded, Ronan was entrusted with the undemanding office of prefect of health for a community much younger than himself.[19] He soon settled in and by 1903 he was spiritual father or guide to the community, confessor to the students, and in charge of religious instruction for the staff. As always he enjoyed being amongst his 'young friends'. His enthusiasm, as in earlier years, led to improvements in the grounds. 'In the spring of 1904', the *Mungret Annual* of July 1908 recalled, 'the abbey walk was made'. It ran from the outer gate along the eastern boundary line of the farm to the playground, skirting the wall of the cemetery and in full view of the abbey. 'Thousands of quicksets, fir, and larch plants were also set along the abbey walk and all over the farm. A conservatory was built in the garden, and a little orchard in the quadrangle between the ambulacrum and the infirmary. All these were carried out under Father Ronan's supervision.'[20] The following year, Ronan had added to his duties that of bursar, and the next year again the role of admonitor to the popular new rector, Father T. V. Nolan.

Under the new rector, improvements and new developments became a feature. Consciousness of the approaching silver jubilee of the apostolic school hastened the raising of the old wing, the building erected in 1857, to a third storey to bring it on a level with the new building, and new refectories, additional bathrooms, and classroom improvements were added. These developments were matched by university examination results in which ten distinctions were gained, including third and fourth place over all in Greek and Latin in second and first arts. The school, as from the start, continued its participation in a range of athletic activities, but in 1906 there was also a class in Solesmes chant, classes in Irish step-dancing, and three ambitious theatrical productions, 'Richelieu' and 'Hamlet' acted by the apostolic students, and the 'Private Secretary' by the lay boys. As usual, interest in debating was high, and members of the Jesuit staff joined with the students in lively discussions. The many faceted education at Mungret was clearly in a healthy state as the college approached its silver jubilee.

The silver jubilee was celebrated over three days in early September 1907. The grounds and corridors were artfully decorated with bunting of every hue, and the boys, just back from vacation, joyfully entered into three days of emancipation from books and classes. The first day was given over to domestic rejoicing. The second day was devoted to a reunion of friends and past pupils, all of whom were invited to inspect the buildings, and to a special lunch. Among the visitors were Lord and Lady Emly, Lord and Lady Clarina, professional people from Limerick and other parts of Ireland, various clergy and past students, including one each from Australia and the United States as representatives of the past apostolic students of Mungret in those extensive regions.

Ronan moved happily among many old friends. After lunch, when Mr. J. Grene Barry, J.P., D.L., rose to propose the toast of

'The College and its Silver Jubilee' he honoured not only the eminent men who formed the original trustees, of whom he was one of the survivors, but also Father William Ronan. To speak of his good qualities in Mungret would be impertinent, he declared, but 'the best eulogy that could be bestowed on him was to ask those present to look around and observe the buildings which through his energy had been raised on the site of the ruins of the ancient foundation'.

A sense of community with the missionary monks of the ancient abbey had been developed from the start of the apostolic school, not only by trustees such as Emly, de Vere, and Grene Barry, but by the apostolics themselves in numerous references, poems and even articles in issues of the *Mungret Annual*. The association was enshrined in the college crest with its symbol of a phoenix rising from the ashes, the apostolic school reincarnating the old foundation. The missionary tradition established by the apostolic school was highlighted by the rector in his response to Mr. Grene Barry's toast, pointing out that in its twenty-five years the school had already sent two hundred students to different parts of the world. He concluded by requesting all to join him in toasting Fr. Ronan's health. Ronan, 'who was received with loud applause', replied in a brief address.

The evening ended with an orchestral concert. Then, 'the concert over, and most of the visitors having departed, the grounds were brilliantly illuminated, and a display of fireworks took place.' The apostolics, in their address to their distinguished guests on the third day, evoked once more the theme of carrying forward the old missionary tradition: presenting the college as the heir to a tradition of sanctity, learning, and missionary zeal which came down from the days 'when the monastery of St. Nessan was the centre of Christian life ... and a nurse of missionaries to Europe'.[21] It was music to Ronan's ears. Indeed, as a contemporary observed not long afterwards, 'Fr. Ronan lived to see how the work of his hands had prospered. His presence at the jubilee celebrations, as it was the source of the deepest satisfaction to all friends of Mungret, so to himself much have seemed to be the crowning of his life, and the fit moment for saying: '*nunc dimittis*'. Nor was the call long delayed ...' [22]

## *Death and Estimation*

In the late afternoon of Tuesday, 10 December 1907, while the students were at supper, news reached their refectories that Fr. Ronan had been taken seriously ill. The apostolics soon learned that he whom they looked upon as a father had gone to the reward of which he had often spoken.

The news came as a shock. Ronan had been apparently in his usual vigorous health a few hours before. Some of the boys had seen him go to the chapel about 5.0 p.m., as he was accustomed to do every evening, to spend an hour in prayer before the Blessed Sacrament. He returned towards his room about 6.0 p.m., visited a father of the community on his way, and after leaving the latter's room appeared to have suffered a sudden apoplectic stroke in the cloister leading to his own room. Here he was found a short time after 6.0 p.m., prostrate and speechless, but still breathing. The rector was summoned and, in the presence of several of the community, administered Extreme Unction. Ronan gave no further sign of consciousness, and stopped breathing as the final prayers were being recited.[23]

News of his death appeared in *The Irish Times, The Irish Independent*, and *The Freeman's Journal* of 12 December. The last named gave a condensed but extensive account of his life. As a missioner, it observed that he 'became well known in almost every diocese and district of the country', and that few were 'more prized as a spiritual director of religious communities of both sexes throughout Ireland and of the clergy in very many dioceses.' His extraordinary devotion to the person of Jesus Christ under the symbol of the Sacred Heart was said to have 'brought manifest blessings on his work'. He also had a marked devotion to the mother of Jesus under the invocation of Our Lady of Lourdes, and he 'attributed the temporal success and prosperity' of his undertakings 'to his confidence in St. Joseph'.

A perceptive, though unsigned article in the *Mungret Annual* (vol. iii, July 1908) captured something of the capacity and character of the deceased. Among the qualities mentioned were those which created problems, at times, for higher authority.

Fr. Ronan was not a man of exceptional intellectual powers, but he possessed what is infinitely more valuable in the race of life: indomitable strength of will, a power of perseverance in the teeth of all difficulties, and a cheerful courage that bore him up and inspired a certainty of success even when events looked most unpromising. He had a clear idea of his purpose and object, and went straight and frankly for it without recking of minor obstacles.

He had a strong faith 'in the all-ruling providence of God', the writer continued, 'and calmly received all eventualities, whether apparently favourable or otherwise', as the outcome of an eternal decree devoted solely to what was best. Hence, he seldom gave evidence of doubt, 'and his cheerful spirit, which he preserved to the day of his death, reacted on all around him'. Endeavouring to pull together the seemingly conflicting strands which abided in Ronan, as in every human character, the author offered the illumination:

> Though a man of stern, determined, fearless character, who flinched before no opposition, and knew not what it was to yield or compromise where principle or what he considered the glory of God or the advancement of God's work was involved, he was in his social relations singularly amiable, and forgiving and considerate. Even to the last he was unusually free from the idiosyncrasies that often accompany old age, and was constantly bantered on his youthfulness of heart.

Adding a human dimension not readily perceivable in Ronan's correspondence, the same author observed: 'Even when he was over eighty years of age, none enjoyed a joke more or bore with better grace the turning of the tables against himself, or told a good story with richer humour, or contributed a more considerable share to the general social cheerfulness which he loved.' Not surprisingly, he had many friends and he was singularly loyal to the claims of friendship. 'His spiritual life and his ascetical teaching bore the impress of his natural character', the writer continued, 'It was founded above all on the virtue of hope; and he always insisted on prayer and union with God as the one means to do successful work in God's service.' Consequently, he attributed little to himself, and when congratulated on all sides during the jubilee celebrations seemed little moved, replying invariably, and meaningfully: 'Thank God! It is all his work; I really had very little to do with it.' The last words attributed to him when still vigorous, shortly before his stroke, were characteristic and fitting: 'How good God is to me. How happy I am to be here'.[24]

Ronan's body was laid out in his room, and during Wednesday, 11 December, the students of both sections of the college visited the remains and prayed by the bier. Next day, after a solemn requiem office and Mass in the college chapel, the funeral cortege proceeded to the cemetery. The pupils of the college went first, followed by the clergy, after these the coffin was carried on the shoulders of the senior students, and was followed by the mourners in considerable numbers. These included some elderly men 'who retained vivid recollections of missions preached by Father Ronan half a century ago.' Amongst the many others present were 'Rev. William Ronan, Newry, nephew of the deceased'- the first chronicled reference to a member of Ronan's family, Lord Emly, General Sir William Butler, K.C.B., Surgeon-Major Holmes, Limerick, and numerous past pupils of Crescent College. Ronan's body was laid to rest in the college cemetery, 'in a spot which he himself had carefully chosen long before', under the shadow of the old abbey 'and facing the window of the college chapel, where the Blessed Sacrament was situated'.[25]

The founding of the apostolic school was regarded by Ronan as the great work of his life, one which he said God enabled him to accomplish as the result of twenty years of constant effort and prayer for its realisation.[26] One other deep experience, however, remained with him to the end of his life, namely, his time as military chaplain in the hospitals in the east. His old friend, General Sir William Butler, was in Mungret during Ronan's final days. They had chatted together, and Ronan recounted anecdotes of his life in the Crimea and of his travels in the United States. One statement which, apparently, Ronan 'always insisted upon when speaking of his work in the Crimea', he repeated to Butler. The words, in the view of Ronan's obituarist in the *Mungret Annual*, were 'characteristic of the man' and, hence, though many of them have been quoted earlier, they are given here as Butler reported them.

'He said to me', Butler recalled, 'some memorable things on that first and last interview I had with him on 9 December. Amongst other things he said:

> 'In the hospital near Scutari I suppose more than one thousand poor soldiers from the Crimea were prepared for death by me. Some of them were able to utter only an ejaculatory prayer - some of them had known little of their faith before that time; but I have never for one moment doubted that every one of those poor souls went straight to heaven; and when I go', he added smiling, 'and meet them in heaven, I think they will elect me their colonel, and I shall stand at their head there'; and again, 'I pray our Lord that he may take me at any moment; I am quite willing to go - but I say, too, that I am ready to stay if he has any more work for me to do.'

Why Ronan saw himself in the unusual position of 'colonel' is difficult to understand, unless, perhaps, it reflected the respect in which he was held by dying men. In the circumstances it did not seem strange to General Butler, who concluded: 'It is an intense satisfaction to me that it was given me to see this grand veteran on the last full day of his long and wonderful life - all his faculties perfect.'[27]

Many past students from different parts of the world wrote to express their appreciation of Ronan and their sympathy to the college. Some expressed the hope that 'a grand monument' would be erected in his memory 'at the old *alma mater*'; one man, however, Rev. T. Shealy, S.J., from New York, wished rather that 'his life will be written. It will be one of the rich inheritances of Mungret; and remain an abiding inspiration for future generations of apostles'.[28] Ronan, it may be presumed, would have approved but mainly in the hope that it might be 'an inspiration for future generations of apostles'.

The apostolate in a global dimension, as has been seen, was his great concern and impetus, and in this he reflected the ethos of the Catholic Church in nineteenth century Ireland. It emerged from the penal laws with a sense of having preserved the faith in order to pass it on. This sense and impulse flowered following Catholic emancipation, and came into full bloom from the 1850s to the 1950s. Ronan, therefore, was to a considerable degree a representative figure, in his relatively simple faith, spirit of prayer, and driving missionary zeal, of the many thousands of missionary priests and religious, and of the innumerable lay men and women who had a missionary and prayerful spirit and reared, taught, and encouraged those who went abroad to share with others the belief and hope entrusted to them.

The apostolic school, which Ronan founded was closed in 1967, partly, and ironically, because the Second Vatican Council recommended that philosophy and theology be taught together, and the Irish Jesuit province in the 1960s, as in the 1880s, did not have sufficient men or enthusiasm for such a venture. A few years later, the shortage of Jesuits and the absence of vocations to the order resulted in the closure of the successful day school. As the new millennium unfolds the buildings erected by Ronan's efforts stand largely empty; while nearby the ruined Abbey of Mungret still evokes the ventures of an earlier era.

# *Appendix*

The Irish Sisters of Mercy who worked harmoniously under Mother Bridgeman in the testing conditions of the Crimea, contained a number of strong-willed, assertive women. None more so, than Mary Joseph Lynch, who spent her later years as a missioner in North America. Her redoubtable, self-willed personality is conveyed in this reconstruction of her singular manner and indomitable spirit. It is given as it appears in printed pages in the archives of the Sisters of Mercy, Kinsale, Co. Cork:

### *Mother Mary Joseph Lynch, RSM, Oregon Founder*
*'I'm Mother Joseph Lynch. The trip to Kansas City was so easy, I can't believe it. It was like sliding down a sunbeam! I'm used to travelling, you know. Came from Ireland on a ship, but once I got here railroads were my favourite mode. I went from Brooklyn to Rochester and back to Brooklyn, then to Grand Rapids, Michigan, and to Big Rapids. I went from Michigan to Minnesota - Mendota, Anoka, Minneapolis, then over to Morris in western Minnesota.*

*Finally I went to Oregon. But I didn't just sit in Oregon, you know. I travelled back and forth to Morris and even to Washington, D.C. On my Golden Jubilee I was stranded on a train in the Rocky Mountains in a snow storm. Didn't even make it to my own party. I heard the guests went up and congratulated my picture! A Sister in Chicago had created a lovely portrait - lovely as one can make from this face!*

*You probably wonder why I trudged all over everywhere (I was even in the Crimea, you know). Part of it was just plain wanderlust. I liked to see new places, meet new people, accept new challenges.*

*Part of it was - I don't like to admit this, but they told me I had to be honest if I came here - that I always had a hard time getting along with people, some people, especially superiors and bishops. They were glad to be rid of me in Kinsale. My work in the industrial school was great. But I was ... ah ... difficult to live with. I was very assertive - well, all right, aggressive. I always wanted to be boss, but no one in Kinsale wanted me for a boss.*

In Brooklyn they let me be Mother Assistant because they were thrilled with my vast experience and expertise with the industrial school and my nursing experience in the Crimea. But the honeymoon was soon over. When I went to Rochester to help them out for a year or so with their industrial school, Brooklyn wouldn't let me come back.

Luckily there was a bishop in Michigan who wanted me. But he didn't like how I handled money. Then I sort of snuck off to Big Rapids without getting real, formal, airtight permission. You know, Sisters, I had particular problems with bishops. I found that they thought they were my bosses. They took very seriously their "ecclesiastical authority" over us Sisters. With me having to be boss and them having to be boss, it was just a headache to try and do anything for the people. I just keep moving on trying to find a bishop that would let me help the people who most needed help. It was always the really poor and the socially outcast who tugged at my heart.

My next and most distressing encounter with a bishop was with John Ireland of St. Paul, Minnesota. Now he's quite famous. You've all probably heard of him. He was really quite liberal - too liberal to suit my taste. I didn't care about liberal, I cared about people and finding the money to help them. I started a school in Mendota, but he closed it. I founded a branch house in Anoka, but he made it a separate foundation and put a newly professed twenty-eight year old green-behind-the-ears Sister in charge. When they had a hard time - I could have told him they would - he kicked them out of his diocese, just sent them packing to Council Bluffs.

I founded a much-needed hospital in Minneapolis. Worked hard to finance it, but when it was really going well, he put the St. Joseph Sisters in charge of it. He had relatives in the order. He sent us packing then too - out of his diocese. If I weren't a Christian woman, I'd say ... Well, some things are best left unsaid! Anyway, it was all God's will, because it was in Morris, Minnesota, that my heart put down roots. There I worked with the Indians. Oh, how my heart embraced the Indian children! We gave them a tremendous education for that time. We relished the work. We didn't care about being paid, but finding enough money to keep the children fed and clothed was a constant *challenge. The government gave us contracts which paid some of the expenses for a certain number of children but it was never enough and the red tape! I'm not at all good with red tape. I want to just take a knife and slice right through it. But, as you might imagine, that didn't set too well with government authorities.*

*Funds were cut off entirely for us by Congress in 1896 and it was clear that we would have to sell our school to the government and find something else to do and somewhere else to go. It broke my heart to pieces to have to leave my Indians.*

*But that's how I got to Oregon. Ah, it was a fresh beginning. I travelled long and hard and frequently. I felt new energy. We opened a house for working women immediately. It had an industrial department, you can be sure. We opened a home for the aged and a school in Mount Tabor and then ... and then - I can't explain it - my energy just ran out. I languished in bed for a few months occupying myself with needle work for bazaars. And finally I was really low and I died. But my work in Oregon didn't die. How many of you have ever lived and worked in Oregon? There's Mt. St. Joseph's, St. Joseph's School in Roseburg (notice all the Josephs), there's Mercy Hospital in Roseburg and St. Catherine's in North Bend, and there were other hospitals, schools and homes that have long since closed.*

*Did you know that to travel from Portland to North Bend in the early days the Sisters had to travel by steamer for 24 hours, cross the bar and almost die of sea sickness? Did you know that travel from North Bend to Roseburg took 24 hours too and the Sisters would be bounced unmercifully around in stage coaches. When they got there they would be bruised from head to foot!*

*I'm getting pretty windy here. I'd better not take up any more of your time. But, Sisters, I just wanted to say: go where you need to go and do what you need to do. Try to get along with ecclesiastical authority (obviously I can't tell you how!) but don't be intimidated and don't stifle your vision. Heartache will come and the poor you can find wherever you go. Please, Sisters, please find them and stand with them. Try not to make the mistakes that I made, but don't be afraid to make a few mistakes of your own. You'll get the job done if you let God be your boss.'*

# *Notes*

## Chapter 1

1.  Information from Anthony Davis, parish priest of Clonduff, Newry.
2.  *Mungret Annual*, 1908.
3.  Francis Mac Polin. *Clonduff Parish: Past and Present*, panphlet, (Belfast 1936), p. 11.
4.  Padriac Keenan. *Brief Historical Sketch of the Parish of Clonduff*, pamphlet, c. 1941, pp. 8-9.
5.  Idem. p. 10
6.  Information from Fr. Davies, parish priest, Clonduff, 1999.
7.  John O'Donovan, in a letter on 20 April 1834. *Ordnance Survey Letters*, RIA, cit. MacPolin, op. cit. p. 37.
8.  Oliver P. Rafferty. *Catholicism in Ulster 1603-1983*, (London 1984), pp. 102-12; Profile in P. Mac Suibhne. *Paul Cullen and his contemporaries*, (Naas 1962), vol. II, pp. 333-53; Ambrose Macauley. *William Crolly, Archbishop of Armagh, 1835-49* (Dublin 1994), pp.120, 261.
9.  Jonathan Bardon. *A History of Ulster* (Belfast 1992), p. 261.
10. S.J. Connolly. *Priests and People in Pre-Famine Ireland, 1780-1845*, (Dublin 1982), p. 33.
11. Idem, pp. 36-7.
12. P. J. Corish. *Maynooth College 1795-1995*, (Dublin 1995), p. 100.
13. Idem, p. 107
14. Idem.
15. Idem, p.108
16. Idem, p. 113.
17. Idem, pp. 113-116.
18. Idem, p. 114.
19. Idem, p. 109.
20. A. Macauley. *William Crolly* ..., p. 439
21. Corish, op. cit. pp. 454-5
22. *Nation*, 12 Sept. 1846.
23. Corish, op. cit., p. 125.
24. Idem.
25. Cit. in *Nation*, 29 May 1847. Italics mine.
26. O. P. Rafferty, op. cit. pp. 127-29.
27. Letter of P. J. Corish to author, 22 May 1997.
28. Letter of Fr. Anthony Davis, Dromore diocese, to author.

# Chapter 2

1. See *Batterby's Register* or the *Catholic Directory* (Dublin 1849), p. 331 and for 1850 p. 258.
2. Idem, 1850.
3. *Catholic Directory*, 1846, p. 258
4. See T. J. Morrissey. *As One Sent. Peter Kenney, S.J., 1779-1841*, Dublin 1996, p. 96
5. Letter of Fr. Nicholas Pope,S.J., Jesuit Curia Rome, 1999, to author.
6. Comment of one of the Mercy sisters in December 1854 before they departed for the Crimea. *Leaves from the Annals of the Sisters of Mercy*, vol. 2, by a member of the Order of Mercy, (N.Y. 1883), p. 157. Copy in Kinsale archives.
7. Jesuit Catalogue for Francia, 1853, p. 14.
8. Jesuit Catalogue, 1853, courtesy Fr. Pope.
9. See David W. Miller 'Mass Attendance in Ireland in 1834' in *Piety and Power in Ireland 1760-1960*. Essays in honour of Emmet Larkin, ed. Stewart J. Brown and David W. Miller, (Dublin and Notre Dame,Indiana, 2000), p. 158.
10. Royal Commission, 27272; in notes by Kevin A. Laheen, S.J., on Jesuit Parish Missions, in Irish Jesuit Archives.
11. In the chapter on the synod entitled '*De Fidei Periculis Extandis*', cit. Laheen in notes on Jesuit Parish Missions in Irish Jesuit Archives.
12. *The Clare Journal* and the *Limerick Reporter* and *Tipperary Vindicator* give the names of Gaffney and Alexander Kyan as Haly's assistants, but the names on the mission cross erected after the mission were Ronan, Dwyer and Gaffney and these are likely to be more exact. See K. A. Laheen, *The Jesuits in Killaloe, 1850 - 1880*, p. 20.
13. *Limerick Chronicle*, 26 Nov. 1853, in Irish Jesuit Archives, Haly papers, see Laheen, p. 22.
14. *Clare Journal*, 22 Nov. 1853; Laheen, p. 20.
15. Ig. Murphy, *The Diocese of Killaloe,1800-1850*, p. 369
16. Cit. Laheen, p. 21
17. Idem.
18. Ig. Murphy, op. cit. p. 169 (Dublin 1992)
19. Martin Harney. *The Great Father of Brittany. Life of Blessed Julian Maunoir, S.J.* (Boston, 1964), pp. 151, 158.
20. *Clare Journal*, 11 May, 1854.
21. Idem.
22. Laheen in 'Jesuit Parish Memoirs 1863-76', Part 1, *Collectanea Hibernica* (Nos. 39-40, 1997-8), p. 281.
23. David Murphy. *Ireland and the Crimean War*, p. 7. Dublin 2002.

## Chapter 3

1. Evelyn Bolster. *The Sisters of Mercy in the Crimean War*, (Cork, 1964), pp. 6-7.
2. English Jesuit Archives (EJA). Letter of John Butt of 88th Regt. Light Division, Crimea, to Lady Georgina Fullerton, 8 Jan. 1855. Section OU/7.
3. Bolster, pp. 11-12.
4. Idem, p. 14.
5. Idem, p. 17
6. Edward Cook. *The Life of Florence Nightingale*, 1, p. 158, (London, 1913) q. Bolger, p. 18.
7. Mary C. Sullivan. *The Friendship of Florence Nightingale and Mary Clare Moore*, (Philadelphia 1999), passim.
8. See Bolster, ch. xiii, 'Army Chaplains'.
9. Archives Srs. of Mercy, Kinsale. 'Crimean Letters', Box 091. Yore to Bridgeman, 24 Nov. 1854; and see Bolster pp. 39, 41- 47. Italics mine.
10. Helena Concannon. *The Irish Sisters of Mercy in the Crimean War*, Dublin, 1950, (Messenger Publications), p. 8.
11. Archives Srs. of Mercy, Kinsale. Idem. Manning - Newman, 30 Oct. 1954.
12. Manning - Mary Stanley, 5 Nov. 1854, q. Bolster p. 53, and see pp. 52-4, 58-60.
13. Idem. See Bolster, p. 59.
14. Idem, p. 61.
15. *Leaves from the Annals of the Sisters of Mercy*, vol. 2, by a member of the Order of Mercy, ( N.Y. 1883), p. 157. Copy in Kinsale archives.
16. James Murray - Cullen, 11 Dec. 1854 in Dublin Diocesan Archives (DDA), Cullen papers, 1854, section 332/1/11, under 'Secretaries'.
17. Bolster, op. cit. p. 89.
18. Kinsale archives, q. Bolster, p. 96.
19. Kinsale archives, q. Bolster, p. 104.
20. Nightingale - Sidney Herbert, from Barracks Hospital, Scutari, Christmas Day, 1854, in Sue M. Goldie (ed.) The Selected Letters of Florence Nightingale. 'I have done my duty'. *Florence Nightingale in the Crimean War, 1854-56*, (Manchester Univ. Press, 1987), pp. 55-6.
21. Idem. p. 59.
22. Mother Bridgeman's Diary in Archives of Srs. of Mercy, Kinsale, p. 10.
23. Goldie, p. 9
24. Idem.

25. Bridgeman Diary, p. 13. Also Bolster, p. 106
26. Idem. Diary, p. 15.
27. Idem, p. 15, and Bolster, p. 106.
28. Diary, p. 57.
29. Bolster, p. 114, pp. 94-5.
30. Manning - Cullen, 4 Jan. 1855, Dublin Diocesan Archives. Cullen papers, Sect. 332/7/1. 'Secular Priests' file.
31. Cuffe - Cullen, 28 June 1855, DDA. idem.
32. Bridgeman Diary, p. 60.
33. Ronan - Cullen, 22 Jan. 1855, DDA. Cullen papers, 1855, section 332/7/11, under 'Male Religious', enclosed in a letter from Fr. John Curtis, Jesuit provincial, to Cullen, dated 5 Feb. 1855.
34. Idem.
35. A.S.D. Crimea. Chaplains' Letters, no. 9, Bagshaw - Grant, 21 Jan. 1855.
36. Bishop Grant - Cullen, 20 March, 1855, which mentions Cuffe's request for Mrs. Moore's recall, DDA. Cullen papers, 1855.
37. Bridgeman's Diary, p. 63. Bolster, p. 116.
38. EJA. Sidney Woollett Diary, 9 Sept. 1855, p.11. Sect. U 1/10/2.
39. M. C. Sullivan. *The Friendship of Florence Nightingale and Mary Clare Moore*, pp. 72-3 and passim.
40. Nightingale - Manning, 21 Aug. 1853, no. 530821 fnm, cit. Erb, *Recusant History*, p. 499.
41. Bridgeman Diary, p. 63 . Italics as in text.
42. 'More recently a charge of converting and rebaptising before death has been made', she wrote Sidney Herbert, 15 Feb. 1855. It was 'reported by me to the Senior Chaplain' (Protestant Chaplain),' by him to the Commandant, by him to the Commander-in Chief. I have exchanged the suspected nun. So sure am I that, give them enough rope and they will hang themselves - that I would, had I not been sincerely anxious for the R. C. cause, have let the matter drop, and not put them on their guard'. Cit. Goldie, p. 90. Italics in text.
43. Bridgeman Diary, p. 113.
44. Idem.
45. For these see  Diary, p. 120
46. Idem, pp. 101-103.
47. q. Bolster, p. 147.
48. Bolster, p. 156.
49. Cuffe - Cullen, 28 Jan. 1855, DDA Cullen papers, 332/7/1.
50. David Murphy. *Ireland and the Crimean War* (Dublin 2002), p. 135.
51. Cuffe - Cullen, 28 Jan. & 2 May 1855, DDA. 332/7/I, under 'Secular Priests'.

52. Bolster. op. cit. pp. 109-10.
53. Cuffe - Cullen, 3 May 1855, DDA. 332/7/1. 'Secular Priests'.
54. A.S.D. Chaplains' Letters, no. 23.  Bagshaw - Grant, 4 May, 1855. 'I have just received orders to proceed to the Crimea in a letter from Mr. Cuffe in which he decrees it beneath his official dignity to tell one anything whatever about our arrangements ...'.
55. Ronan - Cullen, 6 May 1855, DDA. Cullen papers, 332/7/1, 'Secular Priests'.
56. Cullen - Bridgeman, 18 April 1855, Kinsale archives, 'Crimean Letters', Box 091.
57. Idem.
58. Dr. G. S. Beatson, a Scotch Presbyterian, to Dr. Hall, 15 Nov. 1855, declared that these 'estimable women' abided by the instructions of the War Office and were motivated by Christian charity and benevolence. Rev. Thomas Cooney, an Anglican clergyman, informed Dr. Hall on 7 Dec. 1855, that he had had daily contact with the sisters at Balaclava, and far from there being any substance in the rumours against them, he had been struck by the kindness he 'saw displayed by them towards all alike', and by 'how much they seemed to strive to bury any difference of faith which might exist among those to whom they were called upon to minister in the universal love they showed to all'. Cit. Goldie, p. 120, f.n. 28, and see also pp. 89-90; also Bolster, pp. 130-33.
59. Italics mine.
60. Cuffe - Cullen, 28 June, 1855, DDA. Cullen papers, 332/7/I. 'Secular Priests'.
61. Bridgeman Diary, pp. 147-8
62. Idem. p. 148. Italics in text.
63. Sidney Woollett's Diary, 26 June, 1855, p. 3; EJA. U 1/10/2.
64. Cuffe - Ronan, 29 June 1855, DDA. Cullen papers, 332/7/I
65. Cuffe - Cullen, 2 July, 1855, idem. Italics in text.
66. A.S.D. Chaplains' Letters, no. 27. McSweeney - Grant, 20 Aug. 1855.
67. English Jesuit Province *Letters and Notices*, vol. 24, 'Sidney J. Woollett, 1818-1898.'
68. Francis Charles Devas, DSO, OBE., S.J., in *Mother Mary Magdalen of the Sacred Heart* (Fanny Margaret Taylor), Foundress of the Poor Servants of the Mother of God, 1832 - 1900, (London, 1927), p. 42.
69. Idem. pp. 40 - 46.
70. Idem.
71. Woollett's Diary, pp. 1-2; EJA. U 1/10/2
72. *Letters and Notices*, pp. 420-21.

73. Annual Letters of the English Jesuit Province, Account of Frs. Woollett and Strickland, p. 18; EJA. U 1/10/2.
74. Woollett's Diary, 26 June, p. 3.
75. Cuffe - Cullen, 5 July, 1855, DDA. Cullen papers, 332/7/I.
76. Whitty - Cullen, 5 Sept. 1855, idem, 'Secular Priests' file.
77. Woollett's Diary, 5 August, p. 7.
78. A.S.D. Chaplains' Letters, no.26. Cuffe - Grant, 14 Aug. 1885.
79. Idem. Letter no. 39, Bagshaw - Grant, 9 March 1856. The chaplains at 'daggers drawn' with Miss Nightingale were given as 'Woollett, Duffy, Unsworth, McSweeney'.
80. Woollett's Diary, 27 Aug., p. 10.
81. Idem. 31 August- 3 Sept., p.10. And see Bridgeman Diary, p.200.
82. Bridgeman Diary, p. 197.
83. Woollett's Diary, 6 Sept., p. 10.
84. Idem. 17 Sept., p. 11.
85. Idem. 29 Sept. p. 12.
86. Idem. 5-6 Oct., p. 13. Italics in text.
87. Idem. 7 October, p. 14.
88. Idem., 10 Oct., p. 14.
89. Idem., 20 Oct., p. 15.
90. Cuffe - Cullen, 22 Oct. 1855, DDA. Cullen papers, 332/7/1
91. A.S.D. Cuffe - Grant, 5 Oct. 1855, in box file : 'Bishop Grant, War Office, Admiralty and Colonial Service'.
92. Bolster, op. cit. pp. 245-6.
93. Idem, pp. 309-10. Bridgeman-Hall, 21 March, 1856. To the accusation that they had withdrawn from Nightingale's authority, she pointed out that only five of them had been under N's authority, she had disclaimed authority over the rest, and had resigned the General Hospital in Balaclava on 1 October and the sisters did not arrive until 10 October. That the sisters felt a duty to convert Protestants - not true, and no evidence for the charge. That the sisters were extravagant - not true, and Bridgeman had kept a detailed account of all requisitions to prove her case. That the number of sisters was too many for the number of patients - Bridgeman explained in detail why this was not so.
94. Idem. p. 246.
95. Idem. pp. 246-7.
96. Idem. pp. 247-8.
97. Annual Letters English Province, p. 21 . EJA. U 1/10/2.
98. Bolster, p. 270.
99. Mary E. Doona in 'Isabella Croke: A Nurse for the Catholic Cause during the Crimean War' (based on Croke Diary in Archives of Srs. of Mercy, Charleville, Co. Cork) in *Gender*

*Perspectives in Nineteenth-Century Ireland*, ed. M. Kelleher &
J. H. Murphy, Dublin 1997, p. 156. Italics in text.

100. Bridgeman Diary, pp. 412-14.
101. Bolster, pp. 311-14.
102. Bridgeman Diary, p. 370.
103. Idem, pp. 322-3.
104. Mary C. Sullivan, op. cit., p. 200.
105. Nightingale - Herbert, Crimea, 3 April, 1856, cit. Goldie,
     p. 246. Duffy is incorrectly called Michael Duffy in her letter.
106. Sullivan, p. 63, cit. letter of Nightingale to Lieut. Colonel John
     Henry Lefroy, at War office, 5 April, 1856. Also p. 61,
     Nightingale informed Mother M. Clare Moore on 1 April, 1856,
     that the sisters were not distressed by Fr. Duffy's
     attitude, and that 'Mr. Cuffe was very kind'. In Nightingale -
     Herbert, 3 April 1856, Goldie, p. 246, the word 'Irish' is
     omitted.
107. Lord Stanmore *Memoir of Sidney Herbert, Lord Herbert of Lea*,
     vol. I, (John Murray, 1880), p. 412; q. Bolger, p. xv.
108. 'Letters of Mother Mary Bridgeman, 17 July 1856, to her
     Former Children', Kinsale archives, Box 826.
109. *Leaves from the Annals of the Sisters. of Mercy*, p. 171, copy in
     Kinsale archives.
110. Lieutenant-General Sir William Butler in Light of the West
     (Dublin,1918), p. 230.
111. Bolster, p. 142.
112. Correspondence of or about Mother Bridgeman, Kinsale
     archives, Box 826; also in typed pages on 'Father Ronan's
     Contacts with Kinsale', Kinsale archives.
113. D. Murphy. *Ireland and the Crimean War*, p. 138.
114. *Letters and Notices of the English Province*, vol. 24, pp.
     420-21.
115. Bolger, p. 192; and A.S.D. Envelope of letters Cullen to Grant,
     1858.
116. Nightingale - Manning, letter 600225 fnm, cit. Erb, *Recusant
     History*, p. 502.

## Chapter 4

1. DDA. Walsh papers. Ronan-Walsh, 9 Jan. 1891; Section 405/ 3-6.
2. DDA. H. W. Wilberforce-Cullen, 7 Sept. 1857; Sect. 339/8,
   Laity. Wilberforce's observtions on failings in Inishbofin,
   Clifden, in the west of Ireland, in Sept. 1857, seem likely to
   have been relevant to other remoter rural areas - 'Chastity (is)
   at a low level, honesty hardly exists, and drunkenness is
   fearfully common.'

3. *Limerick Reporter* and *Tipperary Vindicator*, 14 Oct. 1856.
4. Sisters of Mercy Archives, Kinsale. Typed pages on 'Fr. Ronan's Contacts with Kinsale'.
5. Archives Carmelite Convent Loughrea, courtesy K. A. Laheen, S.J.
6. Henry Browne, S.J. 'Father Robert Haly' in *A Roll of Honour. Irish Prelates and Priests of the Last Century*, 1905 Dublin, p. 247.
7. Idem. p. 287.
8. Idem.
9. Bishop Cantwell's diary for that date in A. Cogan. *History of the Diocese of Meath*, vol. iii, p. 494.
10. I. J. A. Haly correspondence. Browne-Haly, 19 April, 1858.
11. Consultors of Irish Jesuit Vice-Province, notebook, 1858, 15 February. Residence of Jesuit provincial, Dublin.
12. *Roll of Honour*, p. 286.
13. *Galway Vindicator*, 19 March, 1859.
14. *The Munster News and Limerick and Clare Advocate*, 6 Aug. 1859.
15. *Galway Vindicator*, 24 April, 1859.
16. DDA. Cullen papers. Bp. Joseph Dixon-Cullen, 12-3-1860; Sect. 333/1, File 1.
17. *Munster News* etc., 8 Dec. 1860.
18. *Freeman's Journal*, 19 Feb. 1862.
19. *Galway Vindicator*, 10 May 1862.
20. *Munster News*, 4 June 1882.
21. DDA. Mac Evilly- Cullen, 23 August 1863; Section 340/7, File 1. Irish Bishops.
22. Idem. start of Sept. (no exact date) 1863.
23. Mac Evilly-Cullen, 23 August.
24. DDA. Cullen papers. Ronan - Mac Hale, 30 Aug. 1863, enclosed in Mac Evilly to Cullen early in Sept. (no precise date), 1863. Sect. 340/7, File 1, Irish Bishops.
25. Idem. Mac Evilly-Cullen, 5 Oct. 1868. Sect. 334/8, File 1, Irish Bishops.
26. Consultors' note book. Provincial's residence.
27. DDA. Cullen papers. Ronan-O'Reilly, 30 Oct. 1866, enclosed in a letter from O'Reilly to Cullen, 2 Nov. 1866; sect. 327/6, File 5. Male Religious.
28. Idem. O'Reilly-Cullen 2 Nov. 1866.
29. DDA. O'Reilly to Rev.Mother (no name given), 13 Nov. 1867; sect. 334/5, file 6, Nuns, 1867.
30. Consultors' note book. Provincial's residence.
31. Idem. 12 Oct. 1870.
32. Idem, 26 July, 1872.

## Chapter 5

1. For an account of these see Francis Finegan. *Limerick Jesuit Centenary Record, 1859-1959*, (Limerick 1959), pp. 67, 54.
2. Idem. p. 8.
3. Idem. p. 10.
4. Idem. p. 11.
5. Idem. p. 13.
6. Idem. p. 20.
7. Archives Sisters of Mercy Kinsale, 21 Nov. 1875 in typed pages on 'Fr Ronan's contacts with Kinsale' in box 826: Correspondece related to Mother Bridgeman.
8. Irish Jesuit Archives. Typed transcripts of Ronan's letters by Fr. Redmond Roche, S.J.: Ronan - Tuite, 12 August, 1880.
9. Kinsale Archives, October 1875.
10. Conveyed in a memoir by Lily Doyle, a younger sister of Chalres Doyle, q. Finegan, op. cit., p. 19.
11. Finegan, p. 22.
12. Idem. Miss Doyle's diary, pp. 23-4.
13. Idem. p. 79.
14. Idem. p. 79 - 80.
15. *Irish Times*, 12 Dec. 1907.
16. Most of the material on the apostolic school comes from Irish Jesuit Archives, Papers of Mungret Apostolic School, and transcripts of letters by Rev. Redmond Roche,S.J., and some summaries by same. See also Thomas J. Morrissey, Ph.D. thesis 'Some Jesuit Contributions to Irish Education', vol.1, section on Mungret Apostolic school.
17. Finegan. p. 71.
18. The bishops concerned were: Thomas Croke, Cashel; James MacCarthy, Cloyne; George Butler, Limerick; Michael Flannery, Killaloe (as he was mentally incapacitated the diocese was run by his coadjutor, James Ryan, 1872-'89); Daniel McCarthy, Kerry, 1878-'81, and Andrew Higgins, 1881-'89; John Power, Waterford, 1874-'86.
19. According to Fr. Ronan in the *Mungret Annual*, Jan. 1904, the idea of apostolic schools originated with a Fr. de Foresta, S.J., at Avignon, who linked the school to the Jesuit college there.

## Chapter 6

1. Jn. Fleming & Sean O'Grady. *St. Munchin's College, Limerick, 1796 - 1996*, Limerick 1996, pp. 56-7.
2. Fleming & O'Grady. op. cit. p. 59.

3. Idem. pp. 60-61; and IJA. Papers Mungret Apostolic School, Redmond Roche typed transcripts, pp. 4-7.

4. The negotiations involving the Holy Ghosts is based on an article 'Proposed College in Mungret' by Fr. Sean Farragher in the *Blackrock Centenary Annual 1960*.

5. IJA. Papers Mungret Apostolic School, Roche transcripts, p.8. Italics in text.

6. Idem. p. 8.

7. Idem. p. 11.

8. Idem. p. 14, italics in text.

9. Idem. p. 12.

10. Idem.

11. The memorandum of agreement was signed between - 'The Right Honourable Baron Emly of Tervoe in the County of Limerick, Sir David Vandeleur Roche of Caras in the said County of Limerick Esquire, Baronet Edward William O'Brien of Cahermoyle in the said County of Limerick Esquire, Sir Stephen E. De Vere of Monare Foynes in the said County of Limerick, and James Grene Barry of Sandville in the said County of Limerick Esquire, Trustees of the Mungret Agricultural School and Model Farm' and 'The Reverend William Ronan of Crescent House in the City of Limerick and The Reverend Thomas A. Finlay of Tullabeg College Tullamore in the King's County and John White of Nanteen in the County of Limerick Esquire D.L.'. The latter was a lay man and Protestant whom Ronan was required to have as a signee. IJA. Idem. Roche transcripts, p.15.

12. Roche transcripts, p. 17.

13. Idem. p. 18.

14. Idem.

15. Idem. p. 19.

16. *Mungret Annual*, 1907, p. 34.

17. IJA. Roche transcripts, p. 17.

18. IJA. from a draft article by Roche on 'The Irish Province Apostolic School', p. 5.

19. IJA. Roche transcripts, pp. 20-25.

20. Idem. p. 24.

21. Idem. p. 25.

22. *Mungret Annual*, bound volumes, vol. 3 (1907-11), p. 517.

23. Italics in text.

24. IJA. Roche transcripts in section on 'American Letters', p. 1.

## Chapter 7

1. Most of the material in this chapter is from Irish Jesuit Archives, Papers of the Mungret Apostolic School, Ronan's letters from America, in transcripts made by Rev. Redmond Roche, S.J., last director of the Apostolic School.
2. Britain (England, Scotland, Wales) was not envisaged in the early years as a mission area for students from the Apostolic School.
3. Ronan's entry for 29, 30 Sept. Roche transcripts, p. 4.
4. Idem. p. 4, Italics in text.
5. Italics in text.
6. Ronan-René, 17 Nov. 1884. Roche transcripts.
7. Italics in text.
8. Italics in text.
9. Italics in text.
10. Italics in text.
11. Ronan-René, 30 Dec.; Roche transcript, p. 11.
12. Italics in text.
13. Italics in text.
14. Italics in text.
15. Ronan - 'Dear Friend', St. Bridget's, Memphis, 16 May, 1885.
16. Ronan-René, 20 May, 1885, from St. Louis University.
17. Idem, 2 July, from Loyola College, Baltimore.
18. Italics in text.
19. Italics in text.
20. Italics in text.
21. Italics, idem.
22. Italics in text.
23. Ronan-René, 6 Jan.1886, from Worcester, Mass.
24. Italics in text. Fr. Keller was Assistant to the General.
    The Vicar-General from 1883 was Fr. Anton Anderledy, acting for the ailing General, Pieter Beckx. He became General in 1887. In 1873 the Jesuits had been ejected from Rome and established their headquarters at Fiesole in the monastery of San Girolamo, where they remained for 22 years.
25. Italics in text. Ronan-René, 20 April, 1886, St. Patrick's, Newburge, New Jersey.
26. I.J.A. Typed summary entitled 'The Apostolic School' by R. Roche, pp. 8-9. See also J. Fleming and S. O'Grady. *St. Munchin's College, Limerick 1796-1996*, pp. 64-85.
27. *Mungret Annual*, 1947, p. 29; q. in Roche transcripts.
28. R. Roche's judgement, in his typed summary on 'The Apostolic School', p. 5; I.J.A.
29. Idem., p. 6.

30. Idem, pp.5-6.
31. I.J.A., Roche's typed pages, 7 pages, entitled 'Opposition'.
32. *Mungret Annual*, July, 1908, p. 60, q. Diaries of Apostolic School for 1886.
33. Idem. 1908, p. 61, q. Diary 1886.
34. Idem. p. 65.
35. *Mungret Annual*, July, 1908, including 'Annals of Mungret College 1882-1907', p. 66.
36. Idem. pp. 32-34. See I.J.A., Apostolic School Papers, for copy of Ronan's printed address 'The Case of Mungret College addressed to The Right Honourable the Endowed Schools Commissioners', Feb. 1st, 1890.
37. I.J.A. Roche transcripts of correspondence, 1879-82, p. 13.
38. I.J.A., in Apostolic School Papers, p. 14.
39. I.J.A., Roche's typed pages on 'Apostolic School', and *Mungret Annual*, passim, and especially, 1931-1933.

# Chapter 8

1. Archives Srs. of Mercy Kinsale (A.M.K.): 'Further Correspondence of, and about, Sr. M. Francis Bridgeman' in Box. 826.
2. Irish Jesuit Archives (I.J.A.), *Memorials of the Irish Province*, 1914, p. 63.
3. Idem, pp. 64-5.
4. I.J.A. Admin/1/1890. General's Letters. Fr. L. Martin - Thomas Keating, Provincial, 18 June 1897.
5. Copy in I.J.A., sent to Fr. K. Laheen, S.J., from archives of the monastery, courtesy of archivist, Sr. Philomena.
6. I.J.A. Admin/1/1890. General's Letters. Martin - Keating, 18 June, 1897.
7. I.J.A. Admin/1/1890-1913. General's Letters.
   Idem. 30 July, 1897.
8. Idem. 20 Dec. 1897.
9. Idem. 15 Feb. 1898.
10. Idem. 26 April 1898.
11. Idem. 21 June 1898.
12. Idem. 17 Aug. 1898.
13. Idem. 15 Dec. 1898.
14. Idem. 8 March 1899.
15. Idem. 28 July 1900.
16. Idem. Martin - James F. Murphy, 9 Jan. 1901.
17. Idem. 1 April 1901.
18. Idem. 15 Oct. 1901.
19. Catalogue of the Irish province, 1902-6.

20. *Mungret Annual*, July 1908, p. 81.
21. Idem, 'Silver Jubilee', pp. 125-8.
22. Idem, p. 124.
23. Idem, p. 190. Unsigned article 'Rev. Wm. Ronan S.J., 1825-1907, Founder of the Apostolic School and Mungret College'.
24. Idem, p. 192.
25. Idem, pp. 192-3.
26. Idem, p. 191.
27. Idem, p. 193.
28. Idem, p. 158.

# *Sources*

**Primary Sources**:
Archives of Sisters of Mercy, Kinsale, Co. Cork. Letters and
papers relating to Crimean War, Mother Bridgeman's
diary, also *Leaves from the Annals of the Sisters of Mercy*,
by a Member of the Congregation (N.Y. 1863).
Dublin Diocesan Archives. Papers of Archbishop Cullen.
English Jesuit Archives. Papers relating to chaplains in the
Crimean War.
Irish Jesuit Archives. Papers of Mungret Apostolic School.
Robert Haly Papers. Catalogues of the Irish Jesuit
Province, and 'Memorials of the Irish Province S.J.',
Vol. I, no. 5. (Dublin 1902. Private circulation).
Minutes of the Consultors of the Irish Province.
Irish National Library. Lord Emly Papers. *Nation* newspaper,
1846-'47.
Southwark Diocesan Archives. Papers of Bishop Thomas Grant.

**Printed Source**.
'Jesuit Parish Mission Memoirs, 1863-'76', part I, and part II,
ed. K. Laheen S.J. in *Collectanea Hibernica*, nos. 39, 40
(Naas,1997-'8), no. 41 (idem 1999).
Report of the Educational Endowments (Ireland) commission
for 1887-'88; (c-5546), H.C. 1888, XXX1X; etc.

**Periodicals**
*Mungret Annual*, bound vol. 2 (1904), vol. 3 (1908).
*The Kinsale Record*. Journal of the Kinsale and District Local
History Society, vol. 3 (Cork 1991), vol. 5 (Cork 1995).

**Books and Articles**
Barden, Jonathen. *A History of Ulster* (Belfast 1992).
Bolster, Evelyn. *The Sisters of Mercy in the Crimean War*
(Cork 1964).
Brown, Henry. 'Fr. Roberty Haly 1792-1882' in *A Roll of
Honour. Irish Prelates And Priests in the Last Century*,
no editor given, (Dublin 1905).
Butler, Sir William. *The Light of the West* (Dublin 1918).

Concannon, Helena. *The Irish Sisters of Mercy in the Crimean War* (Dublin 1950. Messenger Publications pamphlet).

Connolly, S. J. *Priests and People in Pre-Famine Ireland 1781-1845* (Dublin 1982).

Corish, P. J. *The Irish Catholic Experience. A Historical Survey* (Dublin 1985) *Maynooth College, 1795-1995* (Dublin 1995).

Devas, Francis Charles. *Mother Mary Magdalen of the Sacred Heart* (Fanny Margaret Taylor) *Founder of The Poor Servants of the Mother of God* 1832-1900 (London 1927).

Doona, Mary Ellen. 'Isabella Croke: A Nurse for the Catholic Cause during the Crimean War' in Margaret Keller and James H. Murphy (eds.) *Gender Perspectives in Nineteenth Century Ireland* (Dublin 1997).

Erb, Peter C. and Elizabeth J. 'Florence Nightingale for and against Rome: Her Early Correspondence with Henry Edward Manning' in *Recusant History*, Oct. 1999, vol. 24, no. 4. Catholic Record Society Publications (Tonton, Hampshire).

Fleming, John, and O'Grady, Sean. *St. Munchin's College Limerick, 1796-1895* (Limerick 1996).

Healy, John. *Centenary History of Maynooth College, 1795-1895* (Dublin 1895).

Hoppen, K. Theodore. *The Mid-Victorian Generation 1846-1886* (Oxford 1998).

Huxley, Elspeth. *Florence Nightingale* (London 1975)

Keenan, Padraic. *Brief Historical Sketch of the Parish of Clonduff* (Newry 1941).

Kelly, James, and Keogh, Daire. *History of the Catholic Diocese of Dublin* (Dublin 2000).

Laheen, Kevin, S.J. *The Jesuits in Killaloe 1850-1880* (Newmarket-on-Fergus 1998).

Larkin, Emmet and Freedenberger, Herman (Eds.) *A Redemptorist Mission in Ireland 1851-'54. Memoirs by Joseph Prost CSSR* (Cork Univ.Press 1998).

Larkin, Emmet. *The Historical Dimensions of Irish Catholicism* (Washington DC, 1984).

Leslie, Shane. *Henry Edward Manning. His Life and Labours* (London 1921).

Lewis, S. *A Topographical History of Ireland*, vol. 1
(London 1837).

Lincoln, W. Bruce. *Nicholas 1, Emperor and Autocrat of all
the Russians* (London 1978).

Macauley, Ambrose. *William Crolly, Archbishop of Armagh
1835-'49* (Dublin 1994).

McClelland, V.A. *Cardinal Manning. His Public Life and
Influence 1865-'92* (London 1962).

McKenna, Lambert *Life and Work of Rev. James Aloysius
Cullen, S.J.* (London 1924).

MacPolin, Francis. *Clonduff Parish: Past and Present*
(Belfast 1936).

Morrissey, Thomas J. 'Some Jesuit Contributions to Irish
Education', vol. I, Ph. d Thesis, NUI 1975.

Murphy, David. *Ireland and the Crimean War*, (Dublin 2002).

Murphy, Ignatius. *The Diocese of Killaloe 1850-1904*,
vol. lll (Dublin 1995).

Newman, Jeremiah. *Maynooth and Victorian Ireland*
(Dublin 1983).

Potter, Matthew. *A Catholic Unionist. The Life and Times of
William Monsell, First Baron Emly of Tervoe, 1812-'94*
(Limerick 1994).

Proudfoot, Lindsay. *Down: History and Society* (Dublin 1997).

Rafferty, Oliver P. *Catholicism in Ulster 1603-1933*
(London 1994).

Smith, Cecil Woodham. *The Reason Why* (Penguin books
1958) *Florence Nightingale 1820-1910* (London 1950,
& 1982 ed.).

Sullivan, Mary C. (Ed.) *The Friendship of Florence
Nightingale and Mary Clare Moore (Philadelphia 1999).*

Taylor, A.J.P. *Essays in English History* (London 1976).

# *Index*

EDINBURGH
EDUCATION AND SOCIETY
SERIES

General Editor: Colin Bell

# The Manpower Services
# Commission in Scotland

edited by
Alice Brown and John Fairley

EDINBURGH UNIVERSITY PRESS

© Edinburgh University Press 1989
22 George Square, Edinburgh

Set in Linotron Palatino and
printed in Great Britain by
Redwood Burn Limited
Trowbridge, Wilts

British Library Cataloguing
   in Publication Data
The Manpower Services
   Commission in Scotland.
1. Great Britain. Manpower
   Services Commission
I. Brown, Alice   II. Fairley, John
354.410083'3

ISBN 0 7486 0126 0
ISBN 0 7486 0141 4 pbk

# CONTENTS

# LIST OF CONTRIBUTORS

**Steve Baron** taught in remedial education before moving into universities in 1978. He is currently a Lecturer in Sociology and Social Policy at the University of Stirling. He is writing in a personal capacity.

**Colin Bell** is Professor of Sociology at the University of Edinburgh

**Alice Brown** teaches Politics and Extra-Mural Studies at the University of Edinburgh

**Tom Burness** is Principal of Glenrothes and Buckhaven Technical College

**Tom Conlon** is a Senior Lecturer in the Computing Department of Moray House College of Education

**Angus Erskine** lectures in Social Policy at the University of Edinburgh

**Archie Fairley** is Director of the Scottish Local Government Information Unit

**John Fairley** is Manager of the PICKUP Scheme at the University of Edinburgh

**Elisabeth Gerver** is Director of the Scottish Institute for Adult and Continuing Education

**Cathy Howieson** is a Research Fellow at the Centre for Educational Sociology in the University of Edinburgh

**Kaliani Lyle** was a community-education worker with the YWCA Roundabout Centre in Edinburgh when her chapter was written

**Stephen Maxwell** is Social Policy Officer withthe Scottish Council for Voluntary Organisations (SCVO). He is contributing in a personal capacity and not on behalf of SCVO

**The Reverend Donald Ross** is the Industrial Missions Organiser for the Church of Scotland

**Bill Speirs** is the Deputy General Secretary of the Scottish Trades Union Congress

**Anne Stafford** works as Social Policy Research Officer with the Royal Scottish Society for the Prevention of Cruelty to Children

**Liz Sutherland** has worked as a teacher and careers officer. From 1983 to 1988 she was organizer for the Scottish Centre for the Tuition of the Disabled. She is currently working as Training Development Officer for the CALL Centre in the University of Edinburgh

**Jim Wright** is retired. He was previously the Training Manager of Ferranti Defence Systems. He was a member of SCOTEC and served on the Board of SCOTVEC from that body's formation in 1985.

# FOREWORD

This foreword is being written at a time that will be looked back on as most interesting: the period following the publication on 7 December 1988 of the White Paper, *Scottish Enterprise: A New Approach to Training and Enterprise* (Cm. 534).

Such are the exigencies of publishing that this book will not be able to make a direct contribution to the debate on the organization and development of training schemes in Scotland, since the official consultations ended on 31 March. And yet this is an ideal time to take stock of the achievements of what was the Manpower Services Commission in Scotland. To use its own language: how it rose to the challenges and opportunities *in Scotland*. For one thing is very clear from what follows: there is as much to be learned about Scotland as there is about the MSC when we consider their relationship. At a time when constitutional issues are once again the subject of daily debate, the systematic consideration of the operation in Scotland of the quasi-governmental agency is of great significance. Scotland after all now has its own White Paper, referred to above, albeit placed in the context of a general framework for training policy in Britain as set out in *Employment for the 1990s* (Cm. 540).

Scotland is a different political environment, and this naturally cuts both ways. There are advantages in the separate and distinctive traditions, say in education. In order to deliver its programmes at all, the MSC had to recognize the differences, say in local government, and yet of course this recognition was not always apparent to those doing the delivering. As this book makes clear there are areas of Scottish policy-making that mediate the implementation of Whitehall's formulations for the whole of the UK.

This book then explores the 'particularities of the Scottish' as much as the 'particularities of the MSC'.

But what, with the benefits of hindsight, are these latter particularities? 'Politically the MSC is a queer fish' is how Cynthia Cockburn (1987 p. 13) puts it in her exploration of sex inequalities and the Youth Training Scheme, *Two Track Training*. But the MSC was neither fish nor fowl. It was only apparently a quango with a faint remaining trace of its tripartite corporatist origins: as it was put to me recently, 'the last vestiges of the Heathite way of doing things'. Nevertheless, it had the powers that we normally associate with the apparatus of the state, whilst

not being directly answerable to elected representatives, let alone participants in the programmes. And, of course, much of its budget came from
the EEC's Social Fund – a fact not much trumpeted about, we might
notice.

It is when contrasted with 'education' that some of the characteristics
of the MSC can be highlighted. Perhaps, as several contributors to this
book point out, 'training' was always different. 'Education', until the
Baker whirlwind anyway – my characterization is of the sleepy Sir Keith
Joseph days – was based on a 'professional' partnership of administrators, teachers and elected officers, whereas the MSC was based on a
'social' partnership of trade unions, employers and administrators. Education is working within a legal framework – hence the Education
Reform Act – but a 'commission' can do anything and will, by contract.
Education is permanent and long-term; the MSC was programmatic.
Education was consultative therefore slow (didn't he learn fast!) but the
MSC was very 'can do' and precipitative in the extreme. Education is
fragmented but flexible, the MSC was centralized and bureaucratic. Education was on the defensive and the MSC on the offensive.

The MSC viewed 'education' with some surprise that it is so unconcerned about its customers: over 50 per cent are failures. Surely things
cannot be right if most customers view education as 'irrelevant'. The MSC
(not 'education') saw that sex-stereotyping was not confronted in
schools and that education has an excessive fear of vocationalism and
employers. Education is backward also in market research and evaluation. Education is too hierarchical, and the MSC would point to the low
status of non-advanced further education. And, of course, the MSC
thought 'education' was paranoid.

The obvious problem with the MSC was that it was too partisan and
committed. Question: What was the difference between the MSC and the
rest of the Civil Service ? Answer: When the MSC said 'Yes Minister' they
meant it. (This was truer in the Young/Tebbit glory days than under
Fowler/Baker.) The MSC was very 'flavour of the monthish'. In comparison with 'education', they had an inexpert field force, lacked 'pro-
fessionals' and had a high turnover of staff (compared, say, to the HMI),
there was constant reorganization and consequently problems of expertise and credibility. I am aware too that neither the MSC nor education
were as monolithic as my ideal typification makes them and that they
changed over time. By 1988 the MSC was clearly not the 'champion'
organization it once was.

The MSC's strengths were that the staff did seem to be highly motivated. It was pro-active and very fast; when it wanted something, it had to
be done *now*. It had short lines of communication and tremendous
'mobility'. It was pointed out to me by a very senior public servant, who
also worked for the MSC, that because they had such huge programmes

(e.g. YTS) an underspend of 5 per cent could give them £40 million to spend elsewhere.

As the contributors to this volume amply demonstrate, there is a great deal of social and policy interest in what the MSC achieved in Scotland. And yet there has not been an easy relationship with those, not only academics, who would have liked to understand more about the workings of the Commission and its programmes. 'Evaluation' has been much talked about but less frequently listened to. As much as anything, this has to do with the speed at which the MSC implemented its programmes in contrast with the normal pace of academic research. I had the experience of being appointed an evaluator, of TVEI pilot projects in Scotland, *after* their extension, and presumably after their 'success' was announced. (See *Liaisons Dangereuses ? Education–Industry Relationships in the first Scottish TVEI Projects*, 1988.) Many academics have, of course, found the contractual, purposive and directed nature of the evaluations somewhat bruising, whilst the MSC found the academics over-sensitive at best; the worst does not bear repeating! The least that can be said is that both sides doubt the other's motives. The money spent on academic evaluation anyway has been small beer when compared to that spent on advertising agencies: Saatchi and Saatchi £2.8 million on YTS: Burnetts £4.2 million on JTS; Yellowhammer £3.4 million on Restart; Davidson Pearce £4.8 million to sort out the confusion between them and on 'Action for Jobs'.

This book is clear evidence that it is possible to produce a systematic analytic account of the MSC that not only draws a picture that will be recognizable to the participants, deliverers and Commissioners, but takes our understanding further. That this picture will not be universally welcomed by those portrayed is inevitable. This is in part because of the almost universal ambivalence that those of us who have had dealings with the Commission feel. This is expressed with a remarkable and uncolluded consistency by the contributors to this book. The MSC is seen as inflexible yet modernizing; pompous and unable to listen, consult and learn, but funding socially valuable projects. Many are critical of aspects of the MSC's operation and yet acknowledge that it released much creative energy. It must be said that there is far less ambivalence about anti-unemployment programmes from the late 1970s.

This is a contribution to our understanding of the governance not just of Scotland but of Great Britain through one of the key agencies in the restructuring of the social and economic order. This book is exceptionally timely and to be greatly welcomed and we are pleased to publish it in the Edinburgh Education and Society Series.

Colin Bell, Editor, E.E.S.S.
Department of Sociology
University of Edinburgh

# INTRODUCTION

This book assesses the impact of the Manpower Services Commission on Scottish society and institutions during the years of its operation (1974–88), by recording the experience of some of those most directly involved. To date most publications on the MSC concentrate on its impact on education and training and the great majority have an English focus. In Scotland there is, of course, a distinct educational system and tradition, a unique local authority structure, a different voluntary sector, a Scottish Trades Union Congress (STUC), and distinct Church organizations. Each of these has been heavily involved in and affected by the MSC and its programmes. Further the economic, social and political environment in Scotland, in which central government labour market policy and MSC programmes have grown, is distinct from other parts of Britain.

The book is divided into four parts. Part I has two chapters. Chapter 1 outlines the main features characterizing the Scottish economy and public policy during the period of the MSC's rapid growth, paying particular attention to the increase in unemployment in the late 1970s and early 1980s. Chapter 2 provides an overview of the development and growth of the MSC, and describes in broad terms its main schemes and the scale of operations in Scotland. This part of the book is a scene-setting introduction for the general reader, who may know little about the MSC's growth, and provides a context for the more closely focused chapters which follow.

Part II analyses the impact of the MSC on Education and Training and consists of four chapters relating to schools, further education, the universities and computing. Part III outlines the influence of the MSC on institutions and organizations in Scottish society. This section includes five chapters on the voluntary sector, the Churches, local authorities, the STUC and the personal views of a training manager working for a major employer. Part IV concludes by examining the effect of the MSC on different groups in Scottish society, and consists of five chapters relating to women, the disabled, the Black/Minority Ethnic community, young people and adults. The authors of these chapters have either conducted research into operations of the MSC, or been directly involved as participants or practitioners in the implementation and delivery of MSC programmes.

# ACKNOWLEDGEMENTS

A number of people have helped us in the production of Part I of this book; we have benefited greatly from their comments and suggestions. We wish to record our grateful thanks to Professor Malcolm Anderson, Wendy Bradshaw, Professor Colin Bell, Alan Brown, Mike Danson, Angus Erksine, Neil Fraser, Dan Finn, Alex Gordon, Cathy Howieson, Norma Hurley, Alan Lawson, Professor Brian Main, David McCrone, David Raffe, Professor Adrian Sinfield and Anne Stafford. We doubt whether we have met all their criticisms, but with their help the text has been improved.

We should also like to acknowledge the assistance received from the Department of Employment Training Agency staff in providing data for the book.

We regret that the Confederation of British Industry in Scotland declined our invitation to contribute to the book.

Finally, we should like to thank our authors for their contributions to the book and for sharing their experiences with us.

# LIST OF ABBREVIATIONS

| | |
|---|---|
| AC | Accredited Centre |
| AEU | Amalgamated Engineering Union |
| AMB | Area Manpower Board |
| ATS | Adult Training Strategy |
| ATO | Approved Training Organisation |
| | |
| BACIE | British Association for Commercial and Industrial Education |
| BTEC | British Technician Education Council |
| | |
| CALLMI | Computer Assisted Local Labour Market Information |
| CEP | Community Enterprise Programme |
| CEPD | Committee for the Employment of the Disabled |
| CITB | Construction Industry Training Board |
| CGLI | City and Guilds of London Institute |
| COSLA | Convention of Scottish Local Authorities |
| CP | Community Programme |
| CRE | Commission for Racial Equality |
| | |
| DAS | Disablement Advisory Service |
| DE | Department of Employment |
| DHSS | Department of Health and Social Security |
| DMC | District Manpower Committee |
| DRO | Disablement Resettlement Officer |
| DTI | Department of Trade and Industry |
| DTS | Direct Training Services |
| | |
| EAS | Enterprise Allowance Scheme |
| EHE | Enterprise in Higher Education |
| EIS | Educational Institute of Scotland |
| EITB | Engineering Industry Training Board |
| EOC | Equal Opportunities Commission |
| ERC | Employment Rehabilitation Centre |
| ESA | Employment Services Agency |
| ESD | Employment Services Division |
| ESF | European Social Fund |
| ET | Employment Training |
| | |
| FTC | Foundry Training Committee |
| | |
| GRIST | Grant Related In Service Training |
| GTC | Government Training Centre |
| | |
| HCITB | Hotel and Catering Industry Training Board |
| HIDB | Highlands and Islands Development Board |

| | |
|---|---|
| HMI | Her Majesty's Inspectorate |
| IMF | International Monetary Fund |
| ITEC | Information Technology Centre |
| JCP | Job Creation Programme |
| JTS | Job Training Scheme |
| LCP | Local Collaborative Project |
| LCU | Large Companies Unit |
| LEN | Local Employer Network |
| MEP | Microelectronics Education Programme |
| MSC | Manpower Services Commission |
| NAFE | Non Advanced Further Education |
| NALGO | National Association of Local Government Officers |
| NAO | National Audit Office |
| NBHS | National Bureau of Handicapped Students |
| NCVQ | National Council for Vocational Qualifications |
| NEDC | National Economic Development Council |
| NJTS | New Job Training Scheme |
| NPSS | National Priority Skills Scheme |
| NSTO | Non Statutory Training Organisation |
| NTI | New Training Initiative |
| NUS | National Union of Students |
| OPCS | Office of Population and Census Studies |
| OTF | Occupational Training Family |
| PAFD | Premium Assisted Funding for the Disabled |
| PBWE | Project Based Work Experience |
| PER | Professional and Executive Recruitment |
| PSBR | Public Sector Borrowing Requirement |
| PTF | Practical Training Facility |
| RNIB | Royal National Institute for the Blind |
| ROSLA | Raising of the School Leaving Age |
| RTITB | Road Transport Industry Training Board |
| SCDI | Scottish Council Development and Industry |
| SCE(EB) | Scottish Certificate of Education (Examination Board) |
| SCRE | Scottish Council for Research in Education |
| SCOTBEC | Scottish Business Education Council |
| SCOTEC | Scottish Technician Education Council |
| SCOTVEC | Scottish Vocational Education Council |
| SCVO | Scottish Council for Voluntary Organisations |
| SDA | Scottish Development Agency |
| SED | Scottish Education Department |
| SEM | Special Employment Measure |
| SEMAG | Special Employment Measures Advisory Group |
| SEPD | Scottish Economic Planning Department |
| SIC | Short Industrial Course |
| SIACE | Scottish Institute for Adult and Continuing Education |
| SIG | Sheltered Industrial Group |

SMDP        Scottish Microelectronics Development Programme
SPAB        Special Programmes Area Board
SPS         Sheltered Placement Scheme
STC         Short Training Course
STEP        Special Temporary Employment Programme
STUC        Scottish Trades Union Congress
SWSG        Social Work Services Group

TA          Training Agency
TAP         Training Access Point
TC          Training Commission
TD          Training Division
TFE         Training for Enterprise
TLCP        Training Linked to the Community Programme
TOPS        Training Opportunities Scheme
TRIST       TVEI-Related In-Service Training
TSA         Training Services Agency
TSAS        Training Standards Advisory Service
TSD         Training Services Division
TSPA        Training for Skills a Programme for Action
TUC         Trades Union Congress

UVP         Unified Vocational Preparation

VTO         Volunteer Training Organisation

WEEP        Work Experience on Employers' Premises
WEP         Work Experience Programme
WIC         Work Introduction Course
WOTP        Wider Opportunities Training Programme
WOW         Wider Opportunities for Women

YOP         Youth Opportunities Programme
YTS         Youth Training Scheme

# PART I

# The MSC in Scotland:
# Background and Overview

# 1

## THE CONTEXT OF CHANGE:
## THE SCOTTISH ECONOMY AND PUBLIC POLICY

ALICE BROWN

The Manpower Services Commission was established by the 1973 Employment and Training Act and began operating in 1974. Initially it was a small agency with a very limited role, co-ordinating the public employment and training services for the whole of Britain. During the 1970s, however, successive governments increasingly used the MSC as their main response to the rising unemployment of those years. Within a decade the MSC had grown enormously in scale and in scope to assume a role which Parliament had not intended in 1973, and which could not have been envisaged when the MSC was formed. By the mid-1980s the MSC was spending more on education, training and unemployment schemes than the total budget for university education in the whole of the United Kingdom. Lord Cledwyn of Penrhos, in a House of Lords debate on the MSC in 1984, quoted a figure of £2 072 million estimated expenditure for the MSC for the year 1984/5 compared with £1 304 m recurrent income for UK universities.

In order to understand its role in vocational training, it is necessary to examine the MSC in the context of changing public policies towards employment and labour market policies. Training initiatives were first used as appropriate social policy responses to unemployment. But as unemployment continued to rise, especially youth unemployment, the MSC came to assume a strategic and central role in the reform of vocational education and training in Britain; and, further, the establishment of the MSC on tripartite lines did much to facilitate the legitimacy and implementation of its main programmes, at least until 1987/8.

As far as Scotland is concerned, there are difficulties in forming a coherent overview of the impact of the MSC. Even after 1977, when some administrative responsibility was transferred to the Secretaries of State for Scotland and Wales, the MSC was a highly centralized agency. While many of its programmes were delivered (and perhaps overseen) by local agencies, there is no doubt that policies were determined at MSC headquarters in Sheffield, or by the Secretary of State for Employment.

The MSC has had a major impact on different groups in Scottish society. Its programmes have had a direct impact on the unemployed, on industry, on industrial training, on schools and on further and higher education. As most of its initiatives were undertaken in partnership, the MSC has also had a significant impact on local authorities, on voluntary organizations, on trade unions and on Churches. Through its programmes and its role as 'catalyst', the MSC has radically affected the ways in which people think about the issues of unemployment, employment, training and education.

This chapter provides an overview of the Scottish economy as a basis for understanding its distinctive features and the context in which policy was developed; and for assessing the extent to which nationally determined training policies were appropriate to Scottish conditions and needs. (Providing such an overview is complex. As illustrated in this and other chapters, there are different interpretations of the available evidence and no general agreement on the state of the Scottish economy. Examples of these differences can be found in comparing government documents and statements with those issued by the STUC or the Standing Commission on the Scottish economy.) Finally it outlines the main aspects of post-war government employment and training policies, again to set current debates within a historical context and to offer some explanation for the extent and pace of change in the last decade.

The chapter does not provide a comprehensive treatment of the Scottish economy or post-war macro-economic policy, but it gives some sense of the overall picture in which the development and growth of the MSC can be understood, and in which its impact on Scottish society can be evaluated.

THE SCOTTISH ECONOMY

### 1. *The Structure of the Labour Market*

The Scottish economy in the post-war period has had features which distinguish it from the rest of Britain. To some extent, the distinctive character of the Scottish economy can be explained with reference to the country's specific historical development. 'As a junior partner to English industrialization, Scotland evolved an economy focused around textiles and heavy industry' (Scott, 1983). The dependence of Scottish economic activity on a declining base of textiles and heavy industry (such as steel, shipbuilding and coal industries) had implications for employment, and, in the early post-war years, unemployment in Scotland was about twice the UK average (Dey and Fraser, 1982).

In the period between 1964 and 1970, the situation changed, and employment prospects improved as the manufacturing sector in Scotland did better than in the UK as a whole. Some writers attribute this change to the success of regional policy, for example Moore and Rhodes (1974) suggest that regional policy brought between 70 000 and 80 000 jobs to Scotland in this period. However, Scott (1983) argues that regional policy did little to improve the situation, although he concedes that it perhaps prevented matters from getting worse. Other factors influencing employment prospects in Scotland were the increase in investment by multinational enterprises and the development of electrical engineering, and the electronics, chemicals and clothing industries, and the growth of the tourist trade. The result was a diversification of Scotland's industrial base, so that it resembled the industrial structure for the rest of the UK and was less dependent on heavy industry. In 1978 the Research Institute of the Scottish Council for Development and Industry claimed that 'for an industrialised country with a population of 5 million the Scottish economy is remarkably diversified' (Scottish Council for Development and Industry, 1978).

The discovery of oil and gas resources in the North Sea added beneficial effects on the Scottish economy in the 1970s. The oil industry required an investment of capital with a spin-off effect on domestic demand, mainly concentrated around the area of Aberdeen. It is estimated that employment in companies wholly involved in oil-related activity or construction rose from 25 000 in 1975 to 47 800 in 1979, and that if the indirect impact of this expansion is included, the figure rises to around 70–80 000 jobs in 1979. After a peaking of oil-related jobs, however, the industry experienced some instability in employment levels.

Industrial production in Scotland grew by 3.6 per cent and total employment by 0.8 per cent in the period 1970 to 1975, in contrast to the UK as a whole, which experienced little or no growth in either. The picture was reversed after 1975, however, as economic conditions changed. It then became evident that the discovery of oil resources was insufficient to correct the underlying structural imbalance of the Scottish economy. Between 1976 and 1979 there was no growth in Scottish industrial production, and Scottish employment experienced only a modest growth of 0.3 per cent. For the same period, UK industrial output grew by 4.3 per cent while employment in Britain grew by 1.2 per cent (Dey and Fraser, 1982).

During the world recession, which was exacerbated by the 1976 oil crisis, weaknesses in the Scottish economy were exposed. As indicated above, to some extent the economy was cushioned by the oil-related activity, but this was insufficient to halt the decline in manufacturing jobs. Dey and Fraser (1982) record that, in the 1970s, 100 000 jobs in manufacturing were lost, and manufacturing's share of total employment fell from 34 per cent to 29 per cent. The decline in the manufacturing sector continued after 1979, and jobs in this area contracted from 29 per cent of the total employment in 1979 to 22 per cent by December 1985. Most of the decline was concentrated in the traditional basic industries of the Scottish economy, such as metal manufacturing, mechanical engineering, transport equipment and textiles (MSC, 1986). Table 1(a) illustrates the changing relation in Scotland between levels of employment in the manufacturing industry and in the service sector; and Table 1(b) shows the relative contributions of these sectors to Gross Domestic Product.

In answer to those who contended that the loss of manufacturing jobs in Scottish industry was not a matter of concern, as they were being and would continue to be replaced by new jobs in the expanding service sector of the economy, Boyle and Jenkins (1987) argued that the Census of Employment 1984 did not support the contention that the service sector of the economy would grow sufficiently to replace jobs lost elsewhere in the economy. Further, they questioned the extent to which the expansion of the electronics and 'high technology' industries would provide sufficient jobs in the future to off-set the decline in the 'old' manufacturing industries.

Table 1 (a). Number of Employees in Scotland, by Sector (1 000s), and as a Proportion of the Total Scottish Employment Figures (%)

|  | 1979 | 1983 | 1984 | 1985 | 1986 |
| --- | --- | --- | --- | --- | --- |
| Manufacturing | 604 | 444 | 434 | 433 | 416 |
| % of total | 28.7 | 23.4 | 22.8 | 22.7 | 22.0 |
| Services | 1 224 | 1 216 | 1 231 | 1 241 | 1 254 |
| % of total | 58.2 | 64.0 | 64.7 | 65.1 | 66.3 |

Table 1 (b). Contribution to the Gross Domestic Product, by Sector

|  | 1979 | 1983 | 1984 | 1985 |
| --- | --- | --- | --- | --- |
| Manufacturing (£) | 4 173 | 5 434 | 5 568 | 6 440 |
| % of total | 28.6 | 24.8 | 24.2 | 25.3 |
| Services (£) | 7 192 | 11 748 | 12 698 | 13 832 |
| % of total | 49.3 | 53.6 | 55.2 | 54.5 |

*Source*: Fraser of Allander Institute, 'A Review of the Scottish Economy: Performance and Short-Term Prospects', paper prepared for the Standing Commission on the Scottish Economy, January 1988.

## 2. *Exports*

An examination of Scotland's manufacturing export performance in relation to the rest of the UK conducted by the Scottish Council noted that Scotland outperformed the rest of the UK in terms of exports per employee. For example, in 1985, Scottish exports per employee in manufacturing were worth £13 290; in comparison the UK figure was £10 525. These findings were examined by Mark Cox (1987). Cox noted that the figures depended heavily on the performance of just two out of the twenty-one industries surveyed: office machinery and data-processing equipment, and food, drink and tobacco. If both these sectors were excluded, Scotland's export performance per employee would lag behind the rest of the UK by a considerable amount. He concluded that Scotland's relative advantage in export performance was narrowly based and a potential source of volatility. To some extent the volatile nature of Scottish exports was exposed by the drop in real value of exports in 1986 by 11 per cent compared with a figure of 1.4 per cent in the UK as a whole.

## 3. Branch Economy Status

The above changes in the post-war Scottish economy led to a number of debates in Scotland over Scotland's position in relation in the rest of the UK and to the world economy.

One major issue was the fear that Scotland was becoming a branch economy and thereby losing control over key economic decisions and strategic sectors of the economy. It is argued that there has been a rising trend of takeovers of control and ownership by English and American interests, and that increasingly Scottish manufacturing and service industries are subject to decisions which are taken outside Scotland. Some writers have described Scotland as a 'regional economy' (Hood and Young, 1984) and, because of the loss of control of key economic decisions within Scotland, others have questioned whether the term 'Scottish economy' can be used in any meanful sense (Keating and Midwinter, 1983).

Table 2 illustrates the importance of overseas-owned companies to Scotland's economy in the provision of employment, and the relatively high influence of American-owned firms.

Concern was expressed that a large proportion of the sectors of the Scottish economy which did experience growth were owned and controlled by interests with headquarters outside Scotland. In 1984, over-

Table 2. Employment in Overseas-owned Manufacturing Plants in Scotland, Selected Years, 1950–1985

|  | 1950 | 1960 | 1970 | 1980 | 1985 |
|---|---|---|---|---|---|
| Total Employment | 26.3 | 56.2 | 108.9 | 97.1 | 72.0 |
| As % of Total Scottish Manufacturing | 4 | 8 | 15 | 17 | 17 |
| Overseas-owned Manufacturing Employment by Country of Ownership | | | | | |
| USA | 76 | 81 | 79 | 68 | 67 |
| Europe | 15 | 10 | 13 | 22 | 21 |
| Other | 9 | 9 | 8 | 10 | 12 |

Sources: Industry Department Scotland, 'Overseas-owned Firms in Scottish Manufacturing Industries – An Overview', Statistical Bulletin, No. A3.1, June 1986; see also Scottish Economic Bulletin, No 33, 1986.

seas firms accounted for 49 per cent of total Scottish employment in the
electrical and instrument engineering industries; 25 per cent in both the
chemical industry and mechanical engineering; 16 per cent in paper,
printing and publishing; and for 20 per cent of the work force in Scottish
manufacturing as a whole. Most of this investment came from the USA,
and American-controlled plants in Scotland provided 50 000 jobs in
manufacturing in 1984 (Buxton, 1986).

Scott (1983) argued that this trend towards declining autonomy can be
traced back to the early days of Scottish industrialization, but that the
post-war period is marked by the rapidity with which autonomy has
declined. He traces the shift in ownership in the post-war period, first
with reference to the nationalization by Labour governments of the
major heavy industries of Scotland – coal, steel and shipbuilding. This
policy resulted in increased centralization of decision making. Second,
he records the extent of English and foreign takeovers of manufacturing
industries in food and drink production and the car industry. Third, he
refers to the shift in control over oil exploration and production in the
North Sea. And finally, he warns against greater outside ownership and
control of the financial sector in Scotland.

## 4. Deindustrialization

Related to this shift in ownership has been the debate over deindustrialization and concern about the decline in Scotland's industrial base.
Buxton (1986) states that there are several different ways of defining
deindustrialization, but argues for a definition which relates to an abso-
lute and sustained decline in industrial employment. On the basis of this
definition, it is contended that deindustrialization in Scotland has proceeded further than in any other advanced industrial nation, with the

Table 3. Structure of the Scottish Economy by Main Sectors, 1973–1984

| Sector | Contribution in 1973, per cent | | Contribution in 1979, per cent | | Contribution in 1984, per cent | |
|---|---|---|---|---|---|---|
| | to GDP | to total employ-ment | to GDP | to total employ-ment | to GDP | to total employ-ment |
| Agriculture, Forestry and Fishing. | 5.1 | 2.5 | 3.6 | 2.3 | 3.3 | 2.2 |
| Energy and Water Supply. | 4.6 | 3.1 | 5.4 | 3.5 | 5.1 | 4.0 |
| Manufacturing | 29.0 | 32.1 | 28.1 | 28.7 | 25.3 | 22.6 |
| Construction | 9.6 | 8.4 | 8.3 | 7.4 | 7.0 | 6.2 |
| Services | 51.7 | 53.9 | 54.6 | 58.1 | 59.3 | 65.0 |

Sources: Scottish Economic Bulletin; Scottish Abstract of Statistics.

loss of 40 per cent of its industrial employment, mostly in manufacturing, since 1959/60. As discussed above, manufacturing accounted for a
reduced share of total employment between the mid-1970s and 1980s.
The figures relating to the contribution to GDP also illustrate a reduction
over the period.

Table 3 illustrates the decline in the contribution of agriculture,
forestry and fishing, manufacturing and construction to GDP and total
employment; it also shows the increase in the contribution of energy and
water supply and the services sectors over the period 1973–84. There is
some dispute as to whether the shift from manufacturing to service
industries should be a matter for concern. Those who believe it is base
their argument on the extent and speed of this shift in Scotland in
relation to other countries; on the evidence that relates the size of
manufacturing in an economy to the level of income per head and the
GDP; and on the interrelationship between manufacturing and trade.
Overdependence on the export of oil and invisible exports they argue,
has a long-term detrimental effect on Britain's balance of payments and
increases the vulnerability of the Scottish economy to changing economic conditions.

## 5. North–South Divide

The trends noted above have contributed to increasing concern in Scotland that the UK economy is divided in terms of the economy and
employment between the North and South of Britain (Ashcroft, 1988).
After the recession of 1979–81, Scotland together with the rest of the UK,
enjoyed a period of economic recovery and growth. In 1986, however,
the relative performance of the Scottish economy deteriorated, and
Ashcroft argues that the principal reason for the reversal in Scotland's
economic fortunes was to be found in the fall in the price of oil during late
1985 and early 1986. This had a spin-off effect on the rest of the Scottish
economy, which was to experience a rise in unemployment at a time
when unemployment in the UK as a whole was beginning to fall.

Ashcroft attributes the rise in concern about the relative performance
of the Scottish economy to the publication of the 1984 Census of Employment in January 1987. The Census highlighted regional disparities in
unemployment rates, and estimated that the employed labour force in
Britain had fallen by 3 per cent between June 1979 and June 1986, in
comparison with a fall in Scotland of 8 per cent. Other regions also
experienced a relatively large fall in the employed labour force. For
example in the North, North-West and Welsh Standard Regions there
was a fall of 10 per cent, 12 per cent and 13 per cent respectively. In
contrast three southern Standard Regions, East Anglia, South-West and
South-East, all experienced positive employment growth of 13 per cent,
5 per cent and 2 per cent respectively. Bodies such as the Scottish
Council, the STUC and the Fraser of Allander Institute also drew attention
to the imbalance between the North and South, which they claimed had

Table 4. Gross Domestic Product Per Head, as Percentage of UK
Average, 1975–1985, by Region

|  | 1975 | | 1985 | | Change 1975–85 | |
|---|---|---|---|---|---|---|
|  | % | rank | % | rank | % | rank |
| East Anglia | 92.8 | 8 | 100.8 | 2 | +8.0 | 1 |
| South West | 90.3 | 9 | 93.8 | 6 | +3.5 | 2 |
| South East | 112.9 | 1 | 114.8 | 1 | +1.9 | 3 |
| Greater London | 125.8 | | 125.8 | | 0.0 | |
| Rest of SE | 103.6 | | 107.7 | | +4.1 | |
| Scotland | 97.1 | 3 | 97.3 | 3 | +0.2 | 4 |
| Wales | 88.7 | 10 | 88.8 | 10 | +0.1 | 5 |
| North West | 96.2 | 4 | 96.0 | 4 | −0.2 | 6 |
| East Midlands | 96.1 | 5 | 95.7 | 5 | −0.4 | 7 |
| North | 93.6 | 7 | 92.9 | 7 | −0.7 | 8 |
| Yorks and Humber | 94.1 | 6 | 91.8 | 9 | −2.3 | 9 |
| N. Ireland | 80.0 | 11 | 74.8 | 11 | −5.2 | 10 |
| West Midlands | 100.0 | 2 | 92.3 | 8 | −7.7 | 11 |

*Note*: Ranking is by Standard Region
*Source*: *Regional Trends*, 1987 (HMSO)

worsened since 1979. This claim that the country was being increasingly
divided in regional terms between the South (East Anglia, the South-
East and the South-West) and the North (the rest of Britain) was vigorously rejected by the government and the Secretary of State for Scotland,
Malcolm Rifkind.

In considering the arguments for and against the proposition of a
North-South divide, Ashcroft argues that there is no simple dichotomy
between the economic performance of the North and the South of
Britain. That is, on the evidence provided in relation to GDP per head (the
measure conventionally used by economists as an index of living standards) there is no simple division between the North and South. Comparing the years 1975 and 1985, Ashcroft notes that Scotland retained its
high third position in the rankings of regional trends, and GDP per head
actually grew somewhat more quickly than the UK average (see Table 4).
However, more recent data indicates a reversal of this trend and a
decline in Scotland's position to fifth place in the rankings. Further
Ashcroft does concede that there is a clear distinction between the job
opportunities available in regions above and below a line drawn from the
Humber to the Severn.

## 6. Occupational Change

The structural changes which have taken place in the Scottish economy
have had a direct impact on employment patterns. For example, the
decline in the traditional areas of employment has meant the loss of
full-time jobs in heavy industry, normally undertaken by men, and the

loss of full-time jobs in manufacturing, which has had an impact on both men and women. The development of the service sector has increased the part-time job opportunities, especially for women. To some extent this is a reflection of the UK picture, but in Scotland the 1984 Census of Employment demonstrates that, at 44.2 per cent, the labour force participation rate of women, is slightly higher than the figure of 43.9 per cent for the whole of Britain. The difference between the two participation rates was solely attributed to a higher rate of female part-time employees within the Scottish labour market. Part-time working has increased significantly for both men and women. In 1951 part-time employment accounted for 4 per cent of all employees compared with 23 per cent in 1986. Figures for the number of vacancies notified to Jobcentres in March 1988 indicate that 27.4 per cent of vacancies in Britain were part-time. In Scotland the percentage of part-time vacancies was 29.4 per cent (Unemployment Unit Briefing, April 1988).

Steve Kendrick (1986) states that the last twenty-five years have witnessed an unprecedented transformation of the Scottish occupational structure. Similarly in the rest of Britain, the most significant feature has been the continuing swing from manual to non-manual occupations. There has also been a shift in the balance within the non-manual group. The numbers of routine non-manual occupations – mainly clerical and sales jobs – have stagnated; and the fastest expansion has been among the professional, managerial and intermediate non-manual occupations. No such clear-cut shift in the balance within the manual occupations is evident. The main impact of industrial change has been met by skilled manual workers, although unskilled workers have also suffered with the disproportionate shedding of unskilled labour within industries in the last fifteen years. This decline has taken place at the same time as the number of personal-service workers has risen and the reversal of the downward trend in the number of employers and self-employed workers. Kendrick argues that the speed of industrial change and its impact have given rise to fears that advanced automation and information technology will bring about unprecedented changes in occupational structures in the future. (see Table 5 for a socio-economic analysis of employment.)

Kendrick (1986) notes that the most important single shift in the labour market since the Second World War has been the entry of married women into paid employment outside the home. The position in Scotland differed from the rest of Britain, because there were proportionately more single women in Scotland, who to some extent mitigated against the participation of married women in the labour market. As a result the economic activity rate for married women in Scotland was only two-thirds that of the national figure in the immediate post-war years. It was not until the 1970s that the labour-force participation rates of Scottish women began to catch up.

Table 5. Employment in Scotland by socio-economic group, 1961, 1971, 1981, as percentage of total employment

| | 1961 | 1971 | 1981 adjusted | 1981 published |
|---|---|---|---|---|
| Employers | 2.6 | 2.2 | 2.3 | 2.2 |
| Managers & Administrators | 3.9 | 5.6 | 7.0 | 7.4 |
| Self-employed professionals | 0.7 | 0.7 | 0.8 | 0.6 |
| Professional employees | 1.7 | 2.7 | 3.8 | 3.2 |
| Intermediate non-manual | 5.8 | 8.1 | 10.8 | 11.3 |
| Junior non-manual | 20.8 | 21.1 | 21.9 | 20.9 |
| Personal service | 4.4 | 5.5 | 6.4 | 6.4 |
| Foremen & supervisors (manual) | 2.4 | 2.5 | 2.7 | 2.7 |
| Skilled manual | 27.6 | 22.8 | 19.8 | 19.2 |
| Semi-skilled manual | 13.4 | 12.9 | 10.8 | 12.1 |
| Unskilled manual | 8.3 | 8.9 | 7.0 | 7.0 |
| Own account workers | 1.7 | 2.0 | 2.4 | 2.4 |
| Farmers – employers and managers | 1.4 | 0.8 | 0.7 | 0.7 |
| Farmers – own account | 0.8 | 0.8 | 0.7 | 0.7 |
| Agricultural workers | 3.0 | 2.0 | 1.2 | 1.4 |
| Armed forces | 1.0 | 1.0 | 1.0 | 1.0 |
| Inadequately described, not stated | 0.4 | 0.5 | 0.7 | 0.7 |
| Total (1 000s) | 2216 | 2164 | 2104 | 2104 |

Note: Socio-economic groups are as defined by the Office of Population Census and Surveys,

Source: Scottish Government Yearbook, 1986.

Comparing the occupational structure of Scotland in 1981 with the rest of Britain, Kendrick summarizes the main differences as follows. First, Scotland has a higher proportion of the work force in manual jobs. Second, the shortfall of non-manual workers in Scotland can be attributed mainly to the lower percentage of managers and administrators (7.4 per cent of total employment in Scotland, compared with 10 per cent in England and Wales) particularly in the private sector. One factor which may account for this divergence is the large number of branch plants and fewer head offices of foreign companies located in Scotland. Third, Scotland has a much lower level of non-agricultural, own-account workers (the non-professional, self-employed, without employees). Only 2.4 per cent of Scotland's employed population were in this group, compared with 4.3 per cent in England and Wales as a whole, although much of the difference can be attributed to the different organization of labour in the construction industry. Kendrick concludes that in addition to the manual/non-manual divergence, Scotland's occupational structure has what he describes as a collectivist bias in relation to England and Wales. That is, a bias away from own-account working and management in the private sector, towards employment in the state sector (central government, local government and the nationalized industries). It

Table 6. Occupational Structure of the Labour Force: Scotland and GB

| Occupation Group | Scotland | | GB | | Scotland as % of GB |
|---|---|---|---|---|---|
| | 1 000s | % | 1 000s | % | |
| Managerial and Admin. | 258.3 | 12.8 | 3231.7 | 14.1 | 8.0 |
| Higher-Level Service | 279.8 | 13.8 | 3424.8 | 14.9 | 8.2 |
| Higher-Level Industrial | 100.5 | 5.0 | 1139.4 | 5.0 | 8.8 |
| Lower-Level Service and Supervisory | 601.2 | 29.7 | 6845.6 | 29.8 | 8.8 |
| Craft and Foremen | 327.9 | 16.2 | 3521.9 | 15.3 | 9.3 |
| Lower-Level Industrial and other | 458.0 | 22.6 | 4802.0 | 20.9 | 9.5 |
| All occupations | 2025.7 | 100.0 | 22965.4 | 100.0 | 8.8 |

*Source:* Labour Force Survey, 1984.

remains to be seen to what extent the privatization policies of the Conservative governments since 1979 will affect these figures in the future. Figures supplied by the Secretary of State for Employment, in answer to a parliamentary question from Michael Meacher MP, indicate that in 1987, 8.9 per cent of Scotland's employed population were self-employed compared with 9.9 per cent in England and Wales as a whole and 10.4 per for the South East of England. The Labour Force Survey of 1984 indicates that the divergence between manual and non-manual occupations within Scotland and the rest of Britain had continued (see Table 6).

## 7. Unemployment

As industrial change has had an impact on occupational structure, so too has it affected the level of employment. Fraser and Sinfield (1987) record that unemployment in Scotland doubled in the second half of the 1970s and again in the first half of the 1980s. As noted above, at the end of the Second World War, the rate of unemployment was about twice the total UK level. By 1961 the situation was unchanged, but in more recent years the differential has reduced to between 15 per cent and 20 per cent. This can be accounted for by the employment effects of the discovery of North Sea Oil and the continuing migration of labour from Scotland. There is an added difficulty in comparing unemployment figures across time, because of changes in the compilation of the official statistics since 1979. The Unemployment Unit has monitored the changes in the official measurement of unemployment in Britain (twenty-four changes between 1979 and 1988) since the election of the Conservative government in 1979, and publishes its own index of the level of unemployment (Unemployment Bulletin, summer 1988). For example, the official number of unemployed people as measured by the Department of Employment in June 1988 was 2 375 300 (seasonally adjusted). The figure

Table 7. Regional Unemployment, adjusted totals and percentage
rates, June 1988

|  | DE Count* | | UU Index ** | |
|---|---|---|---|---|
|  | Total | % | Total | % |
| South-East | 516 200 | 5.6 | 652 583 | 7.0 |
| (Greater London) | (293 600) | (6.8) | (371 171) | (8.5) |
| East Anglia | 52 800 | 5.2 | 67 627 | 6.6 |
| South-West | 140 800 | 6.7 | 183 214 | 8.7 |
| West Midlands | 238 700 | 9.1 | 304 814 | 11.4 |
| East Midlands | 148 800 | 7.6 | 189 254 | 9.6 |
| Yorks and Humberside | 235 000 | 9.9 | 300 689 | 12.5 |
| North-West | 331 200 | 11.0 | 424 203 | 13.9 |
| North | 179 200 | 12.3 | 231 351 | 15.7 |
| Wales | 130 600 | 10.9 | 170 609 | 14.1 |
| Scotland | 286 000 | 11.5 | 364 119 | 14.3 |
| Northern Ireland | 116 100 | 16.7 | 148 257 | 21.1 |
| Great Britain | 2 259 200 | 8.2 | 2 884 943 | 10.4 |
| UK | 2 375 300 | 8.4 | 3 033 200 | 10.6 |

* DE Count percentage rates are on the new 'Workforce in Employment' basis for
June and on the Working Population for May.
** UU Index percentage rates are based on the Working Population for June and the
Employed Labour Force for May.

*Source:* Unemployment Unit, *Statistical Supplement*, July 1988.

Table 8. Scottish Unemployment Rates by Region, ranked by Level,
May 1986

|  | Old Count | | | | | | | New Count | |
|---|---|---|---|---|---|---|---|---|---|
|  | May 1967 (%) | May 1971 | May 1976 | May 1979 | May 1983 | May 1986 | May 1986 (%) | May 1986 | May 1986 (%) |
| Strathclyde | 4.3 | 156 | 177 | 205 | 432 | 489 | 21.0 | 430 | 18.5 |
| Western Isles | 22.9 | 79 | 59 | 57 | 99 | 91 | 20.9 | 80 | 18.4 |
| Fife | 4.2 | 131 | 143 | 162 | 330 | 447 | 18.8 | 393 | 16.5 |
| Central | 3.1 | 155 | 184 | 200 | 536 | 594 | 18.4 | 522 | 16.2 |
| Highland | 5.2 | 119 | 106 | 161 | 277 | 335 | 17.4 | 294 | 15.3 |
| Tayside | 3.2 | 175 | 191 | 225 | 487 | 515 | 16.5 | 453 | 14.5 |
| Dumfries and Galloway | 5.4 | 100 | 131 | 142 | 263 | 282 | 15.2 | 248 | 13.4 |
| Lothian | 2.1 | 224 | 248 | 286 | 618 | 683 | 14.3 | 600 | 12.6 |
| Orkney | 4.6 | 89 | 56 | 126 | 279 | 295 | 13.5 | 259 | 11.9 |
| Borders | 1.3 | 231 | 277 | 269 | 804 | 840 | 13.2 | 738 | 11.6 |
| Grampian | 3.0 | 127 | 100 | 147 | 316 | 330 | 9.9 | 290 | 8.7 |
| Shetland | 8.3 | 58 | 35 | 32 | 96 | 83 | 6.9 | 73 | 6.1 |
| Scotland | 3.6 | 153 | 178 | 203 | 445 | 493 | 17.7 | 433 | 15.6 |

*Note:* 1967 = 100 as index of change.

*Sources:* Scottish Abstract of Statistics, 9 (1980, p. 95), and Department of Employment press releases, with estimates of the old registrant count by the authors
based on data from the Unemployment Unit.

using the Unemployment Unit's index, was 3 033 200 (seasonally adjusted) unemployed people (Unemployment Unit Briefing, July 1988).

Table 7 shows the seasonally adjusted figures of unemployment and the percentage rates of unemployment, broken down by region within the UK, for June 1988, using both the Department of Employment's count and the Unemployment Unit's count. Using the Department of Employment index the percentage rate of unemployment in Scotland was 11.5 per cent in June 1988 compared with average rate of 8.4 per cent for the UK as a whole. Using the Unemployment Unit index, the percentages are 14.3 per cent and 10.6 per cent respectively. These figures show that the level of unemployment is unevenly distributed throughout the UK. But it should also be noted that the level of unemployment is unevenly distributed between and within the different towns, cities and regions of Scotland. The divergence between the unemployment rates in different regions in Scotland was noted by Fraser and Sinfield (1987) (see Table 8). In mid-1986, apart from the Western Isles, Strathclyde had the highest rate of unemployment in Scotland at 18.4 per cent (21 per cent on the basis of the old count figures); and Fife and Central were the only other regions above the national average. In contrast unemployment in the Grampian region and the Borders has been closer to half the national rate since 1970. However, within Grampian region, Forres had the highest unemployment rate for a travel-to-work area in the whole of Scotland at 25 per cent in July 1986, compared with a rate of 7.7 per cent for the city of Aberdeen.

Statistics ranking and comparing local variations in unemployment in the UK in March 1988 indicate that Glasgow Central parliamentary constituency was ranked fourth with an unemployment rate of 22.7 per cent (Department of Employment), 28.8 per cent (Unemployment Unit). This compares with Glasgow Hillhead which was ranked seventy-fifth with unemployment rates of 15.3 per cent and 19.7 per cent respectively (Unemployment Unit, April 1988). Similar variations can be found within the city of Edinburgh where the average rate of unemployment was 10.4 per cent (Department of Employment) in May 1988, but where the worst affected area, Fort/Harbour, had an unemployment rate of 21.8 per cent (Edinburgh District Council, summer 1988).

## 8. Youth Unemployment

In addition to the uneven geographical distribution of unemployment, the impact of unemployment is unevenly distributed between different groups in society. Fraser and Sinfield (1987) state that during the recession the burden of unemployment has continued to be borne disproportionately by certain groups. They refer to the most vulnerable groups, such as young people unable to establish themselves in employment, older workers, who are particularly prone to prolonged unemployment once they lose a job, those with fewer skills, the disabled and those in

Table 9. Destinations of previous session's fourth year summer term leavers, at time of survey, Scotland (%)

| Year of leaving | 1978 | 1980 | 1982 | 1983 | 1984 |
| Survey year | 1979 | 1981 | 1983 | 1984 | 1985 |
|---|---|---|---|---|---|
| **Males and Females** | | | | | |
| Course | 8.4 | 8.1 | 10.2 | 8.7 | 9.3 |
| Full-time job | 72.2 | 55.0 | 40.2 | 33.7 | 31.6 |
| YOP/YTS | 8.3 | 18.9 | 27.1 | 37.7 | 38.7 |
| Unemployed | 9.6 | 16.9 | 19.6 | 16.5 | 16.3 |
| Others/NK | 1.4 | 1.1 | 2.8 | 3.4 | 4.1 |
| **Males** | | | | | |
| Course | 3.0 | 2.5 | 4.4 | 3.7 | 4.6 |
| Full-time job | 76.8 | 60.6 | 46.8 | 35.7 | 32.3 |
| YOP/YTS | 9.6 | 19.4 | 27.2 | 41.8 | 43.2 |
| Unemployed | 9.4 | 16.8 | 19.5 | 15.7 | 16.5 |
| Others/NK | 1.2 | 0.7 | 2.0 | 3.1 | 3.4 |
| **Females** | | | | | |
| Course | 13.9 | 14.6 | 17.0 | 15.0 | 14.9 |
| Full-time job | 67.5 | 48.7 | 32.5 | 31.2 | 30.9 |
| YOP/YTS | 7.1 | 18.2 | 26.9 | 32.6 | 33.3 |
| Unemployed | 9.8 | 17.0 | 19.6 | 17.4 | 16.0 |
| Others/NK | 1.7 | 1.5 | 3.9 | 3.8 | 5.0 |

*Note*: 1978 leavers from grant-aided and independent schools without Highers or O grades at A–C are not included.

*Source*: David Raffe, Centre for Educational Sociology, University of Edinburgh, 1986.

poorer health. One could add other groups to this list, for example married women with low skills or skills which are considered out of date by potential employers; and members of different ethnic minority groups.

Focusing on youth unemployment, Fraser and Sinfield note the difficulty in accurately assessing the extent of the collapse of the youth labour market since 1979, because of the changes in the collection of official statistics referred to above, changes in the benefit entitlement of school-leavers, changes in youth training and special programmes and in the proportion of young people staying on in full-time education. Instead they quote the surveys of Scottish School leavers or Young People's Surveys to illustrate the changes in employment opportunities for young people (see Table 9). The data in these surveys is 'snapshot' and shows the destinations of young people at a given time. The figures, comparing the years 1978/9 with 1984/5, indicate that 72.2 per cent of all fourth year summer term leavers found full-time jobs in 1978/9 compared with only 31.6 per cent in 1984/5; 8.3 per cent went on youth training or special programmes in the earlier period compared with 38.7 per cent in the later period; and 9.6 per cent were unemployed in 1978/9 compared with 16.3 per cent in 1984/5.

Concern about the high and rising levels of youth unemployment was expressed in Scotland and reflected in the Report on Unemployment from the House of Commons Committee on Scottish Affairs: 'The recent levels of unemployment amongst young people and in particular amongst school leavers are a cause for concern' (Parliamentary Papers, 1981–2, vol. 1). The Committee considered written submissions and evidence from a number of witnesses representing a wide cross-section of Scottish society, including representatives from the MSC, local government, training boards, the STUC, the CBI, education, the Fraser of Allander Institute and youth organizations. The Committee identified the factors influencing the level of youth unemployment as demographic change (in the population of young people in the relevant age-group); labour-market competition (resulting from the increase in female participation rates); and the increase in the wage levels for young people in relation to adult workers, especially in the 1970s. But these factors have to be seen in the context of the economic recession, which reduced the demand for all workers, and which affected the demand for young workers disproportionately.

## 9. Long-term Unemployed

The number of people classified as long-term unemployed has also grown more rapidly than the total number of unemployed. Again there are difficulties in making comparisons over time because of statistical changes and especially the changes which affect women. The statistics indicate that all groups have been affected by the increase in long-term unemployment, with older people being at risk and young people under the age of 25 the most vulnerable. Members of this latter group become less and less likely to get a job as they are trapped in a vicious circle of

Table 10. Long-Term Unemployment (LTU), Scotland, January 1986

| Age | Total LTU | 1–2 Yrs LTU | | 2–5 Yrs LTU | | Over 5 Yrs LTU | |
|---|---|---|---|---|---|---|---|
| | | Total | % | Total | % | Total | % |
| Under 20 | 14291 | 9976 | 70 | 4315 | 30 | — | — |
| 20–24 | 27183 | 11576 | 43 | 13341 | 49 | 2266 | 8 |
| 25–49 | 72154 | 25901 | 36 | 31746 | 44 | 14507 | 20 |
| 50–59 | 31934 | 8598 | 27 | 15610 | 49 | 7726 | 24 |
| 60 and Over | 1414 | 662 | 47 | 502 | 36 | 250 | 28 |
| All Ages | 146976 | 56713 | 39 | 65514 | 45 | 24749 | 27 |
| Males | 112626 | 40853 | 36 | 50720 | 45 | 21053 | 19 |
| Females | 34350 | 15860 | 46 | 14794 | 43 | 3696 | 11 |

*Source*: Department of Employment. Quoted in, MSC, Corporate Plan Scotland, 1986–1990.

applying unsuccessfully for jobs for which experience is often required. Figures quoted by the MSC for long-term unemployment in Scotland indicate that since the onset of the recession in 1979, the ratio of long-term to total unemployment has jumped from 25 per cent to 40 per cent as at January 1986, and that the number of under-25-year-olds who have been unemployed long-term has risen dramatically since 1979 when the figure was around 5000 (MSC, 1986). Table 10 illustrates this dramatic rise.

## 10. Women

As more women are participating in the labour market, the level of unemployment among women has also increased. In 1982, before the major statistical change in the employment figures which most directly affected women took place (excluding from the official count women who were not entitled to claim Unemployment Benefit), Dey and Fraser noted that female unemployment in Scotland had increased from 25000 in 1971 to 78000 in 1980 and 93400 in 1981; and that the proportion of female unemployment in Scotland was 9.8 per cent compared with a figure of 7 per cent for Britain as a whole. This increase in unemployment took place within a background of rising employment for women (estimated at approximately 85000 additional jobs). However, the expansion was mainly in part-time work in the service sector, as women, like men, lost full-time jobs in the manufacturing sector during the recession of 1974–6 and after 1979. The increase in female unemployment before 1982 is attributed to an increase in the number of women registering as unemployed and the decline in full-time jobs which occurred in this period, although the extent to which this is a sufficient explanation can be questioned.

Breitenbach (1989) records that these trends have continued since 1982. Women's work has continued to become concentrated in the service sector; part-time work has increased and full-time work has decreased; an increasing proportion of women are now participating in the labour force in relation to men; and unemployment experienced by women is increasing. However, as she indicates, establishing an accurate figure for women's unemployment is impossible for a number of reasons: the government's policy of encouraging married women to register as unemployed from 1978; the sharp increase in unrecorded female unemployment after 1979 as a result of a number of changes in the method of collecting the official statistics, in particular the switch in 1982 to claimant basis which excluded many married women from the register; and the impact of the availability-for-work test for people claiming Unemployment Benefit, which includes questions on child-care arrangements. The pattern of female unemployment in Britain is, therefore, markedly different from other countries using various methods of registration and recording of statistics. Breitenbach concludes that whilst it

Table 11. People Employed, Scotland, 1975–1987 (1 000s)

| Employed | 1975 | 1976 | 1977 | 1978 | 1979 | 1980 | 1981 | 1982 | 1983 | 1984 | 1985 | 1986 | 1987 |
|---|---|---|---|---|---|---|---|---|---|---|---|---|---|
| Men | 1219 | 1210 | 1198 | 1200 | 1209 | 1188 | 1128 | 1097 | 1069 | 1048 | 1036 | 1020 | 1006 |
| Women | 858 | 861 | 873 | 867 | 898 | 897 | 874 | 867 | 854 | 882 | 899 | 866 | 880 |
| Total | 2076 | 2071 | 2071 | 2067 | 2107 | 2085 | 2002 | 1964 | 1923 | 1930 | 1936 | 1886 | 1886 |
| Women as% of Total | 41.3 | 41.6 | 42.1 | 41.9 | 42.6 | 43.0 | 43.6 | 44.1 | 44.4 | 45.7 | 46.4 | 45.9 | 46.6 |

*Sources*: Scottish Abstract of Statistics; Department of Employment *Gazette*.

Table 12. People Unemployed, Scotland 1975–1987 (1 000s)

| Unemployed | 1975 | 1976 | 1977 | 1978 | 1979 | 1980 | 1981 | 1982 | 1983* | 1984 | 1985 | 1986 | 1987 |
|---|---|---|---|---|---|---|---|---|---|---|---|---|---|
| Men | 76 | 105 | 126 | 124 | 117 | 143 | 206 | 232 | 224 | 228 | 240 | 248 | 241 |
| Women | 23 | 39 | 60 | 63 | 65 | 80 | 99 | 109 | 100 | 101 | 106 | 111 | 103 |
| Total | 99 | 144 | 186 | 187 | 182 | 223 | 305 | 341 | 324 | 329 | 346 | 359 | 345 |
| Women as % of total | 23.2 | 27.0 | 32.2 | 33.7 | 35.7 | 35.9 | 32.5 | 31.9 | 30.9 | 30.6 | 30.6 | 30.9 | 29.9 |

* Figures collected on different basis from 1983 onwards.

*Sources*: Scottish Abstract of Statistics; Department of Employment *Gazette*.

is impossible to say how many women are actually unemployed, it can be concluded that the recorded figure is a gross underestimate.

While women have gained real benefits in the labour market in recent years through improved access to jobs previously denied them and opportunities for promotion; and as a result of Equal Pay legislation which has helped improve the income of some women, many problems for women in the labour market still exist. Women are still concentrated in the service sector; they still earn on average only two-thirds of the pay earned by men; more women are in part-time, often insecure, jobs with few employment rights; and more women are unemployed than in the past.

More recent demographic trends, however, indicate a reduction in the number of young workers in the labour market which may result in an increase in demand for female workers and improved job opportunities for women in the future. Projections from the Department of Employment estimate that by 1995 a further 800 000 women will enter the labour market. Employers in some sectors, including health, education, industry and financial services are said to be experiencing skill shortages. Some employers, for example in the financial sector, keen to attract more women workers, have already made improvements to child-care facilities, maternity and pension rights, and have introduced career-break schemes for women. The extent to which these changes will result in improvements for all women in work, however, remains to be seen.

Table 11 shows the numbers of people in employment in Scotland for the period 1975–87, analysed by sex; and Table 12 shows the breakdown by sex of unemployed people in Scotland over the same period.

## 11. Poverty

One of the consequences of high and sustained levels of unemployment is an increase in the level of poverty suffered by the groups most directly affected. A report by the Church and Nation Committee of the General Assembly of the Church of Scotland on the Distribution of Wealth, Income and Benefits (1987) referred to the increase in the number of people living in poverty in Britain ('if we accept the definition of poverty as "living on or below the supplementary benefit rate"') from 6.1 to 8.9 million between 1979 and 1983, a rise from 3 to 6 million in the number of persons in families under pension age, and contended 'Unemployment is, of course, the main cause of increased poverty and three-quarters of persons in families of the unemployed live in poverty. In 1948, one in 33 of the population were dependent on means tested supplementary benefit. Today it is one in eight.'

Long-term unemployment in particular, therefore, has significant and far-reaching implications for the economic wellbeing of those concerned. Similarly, concentrations of unemployment levels in regions, districts and cities has an adverse economic effect in these areas.

### THE POLITICAL CONTEXT

The above changes in the Scottish economy and its impact on employment and unemployment have taken place within a distinct political environment in Scotland. The Conservative Party has held office in Britain since 1979, but increasingly commentators have referred to the political division which is evident between North and South. For the last 30 years the Labour Party has been the majority party in Scotland and does not appear to have been affected by the shift in voting patterns evident in the south of England in particular since 1979. At the 1987

Table 13. Scotland's Electoral Divergence 1983–1987 (%)

|            | Scotland |        |        | England and Wales |        |        |
|------------|----------|--------|--------|-------------------|--------|--------|
|            | 1983     | 1987   | 1983–7 | 1983              | 1987   | 1983–7 |
| Con.       | 28.4     | 24.0   | −4.4   | 45.1              | 45.3   | +0.2   |
| Lab.       | 35.1     | 42.4   | +7.3   | 27.6              | 30.4   | +2.8   |
| All.       | 24.5     | 19.2   | −5.3   | 26.2              | 23.5   | −2.7   |
| SNP        | 11.7     | 14.0   | +2.3   | —                 | —      | —      |
| Lab. lead  | +6.7     | +18.4  | +11.7  | −17.5             | −14.9  | −2.6   |
| Con. + Lab.| 63.5     | 66.4   | +2.9   | 72.7              | 75.7   | +3.0   |

Source: Bochel and Denver Scottish Government Yearbook, 1988.

general election, the Conservative Party won only 10 of the 72 parliamentary seats in Scotland. This was their worst result since 1910 and represented the smallest number of MPs which a government party has ever had in Scotland (Alan Lawson, 1988). In contrast the Labour Party won 50 seats, which represented the highest number for any party since the Liberals won 58 seats in 1910. Further, before the emergence of the Alliance between the Liberal Party and the newly formed Social Democratic Party in the early 1980s, Scotland already had its own third party: the Scottish National Party.

The extent of Scotland's electoral divergence, highlighted in Table 13, is discussed by Bochel and Denver (1988) and Lawson (1988). Election results in Scotland differ from England and Wales in two respects. First, because the two major parties (Labour and Conservative) together obtained a much smaller share of the votes in Scotland than they did in England and Wales; and second, because of the growing dominance of the Labour Party in Scotland in contrast to the dominant position of the Conservative Party in the rest of Britain. The results of the 1987 general election in Scotland were not entirely unexpected, as local government election results leading up to the general election had already given some indication of the current voting trends. The 1988 District Elections reinforced this trend and the Conservative Party came third behind the SNP in their share of the votes (Bochel and Denver, 1989).

Table 14. Party Shares of Votes in Scottish Districts 1974–1988 (%)

|  | 1974 | 1977 | 1980 | 1984 | 1988 |
|---|---|---|---|---|---|
| Conservative | 26.8 | 27.2 | 24.1 | 21.4 | 19.4 |
| Labour | 38.4 | 31.6 | 45.4 | 45.7 | 42.6 |
| Lib/All./SLD | 5.0 | 4.0 | 6.2 | 12.8 | 8.4 |
| SNP | 12.4 | 24.2 | 15.5 | 11.7 | 21.3 |
| Independent | 14.1 | 9.8 | 6.7 | 6.8 | 6.4 |
| Others | 3.4 | 3.3 | 2.2 | 1.6 | 2.0 |

Source: Bochel and Denver, Scottish Government Yearbook, 1989.

Some of the reasons advanced for the divergence in voting and the relative decline of the Conservative Party in Scotland are discussed elsewhere (Maxwell, 1985; McCrone and Kendrick, 1990). Lawson (1988) argues that it is not easy to ascertain the extent to which people increasingly voted anti-Tory either because they wanted some form of Scottish self-government or because they did not like Tory policies, but he also believes that the two reasons may be becoming so fused that the distinction between them has decreased.

For our purposes I am concerned to consider the extent to which the political divergence has implications for implementing policies (especially labour market policies) within Scotland, which have been

formulated and designed outside Scotland. The potential conflict between central government and different countries or regions within
nation states is discussed by Moore and Booth (1986). As the role of
formal corporatist institutions has declined at the nation state or macro-
level in countries in Western Europe and North America which have
shifted to the right politically and adopted the free market as a basis for
policy making, so too have different regions within nation states developed formal and informal mechanisms in order to defend particular
regional or sectoral interests. In analysing and explaining policy making
in Scotland, Moore and Booth identify four variables. First, the political
dimension (the nature of party representation and electoral strengths);
second, the ideological (the influence of socialism, labourism and
nationalism as opposed to liberalism); third, the institutional (the representation of Scottish interests as distinct and their relationships to the
Scottish state as opposed to Westminster and Whitehall); and fourth, the
economic structure of Scotland. They conclude that although the politics
of Scotland are different in significant respects to the rest of the UK, it is
only periodically that these differences have asserted themselves to
challenge the power and politics of the UK state.

Indeed there are areas of Scottish policy making, for example local
government, the STUC and the CBI, which have played a significant part
in terms of the mediation and implementation in Scotland of policies
formulated in Whitehall which relate to the whole of the UK. There was in
the past sufficient consensus of opinion on the benefits of training policy
to make the MSC's schemes and programmes a reality in Scotland.
However, there was some evidence that this consensus was breaking
down before its eventual collapse in 1988.

One response to the perceived relative decline of the Scottish economy
and the high levels of unemployment was the initiative taken by Strathclyde Regional Council and the STUC in holding a Scottish Economic
Summit Conference in July 1986. The decision to hold the conference
was 'triggered by the huge wave of closures and redundancies across
Scottish industry which were announced in the spring of that year and
growing concern that increased centralisation would inhibit Scotland's
prospects for recovery' (The Standing Commission on the Scottish Economy, February 1988). Participants at the Conference were drawn from a
wide range of Scottish industrial, political and social life and included
representatives from CBI Scotland, chambers of commerce, the Scottish
Council (Development and Industry), local authorities, trade unions, the
Churches, education and Scottish political parties. The key points in the
statement adopted unanimously by the Conference included:

    1. Agreement that the economic and industrial situation in Scot-
land cannot be allowed to deteriorate further, the recovery cannot
be relied on to come about unassisted, and the task of reconstruction
must begin now.

2. The importance of striking an appropriate balance in public policy between reliance on oil, services, the new high-technology industries and a modernized and reinvigorated manufacturing sector.

3. Support for urgent measures to deal with the crisis in steel, shipbuilding, railway engineering, the energy industries and clothing and textiles.

4. The need for fresh policies to help bridge the growing gap between those in work and those out of work (The Standing Commission on the Scottish Economy, February 1988).

The Conference also agreed to establish the Standing Commission on the Scottish Economy chaired by Professor Sir Kenneth Alexander to investigate further some of the issues that had been highlighted, and report back to a reconvened economic summit.

This initiative reflects widespread concern in Scotland that increasingly central government policy is insufficiently responsive to the particular needs of different regions and countries within the United Kingdom. It is also suggested that the form of the response, that is its collectivist and corporatist nature, reflects the distinct features of Scotland's political economy. This approach is contrasted to the general trends in the south of Britain. Before examining the growth of the MSC and the development of training policy in Britain and Scotland, therefore, we set out below the macro-economic context within which current developments have taken place.

## MACROECONOMIC POLICY IN THE POSTWAR PERIOD

Before the end of the Second World War, a consensus was reached between all political parties in Britain that the maintenance of a 'high and stable level of employment' (HMSO, 1944) should be a common objective of post-war policy. In other words, it was accepted that future governments would be responsible for adhering to this goal. The White Paper on Employment Policy (1944) listed four main methods for achieving this objective:

1. influencing the location of new enterprises in areas of high unemployment;

2. encouraging mobility between areas and occupations;

3. retraining of labour;

4. using government spending, taxation and monetary policy to maintain aggregate demand or total spending at high enough levels to maintain employment.

The belief that governments were both capable of and responsible for achieving full employment through greater intervention in the economy marked a radical departure from orthodox economic theory, which dictated the adherence to market forces and balanced budgets, and argued that governments could not affect the level of employment in an economy. However, the experience of two world wars and high un-employment during the depression in the inter-war period created a popular demand and belief that governments should and could take responsibility for full employment (Addison, 1977; Marwick, 1970). The demand for full employment gained credence from the intellectual sup-port of the economist John Maynard Keynes and other economists, who attacked the weaknesses in orthodox economic theory, and argued that governments could influence the level of employment by spending and stimulating demand if private investors were unwilling to do so (Keynes, 1936). Keynes' general philosophy was accepted by William Beveridge in his Report 'Full Employment in a Free Society' (1944), where he argued that unplanned market economies were less likely to result in a high level of employment than had previously been supposed. Beveridge went on to outline the foundations for what was to become the welfare state. Although both Keynes and Beveridge were Liberals, their ideas had a significant impact on the labour movement.

Labour was voted into office in 1945 as the Party most likely to imple-ment the policies outlined in the White Paper and the Beveridge Report. However, it was clear that the new orthodoxy in economic management had gained acceptance not just within the Labour Party. Successive governments in the post-war period, both Labour and Conservative, engaged in what has been described as consensus policies, where the principle of an interventionist role for government was accepted, and where political debate was confined to the level or extent of such inter-vention in say nationalization or the redistribution of wealth. Thus the post-war period, at least until the mid-1970s, was characterized by the settlement between the two sides of industry and the adoption of a broad consensus between the major political parties over the acceptance of Keynesian demand management and of full employment policies, nationalization, the welfare state, and the role given to trade unions in British society (Kavanagh, 1987).

In the immediate post-war years British governments were very suc-cessful in maintaining a 'high and stable level of employment', although there is some debate over whether this was due to government policies per se, or the favourable economic conditions of the post-war period (Tomlinson, 1985). In the 1950s and 1960s unemployment was kept low in Britain and other developed countries, and the 'normal' and sustain-able unemployment rate was generally accepted to be of the order of 2 per cent, a figure even lower than that anticipated by either Keynes or Beveridge. Any inflation that did occur in this period was of relatively minor significance, and governments believed that they could success-fully trade off the unemployment and inflation rates with little threat of either increasing uncontrollably.

During this period of relatively full employment, governments had little need to worry about labour market policies, although they did intervene through regional policies in bringing work to the workers and workers to the work. Training of labour was largely undertaken on the job or through the apprenticeship system by the employer. There also existed the tradition of 'voluntarism' in British industrial policy and industrial relations, which holds that within an overall legislative framework and government intervention at the level of macro-economic demand management, employers should be free to make their own decisions on production; and both employers and workers should be free to reach agreement on wages, hours and conditions of work with the minimum of state interference. In addition, trade unions and employers were involved in discussions through tripartite bodies, such as Wages Councils. Wages Councils were first established in 1909 in order to set minimum wage standards and conditions in certain trades, and they had the power to fix legally enforceable minimum rates of pay. The growth of Wages Councils in the 1950s can be cited as an indicator of the increasing use of tripartism and tripartite structures to implement policy in the period, and as an indicator of the consensus over broad objectives which existed (Brown, 1988).

But during the late 1960s and especially in the 1970s, British governments faced the problem of rapidly increasing inflation and unemployment – 'stagflation' – and the belief and confidence that governments could choose between them broke down. Also the broad consensus on the priorities of economic policy and the government's ability to control the economy came unde stress. The new focus of attention then became the fight against inflation, and it is argued that unemployment declined in relative importance in terms of policy objectives. It is less clear when and to what extent full employment was abandoned as a policy objective. While it may have declined in relative importance in the 1970s (although Therborn, 1986, dates the decline of full employment as the priority objective to 1967), it was not abandoned altogether, as the spectacular 'U-turn' of the Conservative government in 1972 demonstrated (Kavanagh, 1987). The Conservative government headed by Mr Heath came into office in 1970 on a manifesto not unlike the manifesto of Mrs Thatcher's first government in 1979; it aspired to reduce government intervention, cut public spending and taxation and restore competition. Eighteen months after taking office, unemployment had risen to almost one million, a consequence which was considered tantamount to political suicide at the time. Jordan (1982) argues that, in fear of the social and political consequences which could result, the government dramatically revised its economic strategy and increased public expenditure.

The Conservatives lost the election in 1974 to the Labour Party. But Labour too was to 'U-turn' on its election manifesto promises. To justify their action, the leadership of the Labour Party argued that Britain's economic problems – Balance of Payments deficit, high inflation, rising unemployment and low growth – made it necessary to postpone manifesto commitments. When an application was made to the International Monetary Fund (IMF) in 1976 to alleviate financial pressures, it was contended that a loan would only be possible if the Government agreed to cut public expenditure and made a commitment to keep within announced targets for the Public Sector Borrowing Requirement (PSBR) and the money supply. Therefore, despite the fear of the political consequences of relegating unemployment in terms of priority objectives, the leadership of the Labour Party was prepared to commit itself primarily to the attack on inflation in 1976. This was illustrated in Mr Callaghan's well-recorded statement, when he was Prime Minister, to the 1976 Labour Party Conference, in which he asserted that cutting taxes and boosting government spending led to increased inflation in an economy and subsequently increased the level of unemployment (Hodgson, 1981). Not only was this statement a rejection of Keynesian analysis, but it was an implicit acceptance of monetarism and the link betwen government spending and inflation.

The new Conservative government of 1979 attempted to distance itself even further from responsibility for maintaining a 'high and stable level of employment'. Instead they argued that their main objective should be to reduce inflation through control of the money supply and to create the conditions in which substantial economic growth could be achieved. In his submission to the House of Commons Treasury and Civil Service Committee on Monetary Policy in 1979, the then Chancellor of the Exchequer, Geoffrey Howe, argued that government could not be held responsible for ensuring high employment. Governments could create the conditions in which it could be achieved, but whether it was achieved would depend on the responses of management and labour. Further, he advocated the reduction of the role of government in economic management to allow market forces to operate more freely (HMSO, 1979/80).

The explicit overriding economic objective of the 1979, 1983 and 1987 Conservative governments was stated to be the reduction of inflation. After an initial increase to a level of over 20 per cent in 1980, the rate of inflation dropped to around 4 per cent in the mid-1980s (although in 1987 the inflation rate began to rise again and is currently of the order of 8 per cent). Critics argued that the initial reduction, for which the government claimed credit, was not the result of the policies advocated by the government, that is not through control of the money supply. They argued instead that inflation had been reduced because the government had dampened demand in the economy and was prepared to allow unemployment to rise to unacceptable levels; and because of the reduction in the cost of imported raw materials (Keegan, 1984).

THE POLITICS OF TRAINING

The reduction of inflation was accompanied by high and increasing rates of unemployment. As unemployment rose to a level not anticipated by

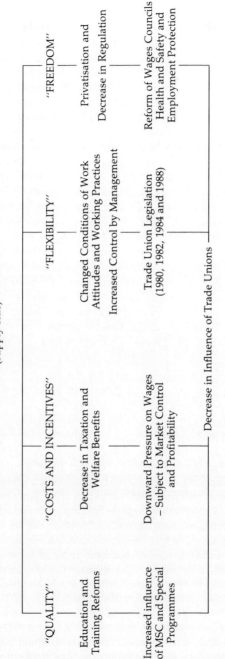

FIGURE 1. Government Economic Policy

Priority Objective:
Reduction of Inflation

As unemployment has increased attention has shifted to Labour Market Policy
(supply side)*

"QUALITY"

Education and
Training Reforms

Increased influence
of MSC and Special
Programmes

"COSTS AND INCENTIVES"

Decrease in Taxation and
Welfare Benefits

Downward Pressure on Wages
– Subject to Market Control
and Profitability

Decrease in Influence of Trade Unions

"FLEXIBILITY"

Changed Conditions of Work
Attitudes and Working Practices

Increased Control by Management

Trade Union Legislation
(1980, 1982, 1984 and 1988)

"FREEDOM"

Privatisation and
Decrease in Regulation

Reform of Wages Councils
Health and Safety and
Employment Protection

* 4 Areas in which Labour Market is to be improved.
(Source: Department of Employment, "Employment: The Challenge for the Nation", 1985.)

the government, with more than three and a half million people in Britain unemployed, more attention was then paid to the problem of unemployment and to labour market reform. In the 1985 White Paper on employment, the government argued, to some extent in answer to critics advocating reflation of the economy, that unemployment was not caused by lack of demand, lack of public sector investment or techno-logical change, but rather by the failure of the market for jobs in Britain: 'the biggest single cause of our high unemployment is the failure of our jobs market, the weak link in our economy.' Thus, the government rejected a Keynesian demand management solution to unemployment in favour of supply side reforms with the objective of creating a more efficient labour market.

The government proposed four main areas of reform (see Figure 1). First, the quality of labour was to be improved, 'so that businesses can find the increasingly demanding skills they need, now and in the future'. This objective relates directly to the education and training reforms of the government. Second, the cost of labour was to be reduced and incentives improved 'so that people are neither prevented from pricing themselves into jobs nor deterred from taking them'. Thus, wages were to be more responsive to market conditions, and reforms were to be made to tax-ation and social-security benefits to improve incentives. Third, improve-ments in flexibility in the labour market were advocated, 'so that employers and employees adapt quickly to new circumstances'. This was to be done by removing barriers to change through trade union reform and by changing conditions of work and working practices and attitudes, and increasing the control given to management. And finally, the government argued for greater freedom in the labour market 'so that employers are not so burdened by regulation that they are reluctant to offer more jobs'. This objective was to be achieved through deregulation of the public sector and reform of employment legislation, provision of health and safety at work and Wages Councils.

The government has made extensive and far reaching reforms to policies relating to education, training, taxation, social and welfare ben-efits, trade-union reform, privatization and employment legislation since it took office in 1979. Indeed for a government which was suppos-edly committed to reducing its role in the economy, the present govern-ment has intervened to an unprecedented extent in the labour market. Further, as Robinson (1986) argues, the labour market policies of the Thatcher governments can be seen as mutually reinforcing, providing a greater coherence than has been provided by any other government since the war.

This shift of emphasis to supply-side labour market reforms may at first sight appear to contradict the government's market philosophy of non-intervention. But this strategy is consistent with the argument that unemployment cannot be tackled by government intervention and stimulation of demand at the macro-economic level, while accepting intervention at the micro-economic level in order to free the market from restrictions and improve the price and quality of the supply of labour. Robertson (1986) provides a useful model in which to analyse the government's strategy. He distinguishes two criteria: whether the principles underlying the policy are social democratic or neo-liberal; and whether policy implementation is active or passive. The 'social-democratic active' strategy – the egalitarian model – is illustrated by the labour market policies of the Swedish government. The Conservative government in Britain after 1979 is categorized as 'neo-liberal active', a market-centred model (Brown and King, 1988). 'The market-centred model combines neo-liberal goals with the active use of state power to remake the labour market' (Robertson, 1986: pp. 279–80).

These two approaches to labour market policy also have implications for the role of trade unions. The egalitarian model is dependent on maintaining trade union consent, which is achieved through the integration or inclusion of the unions in the decision-making process. In contrast the market-centred model implies the exclusion of trade unions from the consultative process in order to reduce potential distortions to market forces.

It is within the above framework that the changes in training policy and the role of the MSC should be analysed. During the post-war period of consensus politics, and particularly at times of full employment, training policy was a relatively non-political issue. Indeed the two main initiatives on training proposed by Conservative governments (1964 Industrial Training Act, which established 23 Industrial Training Boards (ITBS), and the 1973 Employment and Training Act, which created the MSC, a tripartite body involving government, the CBI and the TUC) were subsequently implemented by Labour governments. That is, the consensus on training policy reflected the general consensus on other matters of economic and employment policy, which were embodied in organizations such as the National Economic and Development Council (NEDC). Training policy was uncontroversial, and training reforms tended to be shaped by views held on other issues (Anderson and Fairley, 1982). The intervention by government at this time took place within a framework of Keynesian demand management policies.

Thus the 1964 Training Act was consistent with the growing commitment of the Conservative Party and later the Labour government to economic planning, and with the view that 'voluntarism' in training had failed to secure a supply of skilled labour which was necessary for industrial expansion. Further the form of intervention, that is through tripartite, self-financing ITBS, also reflected Government's changing attitudes to the implementation of policy decisions. Similarly, the Heath government's 1973 Employment and Training Act, which established the MSC, had all party support. The labour movement had campaigned for some time for such a body, and the structure and remit of the MSC was heavily influenced by the TUC.

As unemployment and especially youth unemployment rose during the 1970s, British manpower policy was increasingly directed away from supporting industrial training and towards Special Programmes intended primarily to alleviate youth unemployment, which gave rise to a new division in the MSC, the Special Programmes Division. With the rise in unemployment, and the reduction in the priority given to tackling unemployment through macro-economic policies, it might have been anticipated that training would become an area of political dispute.

But the demands for the government to 'do something' about unemployment, initially at least, appear to have outweighed criticisms of the training policies adopted. Therefore, while it is feasible to have anticipated political controversy over the Conservative government's reforms of the training system in the 1980s, as the government's critics were not supportive of its overall economic management based on the principles of monetarism, there remained a surprising degree of agreement and consensus over the objectives of training reform. The TUC and the Parties in opposition were generally supportive of the reforms, and debates for the most part were confined to the level of payment or 'wages' to be paid to participants, and job-placement rates. In this respect it is argued by some that there was insufficient debate on other aspects such as the quality, content and objectives of training schemes. As a result the opportunity was missed to expose the vulnerability of the government on some of these points, and to provide an alternative training strategy which was significantly different from that already on offer.

To some extent the level of agreement can be explained by the general acceptance of the argument that Britain's lack of competitiveness in world markets could partially be explained by the lack of a comprehensive training strategy and the reluctance of some British employers to invest in training. Examples of training policy were drawn from other European countries, and the government used countries, including West Germany, as 'models' to gain acceptance for the Youth Training Scheme (YTS) and to demonstrate the benefits of training. Another factor contributing to consensus over training policy could be the incremental nature of the reforms that took place as the government attempted to respond to changing economic conditions.

However, as the number of schemes on offer multiplied, the job-placement rates deteriorated, and as MSC policy was subject to greater political control after the 1983 election, the consensus on which training policy was based became more fragile. (For example, Raffe (1984) predicted a breakdown of consensus over aspects of the YTS.) Opposition mounted in response to proposed changes in training, and, as is indicated in some of the chapters which follow, those involved in implementing the government's schemes found it increasingly difficult to meet the MSC's changing criteria. The New Job Training Scheme (NJTS) 1986 which was targeted at 18–25 year olds came under attack for not offering a wage or a proper training allowance. Instead trainees were to receive an allowance equivalent to their existing supplementary benefit entitlement plus some travel costs. Critics accused the government of moving towards a 'Workfare' system based on developments in the United States. The 1987 Conservative Party election manifesto contained further proposals for reform to be implemented in 1988. These included plans for a unified training programme for unemployed adults, the withdrawal of the right to benefit from young people should they refuse to participate in the YTS and the reduction of representation of trade unions on Area Manpower Boards. These changes were proposed without consultation with the trade union movement. It would appear, therefore, that the government no longer considered it necessary to have trade union support for its policies on training.

In recent years, the official level of unemployment has declined although the extent of this reduction has been questioned by a number of commentators, who argue that the reduction is mainly a reflection of changes in the composition of the unemployment statistics, the exclusion of participants on training schemes from the unemployment register and demographic changes which have reduced the number of young workers entering the labour market. It is perhaps none the less paradoxical that the broad consensus over training policy reforms has at the same time broken down. At its 1988 Congress, the TUC voted to oppose the government's most recent and largest training programme. Employment Training (ET), and to withdraw its co operation with the implementation of the scheme. This decision has no historic precedent and marked a radical departure from TUC policy towards participation in training reform.

In September 1988, the government announced two major changes. First, the abolition of the Training Commission (TC); the government had only recently changed the name of the MSC to the TC in April 1988; and second, the transfer of the responsibility for running the government's job training programmes to an agency set up within the Department of Employment (Leadbetter, 1988). Mr Fowler, the Employment Secretary, stated that the TUC's vote was the immediate reason for the decision to abolish the TC, but that relations between the policy making commission and Employment Ministers had become increasingly strained over the previous two years.

The decision followed changes which had already been mooted in Scotland. In the summer of 1988, Bill Hughes, Chairman of CBI Scotland, put forward a proposal to create an agency, Enterprise Scotland, based on a merger between the TC in Scotland and the Scottish Development

Agency (SDA). Under this plan, local employers were to have more influence on training policy and the role of trade unions was to be reduced.

These most recent changes have implications for the tripartite nature of past training policy, as they represent a shift to bipartite decision-making between government and employers, with an increase in the role for employers. Further, they are being pursued in spite of evidence (see for example chapters 3 and 11) that employers have in the past been reluctant to become more involved in vocational education and training. It remains to be seen whether the attempt to link business developments and training at the local level, and the increasing privatization of the delivery of training will be successful in meeting Scotland's training needs in the future.

REFERENCES

Addison, P. (1977). *The Road to 1945* (Quartet Books Ltd).

Anderson, M., and Fairley, J. (1982). The politics of industrial training, *Journal of Public Policy*.

Ashcroft, B. (1988). Scottish economic performance and government policy: a North–South divide? In, D. McCrone and A. Brown (eds.), *Scottish Government Yearbook*.

Beveridge, W. (1944). Full employment in a free society (G. Allen and Unwin Ltd).

Bochel, J., and Denver, D. (1988). The 1987 general election in Scotland. In, D. McCrone and A. Brown (eds.), *Scottish Government Yearbook*.

Bochel, J., and Denver, D. (1989). The Scottish district elections of 1988. In, A. Brown and D. McCrone (eds.), *Scottish Government Yearbook*.

Boyle, S., and Jenkins, I. (1987). Consensus of employment 1984 – an assessment. In *Quarterly Economic Bulletin*, 12.3 (Glasgow: Fraser of Allander Institute, University of Strathclyde).

Breitenbach, E. (1989). The impact of Thatcherism on women in Scotland. In, A. Brown and D. McCrone (eds.), *Scottish Government Yearbook*.

Brown, A. (1988a). Labour market policy in Britain: a critical view (New Waverley Papers, University of Edinburgh, Politics Series, 1).

Brown, A. (1989b). The case against wages councils: the evidence versus the ideology. In, R. Davidson and P. White (eds.), *Information and Government* (Edinburgh University Press).

Brown, A., and Fairley, J. (1987). A Scottish labour market board. In, D. McCrone (ed.), *Scottish Government Yearbook*.

Brown, A., and King, D. (1988). Economic change and labour market policy: corporatist and dualist tendencies in Britain and Sweden. In *West European Politics*, 2.3 (July).

Buxton, N. (1986). Performance and problems of Scotland's industrial economy (Scottish Council for Development and Industry).

Church and Nation Committee of the General Assembly of the Church of Scotland (1987). Distribution of wealth, income and benefits.

Cox, M. (1987). Scotland's export performance – a closer look. In *Quarterly Economic Bulletin*, 12.4 (Glasgow: Fraser of Allander Institute, University of Strathclyde).

Dey, I., and Fraser, N. (1982). Scotland at sea – the government, the recession and Scottish unemployment. In, D. McCrone (ed.), *Scottish Government Yearbook*.

Edinburgh District Council (1988). *Economic and Employment Review* (summer).

Fraser, N., and Sinfield, A. (1987). The Scottish labour force in recession. In, D. McCrone (ed.), *Scottish Government Yearbook*.

HMSO (1944). White Paper on employment policy (Cmd. 6427).

HMSO (1979/80). Letter from Chancellor of the Exchequer to House of Commons Treasury and Civil Service Committee, Memoranda on Monetary Policy (720).

Hodgson, G. (1981). *Labour at the crossroads*. (M. Robertson).

Hood, N., and Young, S. (1984). *Industry, Policy and the Scottish Economy*.

Jordan, B. (1982). *Mass Unemployment and the Future of Britain*. (Blackwell).

Kavanagh, D. (1987). *Thatcherism and British Politics* (Oxford University Press).

Keating, M., and Midwinter, A. (1983). *The Government of Scotland*. (Edinburgh Mainstream).

Keegan, W. (1984). *Mrs Thatcher's Economic Experiment* (Penguin).

Kendrick, S. (1986). Occupational change in modern Scotland. In, D. McCrone (ed.), *Scottish Government Yearbook*.

Keynes, J. M. (1936). *The General Theory of Employment, Interest and Money* (Macmillan).

Lawson, A. (1988). Mair nor a rouch wind blaw in . . . In, D. McCrone and A. Brown (eds.), *Scottish Government Yearbook*.

Leadbetter, C. (1988). In the *Financial Times* (16 Sept. pp. 1 and 13).

McCrone, D., and Kendrick, S. (forthcoming 1990). Politics in a Cold Climate: The Conservative Party in Scotland. *Political Studies*.

Marwick, A. (1970). *Britain in a Century of Total War* (Pelican).

Maxwell, S. (1985). The Fall and Fall of Toryism in Scotland. In *Radical Scotland*. 14 (June/July).

Moore, B., and Rhodes, J. (1974) 'Regional Policy and the Scottish Economy'. *Scottish Journal of Political Economy*, Vol. XXI No. 3.

Moore, C., and Booth S. (1986). Place, power and politics: towards a theory of meso corporatism (Strathclyde Papers on Government and Politics, 48).

MSC (1986). Corporate plan, Scotland, 1986–1990 (Edinburgh).

Parliamentary Papers (1981–2). 17, House of Commons Papers 95–115, Vols. 1 and 2.

Raffe, D. (1984) 'Youth Unemployment and the MSC: 1977–1983' in D. McCrone (ed.) *The Scottish Government Yearbook*.

Robertson, D. B. (1986). Mrs Thatcher's employment prescription: an active neo-liberal labour market policy. In *Journal of Public Policy*, 6 (pp. 275–96).

Robinson, D. (1986). *Monetarism and the Labour Market* (Oxford University Press).

Scott, J. (1983). Declining autonomy: recent trends in the Scottish economy. In, D. McCrone (ed.), *Scottish Government Yearbook*.

Standing Commission on the Scottish Economy (1988). Interim report.

Therborn, G. (1986). *Why Some Peoples are More Unemployed than Others*. (Verso).

Tomlinson, J. (1985). *British Macro-economic Policy Since 1940* (Croom Helm).

# 2

# AN OVERVIEW OF THE DEVELOPMENT AND GROWTH OF THE MANPOWER SERVICES COMMISSION IN SCOTLAND

JOHN FAIRLEY

## INTRODUCTION

This chapter is not a comprehensive and detailed treatment of the MSC's activities in Scotland from 1974 to 1988: such a task would probably require several volumes of text, even if all the necessary data were available. It has the much more limited aim of describing the main structures, policies and programmes of the MSC in Scotland.

However, despite this limitation, the task remains extremely complex. Over the 1974–88 period there were so many changes in all the key aspects of the MSC that even cataloguing the major ones is difficult. This complexity also raises questions concerning the most effective way of organizing the material. Given the nature and the range of the available information concerning the MSC in Scotland, and the broad aims of this book, it would be possible to organize the material in a number of ways, for example around the MSC's major programmes, or around the main objectives which the MSC was asked to pursue, or around the perspectives of the main consumers of the various MSC services.

The structure of the chapter represents a compromise between the need to organize and explain the information which is available about the MSC in Scotland, and the need to complete the background for the chapters which follow and which take a more particular approach to the MSC.

The MSC grew rapidly and became well known to the public primarily through its schemes for school leavers. These schemes were radically changed by the New Training Initiative (NTI) in 1983. Therefore much of the material is organized on a pre-NTI and post-NTI basis. However, the NTI did not have the same immediate impact on the MSC's (smaller) adult schemes. Two of the adult schemes are separately discussed because they were not immediately changed by the NTI, namely the Training Opportunities Scheme (TOPS) and the Community Programme (CP).

The development of the MSC has reflected the changing priorities and policies of successive governments in the 1970s and 1980s. Initially it was a small co-ordinating body based in London, which worked through the Training Services Agency and the Employment Services Agency. By the late 1970s the MSC had grown into a very large state body as a result of being the main response mechanism to rising unemployment. Its three operating divisions were Employment Services, Training Services and Special Programmes, the last of which was the main provider of short-term unemployment palliatives and the fastest growing part of the MSC. Dispersal of the MSC's headquarters to Sheffield was completed by 1982. In 1983, as a part of the New Training Initiative, Special Programmes and Training Services merged into a new Training Division. This in turn was merged in 1987 with the MSC's new schools programmes section into a large Vocational Education and Training Group. In 1987 the Employment Services largely reverted back to the control of the Department of Employment, where they had been before 1973. Over the period some smaller parts of the MSC, for example the Skillcentre network and the Professional and Executive Recruitment service underwent major changes.

As far as Scotland is concerned, the picture has further complexities. In July 1977 some administrative decentralization of responsibility for the MSC's day-to-day operations took place. While not all of MSC's activities were decentralized and separate accounts for Scotland were not available, the MSC's Annual Report for 1977/8 estimated that the decentralized services would have accounted for some £36 million in that year. In October 1977 an MSC Office for Scotland was established, and a tripartite Manpower Services Committee (with Dr Johnston as chairman) was set up to advise the Secretary of State. In May 1979, a Scottish Office Minister was appointed to cover both education and industry, and to co-ordinate the relevant activities of the Scottish Education Department and the Scottish Economic Planning Department. One valuable consequence of this very limited decentralization was that fairly comprehensive data became available for MSC activities in Scotland from the late 1970s (though this did not extend to those MSC acitivities which remained fully centralized). The MSC began to publish forward plans for its activities in Scotland.

The MSC operated through a network of local tripartite advisory organizations, building on and extending a tradition in labour market policy that predated the Commission. In 1975/6, a network of 125 local District Manpower Committees (DMCs) was established throughout Britain. There were fifteen of these in Scotland. The DMCs were subsequently complemented by local Area Boards set up to oversee the Special Programmes, which the MSC implemented as a response to rising unemployment. There were five Special Programme Area Boards in Scotland. From 1983 and the implementation of the New Training Initiative, these local bodies were rationalized into a network of Area Manpower Boards (AMBS), nine of which covered Scotland. They corresponded to the network of eight area offices of the MSC's Training Division, except in the case of the Ayrshire, Dumfries and Galloway Office, which was served by two AMBS. The Boards included representatives of employers and unions who were nominated by the Confederation of British Industry and the Scottish Trade Union Congress respectively. Other interests, for example those of the local authorities, were also represented. A number of chapters in this book reflect on various aspects of AMB representation and effectiveness, in particular Chapters 7, 8, 9, 10, 11 and 13.

At the outset a broad role was intended for the AMBS. Parliament was told in 1983 that the AMBS would develop into planning bodies covering 'the whole spectrum of local training needs and provision'. However, the resources needed to achieve this were never made available. Initially the AMBS were charged with the responsibility of approving new projects under the Youth Training Scheme (YTS) and the Community Programme (CP). All YTS schemes, except those negotiated for the whole of Britain by the MSC's central Large Companies Unit and Youth Training Board, had to secure local AMB approval, as did CP projects. The rapid development and expansion of these schemes put enormous pressures on some AMBS in the initial years.

In general terms Scottish AMBS were overseen by the Scottish Manpower Services Committee, but ultimate responsibility for them lay with the Chairman of the MSC. In the main the AMB system seemed to work smoothly and efficiently, despite regular complaints of crowded agendas and insufficient resources. However, on the very few occasions when conflicts arose and were made public, for example over the proper remit of the Boards, these were resolved centrally, which sometimes caused resentment at local level. In one case, a decision by the Central and Fife AMB led to conflict with MSC headquarters in Sheffield. The subsequent overruling of the AMB led John Pollock, then the General Secretary of the Educational Institute of Scotland, to question publicly the value of the local advisory boards.

Throughout the period from 1974 to 1988, the MSC was generally seen as a highly centralized agency, despite the existence of its local DMC/AMB structures and despite the local delivery of the major programmes. Generally it was felt that control over all the key aspects of policy, of programme changes and of resources lay with the Employment Secretary and with MSC headquarters in England. This aspect of the MSC is discussed in a number of the chapters which follow.

## INDUSTRIAL TRAINING BOARDS

The 1973 Employment and Training Act, in addition to setting up the MSC, reformed the previous arrangements regulating training within industry, namely the Industrial Training Boards. These Boards had been set up under the Industrial Training Act passed by Harold Macmillan's Conservative Government in 1964. This Act also enjoyed the support of all political parties and of both sides of industry. Like the 1973 Act, the legislation permitting the establishment of ITBs was put into effect by an incoming Labour Government. In the 1960s and 1970s the main issues in industrial training did not divide the political parties.

The 1964 Act was a response to the fairly widespread skill shortages which were perceived to have held up economic expansion during the late 1950s and early 1960s. Industry had been left in these years simply to train if it wished to. Many firms preferred to poach skilled labour from wherever they could rather than undertake systematic training (see Chapter 11). Skill shortages remained, and, in the opinion of some commentators, the poaching of skilled labour helped to bid up wages and so contributed to inflation.

The Act empowered the Minister of Labour to establish Industrial Training Boards with statutory powers over their industry. An advisory Central Training Council (CTC) was set up. Responsibility for training efforts remained with individual firms. The Act gave ITBs the power to raise a levy on firms in their industry. The highest levy set by any Board was in engineering. It was set at 2.5 per cent of payroll, the Engineering ITB's estimate of actual training costs in the industry. The majority of ITBs set their levies as a percentage of payroll costs, while a small number set per capita levies.

The Boards were given the responsibility of bringing about an improvement in the quantity and the quality of industrial training in their sectors. They were empowered to collect information about employment and training in their industries in order to facilitate some degree of manpower planning. The ITBs were tripartite bodies on which employers and trade unions had equal representation.

ITBs were set up in a number of phases after the Act. In the first phase were the traditional manufacturing industries: engineering, shipbuilding, construction, wool, jute and flax, and iron and steel. The second phase covered the public utilities gas, electricity and water. Thereafter Boards were set up to cover the range of textile industries, some smaller manufacturing sectors, important technological industries such as chemicals and petroleum and the major service industries in road transport and hotels and catering. In 1969, the Third Report of the Central Training Council recorded the existence of 27 statutory Boards, one hybrid Board later known as the Foundry Industry Training Committee and three voluntary Boards covering Insurance, Local Government and

the Merchant Navy. Together these Boards covered over a million establishments, and some 15.5 million employees (62 per cent of the working
population) (Perry, 1976).

Many firms were unhappy about the new arrangements for training
and in particular about the prospect of external bodies interfering in their
internal employment and training practices. In one sector, Agriculture,
Horticulture and Forestry, employers' opposition to the new proposals
was so strong that the Board abandoned its planned per capita levy
(Perry, 1976). Perhaps reflecting this mixture of apprehension and opposition, the House of Commons Estimates Committee recommended as
early as 1967 that levies should be reduced to a minimum.

Generally, however, the existence of the Boards, and their willingness
to use their powers to raise levies and give out grants for approved
training, led to a rapid increase in training activity. Other benefits followed. The modernization of apprenticeship training began with the
innovation of a first year of off-the-job training (to ITB approved standards) followed by modularized training in subsequent years. The
Engineering ITB introduced these changes from 1968 and other Boards
were quick to follow.

The levy–grant system itself brought about important changes. The
very existence of the levy led to many firms appointing training
managers and looking seriously at training for the first time. The significant transactions which could be involved in the levy–grant relationship with ITBs encouraged many companies to look more seriously
at training issues within broader company planning (see Chapters 4
and 11). The levy–grant mechanism permitted some redistribution of
training costs within an industry. Poor trainers paid their levy to the ITB
while firms which were good trainers could aim to maximize their
income from ITB grants and so lower their net training costs. In some
industries, like engineering, it was possible for the ITB to reward firms
which were willing to train beyond the level required to meet their own
immediate needs. Such firms could receive more in grant than their levy
liability.

The ITBs assisted small and medium-sized companies, many of which
had limited resources for training and only intermittent training needs,
by encouraging them to take a collective approach to training through
locally based group training schemes. A number of such schemes were
started before the 1964 Act, such as the Hawick Hosiery Manufacturers'
scheme, involving 20 employers with some 3 000 employees, which was
set up in 1949. However, the Act gave a push to their formation through
the availability of ITB advice, grants and start-up costs. By 1980 the
Scottish engineering industry had 18 group training schemes involving
601 establishments and 113 400 employees. Group training made a more
significant contribution to first-year apprentice training in Scotland than
in any other Engineering ITB region. In road transport in Scotland, there

were 16 group training associations, involving 519 employers and 19 500 employees. The Construction ITB set up 15 groups in Scotland, involving 340 firms with 19 000 employees.

Whatever improvements may have stemmed directly from the 1964 Act, and notwithstanding the broad cross-party and cross-industry consensus which favoured the Act, the ITB system itself was not welcomed everywhere, and failed during the second half of the 1960s to win over some of the major critics. Some firms with activities in more than one industry had to deal with more than one ITB and complained about the duplication of effort and paperwork. Small firms complained of ITB bureaucracy and, significantly, the Bolton Committee which looked into the situation of small firms argued that they had not been well served by the ITBs. The Hunt Committee, reporting on policy towards the intermediate areas in 1969, argued for closer working relationships between those responsible for education and training and those responsible for regional development. Some argued in the early 1970s that the ITBs had done their work by bringing about a permanent change in industry's attitudes to training and so had rendered themselves redundant. Others who had been opposed to interventionist measures in 1964 had continued to snipe at the ITBs from the wings of the policy making stage, particularly economic liberals, like Enoch Powell MP, who complained to Parliament about the ITBs' 'great training robbery'. More significant at the time though was the large body of feeling that a centralized agency with powers to oversee the ITB network was required to replace the small advisory Central Training Council.

The 1973 Employment and Training Act significantly changed the ITB system, though these changes were overshadowed by the creation of the MSC. After 1973 the ITBs were required to exclude small firms from levies, a change which was generally welcomed by the larger Boards on cost–benefit grounds. More significantly the ITBs were limited by the new Act to a levy ceiling of 1 per cent of payroll costs (a levy limit which was below the actual costs to industry of training in many skill intensive sectors) and the levy–grant system was changed to a levy–grant–exemption system. This new system required Boards to exempt from levy firms which met their own labour requirements as agreed between them and their ITB. Each industry's training needs came to be defined as equivalent to the sum of the short-term needs of the firms comprising that sector. In future it would be considerably more difficult for ITBs to encourage training surplus to the immediate needs of individual firms. Significantly, the new MSC was given the tasks of meeting ITB operating costs and co-ordinating ITB operations, two very different tasks which the MSC would never reconcile satisfactorily.

The 1973 Act weakened the interventionist approach to industrial training which the ITBs had developed. The ITBs' status and ability to influence companies' decisions was undermined, and their overall levy yield declined, from a peak of £382 million in 1971/2 to £71 million in 1978/9 (constant prices). By 1987, only 10 per cent of engineering firms were paying levy to the Engineering ITB, and its levy income had fallen sharply (see Chapter 11).

While the weakened ITB system remained in place throughout the 1970s, skill training through apprenticeship programmes declined. The economic climate facing manufacturing industry worsened reducing the demand for skilled industrial workers and industry's inclination to train. The ITBS lacked the powers required to arrest the downward trend in apprentice training which occurred throughout the 1970s in Britain. Between 1970 and 1980 apprentice numbers in Britain fell by one-third. There were within this overall trend some very large differences between sectors and some variations between Scotland and other parts of Britain.

The sectoral decline over the decade varied between a 64 per cent fall in shipbuilding and a 10 per cent drop in vehicles. In Scotland the decline in engineering apprenticeship occurred later than in England and Wales. The larger industrial ITBS and MSC initiated a number of schemes to boost apprentice training and to try to deal with the growing problem of apprentices made redundant during their training period. In 1981, about one-third of Britain's estimated total of 90 000 apprenticeships was publicly funded, at a cost of about £70 million per year. The MSC supported ITB apprenticeship under a Special Measures programme which ran from July 1975 to 1979 at an overall cost of £132 million. This was succeeded by the TSPA – Training for Skills: A Programme for Action – which commenced in 1979. Through the TSPA the MSC worked closely with ITBS and with non-statutory training bodies. One feature of the TSPA was its attempt to promote responses to cross-sector skills shortages, which the ITBS found difficulty in tackling. In 1982/83, some £56.5 million was spent on TSPA throughout Britain. Over 80 per cent of this support went to the training of young people, including apprentice training, assistance to redundant apprentices, and trainees on the National Computing Centre's Threshold Scheme in computer programming. TSPA funds supported skill training in a wide range of industries. In 1980/1 for example, TSPA allocations in Scotland included £315 000 to support construction and engineering craft-training in local authorities, £20 000 to meet special training needs in rural areas through the Joint Training Group for the Highlands and Islands and £53 000 to the Training Council for Scottish Local Authorities. In 1980/1, some 1 500 training grants and awards were taken up in Scotland boosting employers' recruitment to traineeships and providing additional recruitment. About 80 per cent of those MSC-funded places were in the ITB part of the Scottish economy. While numbers were small, it is important to note that the MSC also funded some teacher training under this programme. In 1980/1, 59 places leading to a qualification for teaching handicapped pupils were supported.

Most of the TSPA programme was incorporated into the Youth Training Scheme after 1983.

The factors behind the rapid decline in skill training were many, though the most important were undoubtedly the long-term trend towards deindustrialization and the very sharp difficulties which faced industry in the late 1970s (see Chapter 1). When it considered these issues, the Scottish Select Committee (1981/2) found that the principal causes of the decline in the numbers of apprentices and other trainees were, economic conditions, changes in industrial structure, rising costs (including pay) and defects in the form and content of courses'. In a memorandum to the Committee, the Fraser of Allander Institute suggested that perhaps only one fifth of the decline between 1970 and 1978 was due to structural economic change. The remainder was explained in terms of declining training rates in industry.

In Scotland, the difficult economic climate, the decline in demand for skilled labour and firms' traditional reluctance to train led to a fairly sharp decline in apprentice training in major industries, like engineering, construction, shipbuilding and road transport. However, the analysis of trends is difficult because, after 1982, the situation was further complicated by major reductions in the ITB network, and by the arrival of MSC proposals for a major change in youth training arrangements.

The decline in apprentice training increasingly led to a problem of underused training capacity. In engineering for example, first-year apprentices could be trained to ITB standards within the industry, or in colleges or group training centres. In Scotland, there were some 2 792 approved first year places in 1980/1, with group provision (51 per cent of the total) relatively more important than elsewhere in Britain, and college places (14 per cent) relatively less important. Overall, however, only 58 per cent of Scotland's capacity was in use (compared with, for example, 70 per cent in London and the South-East). The problem of industrial training facilities becoming uneconomic through underutilization was not immediately helped by the growth in the MSC's anti-unemployment measures which tended to require different kinds of facilities.

## REFORM OF THE ITB SYSTEM

Two MSC-conducted reviews of the ITB system took place. The first was conducted before the 1979 General Election. The second was ordered by the incoming Conservative government (which had made clear its dislike for ITBs during the election campaign) and was conducted on very different criteria. The MSC reviews showed that in 1979/80 there were 23 statutory ITBs operating throughout Britain, together with the Foundry Industry Training Committee. MSC accounts put the total operating costs of the ITBs in that year at £42.5 million, with a further £44 million being spent through their various training grants schemes.

Both reviews were broadly favourable to the ITB system, and neither review recommended that any ITB closures should take place. However, the government's view was that industry should be left to meet its own training needs, and that ITBs were an obstacle to this (see Chapter 1). An enabling Act, the Employment and Training Act 1981, was passed, giving the Secretary of State for Employment powers to create or close down ITBs and to change their industrial scope. These powers were used to close most of the Boards, leaving statutory ITBs in engineering, construction, hotel and catering, road transport, clothing, plastics and offshore oil (the last of which was a new ITB). All of the remaining ITBs had a field presence in Scotland, and some, like the Engineering ITB, regarded Scotland as a full operating region and made available a substantial amount of information about their Scottish operations.

The abolished boards were replaced by some 80 voluntary Non-Statutory Training Organization (NSTOS) most of which were based on trade associations. However, the overall coverage of the ITB system did not immediately change by as much as the closure figures would appear to suggest. Before the closures the ITB network had covered an estimated 50 per cent of employees in employment. After the reforms an estimated 30 per cent remained with the statutory ITB framework.

The remaining Boards were further weakened by a return to industry funding within a general upper levy limit of 1 per cent. Financial pressures increasingly encouraged the Boards to undertake work which would bring in short-term funding, and to move away from the more strategic tasks involved in the encouragement of long-term systematic training in industry. While the MSC role in meeting ITB operating costs ended, the MSC retained some policy control over the Boards. Some ITBS, for example the Construction ITB, became heavily involved in MSC programmes which were intended initially to alleviate unemployment. Others turned more to offering training advice and consultancy services. The Employment Act of 1988 further changed the ITBs by adding additional members, who were generally employers, to the Boards, and by weakening the trade union input. This Act ended the arrangements which had guided and shaped industrial training since 1964, giving employers a majority of places on the Boards, weakening the trade-union input and so formally ending the tripartite arrangements which had prevailed for over 20 years.

THE TRAINING OPPORTUNITIES SCHEME AND ADULT TRAINING

Apart from its involvement with the ITBs, and its wider support for skills training through the TSPA programme, the MSC had other, more direct influences on training for industry. From its formation the MSC was charged with the management of a national scheme for the accelerated training of adults in industrial skills, the Training Opportunities Scheme (TOPS), which was intended to ease problems of redeployment arising from industrial restructuring. (Aspects of the TOPS scheme are discussed in Chapters 4, 10, 12, 13 and 16.) The TOPS scheme was intended to build up over a period of time to a 100 000-place programme. In fact, because of public expenditure restrictions, it peaked at about 75 000 places in 1979/80 (making TOPS a fairly small-scale programme compared with schemes operated in for example Sweden and some other countries).

TOPS was built on an earlier Vocational Training Scheme, which was based primarily in Government Training Centres (GTCs). For some 40 years these had mainly social objectives, such as the rehabilitation of people with disabilities and forces ex-regulars. In the early 1960s the emphasis changed to accelerated adult training for industry as the GTCs were harnessed to tackling the skill-shortage problem. By 1966 Scotland had 7 GTCs, at Dumbarton, Dunfermline, Glasgow (Queenslie and Hillington), Irvine, Motherwell and Port Glasgow. Between them they had nearly 900 training places, with carpentry and capstan setting operating the most important training skills.

TOPS, which offered training to unemployed adults and to those in work, grew rapidly during the 1970s. In Scotland, the number of adults completing TOPS courses rose from 2 000 in 1972 to nearly 10 000 in the peak year of 1977/8. In 1978/9 the numbers dropped to nearer 9 000 and TOPS continued to shrink thereafter. The main TOPS providers were colleges of further education followed by the MSC's own Skillcentres. In 1977/8, two thirds of TOPS completions in Scotland were in further education colleges, with a further 25 per cent taking place in Skillcentres. Relatively small numbers of trainees went through TOPS courses in employers' establishments or undertook training in heavy goods vehicle driving. In 1979/80, 42.5 per cent of Scottish TOPS completions were in clerical and commercial courses, and 20.6 per cent of completions were in engineering and automative skill areas. Management courses accounted for 8 per cent of completions, construction for 5.8 per cent and HGV driving for 4.8 per cent.

Women accounted for a large proportion of TOPS completions: about 53 per cent of Scottish completions in 1977/8. The proportion fell to under one-third in 1984/5, largely because of changes to the patterns of TOPS provision. (This aspect of TOPS is discussed in Chapter 12.) The House of Commons Committee of Public Accounts raised questions about the prominence of office skills in TOPS output as early as the mid-1970s (CPA 1986/87). Gradually the pattern of TOPS began to change to reflect concerns for industrial needs and to serve the short-term market for skills. Attempts were made to increase provision of new technology and small business courses, and to effect some redistribution from the West of Scotland to the relatively more buoyant labour market in the East.

In 1979/80, the first TOPS course specifically aimed at women, the Wider Opportunities for Women course, was run on a pilot basis at Edinburgh University. As a result WOW became a part of the TOPS programme in

1980. By 1986/7 just over 400 women were going through wow courses each year in Scotland, and plans were announced to double this level of provision. (Chapters 12 and 16 discuss wow in Scotland.)

In 1978, and on a number of occasions in subsequent years, TOPS criteria were tightened. Actual or expected short-term placement rates in training trades increasingly became the test of the relevance of TOPS to industry's needs, as rising unemployment and the decline of manufacturing discredited the very concept of training 'for stock' which had underpinned the early years of TOPS. Within the general tightening of criteria which stemmed from the quest for greater 'market relevance', there remained a social concern to combat unemployment and to offer training opportunities to disadvantaged people. (Chapter 13 discusses the importance of TOPS to disabled people.) In the early 1980s TOPS provision began to reflect the new priorities of training for small business start-ups, training for self-employment and pre-vocational courses. The Skillcentres became involved in a wider range of courses as they diversified away from the old-style TOPS provision. Again these changes make it almost impossible to make long-term comparisons of levels of skill training provision through TOPS. Taken together though, spending on TOPS ands Skillcentres fell to about 18 per cent of the total MSC budget in 1982/83 from about 33 per cent in 1978/79.

Financial restrictions were imposed on TOPS from the late 1970s and were felt mainly in the further education colleges. Between 1979/80 and 1982/3, total TOPS completions in Scotland fell by some 2 200 (23 per cent). Within this overall decline, further-education completions fell by 37 per cent and the relatively small number of completions on employers' premises fell by 66 per cent. Skillcentre completions increased by 23 per cent. (Some 994 of the 3 200 Scottish Skillcentre completions in 1982/3 were in the Skillplus scheme which retrained unemployed craftsmen.)

During the 1980s the Skillcentre network was rationalized and then set apart, in 1983 as a semi-independent Skillcentre Training Agency (STA) with its own business plan and operating targets. (The Skillcentres are discussed in Chapters 10 and 16.) The STA quickly had to face up to the task of tooling up in order to increase training in hi-tech areas. By the end of 1984, all of Scotland's Skillcentres had computer numerically controlled (CNC) machine tools, and computer aided design (CAD) had been introduced in the training of draughtsmen at Hillington.

However, with employer-sponsored training still in recession the STA found it impossible to meet its new operating targets. The MSC was criticized by the Public Accounts Committee (1986/7) for purchasing too heavily from the STA when other more cost-effective providers may have been available. In particular Skillcentres were compared unfavourably with further education colleges, although the critics of the new restrictive policy argued that this was an unfair comparison. At any rate the STA was unable to expand its business sufficiently quickly. An identified shortfall of between £10 million and £12 million led to a skillcentre-by-skillcentre review and recommendations for a major reduction in the network of centres. In January 1985, the MSC voted 5 to 4 in favour of closing almost one-third of the Skillcentres. In Scotland the arithmetic was more severe, with 5 out of 11 centres being closed. The Skillcentres at Bellshill, Dundee, Dunfermline, Edinburgh, Glasgow (Hillington) and Irvine were retained. Operating from a reduced base, the STA took steps further to diversify its activities, in particular by concentrating on the establishment of a force of mobile instructors able to train in-company to meet employers' perceived short-term requirements. In 1987/88, using these and other resources, the STA planned to provide some £8 million of training in Scotland.

TOPS training in occupational skills was succeeded by (often shorter) courses run under the Job Training Scheme (JTS). While the JTS was smaller in scale than TOPS – there were 4 300 Scottish JTS completions in 1985/6 – it remained a significant programme, and was particularly important to the STA, providing over 90 per cent of the Agency's MSC-derived income. The MSC was clearly conscious of the link between JTS-type adult training and industrial restructuring. It was claimed that 1985/6 JTS provision was roughly equally divided between courses relevant to the new sunrise hi-tech industries on the one hand, and those needed by the old traditional manufacturing sectors on the other hand. In 1986/7 £10 million was spent on the JTS in Scotland, this sum being nearly 60 per cent of MSC spending in Scotland on adult training.

The MSC's other main direct involvement in industrial training in the 1970s was its Direct Training Services. These services were diverse, ranging from supervisory courses and the use of MSC mobile instructors to train on employers' premises, to courses in international trade procedures. In 1977/8, the number of Scottish firms using these services totalled 1 714, and some 8 457 people underwent training. At this time the output of all the Direct Training Services was growing, with the expansion in employer-sponsored TOPS and employers' usage of MSC's mobile instructors growing particularly rapidly. In October 1979, charges for these MSC services were introduced in the Assisted Areas. In Scotland there was an almost immediate 28 per cent decline in demand for DTS in 1979/80, with a further 35 per cent drop to a total throughput of 4 252 occurring in 1980/1. Over the period 1979/80 to 1982/3 annual DTS completions in Scotland declined by 60 per cent.

In late 1982, the MSC began an experimental programme known as the Open Tech (see Chapter 4). This project was concerned with providing distance-learning facilities for people in work. Training was provided primarily for employees in technician, supervisory and management grades. The budget for the scheme over the initial funding period to March 1987 was £47 million. This budget was used to fund Open Tech projects for a pump-priming period of three years. In early 1984, there

were five Open Tech projects in Scotland with a total contract value of
£0.9 million. Fifteen projects had started by 1985, all with the aim of
becoming self-financing by 1987. Throughout Britain some 120 Open
Tech projects had been supported by early 1987. By 1984/5, before the
implementation of the Adult Training Strategy initiatives, the MSC's
main expenditures on adult training throughout Britain were over £250
million spent on TOPS and related training (including some £7 million
spent on business training), £17 million on the Open Tech programme,
£12.5 million on the National Priority Skills Scheme (NPSS), and about
£11.5 million on various smaller schemes (including £3 million on the
pilot schemes for the new ATS).

UNIFIED VOCATIONAL PREPARATION

While the UVP was a scheme aimed at young people, discussion of it
belongs firmly with industrial training. Unlike the larger YOP and YTS
programmes, the UVP was aimed exclusively at young people in work
(see Chapter 4). The UVP began in 1976 and was aimed at young people in
jobs where there had previously been no systematic training arrangements. Many of the 20 per cent of school leavers estimated by MSC to find
their first job in distribution would have fallen into this category.
Courses were run by employers, colleges and ITBs with MSC support. UVP
courses were often about 13 weeks in duration. While they were short
compared with the first year of ITB apprenticeships, the proponents of
the UVP system argued that these courses were comparable in quality to
many of the 450 'apprenticeships' in the much-lauded West German
training system. In Scotland, UVP was administered by the MSC, the
Scottish Education Department, and the Scottish Economic Planning
Department.

In 1980/1 there were perhaps 20 000 young Scots in the UVP client
group. In that year between 450 and 500 young people passed through
the scheme in Scotland, and plans existed to expand the scheme to a
throughput of 2 000 in 1983/4. By the end of April 1981, there had been 94
UVP schemes in Scotland catering for 1 174 trainees. Fifty-two of these
schemes, with 652 trainees, were sponsored by the Distributive ITB. In
1982/3, 528 trainees took part in UVP in 21 industries in Scotland. After
1982/3, the UVP was incorporated into the Youth Training Scheme.

Clearly then the MSC was heavily involved in a wide range of industrial
training activities. However, the MSC's spectacular growth did not come
about through a large expansion of industrial training. MSC expenditures on training were at times substantial, but from the late 1970s they
were rapidly overtaken by the emerging anti-unemployment programmes. In fact, by the late 1970s, considering all aspects of vocational
training, direct state involvement in skills training for industry was
declining. The ITB network was being reduced and weakened, and the

MSC's own programmes and Skillcentres were similarly cut back. The measures available to assist those areas worst affected by cyclical economic decline were reduced. The drift and explicit objective of central policy was a strengthening of the market and a return to the voluntarism that marked the pre-1964 period. Added to this the government seemed to view trade union involvement in training as at best an anachronism and at worst a restrictive practice. The government wished to reduce union involvement in training, and to weaken the position of unions in the ITB and MSC tripartite structures.

The MSC's rapid growth between the mid-1970s and mid-1980s was based largely on the rapid expansion of its short-term responses to unemployment, and in particular the Youth Opportunities Programme. However, by the early 1980s, these anti-unemployment programmes had formed the basis for a new type of active interventionism (see Chapter 1) led by the MSC and designed to change rapidly the nature and focus of vocational education and training. The changes of the early 1980s were so many and varied that even with the benefit of hindsight there appears to have been a bewildering flood of reviews, consultative papers, reforms, new programmes, programme changes and policy changes.

RESPONSES TO UNEMPLOYMENT

It was the rise of unemployment (see Chapter 1) which proved to be the basis for the transformation of the MSC from a small co-ordinating and planning agency in 1974 into a major government agency, which came to spend more on labour market programmes than the University Grants Committee spent on the whole of university education. The rapid growth of the MSC lasted for a decade from 1976 to about 1986, although during this period there was such a proliferation of MSC schemes and so many changes in the longer lived programmes that it is very difficult to trace the growth through in detail.

The early part of this growth, between 1976 and 1978, took place under a Labour government and involved a major expansion of the MSC itself. The later period of growth took place under Conservative administrations. This growth was remarkable for at least three reasons. First, the Conservative government in 1979/80 was openly hostile to the MSC and some backbenchers were even calling for abolition. Second, the growth took place within the framework of a set of policies designed to control and reduce public spending. Third, much of the 1982–86 growth, though it involved the expansion of MSC budgets, financed activities that were carried out by contractors (public and private sectors) on behalf of the MSC, in such a way that by the late 1980s the MSC itself was increasingly vulnerable to challenge.

A fourth more obvious point should perhaps be added. In relation to the rapidly increased anti-unemployment programmes, the government needed quickly to find training providers (and hundreds of thousands of training places) across the private, public and voluntary sectors. For the sake of national legitimacy and easy local negotiations, the TUC was permitted to retain its network of representatives on MSC tripartite structures, from the Commission itself to the network of local Area Manpower Boards, during a period when policy did not favour tripartism. Generally, though, at the level of the tripartite Commission itself, trade union views and comments were to be increasingly ignored or even overridden, except perhaps in a few notable instances where the union view coincided with that of a majority of Commissioners and with public opinion, as happened for example when the government retracted the initial White Paper proposals (Cmnd. 8455) to make participation in the Youth Training Scheme compulsory.

## THE SPECIAL PROGRAMMES

The first special programme was introduced in October 1975 in the priority regions, as the Labour government's initial anti-unemployment measure. The Job Creation Programme was in part based on Canadian experience in dealing with unemployment. It gave unemployed people temporary work in return for an allowance based on the 'rate for the job.' Compared with susequent MSC programmes, the JCP was a relatively small programme. It was, however, implemented rapidly and quickly outgrew the initial planning figures. The scheme was overseen throughout Britain by six area teams, two of which were based in Scotland. By the end of April 1977, some 1 989 projects with about 22 300 'jobs' had been created in Scotland at a cost to the MSC of a little over £30 million. A little over half of these places were sponsored by local authorities, with the voluntary sector providing about 34 per cent. By the end of the JCP in December of the following year, nearly 42 000 'jobs' (28 per cent of the British total) had been created in Scotland.

In September 1976, the Work Experience Programme (WEP) was introduced to provide work experience for unemployed young people under the age of 19. One unit with nineteen staff handled the whole of the WEP in Scotland with applications coming in at the rate of about 200 per month in 1977/8. At the end of March 1978, Scotland had some 6 500 WEP places on 2 100 schemes. An estimated 84 per cent of WEP graduates went on to secure paid employment after their course.

## THE YOUTH OPPORTUNITIES PROGRAMME

The MSC's first mass programme came as problems intensified in the youth labour market and as awareness grew in government circles of the scale of these problems. In the wake of the Holland Report on the problems of youth unemployment, the TUC pressed the Labour government to mount a quick response. The MSC was given the task of quickly developing the Youth Opportunities Programme and of implementing Holland's main recommendations. YOP was introduced in 1978 and grew rapidly. The MSC's impact on school leavers through the YOP and other programmes is the most researched aspect of its activities (see Raffe, 1988a).

In Scotland the programme more than doubled in two years, rising from 23 600 entrants in 1978/9 to 49 300 entrants in 1980/1 (some 14 per cent of the British total). Over the life of the YOP between 1978/9 and 1982/3, nearly one quarter of a million young Scots entered the programme. Of these over 199 000 entered the various forms of work experience while over 39 000 took part in work preparation. By 1982/3 the YOP was catering for more than half of all the school leavers entering the labour market (Raffe, 1988a). Aspects of the YOP are discussed in Chapters 4, 10 and 15.

The expansion of the YOP was so rapid that the balance of MSC expenditures and activities rapidly tipped towards the new anti-unemployment, social policy measures and away from the more traditional activities of supporting skill training for industry. In 1982/3, the programme accounted for over 40 per cent of MSC's entire budget compared with less than 10 per cent in 1978/9. Within the MSC, the Special Programmes Division was the rapidly growing part. Once again, however, these trends are made impossible to follow by MSC's structural and programme changes. With the introduction of the New Training Initiative (see below) the old distinction between youth training and anti-unemployment measures disappeared, while within the MSC the Special Programmes and Training Services Divisions were merged into a new Training Division.

The emphasis of the YOP was on work experience in order to help young people get some experience of working life which employers would recognize as valuable. Young people on the scheme received a flat-rate allowance.

YOP was supervised by a very large network of scheme sponsors. Eventually there were over 150 000 YOP sponsors throughout Britain. While most of these were private-sector-based, voluntary agencies and public bodies, particularly local authorities (see Chapter 9), played an important role. In Strathclyde, for example, in 1979/80 the Regional Council directly promoted 9 000 out of the total of 21 000 YOP places.

Initially the programme was successful in its primary objective of helping young people find work. Eighty per cent of young people moved on from the programme to paid employment. In Scotland surveys indicated that only 13 per cent of those who entered YOP in September/ October 1978 registered as unemployed when they finished on the scheme. As the programme grew however this type of success declined. The corresponding figure for entrants in January and March/April 1980 was 48 per cent. Over this period the proportion of YOP graduates in Scotland going on to jobs fell from nearly 78 per cent to 39 per cent (Scottish Select Committee, 1981/2).

The YOP was expanded rapidly as a response to worsening youth unemployment. In 1980/1 it was widely expected that the government would reduce the scale of the YOP and cut back on the MSC's expenditures. However, the scheme also proved to be a convenient mechanism for making a quick response to the youth unrest evident in a number of English inner cities in 1981.

As the YOP grew, its popularity declined. The YOP became increasingly criticized as a low quality, 'cheap labour' scheme which was open to abuse by unscrupulous employers. There is no doubt that later MSC initiatives were to an extent tarnished by the poor image held by young people and parents of the YOP in its later years.

The YOP contained a number of different forms of provision. By far the largest part was Work Experience on Employers' Premises (WEEP). Project-Based Work Experience (PBWE) came second, with other forms of YOP being offered in Training Workshops and on Community Projects. WEEP was the cheapest form of provision, with a filled place on WEEP costing less than half of a filled Training Workshop place. Of 1980/1 entrants in Scotland, over 62 per cent did work experience on employers' premises and the four types of work experience accounted for 86 per cent. Some 6 900 (14 per cent) trainees undertook work preparation. Training Workshops, sponsored in the main by local authorities, catered for about 7–8 per cent of Scottish entrants (compared with 3 per cent in Britain as a whole). Interestingly, in view of post-YOP initiatives just over 6 000 of these entrants were engaged in short industrial training courses, with over a third of these being in the engineering and automotive industries where employer-sponsored training had slumped. In its submission to the Scottish Select Committee (1981/2), the Scottish Branch of the Association of Principals of Colleges argued that these short courses were too short for the purpose of significant skill training and were too long to function as 'taster' courses.

Within YOP, WEEP was generally seen as the top of an unofficial hierarchy of different forms of provision. More young people went into WEEP than went to other forms of YOP, and WEEP tended to be best in terms of post-YOP job placement. PBWE had a different image, tending to be associated with the needs of young people with low levels of educational attainment.

However, it was around the WEEP element of YOP that controversies began to emerge around allegations of abuses by some employers. Some trade unionists critizied YOP as a 'cheap labour' scheme, and in some craft unions memories of old disputes over skill 'dilution' were certainly stirred by the scheme. In evidence to the Scottish Select Committee (1981/2), the Scottish Engineering Employers' Association reported some opposition to YOP emerging in larger firms in the central belt area and in Fife.

The MSC's own research indicated that there was a problem of some employers 'substituting' YOP trainees for paid workers. Survey evidence suggested a possible 30 per cent rate of substitution. However the critics of YOP felt that this level probably understated the problem, as it was based on information volunteered by employers. In agriculture, apprentice intake throughout Britain fell by 47 per cent between 1978 and 1982 (Committee of Public Accounts, 1982/3). There was, however, some disagreement between officials of the Agricultural Training Board and MSC over the precise impact of YOP. The memorandum submitted to the Committee of Public Accounts by the Comptroller and Auditor General observed that 'at the level at which YOP was running in June 1982, around 40 000 to 70 000 jobs enjoying normal pay and conditions may have been lost as a result'. It went on to suggest that 5 per cent of WEEP trainees were replacing adult workers.

However, the fears voiced by critics and the allegations raised in some quarters did little to affect the very rapid growth of YOP, or to influence the character of the programme. Over the two years to March 1981 about 130 applications for WEEP schemes were rejected in Scotland, because of the likely substitution effects. Only between 30 and 40 schemes were closed because of identified abuses, out of some 17 000 Scottish schemes operating at the time (Committee on Scottish Affairs, 1981/2).

JOB CREATION FOR THE ADULT UNEMPLOYED

For unemployed adults, the JCP was superseded by the Special Temporary Employment Programme (STEP) in 1978. The initial budget for STEP in Scotland was £5.3 million for 1978/79. The STEP was not as large as the YOP in financial terms and did not grow as rapidly. In 1979/80 there were 22 400 STEP entrants in Britain and some 4 200 entrants to over 470 schemes in Scotland. In 1980/81 as unemployment in the STEP client groups rose nationally by 60 per cent from 400 000 to 640 000, the STEP was reduced to 18 400 entrants. As this time adult unemployment simply was not perceived as a problem requiring a mass response on the lines of the YOP.

In February 1981 the successor to the STEP, the Community Enterprise Programme was launched. Like its predecessor the CEP offered work of community benefit to unemployed adults who received a local 'rate for the job' whilst on the scheme. Like its predecessor the CEP remained a modest programme in relation to the scale of adult unemployment. CEP's target on launch was 25 000 places throughout Britain by March 1982.

However, by 1982 thinking had changed and a massive expansion of adult make-work programmes took place as the CEP was replaced by the Community Programme (CP), which was to become the longest running of the anti-unemployment measures. (Several chapters in this book discuss various aspects of the CP, in particular, Chapters 7–14 and Chapter 16.)

The initial plans for the CP represented more than a three-fold increase over the peak of provision under the CEP. Like the adult schemes before it, the CP offered work of community benefit to unemployed adults. Most CP schemes were based on environmental and building projects. This together with the fact that only unemployed adults who were claimants in their own right were eligible to take part, meant that the CP catered more for unemployed men than for unemployed women (as indeed had been the case in the earlier STEP and CEP schemes). The main dissimilarity between the earlier programmes and the CP lay in the latter's reliance on part-time provision (see Chapter 16). Throughout its life from 1982 to 1986, the CP remained a centralized scheme which the MSC administered for the DE. The criticism that the CP was overcentralized and inflexible persisted over this period, and became particularly important in the discussions in Scotland over the replacement of the CP by the new Employment Training (ET) scheme in 1988 (see Chapters 10 and 16).

For Scotland the initial plan involved the creation of some 16 900 places catering for 26 000 adults by the autumn of 1983. This represented a more rapid increase in Scotland than for Britain generally, in part reflecting Scotland's appalling umemployment problem (the Special Programmes were, to an extent, 'demand-driven'), and the fact that at that time the MSC found there a more enthusiastic welcome for the new scheme. Local government and the voluntary sector were particularly important to the CP in Scotland (see Chapters 7, 8 and 9) accounting between them for 97 per cent of the places in 1987.

In part, the ability of Scotland, and in particular the local authorities, to respond to new Special Programmes, stemmed from the fact that the early programmes were for a time concentrated on the assisted areas. David Young, then Chairman of the MSC, pointed to the experience of areas like Scotland when asked by the Committee of Public Accounts (1982/3) to explain the different rates of take-up of the CP in various parts of Britain.

The CP peaked in size in October 1986, when there were 32 100 filled places in Scotland. In 1986/7 £134 million was spent by the MSC on the CP in Scotland, making the CP the major programme in expenditure terms. By 1988 the CP was able to cater for some 38 000 adult entrants in a full year.

By the time of the New Training Initiative, the MSC had grown rapidly and changed radically as it had taken on the responsibility of responding to unemployment through Special Programmes, like the YOP. MSC expenditures throughout Britain grew from about £730 million in 1979/80 to over £1.1 billion in 1981/2. Expenditure on the YOP accounted for 36 per cent of the total 1981/2 budget. The two main Special Programmes, the YOP and the CP, accounted for some 43 per cent of total expenditure in 1981/2.

### THE NEW TRAINING INITIATIVE

In the early 1980s, two discussions took place at roughly the same time. First, it became accepted that unemployment was likely to be a long-term problem requiring more than short-term programmes of a palliative nature (which the YOP and the CEP were perceived to be). Second, it was widely agreed that Britain paid insufficient attention to labour market training (at this time Britain's record began once again to be adversely compared with that of competitor countries, particularly with West Germany and the West German treatment of school leaver training), and that there was an incoherence about existing provision.

Proposals for change emerged from the MSC, initially in a consultative document. These were, for the most part, eagerly greeted by the Conservative government, which began at this time to perceive ways of pursuing strategic objectives in labour market and education policy (see Chapter 1) through the systematic reform of vocational training and unemployment programmes, and the lowering of wage levels. The government's proposals (Cmnd. 8455) were published in 1981 at the same time as the MSC's considered response to its consultations. In broad aims and objectives there was little between the documents. Nevertheless, there were important differences which were only resolved after the report of a tripartite Task Group set up to consider implementing the proposals.

Initially the government favoured a scheme catering for 300 000 unemployed school leavers. However, the Task Group favoured a larger scheme catering for up to 460 000 unemployed *and* employed school leavers. The Task Group's view prevailed, and initially the extension of the scheme to cover school leavers in work was the feature which distinguished the YTS from the YOP. The government wanted to reduce training allowances for young people and to make their participation in schemes compulsory by withdrawing benefit entitlements from those who did not take part (see Chapter 10). The ensuing public outcry led to the withdrawal of the 'conscription' proposals (though they were finally reintroduced in 1988, see Chapter 15) and the reinstatement of YOP-level allowances.

The New Training Initiative (NTI) carried three broad objectives:

(i) to develop skill training and apprenticeship in such a way as to enable young people entering at different ages and with different educational attainments to acquire agreed standards of skill appropriate to the jobs available and to provide them with a basis for progress through further learning,

(ii) to move towards a position where all young people under the age of 18 have the opportunity either of continuing in full-time education or of entering a period of planned work experience combined with work-related training and education;

(iii) to open widespread opportunities for adults, whether employed or returning to work, to acquire, increase or update their skills and knowledge during the course of their working lives. (Cmnd. 8455)

In themselves the NTI objectives were uncontroversial. Through the consultative process the MSC built up very broad support for them. The CBI and the TUC had helped to formulate the proposals through their involvement in the MSC. Most trade unions and employers' organizations gave their support. The Commission for Racial Equality (CRE) and the Equal Opportunities Commission (EOC) welcomed the proposals, seeing in them the possibility of progress towards greater equality of opportunity in training provision. Local authorities and voluntary agencies supported the NTI. There were very few critics and even fewer dissenters. Through the NTI reforms a Conservative government was once again able to lead and give voice to a national consensus on the need for training reform. In Scotland too there was widespread support for the NTI despite the unpopularity there of other government programmes and despite criticisms of the government's record on unemployment.

THE YOUTH TRAINING SCHEME

The reform of apprentice training and the second objective of the NTI were to be met by the creation and development of a new Youth Training Scheme (YTS). The YTS was intended to bring together and replace the YOP and other smaller youth schemes. Through its extension to young people in work, it was also intended to incorporate the UVP, and wherever possible, the first year of apprentice training.

Throughout Britain, some 460 000 young people would be offered 12 months of work experience with an entitlement of 13 weeks of off-the-job relevant training and education. The initial plans for Scotland involved YTS entry for 45 000 to 50 000 16-year-old school leavers, with provision being offered to unemployed 17-year-olds by 1985. (A number of chapters discuss aspects of the YTS, in particular, Chapters 4, 10, 11 and 13.) Initially, despite the MSC's marketing of the new scheme's 'quality', it remained a scheme which was very firmly based on work experience like its predecessor the YOP. Indeed, young peoples' attitudes to the new scheme were similar to their attitudes to the YOP (Raffe, 1988a).

YTS training was made available in two main forms: mode A, which was employer-based, and mode B, which was community-based. Throughout Britain there were approximately two mode A places for every mode B place. In some parts of the country, notably where the economy was buoyant and the demand for labour was strong, the mode A : mode B ratio was higher from the start. In other areas, where the recession had hit harder and where employers were less willing to become involved in the YTS, mode B was more important. Initially there were two forms of mode B training. One was run by local authorities and education authorities very much on the lines of mode A. The other was run by local authorities and voluntary organizations and provided work experience on a variety of special projects. A small amount of mode B YTS training took place in Information Technology centres (about 1 200 trainees were catered for by the Scottish ITECs in 1986/7), an initiative by Department of Trade and Industry (DTI) that was encouraged to spread from inner West London to cover the rest of the country (see Chapters 5 and 6). While mode B contained different types of provision, it was viewed overall by many as a means of bridging the gap between, on the one hand, places required and, on the other, places which employers could provide. Mode B was often viewed as a 'second best' within a YTS which was very much based on practical work experience. Mode B was the main means within the YTS for catering for school leavers with 'special needs'.

From the start Scotland's innovative Action Plan for the modularization of all 16–18 non-advanced further education was seen to offer opportunities for the YTS which did not exist in the rest of Britain. The MSC was therefore represented on the SED Working Groups which were set up to implement the new proposals. In addition, a YTS Liaison Group, involving the education service, the careers service, SCOTEC, SCOTBEC, and the education trade unions was established in September 1983 to ensure a close fit between the developing YTS and the developing 16–18 education system. In Scotland, there was a general feeling, particularly in education, that the new scheme was 'education-led', and that the MSC did not have the same degree of control over non-advanced further education and youth training as it appeared to have South of the border.

The Action Plan modularized virtually all non-advanced vocational education. These modules, assessed by means of a single National Certificate, became the main source of the off-the-job training within YTS in Scotland (Raffe, 1988b). In 1984/5 and 1985/6, YTS trainees completed over 140 000 National Certificate modules.

In 1983/4, the first full YTS year, there were 40 332 YTS entrants in Scotland, of whom 27 836 (69 per cent) were in mode A. Plans for future years envisaged an expansion of total numbers and of the proportion who would receive their training in the employer-based mode A. The YTS quickly became the largest scheme operated by the MSC. In 1983/4 expenditure on the YTS accounted for £73.5 million out of MSC's Scottish total of £118.6 million on the fully decentralized activities. Of the Training Division's 646 staff employed in Scotland in April 1983, 497 were working on the development and oversight of the YTS. (This compared with 149 staff employed on the running of TOPS in Scotland.) It is clear that the ambitious plans for the YTS led to a substantial degree of overprovision by the MSC. (The Commons Committee of Public Accounts criticized the waste of over £90 million on unfilled YTS places in the first two years of the scheme (1985/6).) As the MSC made adjustments to bring the supply of

YTS places more into line with demand, serious difficulties emerged for a many sponsors, particularly those involved in mode B. From April 1986, MSC paid managing agents only for filled YTS places.

Following a Task Group recommendation the MSC set up a network of Accredited Centres (ACS). The remit of ACS was to deal with the staff training and development aspects of the YTS. The MSC estimated that up to half a million people in Britain required some training in order to deal positively with the new scheme. An AC was set up for each of the eight MSC areas in Scotland.

In the early 1980s it was already clear that the population of school leavers would be in decline in the second half of the decade, and that the problems in the youth labour-market would ease. Once the YTS was established efforts were made to improve its quality, and in particular to make it the permanent part of the vocational education scene which the MSC's Task Group had envisaged. In 1985, the MSC carried out consultations on proposals for a 2-year YTS and the government issued a White Paper (Cmnd. 9474).

The YTS was changed and extended from April 1986. It became a two-year scheme for 16-year-old school leavers, and places for one year became available to 17-year-olds. Due to the characteristics of the education system, entry at 17 became a more important feature of the YTS in Scotland than it was elsewhere in Britain (Raffe and Courtenay, 1988).

The cost implications of the new proposals were considerable. Throughout Britain the 2-year scheme would cost some £875 million in 1986/7, while in Scotland the MSC would spend over £83 million on 42 000 YTS places (36 000 two-year places and 6 000 one-year places) plus some 10 000 places for those who had started at 16 when the YTS was still a one-year scheme.

The two-year YTS was intended to be a quality scheme of vocational training and to become a permanent part of the training system. Considerable efforts were made to emphasize these points and so distinguish the new scheme from the YOP and one-year YTS. From the start, emphasis was placed by the MSC on training for occupational competencies. All trainees were given the chance to pursue recognized vocational qualifications. The MSC worked closely with the new Scottish Vocational Education Council (SCOTVEC) and with lead industry bodies on the task of promoting industry defined standards for incorporation into vocational qualifications. The YTS Certification Board, which covered the whole of Britain, had the task of considering such qualifications for approval for use in the YTS.

The MSC also took steps to raise and standardize the quality of training organizations. A network of Approved Training Organizations (ATOS) was set up to deliver the YTS. In order to become an ATO an organization had to meet ten criteria laid down by the MSC. These were wide-ranging, covering everything from the competence of staff to the organization's need to show a positive commitment to equality of opportunity (MSC Corporate Plan for Scotland, 1987–91). By September 1987, 170 organizations had been awarded full ATO status and 192 had provisional ATO status.

### THE YTS, APPRENTICESHIP AND JOBS

The second NTI objective was also addressed primarily the YTS. However this proved more controversial, because it sharply raised the issues around the relationship between the YTS and apprenticeship and the relationship between the YTS and waged employment. The surfacing of these issues was inevitable, in part because the innovative aspect of the YTS was that it encompassed young people in work as well as those who were unemployed. The issues were, however, difficult to assess, in part because of the nature of the YTS itself. While YTS training was intended to be based on work experience, it was not intended to be specific to any job or occupation. Training was in broad areas of skill known as 'occupational training families' (OTF's), with the entire youth labour market covered by 11 of these 'families'. The early YTS data did not facilitate analyses of the industrial sectors most engaged in the YTS, but did indicate which types of work were most affected. Nearly two-thirds of entrants to the YTS up to the end of September 1985 were in four OTFS: administrative, clerical and office skills; installation, maintenance and repair; manufacturing and assembly; personal services and sales (Committee of Public Accounts, 1984/6, p. 16). The Scottish Council Development and Industry's study of Dundee and Renfrew showed an even greater concentration. Ninety per cent of the trainees were in the same four OTFS. The SCDI commented that it did not believe this to be atypical of broader Scottish experience (Employment Committee, 1985/6). The issues were of most concern to trade unionists. While criticisms were sharply raised, however, and, occasionally, individual schemes were put under the microscope, at no time did these concerns impede the development of the YTS or threaten significantly to undermine trade union support for the scheme.

There were different views on the apprenticeship issue, although the YTS proved capable of retaining the support of almost everyone. As we have seen, apprentice training had declined sharply in Britain and in Scotland. In government circles this was partly welcomed (and had been since the influential Central Policy Review Staff report of 1980), as apprenticeship was viewed suspiciously as a restrictive practice which needed to be removed to free the labour market, and as a means by which the trade unions, particularly the craft unions, acquired undue influence over training matters. Employers had different and varying views. In craft-intensive industries there was a concern at the future supply of skilled labour, but also, perhaps a feeling that employer-sponsored training would not pick up again until trainee wages were lowered. Broadly speaking these different viewpoints saw the YTS as a welcome means of quickly moving forward. In a few sectors characterized by small firms and self employment, but previously with apprenticeship and a tradition of 'timeserving', there were fears that the YTS would lead to a lowering of standards. The President of the Scottish Decorators' Federation described the YTS as the 'latest threat to our industry' (*Glasgow Herald*, 30 October 1987). However such criticisms were very rare on the employers' side. Considering the economy as a whole, and not only those sectors which had a tradition of apprenticeship, the MSC argued that the YTS had a greatly beneficial effect on the level of initial skill training (Committee of Public Accounts, 1985/6).

The situation was no less complex on the trade union side (see Chapter 10). Throughout Britain, educational unions welcomed the scheme, in part because they had argued for improved provision for school leavers and in part because the MSC expenditures would safeguard lecturers' jobs which could otherwise have been vulnerable, for example in college departments that had previously taught employer-sponsored apprentices and trainees. Other unions saw in the general nature of the YTS, with its broad 'occupational training families', a move away from craft concepts of 'skill' and a possible opening up of some areas of work to different forms of unionization.

The craft unions had for over a decade been concerned about the decline in craft training and the effects that this would have on industry as well as on their own ability to recruit young people. In some sectors, like engineering, there remained a level of recruitment to apprenticeship sufficient for trade unionists to feel that they had a basis for opposing the YTS, as a wage-cutting, apprentice-displacing, deskilling scheme. This kind of opposition tended to be local but was perhaps most evident in engineering. Some craft unions felt that the YTS was an acceptable scheme given that apprenticeship training scarcely existed. Some unions saw involvement in the YTS as a possible means of retaining some apprentice traditions which would otherwise quickly disappear. In these cases the unions generally also viewed the YTS as a possible route to increasing recruitment among young people. These factors were partly behind the trade unions' reasoning in the first national agreements to recognize the YTS for the electrical contracting and construction sectors. In the former sector the trade union agreed in effect to a reduction in apprentice rates of pay in order to maintain training rates. In construction, the unions agreed to a scheme which gave the construction ITB the key role in the industry's YTS arrangements. Twenty-two thousand young people entered the CITB's scheme in the first year of the YTS.

If apprenticeship was controversial it was also complex. Much simpler, and potentially divisive, was the issue of 'job substitution'. YTS recruitment to employer-based schemes was, in theory, required to be additional to intended normal recruitment. In practice this was a major issue which affected the spread of the YTS to industries and firms where recruitment and training were collectively bargained since it was relatively easy to see what was additional and what was not (see Chapter 11). However, this situation did not obtain in the majority of workplaces which were faced with the YTS as a practical issue. The difficulty here was that 'additionality' was not a simple concept, particularly if the structure of employment was changing within the firm. For its part, the MSC did not lay down any clear guidelines on this point, and, indeed some of the marketing aimed at employers came perilously close to encouraging them to save on labour costs by substituting. Some early studies claimed to find high 'displacement' rates.

For example, a study commissioned by the Scottish Council (Development and Industry) claimed that the real job substitution rate of the YTS in Dundee and Renfrew was very high. The study tried to identify situations where it was a feasible option to employ a YTS trainee in the place of a paid employee. Among the 98 employers surveyed, the study claimed to find a significant level of substitution (SCDI, 1985; Employment Committee 1985/6). Despite early controversy, the issue soon faded into obscurity. In part this was because every approach to additionality required its measurement year-on-year, so that once the YTS had established itself the problem effectively disappeared. In part it was because the MSC abandoned the additionality requirement in 1985 (Committee of Public Accounts, 1985/6).

ADULT TRAINING

The third NTI objective was initially put on the back burner, at least in so far as the balance of MSC expenditures were concerned. Adult training had always been the Cinderella of vocational training in Britain and the appearance of the NTI did not immediately change things. While there was a growing problem of long-term adult unemployment from the late 1970s, this was not the kind of public political concern that was raised by massive unemployment among school leavers. The problem of skill shortages appeared to re-emerge in the early and mid-1980s, with the critics of government policy pointing out the paradox of shortages coexisting with historically high levels of unemployment. However, the problems were nothing like as severe as in the 1960s. The CBI pointed out that while in the 1960s and 1970s it was not uncommon for 30 per cent of companies to report skill shortages; in 1987 the proportion was nearer 10 per cent (Employment Committee, 1986/7), and this level of skill shortage was perceived to be significant only in the relatively buoyant labour markets in the South of England. At any rate, the problems in the adult labour market did not bring forth any large-scale new programme.

An Adult Training Strategy (ATS) was launched in 1984, following MSC consultations and a government White Paper, 'Training for Jobs' (Cmnd. 9135). At first, the ATS was backed by many fewer resources than had been poured into the YTS. It consisted mainly of MSC attempts to exhort employers to undertake more adult training (through an Adult Training Campaign, which cost some £1.7 million in 1985/6), together with improved marketing of the various, generally small, schemes which the MSC already ran. In February 1985, the Scottish Office Minister for Industry and Education launched the Adult Training Campaign north of the border.

Some new pilot ATS schemes emerged in 1984/5, but again these were very modest initiatives compared with the MSC's main programmes. Initially then, the NTI offered nothing new for adults. There was (as we have seen) some expansion of the Community Programme and the development of some new initiatives like the JTS. However, initially, the absence of a new initiative with the vision of the YTS meant that the adult training picture remained confused, with one very large DE scheme, the CP, and a plethora of smaller MSC initiatives.

The main training programmes for adults did change, and numbers going through MSC adult training increased, even though there was no new significant injection of resources. The TOPS programme was succeeded by three initiatives: first, the Job Training Scheme (JTS) which continued occupational training; second, the Wider Opportunities Training Programme (WOTP) which continued the work preparation courses started by TOPS; third, the small Open Tech programme of distance learning (see Chapter 4). Alongside these the new ATS pilot schemes were developed, though most of these were relatively small in scale.

The Job Training Programme was a grouping of about eight occupationally relevant training schemes. These included: grants to employers, the National Priority Skills Scheme, occupational training under the JTS, training for enterprise, access to information technology and provision for special needs groups (including WOW courses). The types of course offered within the Job Training Programme varied widely, from an average of 7.5 days per trainee in Local Training Grants, to an average of one year in NPSS. The JTS was the largest of the adult training schemes, catering for 183 000 trainees at a cost of £201 million.

The WOTP had 54 900 entrants throughout Britain in 1985/6, at an overall cost of £23.9 million. Over 80 per cent of the short, work-preparation courses offered were structured so as to allow participants to remain in receipt of unemployment or social security benefits.

In Scotland the various adult training programmes together cost over £21 million in 1985/6. There were over 22 700 adult entrants to the various schemes, of which the largest were local grants to employees, JTS and WOTP. Over 5 300 trainees were assisted through grants to employers, while over 5 100 received JTS occupational training. The WOTP had over 4 600 entrants in 1985/6.

Overall though the adult training picture remained patchy, confused and poorly resourced compared with school leaver training. When major reform proposals did emerge in 1987/8 (Cmnd. 316) there were estimated to be 30 different forms of training, work preparation and work experience provided by the MSC and the DE.

REVIEW OF THE COMMUNITY PROGRAMME

The Community Programme was criticized for its lack of skill training and its largely part-time provision. It was also criticized for offering little to women. From the government's point of view the CP was a terribly expensive scheme and would remain so as long as it paid the 'rate for the job' rather than a participating allowance. In addition the scheme did not lead into anything which would encourage adults to move into self-employment, or to create small firms or community businesses. These priorities had begun to be expressed, as we have seen, in Skillcentre and JTS courses, and in the Enterprise Allowance Scheme, which subsidized the initial period of self-employment.

Indeed the CP rules, with their exclusive concern for 'community benefit', worked against the government's growing concern to foster 'enterprise'. In 1986 the MSC had launched its Enterprise Projects Experiment in Strathclyde to explore ways in which the CP could be used to launch new businesses. The CP was reviewed against these new concerns and priorities, and the Conservatives gave notice of major changes to the CP and to payment levels in it as early as the 1987 election campaign (Chapter 16). The perceived threat to the CP as the main Special Employment Measure mobilized considerable opposition particularly from the voluntary sector in Scotland (Chapter 7) but also from trade unions.

The first major departure from the old-style adult Special Programme with its insistence on the 'rate for the job' and the requirement of trade union approval came with the introduction in 1987 of the New Job Training Scheme (NJTS), which caused a lot of confusion because the old JTS continued as a MSC programme. The NJTS caused further confusion by appearing to be a hybrid scheme that combined elements of training and of special measures. The scheme was initially piloted in nine locations in Britain, including Dundee. Plans to expand the NJTS were announced before these pilots had been evaluated.

As an anti-unemployment scheme, the NJTS were radical in that it moved away from the accepted practice of paying the 'rate for the job', offering instead an allowance which was equivalent to the participant's benefit plus some travel costs. The issue of the 'rate for the job' became the main point of criticism, and the NJTS, though small in scale (there were some 3 000 entrants in Scotland by the end of August 1987, less than one-third of the planned figure), became by far the most controversial part of the whole NTI. The government argued that the scheme was better than the CP in that it was a genuine training scheme and that the programmes were individually tailored. However, the individually tailored nature of the NJTS raised the issue of whether it was appropriate for AMBS to vet scheme proposals (and by implication whether there was any role for trade unions at the planning level). Critics of the scheme pointed to the reduced incomes of (most) trainees, argued that there were insufficient resources to ensure good quality training, and alleged that the NJTS was a small step towards the introduction of an American-style 'Workfare' system which would eventually compel the un-employed to undergo 'training' in return for benefit. Opposition to the scheme was perhaps stronger in Scotland than in Britain generally, in part no doubt because Scotland voted differently from the British pattern in the 1987 election. Throughout Scotland local authorities, trade unions, and many voluntary organizations expressed their opposition to the NJTS.

Although the NJTS was a small scheme and a tiny part of MSC activities, the controversies around it were highly significant. On the issue of the appropriate means of paying unemployed adults who participate in special schemes, the broad consensus which had underpinned the growth of the MSC for over a decade began to look fragile (see Chapters 1 and 10). In 1988, when proposals emerged to replace the CP and the other 30 plus adult schemes with a new Employment Training (ET) scheme, the same controversies re-emerged and the fragile consensus finally shat-tered. In Scotland, there was the additional dimension that critics of ET saw it as a scheme perhaps suited to the buoyant labour markets of SE England but hopelessly irrelevant to Scottish needs. From different perspectives the trade unions and leading figures in the Scottish CBI argued for a new and different approach to the reform of adult training in Scotland.

## EMPLOYMENT SERVICES

When the MSC was set up in 1973, it was given the task of continuing the modernization of Britain's Employment Services. This is perhaps the least-written-about part of the MSC's acitivities. Throughout most of the 1970s and early 1980s the level of demand for the employment services increased as unemployment rose. The employment services themselves did not seem to be controversial for most of that period. Opposition voices demanded more resources and civil service trade unions called for better staffing levels, but the policies which shaped the employment services were not in themselves matters of controversy until a number of changes were implemented by the MSC. The major changes that gave rise to controversy were: the ending of the occupational guidance system, reductions in Jobcentre staffing levels (see Chapters 13 and 16), the introduction of voluntary registration, the 'hiving off' of the Professional and Executive Recruitment agency on a commercial basis and the rein-tegration of the employment services with the administration of benefits (see Chapter 16).

By 1979 there were over 550 Jobcentres throughout Britain. These employed over 60 per cent of MSC's local office staff. In Scotland, the network was expanding at this time; 10 new Jobcentres were opened in 1979/80, bringing the total to 74. The system aimed to be flexible in responding to labour market change; a temporary office was set up at Sullom Voe to assist as the work force at the oil terminal grew rapidly to nearly 7 000. The system also aimed to deliver services to the users as efficiently as possible. By 1980, 80 per cent of Employment Services Division (ESD) local office staff were working in the Jobcentres, and despite the pressures of rising unemployment, they were filling over 80 per cent of the vacancies notified to them and finding jobs for one in three of those leaving the unemployment register.

Following 'efficiency reviews,' staffing levels were sharply reduced in the Jobcentres (see Chapters 13 and 16) at the same time as rising unemployment greatly increased the demand for services. By April 1986, there were 980 MSC staff working in Scotland's Jobcentres, out of a total of 1 194 in the Employment Division (ED), and an MSC total of 2 174. In 1985/6 some £16.4 million was spent on Jobcentre services in Scotland, with total ED expenditures standing at £30.8 million. By this time there were over 120 Jobcentres in Scotland.

The Employment Services offered by the MSC included a wide range of activities within which the Jobcentre functions were the largest. These included Professional Executive Recruitment (PER), which had three offices in Scotland. These offices handled over 1 200 placings (11 per cent of the GB total) in 1985/6 and earned fee income for this. PER also filled executive level vacancies in the MSC's Special Programmes and dealt with applications for higher level courses which were sponsored by the MSC's TOPS scheme (though these higher level courses were early casualties of the cuts in TOPS provision). In April 1983, PER was moved on to a full cost recovery basis to operate at arm's length from the MSC.

Up until 1980 an occupational guidance system was operated. Over 4 000 interviews were given each year in the late 1970s. Applications for Training Services Division's TOPS scheme (some 17 600 in 1979/80) were dealt with by the employment services. The ED also administered the Employment Transfer Scheme set up to help people move to available jobs. In addition, the ED offered the MSC's available services to people with disabilities.

In 1985/6 the Jobcentres placed about 8 000 disabled people in Scotland and planned to increase this to 9 500 the following year (3 800 of the placings being in the Community Programme). Some 2 000 places were available for severely disabled people in sheltered workshops. The ED operated 4 Employment Rehabilitation Centres in Scotland, at Bellshill, Hillington, Edinburgh (Granton), and Dundee. During 1984/5 over 2 000 people completed ERC courses at these centres. The impact of these and other MSC services and programmes on disabled people is dealt with in Chapter 13.

THE ENTERPRISE ALLOWANCE SCHEME

The Employment Services also administered a number of the MSC's labour market schemes. The CP, described above, was administered on behalf of the Department of Employment. The next most important of these schemes was the Enterprise Allowance Scheme (EAS). While the EAS was much smaller than the CP it was arguably of some strategic importance in that it directly promoted the government's objective of increasing the level of self-employment and new business growth in the economy (see Chapters 1 and 16).

The EAS was piloted in a number of locations throughout Britain in 1982/3. The Scottish pilot took place in North Ayrshire. The scheme gave unemployed people an income subsidy to assist them in the crucial start-up phase of establishing a small business or becoming self-employed. The pilot catered for some 409 people and was run through the Jobcentres with business support and advice provided by the Scottish Development Agency (Small Business Division).

The EAS was extended to all parts of Britain after the 1983 budget. The scheme supported unemployed people able to show that they had available £1 000 to invest in their business by providing an income supplement of £40 per week for one year. In Scotland the scheme had an initial budget of £10.5 million, and by the end of 1983 over 1 500 people were participating in it. In 1986/7, the last full year for which the MSC had responsibility, the scheme cost £12.8 million and over 8 300 people entered it during the year.

HELPING THE LONGTERM ADULT UNEMPLOYED

The Restart programme was introduced in 1986 with the aim of contacting every long-term unemployed person with the offer of a counselling interview, usually at their nearest Jobcentre. (This programme is discussed in Chapter 16 below.) The programme was widely welcomed (despite its compulsory interviews) as a means of helping to break down some of the isolation caused by long-term unemployment and as a way of securing better take up of the available services by the unemployed. Between July 1986 and March 1988, some 4.4 million people were contacted throughout Britain, of whom 3.5 million were interviewed. The average interview lasted 30 minutes and was estimated to cost £13. The objective was to offer every interviewee an option from the Restart menu, which included: paid employment, a CP place, a Jobclub place, entry to the EAS, a place on a training scheme, a Jobstart allowance for accepting work paying less than £80 per week, and voluntary work. The Employment Service claimed that 89 per cent of interviewees received a positive offer of help through the Restart process.

In April 1988, it was announced that all long-term unemployed people would be called for interview every 6 months and that all 18–24-year-olds unemployed for between 6 and 12 months would be guaranteed, from

September, an offer of a place on the EAS, a place on Employment Training or a place in a Jobclub. Questionnaires were introduced, and the information required of interviewees increased.

Early in 1988, ten areas including Dundee, were used to pilot new Restart interview forms. The purpose of these was twofold: to enhance the interview by providing more background information for the counsellor, and to permit checks to be made on the claimant's availability for work.

Information given to Parliament showed that substantial numbers of claimants were being referred back to their unemployment benefit offices because doubts emerged about the genuineness of their claimed availability for work. In Dundee, for example, 100 claimants were referred back to their UBO in April and May 1988. The re-establishment of the pre-1974 link between employment services and benefits administration made the employment services a matter of political controversy for the first time since the establishment of the MSC. However, by October 1987 responsibility for administering these and other employment services had reverted back to the Department of Employment. In October 1987, the major employment services passed from the MSC to the DE. This involved over £33 million of MSC expenditure passing outwith the remit of the MSC's Scottish structures.

## THE MSC, SCHOOLS AND THE EDUCATION SYSTEM

In 1983, the MSC introduced a new programme called the Technical and Vocational Education Initiative (TVEI) into schools in England and Wales. This initiative was controversial in so far as it had really stemmed from ideas held by David Young, Chairman of the MSC between 1982 and 1984, and was brought forward without the courtesy of the usual consultations. The aim was to introduce more courses in technical and vocational areas for 14–18-year-olds in schools, and to enhance technical and vocational education within the curriculum. (The TVEI is discussed in a number of chapters in this book, particularly Chapter 3. See also Chapters 6, 11 and 13.)

In Scotland, the scheme was additionally controversial in that it was perceived by some to be an English innovation foisted on to the Scottish education system. The main teachers' union, the EIS, remained hostile to the TVEI for some time and delayed the spread of the scheme to all the Scottish education authorities.

In Scotland the encouragement of similar courses for 14–16-year-olds was already underway through new courses at SCE Standard Grade, and for 16–18-year-olds through the non-advanced vocational certificate being developed as part of the Action Plan. Some welcomed the TVEI as a further stimulus to these developments. However, many saw the TVEI as redundant in the Scottish context. Agreement was reached to introduce the new MSC scheme into Scotland in January 1984, after consultations

involving the SED and the COSLA. The TVEI Steering Group for England
and Wales was expanded to include some Scottish representation.

Under the scheme the MSC funded pilot projects designed for 200–250
school pupils. In 1984, five Scottish projects, involving a total of 1 156
pupils, began. These were located in the Renfrew and Glasgow divisions
of Strathclyde, in Fife, in the Borders Region, and in Dumfries and
Galloway. Lothian joined the following year, with a scheme involving
243 pupils. By 1986/7 TVEI was costing £5.4 million in Scotland, and plans
existed to expand this figure to £12.7 million by 1989/90.

In 1985, the MSC's role in schools was increased further through the
TRIST (TVEI-related in service training) scheme. The objective of TRIST was
to offer teacher training which would promote more practical and relevant teaching across the whole curriculum. Applications for TRIST funding were submitted by all Scottish education authorities (except
Shetland, which decided not to take part) to the TVEI unit in London. By
the end of TRIST in March 1987, over 20 000 Scottish teachers and lecturers had passed through its training programmes.

However, MSC's impact on education went far beyond schools. The
YTS programme (along with smaller schemes, like TOPS and JTS) was of
major importance to the further education sector. There was considerable FE involvement in the Restart programme. In 1987 a major £100
million 'Enterprise in Higher Education' initiative was announced, the
aim of which was to introduce some element of 'enterprise' training into
every undergraduate programme in Britain's universities (see Chapter
5).

THE REVIEW OF VOCATIONAL QUALIFICATIONS

In 1985, the government put forward proposals (Cmnd. 9482) to review
the structure of vocational education assessment and certification in
England and Wales. A major improvement to the existing system was
seen as vital to the promotion of opportunities for progression, which
had been a major concern at the time of NTI. The Review was intended
initially to focus on improving the structure of qualifications to meet the
needs of the YTS. It was not intended to extend the review to Scotland,
largely because the progress made under the Action Plan placed Scotland somewhere ahead of England and Wales in relation to these issues.
In 1986 following the Review, the government proposed (Cmnd. 9823) to
set up a National Council for Vocational Qualifications (NCVQ) to effect
the necessary improvements in England and Wales, in particular by
establishing a new framework for vocational qualifications. The 1986
White Paper noted that the NCVQ's remit would not apply to Scotland 'for
the time being'. However, in 1988 the issue of the NCVQ's extension to
Scotland surfaced as a major controversy. The Secretary of State concluded that SCOTVEC should remain the lead organization for these

matters in Scotland, rejecting the proposed extension of the NCVQ's remit to cover Scotland.

## THE TRAINING 'MARKET'

In the 1980s the MSC introduced a number of initiatives which were designed to assist the functioning of the training market, in particular by improving the quality of data at local level, and by encouraging the more effective use of that data. In general, of course, it is believed that markets require good information in order to function. Alongside this there was also the belief that improved information flows might themselves help to reduce unemployment by facilitating the matching up of some of the unemployed to some of the registered vacancies. Overall these various initiatives had as their over-riding concern the better identification of employers short-term skill requirements by employers themselves and by local suppliers of training.

In 1986 the MSC piloted its Computer Assisted Local Labour Market Information (CALLMI) system. The aim was to make the data collection carried out by the MSC's area offices in Scotland consistent and more easily used. This was seen as vital to improving the local effectiveness of service delivery. The initial surveys of employers concentrated on engineering, construction, textiles, hotel and catering and distribution.

In July 1986, the Training Access Point (TAP) initiative was announced (see Chapter 16). The aim here was the rapid establishment of a network of user-friendly access points, based in libraries, Jobcentres and colleges. A number of pilot networks were set up in Scotland in 1986/7. Network Scotland Ltd. established 3 networks covering Glasgow, the rest of Strathclyde and the Highlands. These projects involved 17 TAPS, with one mobile access point in each region covered. Taytec Ltd. set up a project with 8 TAPS, 6 in Dundee and 2 mobile points covering Perthshire and Angus. The Amalgamated Engineering Union (AEU) set up a TAP project run from its Birmingham office, but partly based in Edinburgh, aiming to provide access to training information for union members.

Local Employers' Networks (LEN) represented a new attempt to re-mould the training infrastructure around some 110 local groupings of employers throughout Britain. To an extent the initiative was influenced by perceptions of the West German system in which local chambers of commerce played a very active role. The initiative was supported by the Association of British Chambers of Commerce, the CBI and the MSC, with the objective of establishing at least one LEN in each education authority area (with a £20 000 pump-priming grant). Through the LEN, it was planned to encourage local employers to play a more systematic and forward-looking role in vocational education and training. The first Scottish LEN was established by the Aberdeen Chamber of Commerce, with others following in Dundee and in Central Scotland. Of 14 planned, 11 were in place, or about to start, by the autumn of 1988, with the rural

areas, and those areas without a strong chamber of commerce or Enterprise Trust reportedly proving the most difficult to develop. The Local
Collaborative Projects (LCP) initiative was introduced in 1984, again with
the aim of making the infrastructure more responsive to employers'
perceived short-term needs. In Scotland LCPS were jointly supported by
the SED and the MSC. Particular LCPS have also been supported, directly
or indirectly, by the SDA, local authorities, Chambers of Commerce and
other training organizations. Projects have focused on areas of skill, on
industries and on geographical areas. In each case the aim has been to
produce recommendations for improving the relevance of training on
which the colleges and other providers will act at the end of the project.
By 1987 some 40 projects had been approved in Scotland (see Chapters 5
and 16).

Early in the 1980s, the STUC gave evidence to the Scottish Select Committee (1981/2). The STUC pointed out that at the end of 1980, there were
nearly 75 000 Scots engaged in the main programmes then run by the MSC
and the DE. In itself, this level of involvement was taken as an indictment
of the state of the Scottish economy.

Yet, this was by no means the peak of MSC activity or the greatest
extent of MSC's impact. By the mid-1980s the MSC had become a very large
and wide-reaching agency. Its programmes cost far more in Scotland
than the industrial development activities of the Scottish Development
Agency. By 1986/7, the last full year before the MSC began to contract as
some of its functions were removed, the various youth and adult programmes had grown to formidable proportions, such that the MSC was
directly affecting some very large parts of Scottish society. In that year,
the MSC's Employment Services in Scotland catered for over 8 000 EAS
entrants, some 24 000 Jobcentre placings, and over 147 500 Restart
interviews.

In 1986/7, there were in Scotland, over 51 000 entrants to the YTS and
over 42 000 entrants to the various adult training schemes. Some 38 000
adults entered the Community Programme. Given that the various
training schemes and special programmes were operated through a
network of contractors and subcontractors (including employers,
employers' associations, colleges, training boards, voluntary bodies,
youth organizations, local authorities and churches) the MSC was clearly
affecting in some way a very wide range of organizations and individuals. By 1988, virtually all parts of Scottish society had some contact with
the MSC's operations.

Note: Except where otherwise stated, the data and information concerning the MSC and its programmes has been taken from the Scottish section
of the MSC's Annual Reports, and from the MSC's Corporate Plans for
Scotland.

OTHER SOURCES AND REFERENCES

1. Central Policy Review Staff, 1980, Education, Training and Industrial Performance, HMSO, London.
2. Commission for Racial Equality, 1981, Response to the New Training Initiative, CRE, London.
3. Equal Opportunities Commission, 1981, Response to the New Training Initiative, EOC, Manchester.
4. House of Commons, Committee of Public Accounts:
   i) 1982/83. Special Employment Measures, HC 235, HMSO, London.
   ii) 1985/86, Vocational Education and Training, HC 46, HMSO, London.
5. House of Commons, Estimates Committee, 1966/67, Manpower Training for Industry, HC 548, HMSO, London.
6. House of Commons, National Audit Office 1986/87, Report by the Comptroller and Auditor General, Department of Employment and Manpower Services Commission: Adult Training Strategy, HC 149, HMSO, London.
7. House of Commons, Select Committee on Employment:
   i) 1985/86, Special Employment Measures and the Long-Term Unemployed, HC 199, HMSO, London
   ii) 1986/87, Skill Shortages, HC 197, HMSO, London.
8. House of Commons, Select Committee on Scottish Affairs, 1981/82, Youth Unemployment and Training, HC 96, HMSO, London.
9. Cmnd 8455, 1981, A New Training Initiative, A Programme for Action, HMSO, London.
   Cmnd 9135, 1984, Training for Jobs, HMSO, London.
   Cmnd 9474, 1985, Employment: the Challenge for the Nation, HMSO, London.
   Cmnd 9482, 1985, Education and Training for Young People, HMSO, London.
   Cmnd 9823, 1986, Working Together – Education and Training, HMSO, London.
   Cm 316, 1988, Training For Employment, HMSO, London.
10. Manpower Services Commission:
    i) 1977, Training for Skills: A Programme for Action
    ii) 1978, TOPS Review
    iii) 1980, Outlook on Training, A Review of the 1973 Employment and Training Act
    iv) 1982, Report of the Youth Task Group
11. Perry, P. J. C., 1976, *The Evolution of British Manpower Policy*, BACIE, London.
12. Perry, P. J. C., 1984, *Sand in the Sandwich*, BACIE, London.
13. Raffe, D., 1984, Youth Unemployment and the MSC, 1977–83, in D. McCrone (ed), *The Scottish Government Yearbook*, University of Edinburgh.
14. Raffe, D., 1988a, The Story so far: Research on Education, Training and the Labour Market from the Scottish Surveys, in D. Raffe (ed), *Education and the Youth Labour Market*, Falmer, Lewes.
15. Raffe, D., 1988b, Going with the Grain: Youth Training in Transition, in S. Brown (ed.), *Education in Transition*, SCRE, Edinburgh.

16. Raffe, D. and G. Courtenay, 1988, 16–18 on Both Sides of the
    Border, in D. Raffe (ed.), *Education and the Youth Labour Market*,
    Falmer, Lewes.
17. The Unemployment Unit: regular Bulletins and Briefings,
    London.

# PART II

# Scottish Education and the MSC

# CHAPTER 3. EDITORS' INTRODUCTION

The introduction of TVEI pilot projects in schools in 1982 marked a major shift in the relationship between the MSC and the secondary schools. The pilot projects were introduced specifically to improve the technical and vocational education of 14–18-year-olds. Other programmes such as the YTS had already made an impact directly or indirectly on secondary education, but not to the extent which was to occur under TVEI. The author estimates that by 1988 schools in every region and division in Scotland were involved with the MSC through TVEI.

This chapter, therefore, focuses on TVEI, highlighting the initial suspicion and opposition from teachers within Scotland to the implementation of a programme imposed by the government without the normal consultative process and with its emphasis on technical and vocational education. The impact of this initiative on the curriculum of Scottish secondary schools and the management of secondary education is discussed within the context of the education/vocationalism debate (see also Chapter 4). It is intended that TVEI should extend to all schools by the mid-1990s, but, as the chapter indicates, the long-term impact of the initiative has yet to be revealed and much will depend on the resources available and the willingness of employers to respond.

# 3

## THE IMPACT OF THE MSC ON SECONDARY EDUCATION

CATHY HOWIESON

INTRODUCTION

The announcement of the Technical and Vocational Education Initiative (TVEI) in late 1982 gave the Manpower Services Commission a direct involvement in secondary education for the first time. While some welcomed the announcement of the scheme, the dominant reaction in educational circles, and especially in Scotland, was one of opposition, and indeed shock. Until that time MSC programmes, for example the Youth Training Scheme (YTS), had had little direct impact on secondary education.

TVEI could scarcely have failed to raise many educational hackles: a scheme dreamt up by politicians without consultation with the normal educational channels; funded by an external government agency outside the usual methods of educational finance; administered by a non-elected body, the MSC, whose remit was concerned with training, not education; and as an initiative which had the aim of stimulating the provision of technical and vocational education. TVEI was seen as direct government interference in, indeed control of, the curriculum, and moreover a control that would move it in a vocational direction, ushering in a return to an élitist, selective, educational system in which certain pupils would take TVEI courses while the more able followed an academic curriculum. In Scotland opposition to TVEI had an extra dimension on a number of counts: comprehensive education had become more widely established and supported than in England, and the concept and aims of TVEI appeared redundant in the Scottish context because of Standard Grade and Action Plan developments. As an initiative that bypassed the Scottish Education Department (SED) and was run by an Agency which regarded Scotland merely as another region within its overall structure, it seemed a direct threat to the independence of Scottish education.

The first TVEI projects were self-consciously pilot projects from which lessons were to be learned, but before even the majority of regions had started projects, let alone any pilot scheme run its full course, the government announced the extension of TVEI to all schools in July 1986 in the White Paper 'Working Together – Education and Training' (Cmnd. 9823). TVEI was here to stay whatever the results of pilot projects. It is timely, as the extension of TVEI has become a reality, to consider the impact of the MSC's intervention in secondary education.

It is necessary to make several caveats at this point. It is difficult to write about TVEI in Scotland over the last four years because projects vary enormously, and because their diversity is compounded by the way the stated aims and criteria of TVEI have been interpreted and reinterpreted in those years and the emphases of projects changed. Bearing this in mind, I consider in this chapter whether TVEI has led to the MSC exerting undue control over the curriculum and the way secondary education is managed. The chapter focuses on the Scottish dimension of TVEI: whether there have been particular problems for Scottish education in the face of a British initiative, how the MSC's aims and intentions have been influenced by the current developments in Scottish education and finally it speculates on the longer-term impact of the MSC on secondary education in Scotland. Although the major focus is TVEI, MSC involvement through TRIST (TVEI-Related In-Service Training) is also discussed briefly.

## TVEI IN SCOTLAND

In 1982 and 1983 few in Scotland welcomed the idea of TVEI. The immediate reaction of the SED was to announce that the initiative was not needed in Scotland and would not apply here. It took months of behind-the-scenes negotiation before the Convention of Scottish Local Authorities (COSLA) and the Secretary of State for Scotland accepted the inevitability of TVEI, or at least the impossibility of obtaining the funding by other means. Hence the delay in introducing it into Scotland; it came a year behind the first pilot projects in England and Wales. In 1984 the first five pilot projects started in Scotland, in the Borders and Fife Regions, in Dumfries and Galloway Region and in the Renfrew and Glasgow Divisions of Strathclyde Region. The Lothian pilot project began in 1985, followed by one in Tayside in 1986. By 1988 there were projects in all regions in Scotland and all divisions in Strathclyde.

Under the TVEI pilot, participating local authorities chose a number of schools and colleges and a limited cohort of young people within each institution to take part. Most pilot TVEI projects are based on a consortium of three, four or five schools and an associated college, and on a cohort of 200 to 250 pupils in each of five consecutive year groups. Participation in TVEI is voluntary, but in practice schools and projects have varied in their recruitment policies. The pilot TVEI projects have set out to 'explore and test the ways of organising and managing the education of 14–18 year-olds across the ability range' (MSC, 1984). TVEI's ambition is to give 14–18 year-old boys and girls of all abilities a more relevant and practical preparation for adulthood and working life through a four-year course of general, technical and vocational education.

TVEI programmes consist of a common core and options. Together the core and options typically make up about 30 per cent of Scottish TVEI pupils' timetables. In Scotland the core usually includes information technology, personal and social development, careers education, work experience and a residential experience (a week or so spent in a different environment to help broaden pupils' experience as part of social and personal development programmes). Options include subjects chosen by students to meet their needs and interests such as business studies, computing, catering, textiles, control technology, pneumatics and caring. Many established curriculum areas have also been 'enhanced' through TVEI funding. Such enhancements mean adding to existing subjects by providing resources to give a more technological dimension to the curriculum or to help change teaching methods. English, mathematics, music, art, geography and home economics are all examples of subjects that have been enhanced. Both in these enhanced subjects and in the TVEI core and options, there has been an attempt to introduce technology across the curriculum. Equally important, TVEI is also about changing styles of teaching, learning and assessment. Projects have tried to emphasize problem-solving approaches, experiential learning and more negotiated learning and to move away from traditional assessment procedures.

## SCOTTISH PROBLEMS

The MSC is an agency with a remit that is Britain-wide whose main focus is inevitably England and Wales. TVEI reflects this. It fits into the English education system and as such has created considerable management difficulties for Scottish TVEI projects. This has been particularly evident at the post-16 stage where the Scottish and English systems differ most.

TVEI was conceived as a four-year programme for 14–18 year-olds, but in reality, in both Scotland and England, projects have lost almost half of their cohorts at 16. To compensate for this, projects recruit new pupils at the end of S4 ('infill' in TVEI-speak). Thereafter English projects have been able to retain the majority of TVEI pupils, old and new, who generally stay for the next two years. Scottish projects face further difficulties because of the distinctive characteristics of post-compulsory education in Scotland. They have to cope with the Scottish phenomenon of the Christmas leaver, so that TVEI projects in Scotland experience another exodus of pupils at the Christmas of fifth year. Many more pupils then leave at the end of S5, since in Scotland, unlike England with its two-year A-level courses, less than half of those who complete fifth year stay for a sixth year. TVEI projects in Scotland have had to cope with not one but three significant transition points. These have caused major management and resource problems in coping with TVEI trainees who are over 16, as well as difficulties in providing a coherent and progressive programme for pupils.

The nature of the fifth-year in Scottish education causes a particular difficulty. For the majority in S5 attempting Highers, this year is very pressurized and the timetable crowded because of the nature of the Higher as essentially a two-term course. There is little room for TVEI if pupils have a full timetable of Highers. The consequence has been that usually academic TVEI pupils either have a very limited involvement with TVEI in S5 or drop out altogether. The MSC have been reluctant to sanction variations in Scotland. For example projects have had to argue very strongly to be allowed to 'infill' pupils after Christmas of S5 and the MSC have been particularly reluctant to allow 'infill' after the summer of fifth year.

## THE IMPACT OF TVEI ON THE MANAGEMENT OF SECONDARY EDUCATION

After some initial statements by Lord Young, then chairman of the MSC, that MSC skill centres would be used and other establishments set up if necessary to implement TVEI, it soon became clear that the MSC expected TVEI to be developed and delivered by local authorities. Consequently, from the beginning, TVEI's radical intentions were mediated by its delivery through the educational establishment and thus subjected to existing practices, customs and prejudices. This may have been inevitable, but does seem ironic. TVEI had been allocated deliberately to the MSC, rather than the Department of Education and Science and Scottish Education Department, as an agency which Ministers believed was not hide-bound by traditional educational attitudes and beliefs and which had a history of quick delivery of major new programmes. The consequences of delivering TVEI through existing educational structures have been especially evident in Scotland where both educational traditions and also recent developments have limited the impact of MSC on the secondary-education sector. Nevertheless, to look at the other side of the coin, the delivery of TVEI through local authorities has had an effect on them and their style of management and operation.

### Bidding

In the first place, local authorities were invited to submit proposals to the MSC to take part in TVEI, to make a 'bid' for funding, stating their intentions and justifying their claims. This 'bidding' procedure has been a novel funding arrangement for local authorities in relation to secondary education for which they normally receive central government finance through the Rates Support Grant. Some have found this procedure, especially the meetings that are involved, somewhat disconcerting. 'Put through the wringer' was how it was described by a member of the directorate in one authority. Authorities have had to explain and justify their TVEI proposals, state the planned outcomes for their projects and specify how they are to be achieved and how they will be measured. It is interesting, however, to see how some authorities have adopted MSC devices and practices, for example, by asking their schools to make bids for finance and resources even outside of TVEI, rather than allocating them on the usual per capita basis.

## New structures

One of the most noticeable effects of TVEI in the area of management has been the creation of a new management structure. Project directors or co-ordinators have been appointed to manage each TVEI project and school co-ordinators appointed within the TVEI schools. The post of project co-ordinator cuts across the normal management relationships and responsibilities, in relation to head teachers and to the directorate. Although project co-ordinators are usually responsible to a member of the directorate, at the same time they are also responsible to the MSC for the operation of the project. Crucially, the role and power of the project co-ordinator, especially through the control of substantial resources, impinges on the traditional autonomy of head teachers. Most co-ordinators effectively control the level of extra resources, including staffing, that goes into TVEI schools, and their budgets can be larger than those of head teachers. The project co-ordinator also has responsibility for the school co-ordinator in each school, who is therefore in the difficult position of having two masters: the project co-ordinator and the head teacher. The creation of this new management structure is one reason for opposition to TVEI from the main teachers' union, the Educational Institute of Scotland (EIS). It sees these new posts as creating a separate external decision-making structure which is inimicable to the normal educational management of the school. Most co-ordinators are sensitive to the potential difficulties and anxious to avoid confrontation. Apart from any other considerations, a head teacher can easily hinder or subvert TVEI developments in his or her school. But there have been instances of difficulties between head teachers and co-ordinators.

The introduction of posts such as project co-ordinator and school co-ordinator and additional teaching and guidance posts has created new career opportunities. Particularly in the early days of TVEI, when EIS opposition was strongest, the decision to apply for TVEI posts could be a difficult one, but it has provided an opportunity for promotion and career advancement. Equally it has been the cause of resentment amongst colleagues who have not benefited from the new posts.

Apart from new posts, TVEI has influenced the management of secondary education in other ways. A plethora of committees and working groups has been established; this is not a new phenomenon in education. But they have given much greater emphasis to involving non-educationalists, for example in steering committees and curriculum development groups, and to developing inter-institutional groups. Although schools have worked together before and been in touch with their local colleges, TVEI has promoted co-operation and collaboration among schools and with colleges.

*New Ways to Reform*

It is clear that the speed of operation of the MSC compared to the usual tempo of innovation and development in education has made a marked impact. Some TVEI staff joke feelingly that involvement in TVEI has taken years off their lives partly because of the pace of work and consequent stress. From 1984 when the first pilot authorities had to submit proposals within a two-month time-span, development has been rapid. This has caused considerable difficulties, with rushed preparation for courses which have had to start before equipment arrived, a lack of time for consultation and staff development and to inform non-TVEI staff about the projects' plans and intentions. The speed at which TVEI has been implemented has aggravated feelings of opposition and resentment in many schools. At the same time, some have appreciated the different timescale and attitude of the MSC; it prefers to get something up and running even if imperfect rather than agonize and debate for years over the fine tuning. This is illustrated by the length of time taken to implement the proposals of Munn and Dunning compared to TVEI. In the former case, the first Standard Grade courses were only introduced in 1984, seven years after the publication of the Munn and Dunning reports. The MSC approach has brought its own problems but it has got developments off the ground and generated a great deal of enthusiasm, commitment and even excitement. The MSC has shown another way of operating, which, if not perfect, is at least as worthwhile an approach as the more cautious one usually taken in education.

*Accountability*

The involvement of the MSC in secondary education has introduced a new idea of accountability into education. Indeed, the idea of education being accountable to an external body was and remains a central reason for opposition to TVEI.

This accountability applies financially and in other areas. Projects have had to submit financial information to MSC and MSC internal auditors and the National Audit Office have right of access to projects. Other data, for example on pupils, is required by the MSC. In this context, the MSC's insistence on projects satisfying equal opportunities criteria is noteworthy. Although projects have not succeeded in achieving equal opportunities, for example, in terms of an equal take-up of TVEI subjects and courses by boys and girls, the MSC's emphasis on the issue and requests for relevant information and statistics have forced schools to give greater consideration to the matter. It has led them to think about the relationships between their curriculum, guidance procedures, teaching methods and the take-up and experience of courses by both boys and girls in a way that had not happened in Scottish schools before TVEI.

Another aspect of accountability has been the creation of the TVEI regional advisers. Regional advisers seconded from education to the MSC have overall field responsibility for ensuring that projects are operated and developed as agreed between the local authority and the MSC. A further element is the annual planning dialogue attended by staff from the MSC's TVEI Unit in London, the regional advisers and staff from the projects and local authorities. Projects produce an annual progress report as the basis for discussion at the meeting of the projects' performance over the past year and developments for the coming year.

As part of the process of accountability the MSC have put evaluation very much more to the forefront than is typical in education. Projects have been contractually obliged to spend at least 1 per cent of their budget on internal evaluation. The MSC itself has funded external national evaluations (carried out in Scotland by Edinburgh University and the Scottish Council for Research in Education (SCRE) ).

In practice, staff responsible for the projects have found the production of data for the MSC and the national evaluations a time-consuming, and for them apparently thankless task, sometimes duplicating what is asked for by the SED. Reactions to the MSC's involvement in the running of projects through the regional advisers and planning dialogues are more variable. Most dislike the principle of education being accountable to an outside body, but projects have been surprised at the flexibility and 'hands-off' approach of the MSC. To some extent this reflects the MSC's lack of expertise in educational matters. The regional advisers are seconded from education, but they have been thin on the ground; there was only one regional adviser for all projects in Scotland until 1987. The 'hands-off' approach is also explained by the wariness of the MSC's TVEI Unit in the face of Scottish sensibilities, coupled with its acknowledged unfamiliarity with Scottish education. And on occasion projects have been able to play on this ignorance. The planning dialogues have generally been seen as useful in forcing staff to sharpen up their ideas. Also attitudes to the role of the regional advisers have tended to vary depending on the individuals holding the post and their interpretation of their role, for example whether they emphasized the advisory and supportive function rather than the 'policing' aspects.

The impact of evaluation has been mixed, and in the case of local evaluation its full potential has not been realized. Such evaluation is still quite novel in education. In some cases projects have been unsure how to use their local evaluators and in others staff have not really accepted the value of evaluation. Nevertheless, in a few instances projects have benefited from using their evaluators to tackle areas of concern or weakness. From the point of view of practitioners, the national evaluations have been of limited use and interest, not altogether surprisingly, since their work is to some extent addressed to a different audience. The external evaluation process in Scotland has also been undermined from its early days, since the extension of TVEI from a pilot to a national scheme was announced at the same time as the evaluations were only beginning. Thus, although MSC has promoted the idea of evaluation within secondary education they, or perhaps the government, have also taken a cavalier attitude to it themselves.

## THE IMPACT OF TVEI ON THE CURRICULUM

The prospect of unprecedented resources for curriculum development was a very powerful incentive for involvement in TVEI (£2 million per project over 5 years) but it is also true that TVEI was seen by some teachers and officials as an opportunity to change the curriculum in ways they had wanted to for a long time. They felt that the curriculum was geared to a minority of pupils the academic youngsters aiming at higher education, and as such was inappropriate for the majority of pupils, who were demotivated by a curriculum that failed to meet their needs and aptitudes. The comment that 'TVEI gave us the money to do what we had been wanting to do' is a common one. Moreover, this opportunity to experiment with the curriculum was not led or limited by a change to an external examination system, as is usually the case. The aims and criteria set out for TVEI by the MSC are very broad and have given TVEI projects substantial scope for experimentation. This is evident in the diversity of the projects in Scotland. At first the pilot projects tended to interpret the aims and criteria in an obviously 'technical and vocational' way although even at the early stages there were considerable differences among projects. But gradually projects have developed a broader definition of their aims and criteria, have increasingly emphasized personal and social development and placed more importance on new teaching and learning methodologies. TVEI has given both resources and legitimacy to efforts to devise a curriculum that would interest and motivate those 'turned off' by traditional education, to develop new teaching and learning styles, to take a more pupil-centred approach and use new forms of assessment. This is the so-called 'new pedagogy'. In this, TVEI has reinforced and helped to accelerate the developments in Scottish education already happening with the Standard Grade and Action Plan. It is difficult to disentangle the precise impact of TVEI and determine to what extent changes in learning and teaching methodologies can be attributed to it alone. At least one can say that TVEI resources have facilitated and encouraged the development of new methodologies. In schools and departments where traditional attitudes were strong, it has provided an extra lever for change. In addition, TVEI has demonstrated how well pupils have responded to the new teaching and learning methods.

Generally pupils have enjoyed and been motivated by them. In the Edinburgh University evaluation of TVEI (Bell, Howieson, King, Raffe, 1988), which surveyed all TVEI pupils from the first five pilot projects, the new teaching and learning methodologies emerged strongly as features that pupils liked in TVEI.

One area where a clear TVEI effect can be seen is in the development of short modular courses, very frequently using SCOTVEC National Certificate modules. The use of SCOTVEC modules was partly brought about by the curriculum boycott of Standard Grade courses due to the teachers' industrial action. Whatever the reasons, TVEI promoted the take-up of National Certificate modules in the schools and in particular extended the use of National Certificate modules, to S3 and S4 pupils. The desirability of younger pupils taking National Certificate modules specifically designed for the post-16 age group is a matter of some argument and some would question their value and suitability at this stage. It seems very likely that TVEI, through its stimulation of schools' use of SCOTVEC modules, has had a strong influence on the decision of the Consultative Committee on the Curriculum (CCC) and the Scottish Examination Board (SEB) to introduce short courses for this age group.

New courses developed for TVEI have added to the existing curriculum but have led to charges of unfairness and divisiveness since only some pupils have benefited from the courses and extra resources. On the other hand, proponents of TVEI have recognized that restricting new courses to the TVEI cohort limits the influence of TVEI on the curriculum more generally. In Scotland the idea of 'enhancement' of existing courses has been taken up very strongly and this has helped to alleviate both concerns. Enhancements to existing, usually certificated, subjects, including apparently non-technical or technological ones, such as English, music and history, and available to all pupils within the normal timetabling structure, is perhaps the most potent way TVEI has been able to influence the whole curriculum. Enhancements have helped to counter some of the criticisms of TVEI as divisive by allowing non-TVEI pupils to take part in courses resourced by TVEI and in enabling other subject departments and teachers to share in the 'goodies' possible through TVEI funding. This has helped to offset some of the resentment felt by departments that have witnessed others receiving new equipment and extra staffing through TVEI at a time of financial constraints. The widespread use of enhancements in Scottish projects has meant that there has been a considerable degree of extension of TVEI to other pupils and other departments before the formal extension of the initiative. Nevertheless, some departments have remained outside TVEI and its resources, quite apart from the exclusion of teachers and pupils in non-TVEI schools, so that criticisms of TVEI as unfair, because its resources are only available to a selected number of schools and pupils, have remained.

TVEI is explicitly about changing the curriculum. New courses have been developed as part of the TVEI core and existing subjects altered through enhancements. One can only speculate on the impact of TVEI on the decision to add a technological mode to the Munn modes. (The impact of TVEI on technology in secondary education is discussed in Chapter 6.) In consideration of the impact of TVEI on the curriculum and attitudes to TVEI, the structures adopted by projects are important. Where projects have a centre for teaching TVEI pupils, this has tended to limit the impact of TVEI on the existing school curriculum and increase resentment about the concentration of TVEI resources outside schools and their exclusive use by TVEI pupils. Such centres have certain advantages, for example, providing a focus for TVEI development and certainly seem to have been very successful in motivating young people. But if one of the aims of TVEI is to have a wider influence, then the advantages of a centre are probably outweighed by their disadvantages.

The curriculum development model used by TVEI is one that has been welcomed by schools. TVEI has generally used classroom teachers to develop courses and has provided the opportunity for teachers to influence their own curriculum. TVEI has had the resources to fund such work, for example by financing staff cover for teachers involved in curriculum development. It has shown the enthusiasm and expertise that is available within schools for curriculum development if sufficient resources are available.

## FROM 'EDUCATION' TO 'VOCATIONALISM'?

Many have felt that TVEI would lead to a narrow vocational curriculum geared to industry's needs and in which employers had a determining influence. These fears have not been realized. The general nature of the TVEI aims and criteria give enough leeway for TVEI projects to develop an approach and curriculum that emphasize, for example, the personal development of pupils as much as their technological competence. The lack of a rigid blueprint for TVEI has been reinforced by the terms upon which TVEI was introduced into Scotland. TVEI was extended to Scotland only after acceptance of the demand by the Convention of Scottish Local Authorities (COSLA) that in Scotland TVEI would have to be compatible with Standard Grade and Action Plan developments. This insistence on compatibility with Standard Grade and Action Plan has contributed to the wider interpretation of TVEI in Scotland. All applications for TVEI are judged by a national steering committee, and, although this still decides on Scottish applications, at COSLA's request, amendments were introduced into the procedure for Scottish projects and a COSLA TVEI committee set up to advise on Scottish schemes. The result of these various conditions is that TVEI has been more fully assimilated into the educational mainstream than seems to have been the case in general in England and Wales. Whether this constitutes 'success' or not depends on one's views of the role and purpose of education; it is likely that some of the Ministers who supported TVEI regard this assimilation as a failure, in that it means TVEI has been 'domesticated' by education. That such a process should have taken place in Scotland is partly a mark of Scottish support for comprehensive education and determination that TVEI should not undermine it, but it has happened largely because the broad aims of TVEI (as they have been interpreted in Scotland) and its methodology have coincided with ideas already current in Scottish education. The 'new vocationalism' is not new in Scotland.

Projects and schools have put a great deal of effort into the timetabling of TVEI to ensure a balanced curriculum. In its report 'The TVEI Curriculum in Scotland' the SCRE looked at this in detail and concluded that there is no evidence that TVEI is leading to an unbalanced curriculum as judged against the Munn recommedations, although the national picture does conceal distortions at the level of individual pupils and individual schools. (The main difficulties have been in minority-time subjects such as physical education and athletics, and in modern languages.) The extent and popularity of enhancement is another indication of the way in which TVEI has tended to be seen more as part of the normal curriculum than as a separate entity.

*Limitations of employers' involvement*

The intention of TVEI to make education more responsive to industry's needs and to facilitate a greater and more direct involvement of employers in education has had only a limited success. What is striking is how firmly TVEI has been led by education. Far from industry dominating TVEI, it has proved difficult for education to involve employers. TVEI has highlighted the problems in reaching employers, in sustaining their interest and in transforming promised help into reality. The TVEI experience has clearly illustrated the limitations of some employers' understanding of education, of what they can be expected to contribute and the difficulty of finding a meaningful role for them. It is ironic that an initiative designed to boost industry's collaboration with education has shown that this is far from being a simple matter. The case of curriculum development is a good illustration of this. At the beginning of TVEI, projects started out with the intention of trying to involve industry in curriculum development in response to the MSC's expectations and most projects tried to include industrialists in all of their curriculum development working groups. But the sheer practical difficulties of doing so has meant that TVEI projects quickly moved to an approach of using employers as consultants once staff had crystallized their ideas and decided on specific tasks to ask of employers. Experience has shown that, although industry has much to offer in curriculum development expectations of industrialists have to be limited; it has also shown that teachers should and can determine the process. TVEI has helped to show that the reality of greater industrial involvement in education is more difficult and complex than is usually acknowledged by either side in the debate about the vocational relevance of education. The experience of TVEI is especially pertinent in the light of recent government moves to increase further employer involvement in education and training, for example through participation on school boards and giving them greater control and direction of youth and adult training.

This is not to say that TVEI has not given a powerful boost to education/industry liaison (EIL), but certainly TVEI has not provided the opportunity for industry's takeover of education, even assuming this is desired by industry. TVEI has promoted the development of links with local companies, which have, for example, offered work experience placements, helped in the development of new courses, provided pupils with interview practice and acted as advisers for mini-enterprise projects and the like. TVEI has raised the profile of such vocationally related activities and, in particular, work experience. It has promoted work experience as a normal, accepted and valuable part of the curriculum for everyone, frequently within a certificated course, rather than as a dumping ground for non-certificate pupils. But all of this has been initiated and controlled by the TVEI projects.

## The Impact on the Status of Vocational Education

An underlying element behind the MSC's intervention in secondary education through TVEI has been the intention to use it to change attitudes to vocational education, to remedy what is seen as the low status of vocational education, and to encourage more of the academic pupils to take vocationally relevant courses and consider careers in industry. There is little to suggest that TVEI has made an impact here. TVEI criteria state that projects should cater for pupils across the ability range. Considering the national level, the first cohort was unbalanced in this respect, with a high proportion of pupils at the lower end of the ability range. Subsequently, the balance has improved to some extent at a national level but there are very substantial variations among projects with some failing to achieve anything like a representative spread of pupils. Perhaps, even more crucially, TVEI is *perceived* by many, including employers, pupils, parents and teachers, as being more appropriate for low attainers. For example, some projects have found that guidance staff in schools advise more able pupils against taking TVEI. The Edinburgh University evaluation of TVEI, which involved extensive interviews with employers, found a widespread perception of TVEI as suitable for low attainers. Part of the problem is the almost automatic labelling of any vocational course or initiative as for the less able because of traditional attitudes. But the TVEI projects' lack of success in developing courses that challenge and stretch the most able pupils has also been a problem. The difficulty of combining TVEI with a full programme of Highers in S5, as outlined earlier, does not help matters. Yet the most vital factor in the status of TVEI and vocational education in general is the attitude and behaviour of the 'gatekeepers'. So long as employers and higher education show that they value traditional academic education and certification and do not recognize more vocationally orientated courses, then the image of such courses, including TVEI, will remain poor. Pupils, especially the more able, will take their cue from this. Regardless of the value and quality of such initiatives, there will not be a fundamental shift in the balance of secondary education between the vocational and the academic unless employers and higher education change their attitudes and their recruitment and selection criteria. Whether such a shift should happen and what the correct balance between the vocational and the academic should be, is a matter of much argument. However, it would be ironic if the practices of employers, one of the groups which advocates a more vocationally orientated education, should stifle TVEI, a scheme devised to meet their demands and whose aims many of them say they support.

## TRIST

Apart from TVEI, the MSC has been involved in secondary education through TRIST (TVEI-Related In-Service Training), which started in 1985 to provide training under the themes of shortage subjects, management, industry links and teaching and learning methods. Perhaps the key element of TRIST was its intention to act as a stimulus to encourage thinking and developments in the provision of in-service training. It was a more limited intervention than TVEI, lasting only five terms and with a smaller budget, although the sums of money were substantial in terms of the average in-service budget for Scotland: approximately £3 million were spent by TRIST in Scotland, compared to the average annual budget of £15 to 20 million. Its possible impact on schools was greatly reduced by its timing, which coincided with the teachers' industrial action, so that many planned activities had to be cancelled and much of the proposed training was switched over to the further education sector. TRIST ended in 1987 and there has not been another programme in Scotland as there has in England and Wales.

In a way that parallels TVEI, the TRIST philosophy and strategy very much reinforced existing trends in Scotland, and a common response in TRIST was that MSC money enabled authorities to do what they would have done anyway, if funds had been available otherwise. In other ways the impact of TRIST was similar to TVEI: in introducing accountability to an external agency; in creating a new management structure with steering committees and a co-ordinator's post; in emphasizing evaluation at both an internal and external level; in promoting inter-institutional and inter-regional links; and in the rapid pace of development. Just under a third of secondary teachers received some form of training under TRIST. Teaching skills and management expertise were also developed and authorities forced to think in a new and more systematic way about staff development.

How far TRIST will have any lasting impact on Scottish in-service training without continued resources from the MSC and the discipline of accountability to it is another matter. It seems likely that, without a follow-up programme, any influence TRIST has had on Scottish in-service training will be dissipated. The experience from other initiatives dependent on short-term external stimulus is that such initiatives seldom have long term effects.

## THE EXTENSION OF TVEI

By 1988 the MSC was involved in schools in every region and division in Scotland through TVEI. Its involvement had had effects on the curriculum, on educational management and on the autonomy of schools and education authorities. As well as generating much enthusiasm for new courses and teaching methodologies, it had also caused considerable ill feeling amongst teachers, pupils and parents within TVEI projects and in schools not involved in the initiative. It had done little to raise the status of vocational education: a mixed balance sheet for TVEI.

The extension of TVEI to all schools by the mid-1990s could be seen as further influence for the MSC, but it should be remembered that TVEI as it has been developed in Scotland is a different animal in nature and content than that initially envisaged by the MSC and especially by the politicians who first conceived of it. Education has domesticated TVEI to a very considerable degree in Scotland, so that its extension does not represent a straightforward 'victory' for the MSC.

Extension will at least resolve the question of the divisiveness of TVEI since it will be available to all pupils in all schools. But very much less money will be available, on average about £30 000 per school per year compared with £130 000 in the pilot projects. (To take an example: in one region £11 million is available for extension for 51 schools, 12 special schools and 5 colleges compared with £2 million for the 4 schools and 1 college in its pilot project.) And within schools the money will be spread across whole year groups, rather than selected cohorts of TVEI pupils. The reduced finance is likely to mean less power and influence for the MSC. A reduced level of resources also poses the question of how far the courses and approaches of the pilot projects can be continued: for example, new teaching methodologies depend partly on small class sizes which TVEI has been able to fund. It is unlikely that residentials will be able to continue as a core element in TVEI, while the issue of finding work experience placements for all pupils is causing many worries.

Various management issues will have to be resolved in extension, for example, what should the roles and responsibilities of TVEI staff such as regional TVEI co-ordinators and school co-ordinators be? What sort of consortium model should be used? How far can and should the management of TVEI be integrated into regional and divisional structures? What are to be the links between the directorate and the new structures?

The extent and nature of the longer-term impact of the MSC through TVEI on the curriculum depends on two factors, first, how TVEI is seen to fit into the curriculum and, second, the attitude of employers and higher education to TVEI. If in extension, TVEI is taken to be essentially a set of principles and methods that should be embedded in the curriculum, and the strategy of enhancing existing courses pursued, then TVEI principles could become a permanent and integral feature of the secondary curriculum. If the approach is that TVEI is defined as a discreet entity and offered mainly as a separate option, then this is likely to limit its impact and influence, and especially if such options become associated with low attainers. Here the management strategy adopted by the MSC, in particular the principles of accountability and additionality could be a factor. It will be difficult for the MSC to see how its resources are being used and to what effect, and to justify expenditure to the Treasury if TVEI is subsumed into the curriculum so that no visibly 'TVEI effect' can be discerned. This idea of additionality, the wish to identify specific changes brought about by TVEI, has run counter to the trend in TVEI in Scotland to blur the edges between TVEI and non-TVEI. If the second approach of distinct TVEI courses is followed then it will compound the poor perception and low status accorded to TVEI by employers and higher education. Their attitudes and recognition (or lack of it) of TVEI will be a very powerful determinant of how far TVEI will become a valued and integral part of the curriculum of secondary schools and how far the MSC's original intention of stimulating the technical and vocational education of 14–18 year-olds is achieved.

*Acknowledgements*

Work on this chapter was supported by the Economic and Social Research Council (Grant number XC00280004). I am grateful to my colleagues Colin Bell, Ken King and David Raffe at Edinburgh University and Heather Malcolm at SCRE, with whom I have discussed the issues in this chapter.

REFERENCES

Bell C., and Howieson, C. (1988). The View from the Hutch: Educational Guinea Pigs Speak about TVEI. In, D. Raffe (ed.), *Education and the Youth Labour Market: Schooling and Scheming* (Lewes: Falmer).

Bell, C., Howieson, C., King, K., and Raffe D. (1988). *Liaisons Dangereuses? Education Industry Relationships in the First Scottish TVEI Pilot Projects: An Evaluation Report* (University of Edinburgh: Centre for Educational Sociology and Department of Education).

Bell, C., Howieson, C., King, K., Raffe, D. (1989). The Scottish

Dimension of TVEI. In, A. Brown, and D. McCrone (eds.), *Scottish Government Yearbook 1989* (University of Edinburgh: Unit for the Study of Government in Scotland).

Black, H., Malcolm H., and Zaklukiewicz, S. (1988). *The Gift Horse: A Study of the Management of Change and Resource Implications encountered in Seven TVEI Pilot Projects in Scotland* (Scottish Council for Research in Education).

Black, H., Malcolm H., and Zaklukiewicz, S. (1988). *The TVEI Curriculum in Scotland* (Scottish Council for Research in Education).

Chitty, C. (1985). TVEI: A Perspective. In *Viewpoints*, 1 University of London: Institute of Education, Post Sixteen Education Centre.

Chitty, C. (1986). TVEI: the MSC's Trojan horse. In, C. Benn and J. Fairley (eds.), *Challenging the MSC on Jobs, Education and Training* (London: Pluto Press).

Dale, R. (1985). *Education, Training and Employment: Towards a New Vocationalism* (Oxford: Pergamon).

Department of Employment and Department of Education and Science (1986). *Working Together – Education & Training* (London: HMSO, Cmnd. 9823).

Educational Institute of Scotland (1986). Technical and Vocational Initiative minute 574 (15) (iii) (Annual General Meeting, June 1986, Edinburgh).

Fulton, O. (1987). The Technical & Vocational Education Initiative: an assessment. In, A. Harrison and J. Gretton (eds.), *Education & Training UK, 1987* (Newbury: Policy Journals).

Gleeson, D. (ed.) (1987). *TVEI & Secondary Education: A Critical Appraisal* (Milton Keynes: Open University Press).

Owen, J. (1984). 'TVEI: future control. In *Perspectives*, 14 (University of Exeter: School of Education, TVEI).

MSC (1984). *Technical & Vocational Education Initiative Operating Manual* (Sheffield). MSC (1986). *Extension of the Technical and Vocational Education Initiative* (Sheffield).

Pignatelli, F. (1987). The Technical & Vocational Education Initiative & Scottish educational developments. In, J. Twining, S. Nisbet and J. Megarry (eds.), *World Yearbook of Education 1981* (London: Kogan Page).

Pring, R. (1985). In defence of TVEI. In *Forum*, 28.

Turner, E. (ed.) (1988). *TRIST Management guides: The Scottish Experience* (Sheffield: MSC).

Woolhouse, J. (1984). Technical and Vocational Education Initiative. In *Perspectives*, 14 (University of Exeter: School of Education, TVEI).

*Other sources*: Pilot project and extension project proposals, annual progress reports and other materials from TVEI projects in Scotland.

# CHAPTER 4. EDITORS' INTRODUCTION

Further education had an important and significant role to play in partnership with the MSC in meeting the training and educational needs of the community. As rising unemployment in the 1960s and 1970s and structural changes reduced the numbers of students in 'traditional' areas of work, MSC programmes came to have a major impact on the type of work undertaken by the further education sector and the type of students involved. Further education colleges provided a large proportion of the off-the-job training needs of the new trainees on MSC schemes.

This chapter outlines the response of further education to major programmes such as TOPS, UVP, YTS, Open Tech, TVEI and TRIST and the impact on the student population, certification and curriculum and staff development. The impact on management is discussed here and in Chapters 3 and 5. The author argues that from its relatively modest beginning in the mid-1970s, the MSC developed into a major influence on further education with some colleges receiving as much as 75 per cent of their fee income from the MSC. In spite of budgetary changes which have been a source of instability for future long-term planning needs, further education has been responsive to the varied and changing demands made of it.

# 4

## FURTHER EDUCATION AND THE MANPOWER SERVICES COMMISSION

### TOM BURNESS

#### INTRODUCTION

College education in Scotland is diverse, but it divides neatly into two broad categories: there are a small number of colleges financed directly by central government (central institutions), and there are those funded by local authorities, usually referred to as further education or technical colleges. The latter have had the widest and deepest involvement over the years with the MSC. Even so, a few distinctive, specialized courses were developed in the mid-1970s, at the request of the Training Services Agency (TSA), by certain central institutions to meet the needs of redundant executives who wanted to re-enter the labour market, and for those who wanted help in becoming self-employed.

In the 1960s and early 1970s, further education colleges provided mainly post-school vocational courses for young people in the age range 16–19. Most students were employees who were given one day a week from work to attend a day-release course, leading to a vocational qualification or a Scottish Certificate of Education (SCE), mainly in the fields of secretarial and office studies, engineering and construction. These courses extended typically over three or four years. A growing number of full-time vocational courses (including 'pre-apprenticeship' courses for 15-year-old school-leavers) gradually evolved across the curriculum, again mainly for young people. Adult students were found in all colleges, but in 'traditional' courses they were always part of a small minority. Indeed most adults attended the extensive evening courses and part-time leisure and recreation programmes held during the day.

This chapter illustrates in broad and admittedly eclectic terms how the MSC and the further education service developed their complementary though distinct roles in meeting the training and education needs of the community in a period of rising unemployment and rapid technological, political and economic change.

It will be argued that further education is a flexible, adaptive service, which, despite persistent under-resourcing, has operated as a principal delivery system for national training initiatives, particularly where these correspond to broad educational objectives cherished by the service itself.

By the mid-1970s a growing number of adults were coming into local further education colleges under the Training Opportunities Scheme, which was administered at that time by the Training Services Agency. The Training Opportunities Scheme (TOPS) catered for those who were unemployed and also for those who wanted to give up a job and change direction by retraining. The TSA bought 'exclusive' courses (i.e. courses in which it paid for all the places) and 'in-fill' courses (where individuals on TOPS awards joined existing courses) from the colleges. Many of the exclusive courses ran for a full academic year and most for at least twenty weeks. The largest number of trainees was to be found in business and secretarial departments taking courses in office skills, typing, shorthand and other secretarial studies. Many others attended craft-based courses, such as catering. The vast majority of participants were women, many of whom were home-based, and they seized the opportunity of being paid for the chance to retrain or refresh their skills at government expense. The TSA staff were committed to achieving numerical targets against a general notion of at least training for stock. And although a number of the participants were motivated initially by the lure of the training allowance, for many trainees this was their first taste of continuing education and training since leaving school. For many it proved to be a personal springboard.

For the colleges, there were a number of aspects to the experience. In the main, local further education colleges came of age in the 1960s, and many of the college buildings in use today were constructed in that decade. They were established at that time to cater for a clientele of 15- to 19-year-olds. Most of these were full-time employees who were granted day release for work-related training. But by the late 1960s and early 1970s, a growing number of school leavers were attending one- or two-year full-time courses in colleges. Facilities such as dining rooms and recreational space which were designed to meet the demands of part-time teenagers proved much less suited to the needs of young students who were spending their whole week in college. This problem for many colleges became acute when adults started arriving on TOPS courses with a set of additional expectations, which included provision of quiet areas, separate dining facilities, relaxation of rules on smoking etc. For a number of staff, whose traditional teaching style was accepted uncritically by young students straight from school, this influx of adults forced an adjustment to a more student-centred approach, which many staff indeed welcomed. At the outset the content of a number of training programmes was narrowly focused on very specific, vocational objectives. Paradoxically, this often resulted in a welcome release from the traditional, examination-dominated curriculum and enabled tutors to respond more sensitively to the actual needs and pace of the group as a whole.

## TRAINING OPPORTUNITIES SCHEME

Because of its narrow focus, TOPS training was seen initially by many colleges as at best a social service and at worst an inevitable burden, especially by those colleges which already attracted large numbers of traditional students for broad-based courses and had little spare accommodation. In some local authorities, the resulting income went into central coffers and the college got neither return nor incentive. For many the story was different: Other colleges welcomed the new clientele: forward-looking authorities invested the income in equipment and additional staffing. Senior TSA officers gradually accepted arguments for a broadening of the curriculum in many courses as the relationship of mutual respect was built between civil servants and educationalists. Nor was the adjustment one way: many senior college staff had to accept personal accountability for the quality of their offerings in ways that might have been unthinkable for other parts of the college curriculum.

It is a tribute to the essential flexibility of the further education service and the personal qualities and drive of the relatively few senior TSA officers who were involved in the mid-1970s that so much was achieved in terms of training places and courses throughout Scotland. These relationships became the bedrock of a considerable expansion and diversification in adult provision and at a later stage of the response to the growing problem of youth unemployment. It also meant that TSA planning staff were able to build a comprehensive picture of the relative strengths and responsiveness of organizations and local authorities throughout Scotland. When it came to 'backing winners' especially when a project was experimental or innovative, the views of the TSA were informed by direct experience.

For a number of colleges this was important, especially for those which are not located in the central belt of Scotland or in main concentrations of population where new courses were usually launched. The Training Services Division (TSD), as it was called by the late 1970s, accepted full-time course proposals from a number of colleges, discussed them fully with the proposers (including evidence of demand) before agreeing to fund them. On this basis, new, certificated full-time courses in industrial relations, production control, industrial security and a number of related areas were offered in selected colleges on a national basis. These new courses ran for several years, until the rules changed.

Change is a constant factor in the evolution of the MSC – change in title, personnel, targets, basis of funding and internal organization – and these occur at a speed which makes it difficult for any delivery system to cope, let alone one as large and diverse as further education. But many colleges did become reasonably adept at keeping up, and their local authorities supported them in these efforts. When the MSC moved significantly away from commissioning the longer, one-year certificated programmes in favour of pushing larger numbers through shorter, sharper 'skills plus' courses, many colleges responded with tailor-made programmes which could be repeated at different times throughout the year, and many were able to catch windfall funding as the end of the financial year approached and the MSC put on a spurt to achieve annual throughput targets.

## INDUSTRY TRAINING BOARDS

By contrast, Industry Training Boards were only marginally involved with further education in providing direct training for adults. The levy system operated in such a way that those companies who met the criteria set by the Boards were exempted from payment on the grounds that they were already meeting training requirements. This training was often done by the company's own staff or by buying courses or places from interested colleges or private consultants. From the point of view of further education, the output represented a distinctive but statistically small proportion of all MSC training activity. But the Training Boards were heavily involved directly and indirectly through member companies with further education in the design and delivery of training for apprentices, junior operatives and certain undergraduates in engineering. In some colleges, the craft and technical courses which were laid on to meet this demand constituted the single major teaching commitment of certain key departments, and those colleges were particularly badly hit when the economic changes of the late 1970s and early 1980s led to the virtual collapse of the apprenticeship system. But by then, the further education service had become quite heavily involved in the growing problem of general youth unemployment. The seeds of this involvement were sown just after the mid-1970s.

## THE IMPACT OF RISING YOUTH UNEMPLOYMENT: SPECIAL MEASURES AND THE YOUTH OPPORTUNITIES PROGRAMME

The problem of rising unemployment was perceived as one which related to an important but still fairly small group of school leavers, mainly low-achieving and non-certificate pupils, who were found wanting by employers and who needed help to make themselves more acceptable in the labour market. The same TSA staff who were heavily involved in setting up TOPS courses were given the task of persuading the colleges and local authorities to extend the notion to 16-year-olds, and a wide range of short vocational programmes were born, which typically were full-time courses of ten to thirteen weeks. Participants in these 'Special Measures' courses were paid a training allowance, and for many young people this was the main reason for joining or staying on in such courses. Even so, despite their length and concentration, these courses were surprisingly successful, particularly in alerting sponsoring employers to the real value and qualities of many young 'non-academic' people and their ability to do the job well. For many of these young people, some of whom lacked initial motivation, the courses provided a genuine bridge between school and work which had not previously existed. Many of these short training courses also included a planned supervised period of work experience in a company willing to co-operate with the college. Colleges were able to offer these short courses at the start of each term and especially in January for Christmas school-leavers. An unpredicted consequence of this was that a number of young people also chose to leave their one year full-time further education courses at Christmas and join one of the range of Short Training Courses in order to qualify for the allowance. A number of 'traditional' further education courses collapsed at that point or staggered on till Easter with very low numbers. The incoherence of the funding system for young people between 16 and 18 has resulted in many making career decisions on the basis of short-term financial advantage. However, as the problem of youth unemployment grew and there were fewer jobs to train young people for, the Youth Opportunities Programme embraced the idea of placing young people in training places for a year with employers where they would be supernumeraries; they were guaranteed a minimum period of off-the-job training, typically on day-release to a local college. The scheme had many successes and led to jobs especially for the less well-qualified. But it was also abused by many employers, either deliberately or because they did not fully understand and accept the obligations placed on them to provide the young people with foundation training at their expense. In particular, in the Work Experience on Employers' Premises Scheme (WEEP), administered by the Special Programmes Division, many young people themselves felt they were used for a year as cheap labour, given no systematic training and then thrown back onto the unemployment register no better off than when they began. Whatever the strengths or inadequacies of YOP it did, however, influence the further education system and paved the way for YTS, a permanent scheme which emphasized the notion of training and built this into its core for both employed and unemployed young people.

RESPONSE OF THE SYSTEM: OPPORTUNITIES AND BARRIERS

The response of the colleges to all of this varied. For some, the MSC enabled them to attract young people (albeit because of the training allowance) who would never otherwise have dreamed of crossing the threshold. Once the young people were in the learning environment, it was up to the colleges to persuade them that further education was very different from school and that they could actually come to value the experience, as the first opportunity, the colleges might hope, in a lifelong process of continuing education. And some colleges succeeded precisely in this ambition. They resisted the easy administrative temptation to put YOP students into YOP classrooms with YOP-financed staff and deliberately set their faces against this type of ghetto-thinking by integrating all three with existing students, facilities and staff.

This involved considerable adaptation on the part of staff, not least because it moved the learner and his or her needs positively to the centre of the curriculum.

CERTIFICATION

Staff found it practically impossible to extend nationally recognized certification to this new student-centred curriculum, and this was a major drawback. With the exception of the innovative and commendably flexible City and Guilds Foundation courses (which were *validated*: the college chose its own preferred balance of internal and external assessment) the main route to certification was through the formal examinations of the established national examining bodies and these were normally held at fixed times in the year and were designed to test centrally devised curricula. Many trainees of course were able to attend regular classes and many did attain nationally recognized group certificates.

But for many more this was not possible either because of fixed starting and finishing dates or because no suitable course was available, and therefore a great deal of genuine learning was 'certificated' only on the basis of locally produced college certificates, which complemented scheme-based profiles. This problem continued into the 1980s and was eventually solved in 1984 by the HMI-led Action Plan, which resulted in the development of the modular National Certificate with its focus on the student and the achievement of agreed learning outcomes.

CURRICULUM DEVELOPMENT

But many of the more innovative colleges made a virtue of necessity so far as certification was concerned before 1984. The disadvantage of a system of national examination is that assessment will almost certainly dominate and indeed determine the curriculum. Release from the constraints of examination syllabuses meant licence to devise from scratch innovative programmes which, if they met the broad aims laid down by the MSC, could incorporate ideas and values for which there was little scope in the traditional syllabus. This opportunity gave valuable experience to many lecturers because their traditional role normally meant they were involved in only one major element of the curriculum, namely the formal delivery of syllabus content. In mainstream courses they played no part in defining the aims or the framework of the curriculum, which, if indeed it was done explicitly, was the task of a central examination board. Unless they happened to be markers, lecturers had no place in the examination system. By contrast, those lecturers involved in formulating the aims of a YOP course, deciding its content and methodology and then specifying how they would go about testing whether the aims were being achieved were involved in a much more demanding and ultimately more satisfying professional task. The experience for such staff had much in common with the brief excitement generated by some of the best curricular initiatives arising from ROSLA (Raising of the School Leaving Age), which were refreshingly free of examination constraints in the early 1970s but which ultimately sank under the weight of the O grade imprimatur. A closer more systemic comparison may be made with the impact the CNAA (Council for National Academic Awards) made on staff in central institutions in the early 1970s. Staff had to be trained quickly to meet the requirement of the CNAA that each degree course proposal must state clearly the aims of each course, the syllabus content, the methods of testing the achievement of the stated aims and the teaching methods to be used.

## STAFF DEVELOPMENT

This was a genuinely subversive experience. Staff who were involved in large-scale YOP initiatives of this sort (and survived) were permanently changed. If they returned to the more circumscribed requirements of the mainstream curriculum, they did so with a much greater awareness of its limitations. This factor amongst many others perhaps goes some way to explaining why the Action Plan was implemented so speedily in further education, particularly in those colleges where curriculum innovation was strongly established. Certain colleges and, more significantly, some local authorities were slow to become involved in this aspect of work-related education. Some, like Grampian, had relatively low levels of youth unemployment; others felt it was a task more appropriate to the community education service. Whether this was justified or not, the decision to bypass their colleges amounted to the loss of staff development opportunities of significant and far-reaching proportions.

## SPECIAL LEARNING NEEDS

It has been said that 'the MSC had the money and education had the ideas.' This is an exaggeration, bordering perhaps on insult. The MSC did, however, act as paymaster to those colleges whose ideas met its criteria. But the MSC was also an important purveyor of ideas itself. In particular, the MSC deserves credit for its early and continued support for young people with special learning needs. The Work Introduction Courses (WIC) pioneered in the 1970s provided a sheltered transition to work for school leavers at a time when there was no such local-authority follow-on course available to young people leaving statutory education. This practical concern has been carried through all subsequent scheme arrangements up to and including the current two-year YTS.

UNIFIED VOCATIONAL PREPARATION

In the same period, the MSC developed pilot schemes of Unified Vocational Preparation (UVP) for young people with no formal qualifications who had secured employment but were in jobs where little or no training was given by employers (traditionally known as dead-end jobs). The MSC brought employers and further education together and paid them to design integrated programmes of training and education. This was a small-scale initiative compared to those provided for the unemployed but it was significant in that it demonstrated the value of training on an integrated basis. The scheme was later taken up by some Industrial Training Boards, particularly the Distributive Industry Training Board, but it remained undervalued by companies at the time. In fact some employers remained convinced that UVP was unnecessary since general or broad education was the task of the state and they argued that it simply raised expectations amongst young people and unsettled those who were otherwise content, thereby adding to labour turnover and increasing company costs. But UVP did demonstrate some of the difficulties of persuading companies to the value of training as an investment. However it also provided a lot of valuable experience both to participating further education colleges and to the planners of future national programmes of vocational preparation. There is perhaps a closer relationship between the elements of the current two-year YTS and UVP than between YTS and most of the better known programmes designed for the unemployed in that UVP schemes were jointly planned by industry and college and sought to integrate both off- and on-the-job learning by delivering the content on the basis of a joint teaching approach involving staff from college and company.

THE YOUTH TRAINING SCHEME

The differences between the new one-year Youth Training Scheme introduced in 1983 and its predecessors were significant. In the first case, the emphasis was on *training*, and the scheme itself was launched as a permanent provision. It was to be employer-led, and a new infrastructure of managing agents was created who were funded to deliver the scheme to standards laid down by the MSC. The scheme was not designed simply for unemployed young people but for all trainees including those recruited as permanent staff, a point not fully appreciated for some time by many managing agents and companies.

The decision by the MSC to shift funding from the traditional providers of youth training (mainly the colleges) to the consumers (mainly companies as managing agents) was important for further education. Some colleges became managing agents in their own right, others were specifically excluded from that option by their local authorities who themselves acted as managing agents. Some colleges became involved for the first time in any significant way in the provision of off-the-job training as a result of their local authority sub-contracting the work to them. For some colleges, this came as a shock; they were obliged to deal with problems of a sort which had been encountered by many colleges in earlier schemes, such as student behaviour and motivation.

At the same time, further education was on the threshold of a major curriculum-led change with the introduction by the SED of the 16+ Action Plan timed for implementation in August 1984 ('The Empire Strikes Back', to quote a contemporary observer). In the four years which followed, the Scottish Vocational Education Council (SCOTVEC) was set up and took over administration of the competence-based modular National Certificate. Since 1984, the process of development, certi- fication and integration of students regardless of employment status has continued apace. Colleges are generally more learner-centred and can respond very quickly to requests for admission of trainees to relevant modules of study on a class-attendance basis and even more quickly on an individual basis using open learning materials and flexible learning workshops.

The Action Plan was strongly supported by MSC officers and many Area Manpower Boards. Those MSC Accredited Training Centres oper- ated by local authorities played a useful role in providing staff training where YTS and Action Plan interests overlapped, and this complemented locally financed in-service arrangements.

It is clear to many that this model could cope admirably with the experimental New Job Training Scheme for the adult unemployed once it has been reshaped into a more acceptable form. The further education service has complained for years that the adult equivalents of YOP (such as the Community Enterprise Programme and later the Community Programme) contained no funding for serious skills training and there- fore denied the adult unemployed the benefits available to young people. An adult version of YTS, suitably amended and with an emphasis on training, would make sense to many and would be well-served by the 'new' further education service.

OPEN TECH PROJECT

In 1982, as part of the Adult Training Strategy, the MSC launched its Open Tech Project with a budget of £47 million. The target was the adult employee at supervisory or technician level who needed updating or retraining, and the intention was that he or she should be able to get access to appropriate materials at a time and a place of the employer's choosing. The whole project was an experimental intervention to widen access and extend the training system, and it attracted criticism on a number of counts. It was considered narrow in focus (aimed at tech- nician employees) and was not based on any credible research into genuine training needs: there seemed to be an absence of any quality guide-lines. Even so, the total budget was small in comparison with the sums spent under other heads by the MSC over the same five-year period, and its aims included pump-priming initiatives which would become self-sustaining after three years.

The Open Tech Project was managed nationally from Sheffield, and a number of projects were funded in Scotland. In general, the OTP staff responded to proposals which appeared to meet their criteria. In the initial stages, this meant that projects were funded to develop open learning study materials. Contracts were issued to a number of colleges in Scotland including Telford and the then Leith Nautical College. Since much of the early emphasis was on new technology, the MSC accepted that users of the materials would certainly need not only home-based kits related to the packages but access to specialized equipment and expertise. To that end they developed a network of twelve Practical Training Facilities (PTFs) in the UK, the first of which was located in Glenrothes College. The MSC funded training support for the staff, and the Scottish Training and Support Unit (SCOTTSU) was established in what used to be Dundee College of Education. A community-based PTF was later established on a joint basis between Central and Borders Regions. At a later stage in the life of the Open Tech Project, the notion of the delivery project was developed. These infrastructural projects were designed to harness the efforts of a number of providers in a geographical area under a single turn-key organization that could serve the needs of the whole area more effectively than any of the individual bodies. The North of Scotland Open Tech Development Unit based in Invergordon was set up by the Scottish Council for Educational Technology (SCET) in collaboration with the Regional and Island authorities of Grampian, Highland, Western Isles, Orkney and Shetland, the HIDB and others. Taytec was established in Dundee by Tayside Region and the colleges based in the region.

Many small-scale projects were funded or pump-primed with OTP finance. The pilot broadcasting course based in Radio Tay's studio led to the establishment of Campus Radio. The Inter-Regional Feasibility study undertaken by Fife, Central, Lothian, Borders, Tayside, and Dumfries and Galloway regions with OTP funding provided the original basis for what has become the Scottish Open Learning Consortium, which now includes all local education authorities in Scotland. (This organization has been set up to develop National Certificate modules on an open-learning basis.) The MSC-funded Technical and Vocational Education Initiative (TVEI) Open Learning Project is closely associated in its origins with the OTP-funded project in Glenrothes College.

There is an accelerating interest in Scotland in the development of open and flexible learning. There are many reasons for this, not least that further education realizes it has to be more concerned with meeting the needs of its users or customers in a much more responsive way. That means providing ready access to learning materials, tutors, assessment support and guidance. By providing finance on a pump-priming basis at a crucial point, the MSC gave the Scottish system a significant boost which coincided with other developments in the system. It is interesting to note that all of the projects referred to above exist today in one form or another albeit no longer financed by the OTP.

## TVEI AND TRIST

By contrast, the Technical and Vocational Education Initiative (TVEI) has made little impact on further education in Scotland. The first pilots are now at completion stage after five years and a number of authorities are now well into the extension phase, which will eventually involve all schools. Some distinctive developments have occurred, but generally the main effects are to be found in improved linkage between schools and colleges, particularly where they were weak before TVEI. There is a slightly improved transfer rate at 16+ from school to further education but the numbers in total are still disappointingly low. The methodological innovations built into TVEI by and large coincide with those which underpin Action Plan, and a number of colleges involved in pilot schemes had difficulty in meeting the MSC's initial request for evidence of how the curriculum was to be 'enriched' when it had so recently been reformed. In this instance, as in some others, we have to look at TVEI as a scheme devised to solve problems in the English system. But it was a scheme so substantially resourced that Scotland could not hold back from pursuing its share. As in the OTP and other Sheffield-led schemes, the MSC officers were more than anxious to be informed of the Scottish dimension and to adapt the requirements of the scheme accordingly.

Perhaps more significantly for further education in Scotland, the TVEI-related In-service Training (TRIST) initiative in 1985/6 made funds available for staff development. The money was provided to local authorities on the understanding that it would top up their own efforts and would be used generally to support staff involved in technical and vocational preparation (not simply those involved in TVEI schemes). Its value to the system was in part that it was 'earmarked' and also that it required the participating authorities to establish an appropriate infrastructure to co-ordinate, deliver and evaluate the training the money was spent on. This too was a scheme designed for England, and MSC funding was to be used as a bridge for a period to allow the DES to put in place a scheme supported from its own funding under the Educational Support Grant (ESG). In England, TRIST gave way to GRIST, and now exists under another acronym. In Scotland, the system of earmarked funding for special purposes is not favoured by COSLA, and local authorities prefer to make their own decisions on spending matters. As a result, although proportionate sums of money are included in the rate support grant they are not earmarked. In Scotland the TRIST initiative finished with the explicit ending of MSC funding and the infrastructure which supported it accordingly ceased as a network. The ESG system has been used by the DES in England to steer the further education system and to build on other MSC initiatives, the most recent of which includes arrangements for stimulating interest in open learning, support for adult literacy and expansion of educational guidance for adults.

## WORKRELATED NONADVANCED FURTHER EDUCATION AND SCOTLAND

It is one thing to accuse the MSC of applying to Scotland schemes designed to deal with problems which are essentially English: it is another to suggest that Scotland might well have benefited from an MSC scheme from which it had been deliberately excluded.

The White Paper of 1984, 'Training for Jobs', transferred to the MSC 25 per cent of the Regional Support Grant given by central government to the LEAS in England for non-advanced further education. Scotland was specifically excepted because of the progress being made with the Action Plan. In fact, the paragraphs came as a surprise to the Commissioners, who saw them for the first time some four hours before they were published in the White Paper. In the event, the new MSC Chairman, Bryan Nicholson, treated the whole issue sensitively; what first appeared as an unwelcome imposition by the LEAS became a positive strategic benefit. To convince the MSC that it should release the 25 per cent funding which relates to Work Related Non-Advanced Further Education (WRNAFE), LEAS were obliged to look not only at that specific item but at the whole further education provision for their areas. As a result, the better authorities have now evolved a more considered strategic framework for the service and this is updated annually. Within this, decisions – including decisions on the unexpected – can be taken on a more informed and rational basis. In turn, this has meant that individual institutions have seen the advantage of developing academic plans which extend over a longer perspective but can be adjusted on an annual basis to take account of the short-term. This sort of strategic thinking has no widespread counterpart in respect of further education as yet in Scotland although pressure of events and the prospect of government legislation will certainly push the system in that direction.

## CONCLUSION

From modest beginnings in the mid-1970s in schemes designed for adults such as Job Creation and TOPS, the MSC in its various organizational guises developed into a significant force in further education over the period till 1988. Almost every college derived a significant proportion of its fee income from the MSC, amounting in some cases to as much as 75 per cent.

Yet despite frequently voiced fears of undue influence on the part of the MSC over the curriculum and intrusion into the ambit of the professional teacher, these anxieties remain largely unrealized. The narrow training philosophy stated initially by the MSC was accepted by colleges in certain circumstances as the legitimate demand of a customer; just as often at local level, by tacit agreement, it was translated into more broadly based course provision.

As youth unemployment grew, official acknowledgement by the MSC of the importance of 'social and life skills' led to an interest in supporting innovative or alternative methods of delivery, such as short residential programmes and experiments in work-based learning activities of a kind that further education has always valued but normally had to underake outwith the formal curriculum.

For colleges with ideas of their own, the MSC has always been viewed as a source of potential financial support. It is interesting to note the extent to which the MSC has allowed its own requirements to be adapted to harmonize with college objectives when they lead to a mutually acceptable outcome.

The MSC has shown a welcome predisposition to gather views and consult at different levels, whether through the Committee for Scotland, the Area Manpower Boards, the TVEI Committee for Scotland or less directly through the Scottish Education Consultative Group (consisting of representatives of the main education trade unions) as well as at college level. But frequent staff changes within the MSC itself (matching the equally frequent changes in programmes and schemes) has meant that although good working relationships between MSC and college staff have always existed, they have been difficult to build upon and develop further.

The MSC is itself a complex organization, and problems arise for colleges as a result. College principals have found themselves dealing with MSC officers from different branches or divisions who reflected quite contrasting approaches to the same training problem and who were themselves not fully aware of differences in each other's perspective. Those programmes which were handled centrally, from the MSC's Sheffield headquarters (such as the Open Tech Project), could result in college-based developments which the Area (or even Regional) manager was not fully aware of.

But, for further education, a more significant difficulty in dealing with the MSC has been coping with the basis of the funding of its schemes and in particular predicting the budgetary implications of the frequent and significant policy changes. This has meant that further education has been obliged to take a short-term view of investment in human and material resourcing particularly in relation to the employment of staff (on short-term contracts) and capital expenditure (virtually nil since a one-off allocation in the late 1970s). The relationship between further education and the MSC is perhaps seen at its best as a partnership cutting with the grain of forward-looking opinion in Scottish education. A great deal is demanded of further education – the 'Cinderella' service – in its social as well as its vocational role. This is usually expressed in terms of short lead times, a rapid-response requirement and an absence of long-term planning. Not altogether different from the MSC – apart from the money.

# CHAPTER 5. EDITORS' INTRODUCTION

The MSC had less to do with the university sector of education than it did with the schools and colleges. Nevertheless it had an important and growing impact on the universities. Directly, it funded research programmes in employment, education and labour market studies. Some vocational courses in universities were funded by the MSC. In 1987, the MSC launched its Enterprise in Higher Education (EHE) programme, which was its first major programme in the university sector, and which was intended to affect every undergraduate programme.

Indirectly, and perhaps more significantly, the MSC through its main programmes pioneered a new style of educational management. This became a strong influence on all sectors of education, including the universities.

# 5

## TOWARDS A SELF-SUSTAINING RÉGIME: THE MANPOWER SERVICES COMMISSION AND THE SCOTTISH UNIVERSITIES

STEVE BARON

At first glance the MSC and the universities seem to have few direct relationships, the one providing training for the age of mass unemployment, particularly among young people, the other providing advanced academic education for four per cent of the age cohort. In this paper I analyse those direct relationships which do exist but I suggest that the more significant impact of the MSC on the universities is to be found in less obvious ways. Of necessity, I develop these arguments in the context of the development of the university system of the United Kingdom as a whole, but with particular emphasis on the Scottish universities and with a case-study of the University of Stirling.

### THE SCOTTISH UNIVERSITIES IN THE ROBBINS ERA

We may start by sketching something of the trajectory of the Scottish universities and the UK university system over the past thirty years. The University Grants Committee quinquennial report for 1957–62 (published in 1964) noted the expansion of the university system from catering for 89 866 students in twenty-four institutions in 1956/7 to a population of 113 143 students in thirty-two institutions in 1962/3. The report also noted the approval by the government (1958–61) of the founding of seven completely new universities in England.

The Scottish share of this expansion was an increase in student numbers from 13 877 to 19 433 with the number of institutions rising from four to five. Conceiving universities to be community-based with more or less definable catchment areas, the UGC rejected founding a new university in Scotland on the basis that the post war birth-rate had been lower in Scotland and that the proportion of young people in Scotland qualified to proceed to university would rise less rapidly than in England.

The last years of the 1957–62 quinquennium saw the establishment of the Robbins Committee on Higher Education, which reported in October 1963. Not only did this committee recommend the further expansion of the university system to provide 350 000 places in 1980/81 and 430 000 in

1985/86, it saw as 'incontrovertible' the need for one new university in Scotland as well as the conversion of some existing institutions to university status so as to provide some 55 000 places by 1980/1.

The rationale for this expansion was contained in six remarkable pages of 'Aims and Principles', in which the committee sought to set the terms of debate for universities (and indeed the whole of Higher Education) into the 1980s. The committee noted the haphazard development of the universities ('it would be a misnomer to speak of a system of higher education in this country') and argued for a 'system' on the grounds of accountability for public funds, of consistency of objectives and co-ordination of activities. The report was at pains to make clear that this was not to be equated with central control. According to the first of 'The Aims for Higher Education' it is 'reasonably certain' that 'no simple formula, no answer in terms of any single end, will suffice ... to do justice to the complexity of things', 'it is necessary to acknowledge a plurality of aims' for Higher Education.

This delicate balancing act of central co-ordination and pluralism resulted in four objectives: 'instruction in skills', the production of 'cultivated men and women', 'the advancement of learning' and 'the transmission of a common culture and common standards of citizenship'.

In order to realize these aims and objectives into a practical university system the committee adopted a series of guiding principles, the most famous of which was 'that courses of higher education should be available for all those who are qualified by ability and attainment to pursue them and who wish to do so'. This principle was justified on the familiar social democratic grounds of the happy coincidence of justice with economic efficiency whereby individual self-actualization results in the economic good of the community; 'the good society desires equality of opportunity for its citizens to become not merely good producers but also good men and women'. The Report was coy about giving target figures for different subjects but, on the basis of a generalized need for more scientifically trained people, it recommended that the percentage studying science and technology should rise from 45 per cent in 1963 to 50 per cent in 1980 by the faster expansion of science and technology provision.

At an institutional level the Report argued for differentiation of function but parity of esteem based on the recognition of attainments wherever they might be found. In order to attain these goals institutions should be 'free to experiment without predetermined limitations' and there should be 'freedom to experiment with new types of institution'. Any conflict between the (already noted) need for a *system* of higher education and these principles the report would hold 'to be the very bankruptcy of constitutional invention' as such initiative 'has always (been) held to be one of the main essentials of intellectual and spiritual health'.

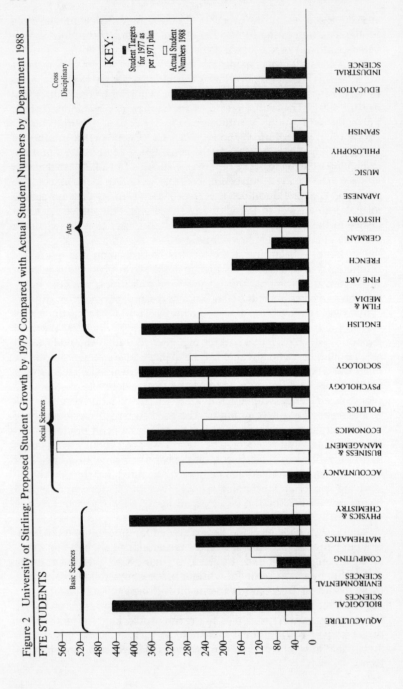

Figure 2   University of Stirling: Proposed Student Growth by 1979 Compared with Actual Student Numbers by Department 1988

In Scotland the Robbins Report led to the creation of the Universities of Strathclyde and Heriot Watt from existing colleges and the University of Dundee from existing parts of the University of St Andrews. The recommendation that a new university should be set up in Scotland was accepted by the UGC in 1963 (despite its concurrent rejection of the case in its quinquennial report noted above) and in July 1964 Stirling was named as the location.

The new foundation at Stirling can be seen as a self-conscious expression of the Robbins ethos as taken up in a Scottish educational tradition. The First Report of the Academic Planning Board in 1965 took the four Robbins objectives as given and argued that the broader school education in Scotland should lead into a flexible university education in which specialization was delayed until half way through the second year. Even then much emphasis was placed on broad General degrees and joint honours degrees ranging across the curriculum. The constitution of the new university outlined in the Second Report of the Academic Planning Board was designed to this purpose, 'to avoid the rigidities of the traditional faculty structure and to facilitate flexibility in the structure of courses and the development of inter-disciplinary studies'.

The new university was planned on an equal division of students between arts, social science and basic science with a target student population of 3 500 by 1975/6 and 'organic' growth thereafter to 'at least double this' by 1980/1. Full details of the intended shape of the new university were specified in the 'Quinquennial Submission 1972-7' published in 1971. Fig. 2. contrasts this plan with the reality of student numbers in the autumn of 1988.

The discrepancy between the submission (in accordance with UGC guidance) for a balanced university of 4 000 students by 1976/7 and the reality of 3 250 students in 1988/9 (eight years after growth was assumed to have resulted in a student population of 7 000) is striking. Similarly striking is the very different subject mix from that intended with the arts and social sciences (excluding business subjects but including a few minor unanticipated innovations) in approximate balance and with the sciences much smaller than anticipated. Most striking of all are the business subjects intended to be 1.4 per cent of the student body in 1976/7 but in fact representing 25.5 per cent of students in 1988.

While not a microcosm of the Scottish university system as a whole, some of the discrepancies found at Stirling between the plans of the Robbins era and the realities of the 1980s are paralleled in the system. Intended to provide 55 000 places by 1980, the Scottish system had 44 448 places in 1980, 47 230 places in 1986/7. In 1986/7 science and technology accounted for 52.25 per cent of students compared with 55.7 per cent twenty years earlier. Because of a change in the statistical series it is not

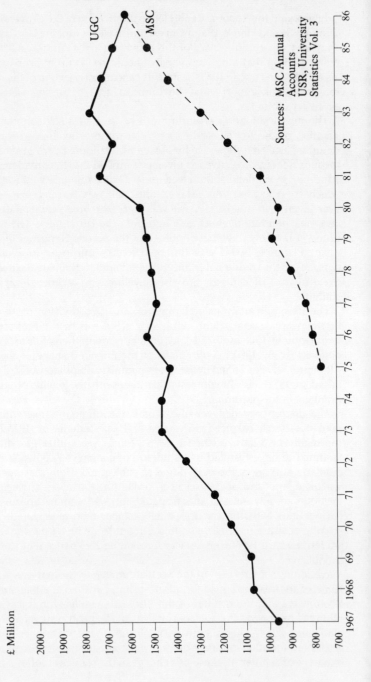

Figure 3   Recurrent Income of the UGC & MSC 1967-86 at Constant Prices

£ Million

Sources: MSC Annual Accounts
USR, University Statistics Vol. 3

possible to quantify the growth of Business subjects on a comparable basis to that used above.

## THE MSC AS COMPETITOR

The mid-to-late 1970s and the 1980s clearly saw the radical non-fulfilment of the plans of the university sector. Such a gap between plans and outcomes is mirrored in the growth of the MSC: as noted in Chapter 1, the MSC was originally intended as a small co-ordinating agency but, by the mid-1980s, it had an enormous clientele and its budget exceeded that of the university sector as a whole.

As Fig. 3. graphically shows, state funding for universities grew relatively rapidly during the late 1960s and early 1970s as student numbers grew. Thereafter funding grew less slowly and began to fall away in the 1980s with the crude funding per student declining by approximately 25 per cent. The period of the slow-down and then reduction of, funding for the universities corresponds almost exactly with the meteoric growth of funding for the MSC. This allows us to suggest the nature of the first impact of the MSC on the Universities: the arrival and rapid success of a competitor for increasingly limited state funding.

Such a conceptualization of the relationship between the Universities and the MSC is very real but very limited. It tends to rely on treating the Robbins principles and plans as sacrosanct, any deviation from them being self evidently for the worse. While there is still resonance in much of Robbins this can be made use of in the 1980s only by understanding the political settlement that Robbins represented, how it held temporary sway enabling the expansion of the universities (and higher education more widely) and how it was rapidly demolished in the 1970s and 1980s making way for an aggressive New Right settlement of education. Appealing to the principles of a quarter of a century ago without understanding their changed meaning in the context of the 1980s and how they could be translated into a coherent educational settlement is to thrash thin air.

Further objections can be made to thinking of the MSC simply as a competitor for state funds. There are good educational grounds and grounds of social justice (themselves pillars of Robbins) for welcoming the resourcing of post-compulsory education for the non-qualified school leaver (perhaps the major lacuna of the post-war expansion of education). Similarly there are grounds for regretting the halt in the expansion of nursery education. The comparison of costs, albeit crude, in Table 15 suggests that the university case is one to be made rather than assumed.

It is to a more complex understanding of the rise and fall of different sectors of education that we must turn if we are to understand the relationship between the MSC and the universities more fully.

Table 15. Comparative Costs of different forms of education and training, 1986/87

| Form of education | Cost per place (£) |
| --- | --- |
| Nursery School | 1405 |
| Primary School | 913 |
| Secondary School | 1440 |
| Youth Training Scheme | 2380 |
| University – total | 3750 |
| – minus 33% research fund | 2512 |

*Source*: Educational Statistics.

THE DIRECT RELATIONSHIPS BETWEEN THE MSC AND THE SCOTTISH UNIVERSITIES

As hinted above, the direct relationships between the MSC and the universities appear few and far between with little coherent pattern. In its early position statement 'Training Services Agency: A Five Year Plan' the MSC locates itself unambiguously in the field of industrial training with scarcely a sideways glance at higher education, whose role was seen as limited to the 'formal off-the-job' development of managers, the retraining of people in the wrong career or whose skills were outdated and the provision of research services. While these areas of contact were seen as legitimate they were marginal to the main thrust of the MSC's work: the Industrial Training Boards, Colleges of Further Education, the direct provision of training and training in firms.

In 1977 the chair of the MSC, Richard O'Brien, addressed himself explicitly to higher education in the Josiah Mason Lecture at the University of Birmingham. While reiterating the themes of the 'Five Year Plan', he went further to suggest that higher education would need to become part of a comprehensive manpower policy responding more to economic imperatives, shifting the balance between academic considerations, 'the needs of industry as far as they can be discerned' and individual student preferences. This was to be accomplished by increasing the output of 'technicians' from the universities and, most effectively because of the difficulties of the precise planning of personnel, by 'increasing the flexibility of the labour force' through education, training and personal experience.

These themes, while articulated early in the life of the MSC, were not developed as the crises of unemployment and youth unemployment developed in the late 1970s and early 1980s. Attention was focused on the succession of schemes to reduce unemployment, to give people work experience and to initiate the non-qualified school leavers. Unambiguously the two-thirds of school leavers hostile to further education or training were the reference group for the MSC in this phase of its development. Throughout the thousands of pages of MSC reports, corporate plans and Employment Committee reports of the House of Commons in the late 1970s and early 1980s, universities scarcely appear.

## 1. Project Resources

These various MSC schemes to combat unemployment, however, gave the universities the opportunity to use the MSC as a resource for funding work which would not otherwise be funded. No national data are available about the extent of this but data are available for Stirling. Stirling University Library was able, through the MSC, to employ un-employed graduates to construct an index of the local newspaper and to help set up the Grierson Archive preserving material related to the development of the British documentary media. Funds totalling some £70 000 were received over a period of four years by the Library (providing some 2.5 per cent of the Library budget in 1986/87). Both of these developments represent valuable academic resources which otherwise would not have been made available with the reduction of routine funding. Less significantly the Estates and Buildings department received some £2 400 for development work around the Loch (some 0.06 per cent of the Estates budget in 1983/4).

## 2. Research Funding

The MSC has also had an impact on the universities as a contractor of research. From its inception the MSC has been active in research as a basis for developing a comprehensive manpower policy. The MSC began to act as a clearing house for Training Research, and published the *Training Research Register* in 1974/5 with follow-up editions and updates giving synopses of research relevant to training.

Much original research was carried out in-house by the MSC with no specific costs attributable: in 1976/7 some 65 MSC staff were in involved in research for part of their time. Figures for later years are not available. The cost of the MSC's external research programme grew from £708 000 in 1974/5 to £3 086 000 in 1986/7. This represented between 0.09 per cent and 0.28 per cent of the annual budget of the MSC. In addition to this must be added the sums spent by MSC contractors on evaluation at the MSC's insistence. It was, for example, a condition of the Technical and Vocational Education Initiative that at least 1 per cent of MSC funds be spent on evaluation.

While universities were not the sole contractors in the field in 1986/87, 80 per cent of MSC external research money went into universities. This represented 0.5 per cent of university research income. The Scottish share of this was some £114 000, placed with the Centre for Educational Sociology (CES) at Edinburgh University. This sum represented 0.18 per cent of the research income of the Scottish Universities, 0.6 per cent of the Edinburgh University research income and a significant (but currently unquantifiable) proportion of the CES income. Three MSC grants can be identified as having been held at Stirling: two research projects in the 1970s into the training of divers (£26 000) and a TRIST evaluation project in 1986/87 (£2 000). This latter project represented 0.02 per cent of research grants current at Stirling in 1986/87.

In funding research the MSC has been at the forefront of restructuring the relationship between funder and researcher. It has funded research on very specific issues with tight definitions of the research problems; there is little evidence of the MSC's funding research which is less directed, more exploratory. During the 1980s other government agencies, notably the SED Research and Intelligence Unit, have followed this path of defining precisely the problems addressable in funded research.

During the 1970s and early 1980s the MSC funded a research unit at Warwick to produce manpower forecasts. The MSC would not reveal the forecasts of unemployment which this unit made to the Employment Committee of the House of Commons in 1979/80 as their figures did not agree with official government forecasts of 1.65 million unemployed in 1982. There appear to have been similar incidents where unpopular research findings have had difficulty in finding the light of day. In 1976/77 the policy was that 'results of major projects and of projects which are likely to be of general interest should be published' alongside the normal publishing activities of the academics involved. By 1980/81 this had changed to 'all information and results derived from research carried out under contract from MSC are the property of MSC' with publication being encouraged 'as much as possible'. In the years following this other government agencies have taken this line, notably the DHSS, which makes publication by permission of the funder.

### 3. Short-Course Provision

In 1977 O'Brien made a speech suggesting two further roles for universities over and above research: the updating of skills and the provision of management education. The Universities Statistical Returns show that the number of short courses in all subjects provided by universities in Great Britain rose from 17 264 in 1980/81 to 21 186 in 1986/7 (a rise of 23 per cent) while the number of courses in Administrative, Business and Social Studies in Scotland rose from 291 to 460 (a rise of 58 per cent). Within this category in Great Britain the contact hours in business management rose from 771 800 to 1 059 300 (a rise of 37 per cent) accounting for 43 per cent of hours in the category (37 per cent 1980). At Stirling the number of courses provided in the category grew from fifteen in 1980 to thirty-five in 1985/86 falling back to twenty-four in 1986/87. All these figures must be treated with caution as the category is very wide encompassing nine subheadings (disciplines) and, even for those courses which were in Business Management, the role of the MSC is not clear.

We can be more certain about the role of the MSC in university courses through the Stirling case-study. The MSC has funded the activities of the Scottish Enterprise Foundation at the university since 1984/85 (£105 503) with grants totalling £278 025 in 1987/88 (1.7 per cent of university recurrent income). Part of this funding goes on short course work for business owners and managers.

The Action Learning Programme (1984 to date) linked a staff member with a group of six small businesses sharing some common problem (e.g. exporting or the problems that exist for entrepreneurial women). After a series of initial workshops a counselling visit was paid to the business by the staff member leading into a series of monthly meetings in which the group tried to resolve the issues in question. The Gateway Overseas Programme linked a language graduate with a company wanting to break into the export market providing support for both to learn the skills necessary.

The MSC has also supported short courses designed to help people become business owners for the first time. Two courses, Business Start Up for Women and Women as Business Advisers, provide such an entry for women. Graduate Enterprise has spread from Stirling to other Scottish higher education institutions aiming to recruit and support graduates with business ideas enabling them to start up on graduation. In addition Stirling has provided a short course for the training of trainers to train entrepreneurs how to be creative and innovative and a course on Computer-Aided Design/Computer-Aided Management with MSC funds.

The University at Stirling is also a member of three Local Collaborative Projects (LCPs) in which local businesses and the university pool resources to meet local training needs. One LCP sought to define the training needs of firms in Central Region while another looked at the impact of new technology on the Region's business. One LCP is in the process of gathering information to assess the impact of 1992 EEC unitary market on Central Region.

## 4. Information Technology Centre

Stirling is also unique in that the University runs an Information Technology Centre (ITEC) funded by the MSC through the YTS. This has been funded since 1984 at approximately £155 000 p.a. (1.5 per cent of university recurrent funding). The ITEC is not only housed in the university but is also managed by the university through an *ad hoc* Board of Management, and some of the teaching is by university staff. At its inception the place of the ITEC in the university structure was the subject of some debate as to whether it should be integrated with the academic management structure or left outside it as an *ad hoc* venture. The latter position was adopted on the grounds that the ITEC might prove a Trojan Horse for reducing the level of work carried on by the university. It provides 47 places on three training programmes with a 72 per cent occupancy. The programmes are in computing, electronics and the electronic office but the ITEC is used in the evening for local employers and other people, and it acts as a resource for training in computer literacy and in life and social skills for other YTS schemes.

In the contacts between the MSC and the universities outlined above we can see that part of the agenda mapped out by O'Brien has been fulfilled: the updating of skills and the development of business and management education. From these interventions the desire of the MSC to move towards a comprehensive manpower policy seems not to have impinged on the universities. Most striking about these contacts are their small scale (repeatedly the percentage of university funds provided by MSC is tiny) and their unco-ordinated, *ad hoc* nature. Few links between MSC interventions seem to exist and no *programme* is obvious. It was only in December 1987 that such a programme emerged: Enterprise in Higher Education (EHE).

### ENTERPRISE IN HIGHER EDUCATION

At first sight EHE is an astonishing initiative planning the fundamental restructuring of the higher education curriculum through money to be found, unplanned, in the 'normal estimating error' of the MSC budget. Its origins lay in a paper written by the director of the MSC, Geoffrey Holland, 'Higher Education: An Enterprise Programme'. Ministerial interest had 'been known for some time', and a meeting was held in January 1987 between the Secretaries of State for Employment and Education and Science, MSC and 'a number of senior representatives of higher education'.

Holland noted initiatives such as those reported above arguing that they were too limited, insufficiently focused and not disseminated effectively. 'We need to do more, and to weave together existing strands of activity into a more coherent whole. What *is* enterprise in the context of higher education?' Holland then went on to define enterprise as the appreciation of the economic and business setting, the acquisition of specific competence and the development of initiative and imagination. The majority of students, he noted, were 'untouched by enterprise activities' and thus they and the economy suffered.

The initiative Holland proposed was 'to take a major step forward so that every person seeking a higher qualification ... should be able to acquire key management/business competence and develop associated aptitudes, whether in the course of, or as an additional element to, their main area of study'. He then went on to outline the areas of higher education needing reform.

Access was to be widened through accepting achievements other than examination grades. The curriculum needed to be widened, made more relevant, more motivating, stimulating, practical, esteemed, assessed and the results marketable. To achieve this in a dispersed system of higher education needed the identification of desired competences, the reviewing of existing curricula, the implantation of the required elements, the monitoring of this implantation and the evaluation and dissemination of results. The privileged method for achieving these aims was thought to be business placements with assessment shared between university and employers. In order 'to develop teachers/lecturers' staff development programmes should give 'the opportunities to deploy their skills outside an HE context'.

The methods of mounting the programme proposed were innovative. Proposals had to come from an institution as a whole and not from a faculty or department, and they were to be submitted with evidence of commercial collaboration and financial support. Proposals crossing institutional lines (e.g. from consortia of higher education institutions or if linked with TVEI) were to be welcomed. MSC funding was to be limited to £200 000 p.a. per institution for five years and was to be dependent on commercial funding of at least £50 000 in the first year, increasing in later years. The timescale proposed was immediate so that 'the changes concerned could . . . begin to bite from 1988/89'.

This paper was sent to the Secretary of State for Employment, who asked MSC to mount the programme as soon as possible. In the paper presented to the Commission different inflections were present from those in the original paper. Firstly the coverage of the 'Enterprise Plan' is more firmly defined as the whole institution even those departments which 'prefer not to'. The enterprise elements of the curriculum were no longer to be 'bolt on' modules but integrated into the mainstream learning activities of the institution, 'enterprising graduates emerge from an enterprising system of education'. To this end the 'development' of staff was seen as more important than new curricula. Students would have no longer the option but the requirement of a placement in businesses (although this was still publicly referred to as the 'opportunity'). Funding, while for a five-year plan, would be on the basis of an annual contract renewed 'subject to satisfactory performance' and on the basis of the commitment to continue the programme beyond the five-year funding period.

UNIVERSITY AUTONOMY

In order to understand the Enterprise in Higher Education Programme we need to step back to chart its strategic importance. No longer is the game one of management education here, updating skills there together with cautious attempts at manpower planning towards more science (the O'Brien agenda) but, I suggest, a fundamental attack on university autonomy (and the consequent but not identical practice of academic freedom). The logic of this is to eradicate one of the more persistent points of resistance to the New Right cultural revolution and finally to subordinate 'education' to the servicing of 'the economy'.

University autonomy is a slippery concept but one crucial to the proper functioning of universities. One of the last acts of Sir Hector Hetherington, former Principal and Vice Chancellor of Glasgow, was to define university autonomy in a paper to the International Association of Universities. In this he argued that the core logical component of the concept 'university' was a community of scholars, holding various perspectives while seeking better to understand truth. From this definition he deduces that autonomy is a necessary condition of the existence of universities and that it resides in the freedom of universities to appoint staff, select students, define a curriculum and the standards required, determine a research programme and the allocation of funds received as they see fit in pursuit of truth. As J. M. Fraser argues in his meticulous 'The Decline of Autonomy of British Universities in the Robbins Era 1963–1983' this definition coincided with the definition of autonomy developed historically by the University Grants Committee (which indeed added a further test: that the institution should define its own size and growth).

If we consider the Enterprise in Higher Education programme according to these criteria we can see it as a precise attack on university autonomy and academic freedom. All aspects of the curriculum are to be reworked to conform to an 'enterprising' perspective, existing staff competence changed (and thus by extension new appointments determined) to conform to this perspective, criteria for student admission altered to advance this perspective, assessment procedures be modified to include those prominent in enterprise and the allocation of funds determined to these ends by an external body.

Offering £200 000 p.a. for a maximum of five years (less than 1.5 per cent of Stirling's income, 0.2 per cent of Edinburgh's income) why should any university participate in the enterprise programme? The first round of applications closed in May 1988 and a substantial number were submitted; Glasgow's was the one successful Scottish application. The Stirling application was for the university to co-ordinate and provide central services for a consortium of ten Scottish institutions each of which would be altering its curriculum to meet the demands of the programme. This application failed the first time (reputedly since Stirling was already seen as enterprising enough) but success is expected in the second round.

It is in explaining this enigma that the impact of the MSC on the universities over the past fifteen years can be assessed.

## THE MSC AS PARADIGM

While the direct effects of the MSC on the universities have been scattered and limited the indirect effect of the MSC providing a new model of utilitarian training has been central to the restructuring of the universities. I am *not* pivoting this analysis on a suggestion of conspiracy (a latent agenda to restructure the universities existing from 1974 and only now becoming explicit) but on the convergence of many factors which have created the MSC both as a paradigm of new state agencies and as a paradigm of 'education'. The combination of these two features has enabled the MSC to articulate a new educational ideology and to have in place the administrative procedures to establish this in practice despite considerable opposition.

This configuration was first developed in the area of post-school education and training. Within two years of its foundation, the speed and agility of the MSC had contributed significantly to a scathing review by the Expenditure Committee of the House of Commons of educational management by the DES. In its report the Committee notes that 'the TSA has moved at a tempo which DES could not (and indeed should not try to) emulate'. The extensive evidence taken by that Committee revealed bitter complaints from a galaxy of other educational institutions that the MSC was proceeding inappropriately. Challenged on this the Chief Executive of the TSA, K. R. Cooper, responded,

> We have established systems there which give managers in those agencies a kind of commitment to programmes which has not been usual in the public service, I think. As a matter of fact, managers in those agencies have measures of discretion to carry those programmes through which have not been altogether traditional in the public service . . . we are very much concerned with the service to people in the market place and we try to make the measure of what we do the effectiveness of that service. So that I think as a result of the agencies being established there is a measure of urgency perhaps unconventionality, a measure of liberty to be more open . . .

The core elements of the product of this liberty can briefly be delineated. Firstly the MSC has been responsible for bringing into the ambit of 'education' groups traditionally hostile to it. In doing this it has operated initially by offering 'opportunity' and then by making this opportunity a practical compulsion through financial pressure on the individual (e.g. those on YTS). Once within the ambit of the new educational practice, trainees are subject to a new form of curriculum which disqualifies previous organizations of knowledge. In particular existing units of knowledge, which act as power bases for various groups, are broken in favour of new organizations (e.g. time-served craft knowledge giving way to generic skills). Such new organizations seek to fit knowledge closely to perceived needs of the existing forms of production. In particular modularization fosters the flexibility of labour, social and life skills, and the conformity of labour to existing authority structures (e.g. YTS).

The subjects of this new education are relentlessly assessed against detailed checklists of cognitive and affective characteristics with such assessments often being made by employers and being made available to potential employers (e.g. City and Guilds 365). In this model staffing is radically revised. Training may be a profitable activity in its own right rather than a public good (e.g. commercial training companies) while existing public service staff may have to abandon old competencies for new ones (e.g. TRIST). Teaching packages, centrally determined or centrally approved in detail, cut local deviations from policy to a minimum (e.g. the Action Plan).

The boundaries between existing institutions are blurred allowing the easier transfer of functions and the lessening of resistance from institutions to the outward growth of the MSC from further education (in e.g. TVEI). The new system is managed in a radically different way from the old. Reliance on notions of 'professionalism' (of the largely self-regulating expert) all but disappear in favour of a version of management by objectives, the setting of criteria of procedure and performance in a hierarchical reporting system (see, e.g. the contrast between Her Majesty's Inspectors of Schools and the Training Standards Advisory Service).

This new model is made to run through straightforward financial pressure: the decline of funding for activities of the 'old' model and the ready availability of funding for the activities of the new. As the Expenditure Committee put it as early as 1976 the MSC has 'the money bags'. Control is exerted not only through simple financial pressure but also through its use in short-term contracts. Funding for institutions is not secured and new contracts depend on past compliance and responsiveness to new demands.

Above all the model represents the systematic and single-minded subordination of educational goals and practices to one end: meeting the perceived needs of the economy in all its changing forms. While each element of this model may be traced back beyond the MSC or may be shown to be part of the educational practice of another agency, the combination which the MSC has forged is, I suggest, aggressively new.

## THE RESTRUCTURING OF THE UNIVERSITY SYSTEM

The rush of the universities to embrace Enterprise in Higher Education can be explained in terms of the MSC model already largely imposed on them as autonomy has been dismantled. The series of progressive cuts in funding initiated in July 1981 left the universities vulnerable with high fixed costs, rapidly increasing student demand but diminishing resources. In each of the areas of autonomy outlined above, restructuring has caused the universities to move away from practices governed by community, scholarship and truth towards the practices of contract-bound suppliers of services to the economy.

As Fraser argues, the autonomy of the university system historically has relied on the trinity of the constitution of the UGC, the block grant system and the quinquennial allocation of recurrent grant in response to submissions from each university. The block-grant system, whereby each university had freedom to allocate resources within the sum granted by the UGC, was the first to decline with the expansion of Higher Education after Robbins. In 1966/67 the UGC gave broad student targets for the system and for individual institutions. In 1970 guidance was given in very general terms about departmental developments with detailed student numbers for institutions given in 1972. The quinquennium system did not survive the inflation of the mid-1970s; it collapsed in 1975 and was replaced by cash-limited grants on varying planning horizons, for which the actual sum for any one year would only be determined as (or after) the year began. These grants have become increasingly more *dirigiste* so that now the UGC is determining the funding of single posts in universities.

The UGC itself has not survived the 1980s; it is being replaced in 1989 by the Universities Funding Council. Developed from 1889 as a buffer between state and universities, the UGC was reviewed by the Croham Committee in 1987. This Committee (dominated by industrialists) recommended that a new body be formed not by representation of academic interests but by simple nomination by the Secretary of State. Details of allocations and the management of the system were not to be the task of the new body but the executive action of the Chief Executive and the civil servants on the basis of performance indicators. The Secretary of State was to have the right to direct the new body. Universities were to be funded on a three-year contract basis in which detailed student numbers per subject would be specified with positive and negative earmarking of funds accordingly. Further selectivity of research funding was to be introduced so that some institutions might no longer be funded to carry out research.

Existing institutional boundaries have been softened, if not yet remoulded. In the early 1980s Stirling felt it prudent to consider, and ultimately to reject, merger with Paisley College. The academic plans of St Andrews, Dundee and Stirling have to be co-ordinated before submission to the UGC, where they are considered side by side. Collaboration is a condition of consideration of further funding by UGC, and merger into a University of Tayforth is openly on the agenda.

The move away from autonomy seen above at the level of the UGC is reflected in the management restructuring of the universities recommended by the Jarratt Committee for Efficiency Studies set up by the Committee of Vice Chancellors and Principals in 1985. The thrust of the Jarratt Report was to introduce line management techniques in universities and move away from methods of government and administration based on collegiality and professional autonomy towards the hierarchical reporting systems and management by objectives. The Vice Chancellor and Principal was to become the Chief Executive and many issues decided administratively by executive action.

Assessment of students has traditionally been seen as a core area of university autonomy, as therein lies the discretion to award a degree or not. As pressure to produce immediately employable graduates increased, so did pressure to involve outside accreditation agencies who could control access to privileged parts of the labour market. The Reynolds Committee on Academic Standards in Universities set up by the Committee of Vice Chancellors and Principals, in its report of 1986, suggested codes of practice to extend the role of people external to a university in the assessment of students, as well as codes for the tighter control of staff.

The position of academic staff as individuals has been radically altered. Individuals whose activities do not figure in the future plans of a university (the Peter Tebbitt formulation used at Aston) have been put under intense pressure to take early retirement, to resign or to transfer to another university. Those who have resisted have often seen the material base for their work disappear. Tenure, the bulwark of the individual academic to hold opinions unpopular with those in authority, has been outlawed (for all contracts since 1987) as Parliamentary Commissioners are being sent round to revise Charters. More detailed surveillance of the work of individual academics has been introduced now that participation in appraisal and staff development schemes have become compulsory under the 1986 pay settlement, while the right of individuals to conduct research (one of the dual roles of academic staff) is threatened by selectivity exercises.

The administrative procedures necessary to convert the university ideal from that of a community of scholars holding diverse perspectives in the pursuit of truth into one of a centralized training organization for the labour market are thus substantially in place. Enterprise in Higher Education represents the next stage of the buy out of education already almost complete in further education and substantially complete in secondary education.

PROSPECT

The objections which may be made to the narrow utilitarianism of the MSC model of education are legion. I want to finish by considering a subset of these which seems most pertinent for higher education and then by suggesting how higher education might seek to inhabit the new political climate while retaining a firm commitment to community, diversity and the pursuit of truth.

One reaction to the increasing imposition of the 'world of work' as the reference point for universities, more attributed than real, is to deny the legitimacy of utilitarian concerns for universities. This is demonstrably incorrect historically (universities would have to be seen as rarely having been universities if at all) and easy to demolish politically (hence its attribution to those resisting the new vocationalism). The question seems to me to be not whether universities should engage with production but how they should.

A second reaction to the MSC model is to argue a pluralist case from philosophy. In any society, so this argument goes, there are many interests which should be represented and developed in universities. The new vocationalism is the attempt by one perspective to disqualify others and to install itself as the central, dominant motif of universities. At the heart of this objection lies some notion of balance: that a certain vocationalism is legitimate but that there should not be too much of it and that it should not be too intrusive. Such objections have strong grounds in theories of democracy and political tolerance, but the theoretical and practical difficulties of defining the 'balance' can make objections appear arbitrary.

More telling from a pluralist perspective is the epistemological argument that our knowledge is always provisional, tentative and subject to falsification and that it is impossible to predict from where new knowledge might start. To rely on one definition of useful knowledge is both to run the risk of that definition being falsified with no developed alternatives at hand and also to inhibit the development of that definition by limiting the number of available hypotheses through which it might grow. Such an objection seems to me to carry substantial weight but ultimately to be limited by an inability to explain the boundaries between hypotheses unacceptable to the current orthodoxy but still admissible to the higher education discourse and hypotheses which are both unacceptable and inadmissible.

This brings me to the final series of objections for these purposes. These objections revolve around arguments about knowledge and power which see knowledge not as neutral disciplines but as both expressive and constitutive of power groups in society. From this perspective the logic of the MSC model is to subordinate all forms of knowledge to the knowledge of the group currently controlling production and, in particular, to present this knowledge as objective and indisputable, as primary.

The nature of this objection suggests strategies for universities to inhabit the MSC model but in a way which does not uncritically assume the perspective of employers. Accepting the nature of production and the reproduction of the labour force as legitimate issues (being the basis of daily life for most of the population), universities committed to a rounded consideration of the issues would want to start teaching and researching on the themes thrown up by, for example, mass youth unemployment: not only why employers find young people lacking in 'employability' but also what young people leaving school want to do with their energies, what it is that prevents from doing that, why the jobs that were once available are no longer available, why it is that employers are demanding certain things of young people, how young people define their needs for further education etc.

Clearly such a version of the academic analysis of the world of work would not easily be won. It would depend on universities opening themselves to groups traditionally excluded, reforming curricular and research programmes to encompass issues previously excluded, taking new reference points from the social context and developing new methods of government. In short it would depend on universities developing into popular institutions applying the highest intellectual resources to the real-life issues of the moment with all the different perspectives involved. The declared aim of Enterprise in Higher Education is to move higher education towards 'a self-sustaining regime'. The question is whether it is to be sustained by the money of the powerful or by the support of ordinary people.

*Acknowledgements*

In researching this chapter I have been greatly helped by many people who have gone out of their way to find information for me. I am very grateful to them all but would like specifically to acknowledge my debts to the ever-patient John Fairley and the ever-helpful Carolyn Rowlinson.

REFERENCES

At the request of the editors I have not given detailed footnotes and references in the usual manner. The major sources used were the Annual Reports, Corporate Plans and Research Reports of the MSC, the Quinquennial, Annual and Working Party Reports of the UGC, the various Reports of the CVCP and the Grierson Archive material on the development of the University of Stirling (University of Stirling Library). In addition heavy use was made of the Command Papers of the House of Commons and the statistical series on Universities published by HMSO. One work which I have found extremely stimulating is James M. Fraser, 'The Decline of Autonomy of British Universities in the Robbins Era, 1963–1983', unpublished dissertation submitted in part fulfilment for the Degree of Master of Education, University of Stirling, 1983. Any specific questions about sources may be addressed to the author at The University of Stirling, Stirling FK9 4LA.

# CHAPTER 6. EDITORS' INTRODUCTION

The MSC had a very important influence on aspects of computing and information technology (IT) education, and acquired a fairly strong presence in these areas, partly because it wished to present itself as the modernizing force in education which was concerned with the essential skills of the future, and partly because the inclusion of some computing/IT elements made it possible to recoup funds from the EEC Social Fund to help finance major programmes like the Youth Training Scheme.

The MSC also helped to push particular approaches to computing education. This was clearest in the schools-based Technical and Vocational Education Initiative (TVEI), which is the focus of this chapter. (A broader assessment of TVEI is presented in Chapter 3.) The MSC's approach to computing IT is compared with that of the Scottish Education Department.

# 6

## THE 'BATTLES OF YESTERYEAR': COMPUTING, THE SED AND THE MSC

TOM CONLON

> ... I want to try and ensure that the kids of today are trained with
> the skills that gave their fathers and grandfathers jobs. It's like
> generals fighting the battles of yesteryear ... And that is the reason
> why we've pushed ahead with computers into schools. I want
> youngsters, boys and girls leaving school at sixteen, to actually be
> able to operate a computer.

With these stirring words Kenneth Baker, as the newly appointed Minister for Information Technology, launched the 1981 Department of Industry (DoI) scheme to provide half the cost of a microcomputer for every secondary school (Wellington, 1988). Both north and south of the border the initiative was widely welcomed. Especially optimistic in Scotland was the minority of teachers who were computing enthusiasts and who had long been left waiting for any official support for their efforts. Although some doubts were expressed, these were mainly at the pragmatic level: were the teachers sufficiently prepared, was there enough software to make the hardware usable, who would pay for repair of the machines when they broke down?

Important though these questions were, they left unchallenged the assumptions which underpinned Baker's rhetoric. Why was an Industry minister intervening in schools? Since when had it been the role of school education to provide vocational training? Where was the evidence that jobs in the 'sunrise industry' of computing would be the reward for pupils trained in the right skills, even assuming that the schools could offer them? And how could the provision of a single half-price machine make a serious contribution to anything? For the most part these questions were left unasked. Sadly, the shallow response of Scottish education to the 1981 DoI scheme was to foreshadow a decade in which the relationship between education and computing was seldom effectively scrutinized.

That computing has had an injection of resources, and this at a time when public education generally has been starved of them, is not in doubt. Since 1981 the UK government has centrally committed more than £40 million to the school micro and the resources associated with it. This is more than any other item of educational technology in the history of schooling (Wellington, 1988). Yet even this sum is dwarfed by the £200 million which has been invested overall in the MSC's Technical and Vocational Education Initiative (TVEI). The political return for the money spent has been apparent in the numerous Conservative party political broadcasts which have portrayed a smiling Baker (later elevated to the rank of Education Minister) surrounded by eager youngsters in a hi-tech classroom. But what is the educational reality behind the media gloss? Who has controlled the computing budgets and in what ways have the schools been affected?

In Scotland the responsibility for implementing government policy for school computing has been shared between the Scottish Education Department (SED) and the MSC. The contrast between these two agencies, both in terms of their published agendas and their styles of work, has sometimes been sharp, but each in its own way has been pursuing the vocationalist outcomes which were offered by the 1981 rhetoric. I shall argue that the vocationalist rationale for school computing lacks credibility. In its pursuit, the SED and the MSC have each been guilty of misleading pupils and parents whilst allowing much of the very real potential that existed for computing in Scottish education to go untapped.

## PERSPECTIVES FOR EDUCATIONAL COMPUTING

Hardly anybody denies that computers, and more generally Information Technology (IT), *do* have a valuable contribution to make to school education. The issues are really those of what the precise goals should be and of how these can best be achieved. It will be useful here to describe briefly some recent thinking.

During the 1980s educationists in many countries have reached a clear consensus over what should be the most important role for IT in schools. This consensus says that the technology ought to be harnessed to support teaching and learning in the *existing* curriculum. Computers should best be regarded as another type of classroom aid, like the overhead projector or the textbook, but potentially far more powerful. There is much evidence to suggest that learning in almost any subject, and at almost any age and stage, can benefit from software which either teaches the subject directly or (much more typically) plays a supporting role to the classroom teacher. It is recognized that pupils will certainly acquire IT skills in this way, but these are seen as a by-product rather than the main aim. The success of this 'curriculum computing' approach in practice is known to be critically dependent on the availability of good computing resources and on the teacher preparation needed to ensure that the new opportunities are taken up.

The 'curriculum computing' approach definitely regards the study of computing *per se* as a secondary, less important matter. However, at least three rationales can be made in favour of computing courses of some kind.

Some education writers, including Caroline Benn (1987), have presented 'computer literacy' arguments. Typically these attempt to identify a core of computing knowledge and skill which are claimed to be desirable for *all* learners: the reasons given are mainly social (that in a 'technological culture', to lack computer understanding is to be isolated) and political (that lack of knowledge is denial of power). The problem for schools is to decide how computer literacy will be achieved. It is important to recognize that computer literacy is presented analogously with basic numeracy and with fundamental skills in reading and writing: it represents a target for all pupils and hence demands a response in the *core* curriculum. But this does not necessarily imply a need for formal computing courses. The knowledge and skill levels suggested by computer literacy arguments are typically low enough that they should easily be overtaken by an effective 'curriculum computing' policy, together perhaps with suitable adaptations within the social science elements of the core curriculum. It can also be agued – somewhat ironically – that if the technology really is as socially all-pervasive as the claims suggest, then (eventually) no special educational provision should be needed for the children will surely become as casually accustomed to IT as did their parents to telephones and cars.

A different rationale for computing courses is one which proposes that computing science should become an option (perhaps like Russian or Botany) in the secondary school curriculum. It is quite easy to find computing scientists who will argue vigorously that their subject has now become a rich and important area of human knowledge. It is much harder to find among them any two who can agree upon precisely what their subject is actually about. What, the perplexed observer of the computing scene may wonder, is held in common between on the one hand, the blue-suited employees of International Business Machines Ltd. (IBM), whose smooth selling talk is of executive productivity tools and management information systems, and on the other hand, the renowned researchers in artificial intelligence who pronounce boldly that for them the goal 'is to build a person, or more humbly, an animal' (Charniack and McDermott, 1985)? But this very diversity can be a source of excitement. Even within the apparently staid world of IBM there is a massively funded research programme in which new discoveries and developments in the uncharted waters of computing are made regularly. The absence of centuries of prior work has the advantage that computing is refreshingly free of the usual rigid taxonomies of topics and domains. Thus Robin Milner, Professor of Computer Science at Edinburgh University, has noted that we all find it baffling to try to demarcate between the sciences of Computing, Intelligence and Cognition. Fortunately, there is so much to do that no-one finds any value in boundary disputes! (Milner, 1986)

If this same spirit of openness and enthusiasm could permeate a school's treatment of computing science, then there seems every hope that it could provide an excellent experience for learners. Certainly there are opportunities as well as difficulties in facing up to a subject in which not only the correct answers but also the correct questions are yet to be determined. Given a willingness to reflect the diversity and to experiment with a variety of syllabus formulations, there seems to be no reason why computing could not be implemented so as to be consistent with wider educational goals, such as the development of scientific thinking skills for example. Pupils taking computing as a special interest in this way might in consequence become attracted to further or higher education courses in computing science.

The crudest rationale for computing courses is the vocationalist one. This regards IT training as the task for schools, and the main problem becomes an accurate identification of what skills the market demands. It follows that teachers should implement courses which offer the precise blend of skills that will match pupils to the available jobs. During the 1980s this rationale has explicitly or implicitly underpinned much of the policy for school computing, and indeed in Scotland it has scarcely been challenged. This fact is all the more remarkable since the evidence to justify this position is extremely hard to find.

## COMPUTING AND VOCATIONALISM

Of course there are some strong contradictions within the vocationalist position. First, the new technologies are upheld as the means by which the quality of life should be improved, and the 'leisured society' attained: yet this advance is implied to depend upon an 'industrialization' of the school curriculum, with job-oriented skills partially supplanting studies in the cultural and aesthetic areas. Second, the citizen best equipped for an advanced technological society is widely agreed to be an adaptable, flexible problem solver who can rapidly acquire new skills and who will probably hold many different jobs in a working life: yet we are asked to move towards not the broad, liberal education which seems ideally suited for such a prospect, but instead towards a schooling which looks more like a specialist training. Third, the vocationalists emphasize the rapidity of technological and structural change: yet they claim to be so confident about the precise skill requirements of future employment that educational policy can be safely based on their predictions.

The vocational ideology seems to suffer from an extreme case of internal inconsistency. But more pragmatically, it founders through an almost complete lack of allies from inside the camp where they might be thought to be most numerous: that of the employers and of industry itself. A great amount of research has been conducted during the 1980s into the employers' needs for IT workers, and it will be useful briefly to review this now.

The studies all more or less concur on the main points. They show that, for specialist IT employees, the skill requirements are high and rising fast; they are already well above the level that can be reached by TVEI, schools, the MSC's ITeCs (Information Technology Centres), and the non-advanced vocational initiatives generally. For example, the report *IT Manpower into the 1990's* produced in 1986 by the Institute of Manpower Studies confirms that IT skills shortages are widespread and will get worse, but the demand is largely for personnel at graduate level and above. The Engineering Industry Training Board 1987 report *Trends in Computing Qualifications* confirms the high-level skill requirements which will be expected of future IT employees, with employers looking for qualifications generally in excess of those obtainable at the lower levels of further education or through initiatives such as the Threshold or ITeC programmes. The DoI's IT Skills Shortage Committee's Butcher Reports similarly identified graduate supply shortfall as the main cause of concern.

But what of employees other than IT specialists? Of course many of them will use IT, but most research suggests that the IT skill requirements are simple and are best met by specialized on-the-job training. There is no employer-led demand for an effort on the part of schools to pre-emptively supply this training. Sheffield University's report *Skills for the Future* (1987), which was commissioned by the MSC, contacted over 1 000 employers and discovered that 'employers do not favour a narrow, skill-based approach to IT education at school level ... few suggested that Computer Studies is a valuable qualification at O or CSE level'. Many employers, however, were recruiting IT staff at graduate level and above and consistently they suggest that schools should encourage more young people to go on to further and higher education in IT-related subjects. An Exeter University report *Job Skills in the Computer Age* (1984), based on a survey of 145 companies, states that employment demand for low-level computing skills is likely to diminish. It advises young people to avoid computer studies at school and follow traditional disciplines, although 'keyboard skills' are identified as important. The report *New Technology and Mathematics in Employment* (1985) from the University of Birmingham examines 31 companies and concludes that thanks to 'user-friendly' systems, most employees had adapted without difficulty to working with the new technology.

It is of passing interest to note that 'keyboard skills' look much less important now than they did five years ago. Most modern computer systems have sophisticated graphical interfaces, so-called 'WIMP environments' (Windows, Icons, Mouse, Pull-down menus), which largely bypass the keyboard as the means of communicating with the machine. There still exist a few applications, with word processing as the most notable example, in which the keyboard remains dominant, but the existence of several current projects (including one at Edinburgh University) to develop speech-driven word processors suggests that even for these the keyboard may soon become of secondary importance. This underlines the danger of stressing specific skills, even apparently 'safe' ones: in computing they become obsolete very quickly. Indeed, it can be argued that the best answer to those educationists who demanded 'computer literacy' in human beings has come from a computing science which is increasingly building 'human literacy' into computers.

From industry, then, we have a picture which Reinecke's study, *The Micro Invaders* (1982), of skill changes in the telecom industry summed up as 'taking out the middle'. Reinecke writes that:

> The technology demands either very skilled electronic engineers or those with straight physical skills needed for functions such as lifting, carrying and simple installation. All the skills in between become redundant.

Employers are worried about IT skill shortages, but they know that the answer does not lie with the schools. The demand for vocational computing courses, which is explicit in Baker's 'battles of yesteryear' rhetoric actually flies in the face of the advice which comes from industry itself.

So why make such a speech at all? At the most generous interpretation, the government has been guilty of making wildly false predictions. But it is hard to avoid relating the motives instead to a more cynical calculation over the wider political agenda for education which has dominated the 1980s. This agenda has included some potentially very unpopular policies: for example, the introduction of compulsory testing at the ages of 7, 11 and 14; the proposals for school boards and the 'opting-out' of schools from elected local authorities; the centralization of the curriculum; and the transfer of power in many areas of education into the hands of business representatives. Clearly the acceptability of these policies might be increased by creating in the public mind a perception that comprehensive schooling was in some sense 'out of date' and no longer capable of serving society's changing needs.

## COMPUTING GOALS FOR THE SED AND THE MSC
### 1. The SED

What then have been the objectives of the SED and MSC in the educational computing area?

From the SED in the 1970s the policy was set out in the Bellis Report of 1972. Bellis, who was headteacher at Daniel Stewart's College, a private school in Edinburgh, recommended that

> work relating to computers should generally be incorporated into the teaching of the various school subjects. Computing Studies

should not be developed as a subject discipline in its own right (Bellis, 1972)

The Report proposed that to underpin this 'curriculum computing' approach all pupils should be provided with some computer literacy:

an appreciation of the working and potential of computers as a necessary basis for future applications in many subjects.

The idea that for some pupils the new area of computing science might have the potential to become a worthwhile subject for study is dismissed:

they [i.e. pupils] could only do this by studying the subject as an alternative to some other of wider acceptability ... Computing becomes meaningful in its application within the area of activity it is serving.

In some respects the Bellis Report represented an enlightened position. It contained no hint of vocationalism and its concern was for schools to respond to computing in such a way as to benefit the all-round education of the majority of pupils. But the committee's dismissal of the educational potential of computing science has a strong flavour of academic snobbery. And because of the SED's well-known centralist, top-down style of policy making, Bellis effectively excluded the subject from all Scottish schools throughout the 1970s. Evidence of the completeness of the exclusion is the absence of any mention for computing in the influential 1977 Munn Report on the secondary school curriculum. In contrast, teachers south of the border were able to negotiate money for resources and had the freedom to experiment with a variety of new computing courses.

With little school access to machines, the Bellis 'curricular computing' strategy had negligible impact. But with the arrival of microcomputers in the late 1970s prospects looked better. Micros meant that computing 'incorporated into the teaching of the various school subjects' might at last become a reality. The SED set up the Scottish Microelectronics Development Programme (SMDP) with a four-year remit costing £1 million to develop educational software and to provide support for schools. In England and Wales the Microelectronics Education Programme (MEP) was established, with a fairly similar set of objectives.

Very soon there began to emerge disquieting stories about the SED's management of SMDP. The 'official' line was that all was going well, and when J. G. Morris, an SED HMCI (Chief Inspector) and the chairman of SMDP's steering committee, described the experience of the first two years of SMDP in the 1982 *European Journal of Education*, he did so in tones of confident complacency:

Much has been learned in two years about the process of integrating computers into education. The hardware needs of the main curriculum subjects are clearer and there is enough software to support training courses. The experience of these two years in Scotland may the better inform any educational group or system which in 1982 is at the beginning of micro-integration.

But a sharply contrasting picture of the experience came from elsewhere. In that same year an independent evaluation of SMDP was published by two Edinburgh University researchers. Their study pointed to major problems in the centralist, SED-directed control of SMDP, the work of which was being rated poorly by teachers in comparison to that of the decentralized MEP. The internal conflicts had led to the resignation of SMDP's Depute Director in September 1981 and relationships with SED had been brought 'near to breaking point' (Odor and Entwhistle, 1982). The Edinburgh Report also pointed out that 'curriculum computing' would require far more resources than the SED had been willing to spend. It identified major problems in the lack of hardware; in the time required to develop good software; in the requirement for teacher education and preparation; and in the absence of an adequate research and development programme. The report concluded:

The potential is there – but teachers will need encouragement, support, and release from class contact to be able fully to grasp the opportunities offered by the microelectronics revolution.

The implication that heavy and recurrent further expenditure would be necessary would hardly be welcomed by the SED. Indeed the researchers themselves describe an interview with the Minister, who at that time was Alex Fletcher. Fletcher is quoted as saying:

I was delighted ... that for a relatively small amount of funds we could get something off the ground, as we did. It is not an expensive operation in terms of value.

At about that time the SED dramatically changed its line on computing studies. Morris (1982) mentions the matter casually in his article:

A joint SCEEB/CCC [Scottish Certificate of Education Examination Board/Consultative Committee on the Curriculum] committee decided in February 1981 that it was time to offer 'O' Grade computing in Scotland. ... It has therefore been agreed by the Secretary of State to run a pilot 'O' grade in 17 schools starting in August 1982

This switch was all the more surprising in view of the fact that plans were already well under way to withdraw all existing O grades in favour of the new post-Munn Standard Grade curriculum. To introduce an O grade in a new subject at that point meant not just a policy reversal: it demonstrated an urgency which looked close to panic.

It is often difficult to fathom the SED's motives; in this case the explanation probably has at least four parts. First, the 1981 DoI scheme to provide schools with micros had been launched on the vocationalist hype characterized by Baker's 'battles of yesteryear' speech. Without computing courses of some kind in the schools the propaganda would look ridiculous. Second, 'curriculum computing' was proving to be tricky and expensive: an O grade in computing may have seemed an opportune means to prevent the machines from gathering dust and becoming too much of an embarrassment. Third, there was some genuine pressure from teachers for the move, especially from those whose enthusiasm (and possible promotion) had been blocked by the Bellis policy through the 1970s.

But the fourth and most important factor may have been the MSC. The MSC at that time was at the height of its expansionist phase and was on the verge of extending its educational tentacles outwards from the FE colleges and into the schools. The SED will have known that the MSC was about to unleash its TVEI programme: rumours abounded that the SED was making a bid to intercept Scottish TVEI funds *en bloc*. The sudden announcement of the new O grade in computing may well have been partly an attempt to give the SED some credibility in its bureaucratic struggle to fend off the MSC.

Yet the SED was clearly in trouble. The strain of implementing mass-scale Computing Studies courses was likely to damage badly the impact of 'curriculum computing', since these two were in direct competition for scarce skills and resources. Furthermore, after a decade of non-engagement with the subject of computing the prospects for high-quality courses were distinctly poor: teacher training was almost non-existent, for example. Computing-science graduates had been consistently deterred from joining the Scottish teaching profession, not just because of its pay and conditions but also because throughout the Bellis period their subject had gone unrecognized by the SED.

In these circumstances a genuinely sound curriculum development might still have been feasible, but it would have had unattractive implications to the SED. It would necessitate a gradual exploration of the new subject which could slowly accumulate a range of pointers to the most promising interpretations of educational aims, content, teaching and learning styles, and so on. Such a process would be lengthy and its outcomes (and hence its contribution to political propaganda) would be unpredictable. Perhaps worse, a genuine exploration of the subject's potential would probably have required a classroom-led, 'bottom-up' development which would put the teachers in control. Diversity would be inevitable. This would hardly have appealed to the SED with its propensity for leading by the nose.

In this context the SED's conversion to the need for computing courses which were vocationally orientated can be understood. Such an orientation was not only clearly favoured by Ministers: it was also the least demanding in the requirement for trained teachers. A skills-based prescription of approved content, suitably embellished with a rhetoric which was careful to appeal to computer literacy and even computing science arguments as well as to the vocational ideology, could be centrally produced quite easily. And to the SEDs' HMIS, who were overwhelmingly themselves the products of more traditional academic disciplines, 'practical', work-related courses in computing might be the only kind which could make sense. The old Bellis view that 'Computing becomes meaningful in its application within the area of activity it is serving' still carried a lot of weight, even although the Inspectors would have been indignant had the same comment been made about Mathematics or English for example. Thus Morris announced that for the new O grade syllabus: 'the emphasis will not be on hardware or logic but on applications' (1982).

By 'applications' the SED meant business and industrial computing skills. It was a decision which maximized the likelihood that the course could be running inside a large number of schools within a short period of time. But it also committed computing to the vocational line, and certainly the concept of a creative investigation of a new science was nowhere apparent.

The SED's Standard Grade computing studies course which rapidly followed on from the introduction of the O grade developed these trends still further. Specified by a working group which substantially comprised individuals who had constructed the O grade syllabus, the Standard Grade prescribes a training-style 'case study' approach as the only permissible classroom methodology. Teachers are expected to make their 14–16-year-old charges into adept users of business data processing systems such as those for mail order, stock control, word processing, and seat booking. Pupils operate junior versions of these programs (scaled down to fit their BBC Micros) and role play what is portrayed to be the typical work of an IT operative.

Certainly the SED had achieved one thing. Within O grade and standard grade computing classrooms there was no risk of 'demarcation disputes' between the boundary areas of Milner's 'sciences of Computing, Intelligence and Cognition': none of these things were to be allowed to interfere with learning. Computing was to be interpreted as an arm of commerce, with the 'electronic office' rather than the research lab upheld as the centre of progress. As surely as in the 1970s the subject was decreed not to exist, so in the 1980s its existence, and the dogmatic interpretation of its rationale in commercial applications and vocational opportunities, was decreed also. Sadly, the new position generated scarcely any more debate than the old.

## 2. The MSC

The MSC's announcement in 1982 of the TVEI programme came as a shock to many in education. According to the MSC, the scheme would fund projects aiming to provide 'a four year course combining general with technical and vocational education'. In a letter to local authorities David Young, the former banker who had been appointed to the chair of the MSC by Mrs Thatcher earlier in the year, indicated that the general objective was to widen and enrich the curriculum in a way that will help young people prepare for the world of work ... In a time of rapid technological change, the extent to which particular occupational skills are required will change. What is important about this initiative is that youngsters should receive an education which will enable them to adapt to the changing occupational environment (quoted in Dale, 1985).

Where the SED's goals seemed often difficult to discern, the MSC was avowedly open about its vocationalist intentions. Young had publicly accused the comprehensive schools of helping to keep the UK economy in recession by failing to 'vocationalize the curriculum' and he had suggested simplistically that much of the problem would be solved if schools trained youngsters to fill available jobs (Young, 1984). For TVEI, the MSC supplied a written set of seven aims with six supporting requirements. The aims were:

In conjunction with LEAS to explore and test ways of organising and managing the education of 14–18 year old people across the ability range so that:

*i*) more of them are attracted to seek the qualifications/skills which will be of direct value to them at work and more of them achieve these qualifications and skills;

*ii*) they are better equipped to enter the world of employment which will await them;

*iii*) they acquire a more direct appreciation of the practical application of the qualifications for which they are working;

*iv*) they become accustomed to using their skills and knowledge to solve the real-world problems they will meet at work;

*v*) more emphasis is placed on developing initiative, motivation and enterprise as well as problem-solving skills and other aspects of personal development;

*vi*) the construction of the bridge from education to work is begun earlier by giving these young people the opportunity to have direct contact and training/planned work experience with a number of local employers in the relevant specialisms;

*vii*) there is close collaboration between local education authorities and industry/commerce/public services etc, so that the curriculum has industry's confidence.

Local authorities were invited to submit proposals for projects which were consistent with these aims: the projects would be managed at local level but be assessed and monitored by the MSC. Many of the fears which were voiced in response to this development saw TVEI as much more than a vocationalist initiative. It was suspected of being an attempt by the MSC to take control of secondary education and even 'to break up the comprehensive system and reestablish ... differentiation at all levels' (Chitty, 1986). Initial opposition to TVEI was very strong, and in Scotland the largest teacher's union, the EIS, added a partial TVEI boycott to its escalating campaign of industrial action against the SED on pay and conditions.

But TVEI went ahead. Three local authorities (Strathclyde, Dumfries and Galloway, Fife) began TVEI pilot projects in 1984. Others, including Lothian, followed the next year and in February 1988 the MSC announced that 9 000 Scottish pupils were undertaking TVEI courses and that all Scottish regions would soon be supporting the scheme. Although there is still considerable hostility towards TVEI from many teachers – enough indeed to persuade an EIS special conference in October 1988 to pass a motion urging a total boycott – it is clear that TVEI has to a large extent ridden out its harshest critics.

Several factors have combined to produce the change of attitude. First and foremost TVEI has been welcomed by teachers as a source of re- sources, meaning the additional staffing required to support curriculum development as well as cash for books and equipment. Teachers in the TVEI pilot projects have been provided with time to meet, to discuss experiences and to exchange ideas and materials: this is a rare treat for those in today's cash-starved education service and it provided a sharp (and sometimes bitterly felt) contrast with the under-resourcing of the SED's Standard Grade, which had been a direct cause of the teachers' industrial action. Second, it soon became clear that the MSC did not intend to impose its will on the details of teaching content, or at least, no more so than the teachers had long become accustomed to accepting from the SED. In fact it is clear that in comparison to the extremely centralized, 'top-down' model favoured by the SED, TVEI to a significant extent adopts a 'bottom-up' philosophy. Thus researchers from the Scottish Council for Educational Research (SCRE), in evaluating Lothian's pilot project, wrote that the 'MSC had identified broad targets or in- structions' but also that:

> It was left to the teaching staffs in the various projects to develop their own solutions ... It was considered important that the ma- terials used in the TVEI courses had been produced by groups of volunteer staff, all of whom were classroom teachers. This was seen as being in contrast to, for example, the model used to develop Standard Grade. (Beck and Black, 1987)

Third, the seven aims of TVEI include at least one (v) which could be largely supported from a liberal standpoint. In Scotland the managers of TVEI have often argued that the existence of this clause in particular enables local authorities to accept MSC funds for work which they would have been trying to do anyway: they could 'take the money and run' and be reasonably confident that they might get away with it. Correspond- ingly, within the Scottish projects the commitment to vocationalization has usually been played down in favour of more 'respectable' edu- cational goals such as 'student-centred learning'. Sometimes indeed the

TVEI organizers have even felt confident enough to go onto the offensive, contrasting TVEI's pursuit of 'relevance' with what is portrayed as a sterile SED-led traditional curriculum from which many learners have become alienated. For example Michael Roebuck, Lothian's TVEI co-ordinator, has recently suggested that it is not TVEI but the educational establishment which has sold itself to vocationalism:

> TVEI is fundamentally a curriculum development project which seeks to explore ways of making the experience of young people in schools more relevant and useful to them. There is a strong emphasis on student-centred learning ... Too often, general education pays little heed to the mode of learning which, in terms of the personal growth and development of the individual, may be more important. Intrinsic educational values have been subordinated to the extrinsic need to provide tickets to employment ('O' grades/Highers). Often the content of these examination subjects has very little relevance or usefulness to young people (Preface to Beck and Black, 1987).

Thus critics of TVEI are invited to reflect upon the reality of what has gone before it. It has been an obvious tack and probably a highly successful one. The need for curriculum reform in Scottish secondary education was widely agreed upon and there had been high hopes that the Munn and Dunning Reports of the 1970s would make it happen, but by the mid-1980s disillusionment with the government's implementation of these Reports was widespread. Even now, long after the teachers' industrial campaign has ended, evidence of their anger at the SED's imperious and tight-fisted implementation of the Standard Grade programme is everywhere and on 17 June 1988 the *Times Educational Supplement Scotland* reported under the headline 'Convener battles against ditching Standard Grade' how within the EIS at least the strength of feeling was undiminished. Little wonder then that some of the most dynamic teachers looked to the MSC as a more likely route to influence educational change. But what of TVEI's contribution to computing in schools? All Scottish TVEI projects have featured computing heavily but the certification has been provided not by the SED's traditional examining arm, the Scottish Examination Board, but by the National Certificate programme of forty-hour modular courses (which had hitherto been associated solely with the post-16 stage) controlled by SCOTVEC. Typically TVEI pupils have enrolled for one or more SCOTVEC modules, of which the following represent typical titles:

1091: Introduction to Computers
2102: Keyboarding
2129: Introduction to the Information Technology Office
2150: Word Processing
1110: Computer Graphics
4807: Introduction to Computer Aided Draughting

As has been argued above, the vocational case for studying such modules as these is highly tenuous. Frequently claims have been made that their study is 'student-centred' and brings desirable side effects in terms of the 'personal development' of individuals, but of course similar claims about side-effects have been made on behalf of numerous topics and subjects in the past. And it is difficult to avoid the suspicion that the 'student-centred' aspects mean little more than that pupils occupy many hours in sitting at solitary keyboards performing low-level tasks (for which many seem to have an astonishing tolerance). Overwhelmingly these modules present computing at a machine operator's level. It would be the 1980s equivalent of learning how to tend the looms and mind the boilers that were the industrial technology of times past; except that jobs for 'machine operators' in the IT era simply do not exist. This news could come as a cruel blow to the 60 per cent of TVEI pupils on the SCRE survey who believed that TVEI would help them find a job (SCRE, 1988).

This is not to deny the possibility that some TVEI computing money may have been usefully spent. A portion of the cash has been allocated to funding 'enhancements' to existing subjects: a strange MSC euphemism for extra cash injections into the budgets of those school subject departments which offered to spend it in a manner compatible with the MSC aims. This opportunity has generated some imaginative proposals from teachers who have found ingenious alignments between their educational goals and the visions of David Young. Some welcome resources for 'curriculum computing' have been won from the MSC in this fashion, and it seems unfortunate that the Scottish Local Authorities did not succeed in diverting more of the money in this direction rather than towards the SCOTVEC modules.

TVEI has been the subject of several independent evaluations, often conducted by university education departments and usually paid for by the MSC itself. This shows another sharp contrast with the SED: the latter has its own 'in-house' inspectors in the shape of the HMI, but, among teachers at least, the credibility of the Scottish HMI's role as dispassionate evaluators of the SED's own initiatives has not been high in recent years. A Scotland-wide curriculum evaluation of TVEI has been carried out by the SCRE. Although the SCRE study offers no evaluation of the educational validity of the TVEI rationale, it does provide some evidence that the damage inflicted by the scheme has not been so great as the early critics had predicted. The SCRE suggests that with the exceptions of technology and computing, the curriculum balance of TVEI pupils is not significantly different from that of non-TVEI pupils; that for every 2 girls doing TVEI there are 3 boys; and that TVEI courses were attracting pupils from across the attainment range, although there has been a skew towards the lower bands. But the researchers warn that figures such as these represent a summary view which conceals the fact that 'projects differed greatly in most characteristics' (SCRE, 1977).

## COMPUTING TEACHERS AND THE MSC

Many Scottish teachers have opposed the MSC, but computing teachers have been largely acquiescent or even supportive. There seem to be many reasons why this may be so, apart from the obvious (and probably most important) one that MSC was seen as a 'gift horse': a source of equipment and cash for staffing which would make developments in their classrooms a possibility.

Undoubtedly the unpopularity of the SED has been to the advantage of the MSC. Not only has the SED been seen by the vast majority of teachers as the principal antagonist in the bitterly fought industrial action, but it is the SED also which is blamed for delivering the full force of Thatcher's education policies, from the legislation on 'opting out' to primary-school testing and the school boards. The MSC, although clearly recognized as a government agency, like the SED, has been identified with a much narrower band of policy.

For computing teachers especially, the arrival of TVEI has meant an opportunity to have a direct influence in the construction of the curriculum. It has been a taste of the 'bottom-up', classroom-led approach which has been hardly known since the 1970s. That they like the taste probably explains to a large extent why their attitude to MSC differs from that of the majority of teachers in other subjects who have been scarcely touched by TVEI.

But why then have the TVEI computing courses not broken from the vocational mould? Why have teachers not experimented with the scientific or liberal problem-solving approaches to computing, for example? First, there was limited opportunity. As the SCRE researchers pointed out, the MSC set the basic parameters of what would be tolerated and the scope for teacher influence lay more in interpretation of method than in revision of philosophy. Second, it must be admitted that vocationalism (along with its ideology of a 'practical' curriculum for 'non-academic' pupils) has been a persistent tradition in Scottish education. It has been particularly nurtured in the secondary school technical and business studies departments, for example, and it would have been an easy tradition for computing to inherit even without the propaganda of Baker and the MSC. Third, the teachers have generally been woefully undertrained and greatly overworked. This probably explains why nobody in Scotland pushed hard at the MSC to establish limits of TVEI's tolerance to educationally based proposals. In the pressure of school life, and in the absence of alternative models of what might be done, it would have been very hard for teachers to do other than implement variations upon the standard machine operator's approach, which had after all been sanctified by the SED in the Standard Grade Computing Studies, syllabus and by SCOTVEC in the IT training modules which had emerged from the FE colleges.

INTO THE FUTURE

The story of computing provides an illuminating insight not just into two government agencies, the SED and the MSC, but also into Scottish education itself. It is the kind of story which should make the starting point for the reform of Scottish education, if and when a Scottish Parliament is given the chance to confront such a task.

Walter Humes has conducted an extensive study into the 'leadership class of Scottish education': the class comprised one or two hundred individuals who 'set the agenda' for education in Scotland. He contrasts the image of Scottish education which is usually presented by this 'leadership' class with the reality which his study uncovered:

> those aspects of the received wisdom which stress the democratic and egalitarian character of Scottish education and which appeal to notions of partnership and consensus rest very uneasily with the extremely hierarchical way in which the system is organised, the endless pursuit of marks of status by individuals and organisations, and the concentration of power in the hands of a relatively small group of mutually admiring hands of a relatively small group of mutually admiring people (Humes, 1986).

Certainly the SED's treatment of computing has been characterized by its liking for hierarchy, uniformity and the judgement of a few 'favourite children'. But the SED has also managed to combine these characteristics with a pragmatic willingness to perform an about-turn whenever it seemed in its bureaucratic interests to do so. Thus the SED committed Scotland to the Bellis 'curriculum computing' policy at a time when it was barely meaningful, and then deflected resources away from it when the arrival of microcomputers made its success seem a possibility. The SED excluded the subject of computing from Scottish schools largely out of an academic disdain in the 1970s and then in the early 1980s it introduced vocationally inspired computing courses wildly and almost overnight, using prescriptive syllabus formulations which effectively excluded liberal and academic interpretations of what the subject might be. Perhaps what is most surprising is that the SED has managed to do these things in the almost complete absence of scrutiny, and still less criticism, from anyone inside or outside Scottish education.

Humes has also suggested that 'the MSC has represented a challenge to the traditional leadership class in Scottish education'. But, noting the appointment (in 1984) of the Chairman of the Consultative Committee on the Curriculum to the Chair of the MSC in Scotland, Humes predicted that there would be 'concern to arrive at an acceptable *modus vivendi*, and to ensure that the various territorial sensitivities are not too outraged'.

From the standpoint of computing this prediction has been borne out. Indeed it has been remarkable to watch the development of the SED's and the MSC's initiatives as two parallel structures, each with their own separate policies, personnel, courses, assessment arrangements, management hierarchies, and provision for teacher training. An outsider (after he or she has overcome the shock at finding everything done twice over) might be forgiven for expecting to find some public evidence of tension, of rivalry even, between these two empires. In fact, apart from some murmurings among the lower ranks there has been none.

In the eyes of teachers it may be that the MSC has seemed the less disagreeable of the two agencies. It is open about its goals, reasonably predictable, openly evaluative (albeit on its own terms), and those prepared to play by its rules have found its pockets to have been unusually well lined. It is clear that the MSC has managed to tap the energy and creativity of at least some teachers, whereas the SED, with its imperious top-down style, has usually made them *en masse* only angry and alienated.

It is less clear whether learners should feel inclined to distinguish the two. The computing courses on offer do not greatly differ in character: both the SED's Standard Grade and the MSC's TVEI modules are vocationally orientated, although the SED would quibble about the label whereas the MSC would not demur. It may or may not strike TVEI pupils as a merciful relief that their modules each occupy only a quarter of the time required for the Standard Grade. No doubt pupils should feel grateful for the fact that a TVEI classroom has probably been better equipped than its non-MSC-funded Standard Grade counterpart. (But that will change: now TVEI is to be extended to all schools and it is certain that the funding levels of the pilot phase will not be maintained.)

The vocationalism which has engulfed school computing has not only misled pupils and their parents. It has also distracted attention away from 'curriculum computing'. There are many examples in the primary schools which show what can be done when the technology is harnessed to learning across the existing curriculum. A major advance for the secondary schools would be to relieve computing teachers of the burden of the TVEI courses and the Standard Grades and to enable them to use their skills as 'consultants' for their non-technical colleagues, so that computing might be used by pupils in the context of learning subjects of all kinds. A Scottish Parliament should set this project high on its educational agenda.

There is a second project which badly needs attention. Since vocational courses are shallow and often dull, they do little to enhance the status of computing as a subject. Youngsters who are presented with a view of computing which is based on programs for mail order, stock control and seat booking see no reason to become excited: they cannot be expected to guess that above and beyond the routine commercial world of data processing, there is a new and exciting science unfolding. Perhaps this is part of the explanation for the falling computing science enrolments into the universities. Scottish computing teachers have tremendous talent, which so far has scarcely been allowed to flower: they need the time, space and encouragement to rebuild the curriculum of computing in ways which are educationally justifiable. If they succeed, then youngsters should find the subject stimulating, and the numbers who consider it worthy of further study will grow. Such a project will take time, and it is unlikely to impress those whose careers have been inflated by the hot air of Kenneth Baker's battles of yesteryear rhetoric. On the other hand, to the future of a modern, science-based Scottish economy, it might actually be a matter of some importance.

REFERENCES

Beck, L., and Black, H. (1987). What is good practice in TVEI? (SCRE Project Reports).

Benn, C. (1987). Technology, education and training (SEEDS, Brighton Technology Conference).

Charniack, E., and McDermott, D. (1985). *Introduction to Artificial Intelligence* (Addison Wesley).

Chitty, C. (1986). TVEI: the MSC's trojan horse. In, C. Benn and J. Fairley (eds.), *Challenging the MSC* (Pluto).

Dale, R. (1985). The background and inception of TVEI. In Dale, R. (ed.) *Education, Training and Employment: Towards a New Vocationalism?* (Pergamon/Open University).

HMSO (1972). Computers and the schools ('Bellis Report') (Curriculum Paper 11).

HMSO (1977). The structure of the curriculum in the third and fourth years of the Scottish secondary school ('Munn Report').

Humes, W. (1986). *The Leadership Class in Scottish Education* (John Donald).

Milner, R. (1986). Is computing an experimental science? (Laboratory for Computer Science Report Series, University of Edinburgh).

Morris, J. G. (1982). Computers in Scottish education. In *European Journal of Education*.

Odor, P., and Entwhistle, N. (1982) *The Introduction of Microelectronics into Scottish Education* (Scottish Academic Press).

Reinecke, I. (1982). *The Micro Invaders* (Penguin, Australia).

SCRE (1977). TVEI students and studies two years on (Edinburgh).

SCRE (1988). The proof of the pudding: a study of the views of pupils on Lothian pilot TVEI schools (Edinburgh).

Wellington, J. (1988). Appendix to policies and trends in IT and education (ESRC Occasional Paper ITE/28e/88).

Young, D. (1984/5). Speech reported in *Sevenoaks Chronicle* (14 Dec.) and *Times Educational Supplement* (4 Jan.).

# PART III

# Institutions, Organizations and the MSC

# CHAPTER 7. EDITORS' INTRODUCTION

The voluntary sector played a very important role in some of the MSC's larger programmes for the adult unemployed, notably the Special Temporary Employment Programme (STEP) and the Community Programme (CP). A wide range of voluntary agencies sponsored schemes and employed staff through CP funding in efforts to assist the adult unemployed. Many old established voluntary agencies became involved in the CP, and some new ones were set up to respond to the opportunities created by the availability of MSC funds. In some cases, MSC funds permitted voluntary bodies to expand their operations and provide new services (examples of this are also discussed in Chapters 13 and 14) at a time when increasing unemployment and poverty were placing new and increased demands on much of the voluntary sector.

MSC funds made possible an expansion of voluntary sector activity in employment and training. However, many voluntary agencies experienced difficulties in their relationship with the MSC and its programmes. Difficulties arose from frequent rule and guide-line changes, from the high and regular turnover of CP staff, and, at times, from an apparent lack of understanding of the voluntary sector on the part of MSC staff. The MSC was often felt to be overcentralized and inflexible, and unwilling to consult or listen properly.

# 7

## THE MANPOWER SERVICES COMMISSION AND THE VOLUNTARY SECTOR IN SCOTLAND

STEPHEN MAXWELL

After its formation in 1974 the MSC was the most important single influence on the development of the voluntary sector in Scotland. As always, the most interesting questions are the most difficult to answer. It is easy enough to describe the MSC's impact on the voluntary sector in quantitative terms: its effect on funding, on the number of voluntary sector employees, on the emergence of new agencies, on the scope of voluntary sector activities. It is relatively easy to trace the MSC's effect on the voluntary sector's relationships with other institutions, the Department of Employment, the Scottish Office, the local authorities, trade unions. It is less easy to establish what the impact of the MSC has been on the different groups of clients the sector seeks to serve. And it is not at all clear what the impact of the voluntary sector's support for MSC programmes has been on the wider society, in terms of its contribution to the restructuring of the labour force, lowering expectations, weakening the power of the trade unions and path-breaking for new forms of social care provision. The voluntary sector itself was disinclined to spend much time on such speculative ventures.

Some will attribute this reluctance to the limitations of the voluntary sector's social vision. Others may find at least part of the cause in an uneasy conscience.

The voluntary sector's involvement with the Manpower Services Commission began with the earliest MSC programmes for unemployed people, the Job Creation Programme (JCP), launched in 1975, and the Work Experience Programme (WEP), launched in 1976.

The JCP provided work of community benefit to long-term unemployed adults, while the WEP was aimed at unemployed school leavers in the 16–18 age group. In a pattern which quickly established itself as characteristic, both programmes went through several mutations before becoming respectively the Community Programme (CP) in 1982 and the Youth Training Scheme (YTS) in 1983.

From the beginning some voluntary organizations, mostly those in the areas of chronically high unemployment supported the programmes.

But while the voluntary sector's involvement in the Job Creation Programmes continued to expand until the replacement of the CP by Employment Training in September 1988, the sector's interest in youth training was a less robust growth. While voluntary organizations which had supported the Youth Opportunities Programme continued their interest into the Mode B stream of YTS (training for special needs groups and in 'caring' services) the change to a two-year YTS with a different funding base in 1986 brought their support to an end.

While some of these early programmes were ambitious in scale, their significance to the voluntary sector lay more in the part they played in alerting voluntary organizations to the emergence of a new source of funding and a new range of state sponsored opportunities for organizational growth than in the volume of resources they provided.

THE COMMUNITY PROGRAMME

The CP emerged as a funder of voluntary sector activity at a spectacular rate (see Table 16). Compared to the CP other sources of MSC funding have been insignificant.

Table 16. Scottish Voluntary Sector
Income from the MSC for the
Community Programme
1982/83–1987/88

|        | £ million |
|--------|-----------|
| 1982/3 | 7.3       |
| 1983/4 | 16.8      |
| 1984/5 | 22.6      |
| 1985/6 | 27.9      |
| 1986/7 | 44.4      |
| 1987/8 | 59.2      |

*Sources*: 'Third Sector', Focus on Fact, 2 (Apr. 1987): *MSC Programmes in Scotland*, 4 (Feb. 1988); *Funding the Voluntary Sector*, SCVO (1987 and 1988).

Scottish expenditure by the Voluntary Projects Programme, which funded voluntary agencies to provide work experience and training for unemployed people on an (unpaid) volunteer basis never exceeded £1 million annually. And, as we have seen, by 1986/87 the voluntary sector had virtually withdrawn from the YTS. So the story of the MSC's impact on the voluntary sector is substantially the story of the Community Programme.

The growth in CP expenditure from 1982 in Scotland quickly established the MSC as by far the largest single source of public funding for the voluntary sector excluding the housing association movement (see Table 17).

Table 17. Main Sources of Public Money (excluding the Housing
Corporation) in the Scottish Voluntary Sector 1985/86 – 1986/87
(£ million).

|  | 1985/6 | 1986/7 | % Increase |
|---|---|---|---|
| Scottish Office |  |  |  |
|   Direct Grants | 7.96 | 9.01 | 17.2 |
|   Urban Programme | 11.7 | 16.6 | 41.9 |
| Unemployed Voluntary |  |  |  |
|   Action Fund | 0.52 | 0.54 | 3.8 |
| MSC | 36.9 | 59.2 | 60.4 |
| Local authorities |  |  |  |
|   (excluding rate relief and fees) | 17.0 | 18.53* | 9.0 |
| Health Boards | 1.05 | 1.8 | 71.4 |
| Total | 74.86 | 105.68 | 41.5 |

* Estimate based on the same % increase as previous year.
*Sources*: 'Third Sector', Focus on Fact, 4 Feb. 1988;
*Funding the Voluntary Sector*, SCVO (1988); Figures from the Scottish Office; SCVO
Estimate of MSC Expenditure; Charity Trends 1986/87, Charities Aid Foundation.

Despite the spectacular growth in the voluntary sector's income from
the CP in Scotland the Scottish voluntary sector was slower to take up the
CP than the voluntary sector in England. Three years into the Programme
it provided only 24 per cent of the 19 000 places in Scotland, a share
nearly 20 per cent smaller than the share achieved by the voluntary
sector in England (see Table 18).

In succeeding years the gap has narrowed without closing completely.
By early 1988 the Scottish voluntary sector was supplying about 40 per
cent of Scotland's 30 000 filled CP places.

The low initial take-up by the voluntary sector probably owed more to
institutional factors than to ideological reservations. The voluntary sector in Scotland was less developed and until recently less diversified than
the voluntary sector south of the border. There was no national Scottish
voluntary organization with either the ambition or the organizational

Table 18. Community Programme Places: Percentage Share by Sector,
1985

|  | England | Scotland | Wales |
|---|---|---|---|
| Voluntary sector | 44.2 | 23.8 | 27.5 |
| Local authorities | 42.6 | 70.8 | 51.2 |
| Private sector | 2.06 | 0.97 | 0.29 |
| Others | 11.04 | 4.26 | 20.9 |

*Source: The Voluntary Sector and the Future of the Community Programme*, report of a
NCVO conference (NCVO Employment Unit, July 1986).

capacity of the National Association for the Care and Resettlement of Offenders (NACRO), which by 1986 was providing 17 000 CP places.

Significantly, the largest Scottish providers of CP places have been local voluntary agencies such as Glasgow Council for Voluntary Service (GCVS), Buckhaven Parish Church Managing Agency in Fife, the Volunteer Centre in Glasgow and Community Opportunities West Lothian (COWL). The voluntary sector in Scotland also faced tougher competition for places from local authorities whose desire to be seen to be reacting to the record levels of local unemployment after the 'shake-out' of manufacturing jobs in 1980–2 overrode political objections to the Programme.

The voluntary sector's appetite for a larger share of the places grew with the increase in size of the Programme. The Government announced an increase to 230 000 places in Great Britain in the spring of 1985 while the budget statement of 1986 contained provision for a further expansion to a total of 255 000, of which Scotland was allocated 12.7 per cent. The MSC's receptiveness to the voluntary sector's case for a larger share was increased by the judgement of an efficiency report that no fewer than 45 per cent of places on local authority schemes in Scotland were in the 'low skill' areas of environmental improvement and gardening (Department of Employment, 1986). 1986 also saw the beginning of a rapid growth in energy conservation schemes in Scotland led by the voluntary sector in the shape of Energy Action Scotland.

The CP has dominated the organizational development of the voluntary sector since 1982 as it has dominated its public funding. It provided the resources through which established voluntary organizations including Glasgow Council for Voluntary Service (GCVS) and Dundee Association of Social Service (DASS) developed their work into new areas particularly in the 'care in the community' field. By the end of 1987 the GCVS agency was managing a 1 000-place programme with a budget of £5 million. Its own core income meanwhile was £93 000. It earned an equal amount in management fees from its Community Programme agency.

Many Scottish voluntary organizations, including Gingerbread, One Plus, and Shelter Scotland also used the Community Programme to extend their activities or to develop into new areas. By 1988 Crossroads (Scotland) Care Attendant Schemes were funding 25 of their 43 schemes through the CP at an annual cost of £1.7 million.

## THE THIRD SECTOR

The Community Programme also served as midwife to a new breed of voluntary organizations as much interested in promoting economic development as in providing caring services on the traditional voluntary sector model.

On the second birthday of one such organization, it explained the difference between the new and the established agencies:

Traditional community and voluntary organisations have been associated in people's minds with the provision of services under the broad banner of social welfare. However, today's community and voluntary organisations are now involved in a much wider sphere – i.e. employment, economic development, income maintenance and so on ... One crucial factor in the response has been the opportunities created by the availability of finance to instigate projects through the Manpower Services' Commission programmes, i.e. Youth Training Scheme, the Voluntary Projects Programme and the Community Programme (COWL, 1985).

Other notable examples of the new generation were the Buckhaven Parish Church Managing Agency, which used the Programme to provide work experience, workshop training, enterprise training and job-search facilities in eastern Fife; Glasgow Heatwise, which began by providing home insulation in some of Glasgow's unemployment black-spots and soon diversified into jobsearch, enterprise promotion and environmental improvement; and Community Business Strathclyde which was a leading user of the 'business starter' element of the Programme. The growth in Scotland of a 'third sector' of the economy – a 'not for profit' sector outwith the public sector – would have been even slower in the absence of the CP.

As it responded to the opportunities opened up by the Community Programme, the role of the voluntary sector as an employer increased dramatically. By 1987, in addition to an estimated 10 000 permanent jobs, the voluntary sector was providing 13 000 temporary jobs through the Community Programme with probably another two hundred 'semi-permanent' jobs in the managing or sponsoring agencies. With a total labour-force of approximately 24 000 by 1988, the voluntary sector became an important employer, providing directly more jobs than coal-mining, steelmaking or shipbuilding.

Between 40 and 50 per cent of the voluntary sector's Community Programme places were in 'social care' services for such groups as the elderly, single parents, disabled or handicapped people, pre-school children, the chronically sick and low-income households. In 1987 the estimated MSC expenditure on these voluntary sector services was £25–8 million. At a time when the government was putting more rhetoric than resources behind its 'care in the community' policy, the voluntary sector, through the CP, was probably the fastest growing source of 'care in the community' services in Scotland. If we can assume that approximately half of the voluntary sector CP places were consistently devoted to care in the community services, voluntary sector expenditure through the CP grew from £3.6 million in 1982/3 to £29.6 million in 1986/7, while joint support finance for community care grew from £2 million to £6 million (SCVO, 1988).

The total net value to the Scottish taxpayer cannot be calculated, but Crossroads (Scotland) Community Care Schemes estimated that their twenty-five schemes funded by the CP at a cost of £1.7 million were saving the National Health Service £36.5 million a year (Crossroads (Scotland) Care Attendant Scheme, 1988).

## DISSENT

This collation of figures may leave the impression that the voluntary sector gave its support to the CP without misgivings. In fact, from the launch of the Job Creation Programme in 1975 by a Labour government, the role of the voluntary sector in the government's special employment and training measures was an issue of continuing and troubled debate among voluntary sector workers. As the CP – and its finances – expanded through 1985 and 1986, more and more organizations came to accept it as too big an opportunity to reject. But there were dissenters. In December 1984 the directorate of Age Concern Scotland circulated a paper identifying the problems of using short-term funding to provide services on which older people could rely. In terms which were to become familiar in voluntary sector discussions, the Age Concern report noted the difficulties of forward planning when the number of future places was uncertain, the lack of funding for development work, the insufficient length of a twelve-month placement, the difficulty of promoting a self-help or community development response within the constraints of the programme. In a pertinent aside, it identified a lack of expertise in the MSC itself:

> Service development which depends increasingly on short-term funded projects will tend to be ephemeral and patchy, particularly when those controlling the funds have no strategy or overview regarding the needs of older people and their services i.e. central Government.

And it raised the issue of the political role of the Community Programme:

> Is the movement in danger of creating through these projects an illusion that the needs of older people throughout Scotland are being adequately and universally met? (Age Concern Scotland, 1984)

But while such questions became familiar to voluntary sector activists, few adopted Age Concern Scotland's answer of refusing to participate in the Programme.

## REPRESENTATION

There was no provision in the legislation establishing the MSC in 1973 for voluntary sector representation on the Commission itself. As the voluntary sector built up its share of CP places to 50 per cent in England and Wales and over 40 per cent in Scotland, both the National Council for Voluntary Organisations (NCVO) and the Scottish Council for Voluntary Organisations (SCVO) pressed their claim for voluntary sector representation alongside the trade unions, business, the local authorities (in-

cluding one representative of the Scottish local authorities) and
education. The government's response was that a change in membership would require legislation which the government was not considering and that the voluntary sector was anyway represented on the Special
Employment Measures Advisory Group (SEMAG) and the Area Manpower Boards (AMBS). The SCVO pointed out that the voluntary sector
could be given representation on the Manpower Services' Committee for
Scotland without legislation only to be told that a change in membership
could not be considered separately from a change in the membership of
the Commission itself. So the voluntary sector's formal representation in
the MSC's structure was limited to SEMAG at the Great Britain level and the
local AMBS.

SEMAG was the main advisory body to the Commission on the Special
Employment Measures, comprising the CP, the VPP and the Enterprise
Allowance Scheme. Membership paralleled that on the Commission
itself with the addition of separate representatives of the English, Scottish and Welsh voluntary sectors.

At the invitation of the Employment Secretary, the Scottish representative was nominated by the SCVO from among its full-time staff after
consultation with some leading voluntary sector CP agents. The justifi-
cation for this undemocratic procedure was that the representative
should be independent of any CP managing agency and that liaison and
consultation with the voluntary sector as a whole could best be secured
through a central representative body.

SEMAG met normally at two-monthly periods, from 1985 under the
chairmanship of Sir Bryan Nicholson. Its regular membership included
the senior MSC officials responsible for each of the three 'special
measures' and, as observers, a senior representative of the Department
of Employment, usually an Assistant Secretary, and representatives of
the Scottish and Welsh Offices.

The voluntary sector was the dominant non-governmental voice on
SEMAG. Indeed an outside observer might have concluded that SEMAG's
remit was to provide a forum for a dialogue between the voluntary sector
and the MSC. The voluntary sector representatives were the most regular
attenders. The same individuals filled the positions from 1985 to the end
of SEMAG in 1988, and the English and Scottish representatives had
regular meetings with their voluntary sector constituencies.

In Scotland the SEMAG representative from his SCVO base convened
regular meetings of voluntary sector CP managing agencies. Initially
these meetings were for the purpose of discussing the SEMAG agenda or
of reporting back from SEMAG meetings. But by 1986 these functions were
taken over by a Standing Forum on Special Employment Measures with
a remit to discuss the range of special employment and training issues
affecting voluntary organizations and to bring common concerns to the
notice of the policy-makers in the Department of Employment and the

MSC. The Forum attracted attendances of between 20 and 60 people, mainly from the voluntary sector managing agencies but including sponsors of local projects, local authority managing agents and trade unions. Speakers included the MSC Chairman, Bryan Nicholson, his (part-time) successor and Chairman of the Committee for Scotland Sir James Munn, Labour Employment spokeswoman Clare Short MP, Lex Gold, Director of the MSC's Office for Scotland, the MSC's Director of the Community Programme Unit, Jeremy Walker, and Bill Hughes, Chairman of CBI Scotland. In addition to these contacts, the Standing Forum made representations to government Ministers and senior MSC officials, and from 1987 on had increasingly close links with the Convention of Scottish Local Authorities (COSLA) and the Scottish Trades' Union Congress (STUC).

Much of this effort to ensure a clear and authoritative voluntary sector voice on SEMAG was wasted. The voluntary sector voice was listened to on the technical or presentational issues, but largely ignored on the substantive policy issues such as wage levels for participants, funding for development, and training strategy. Indeed, on key developments of the Community Programme, for example on questions of eligibility criteria and training strategy, there was often not even a pretence of consultation in advance of key decisions. After his first annual round of SEMAG meetings, the Scottish voluntary sector representative offered the opinion:

> SEMAG has very little influence on the MSC or the Department of Employment. MSC regards SEMAG in the same spirit as it regards Area Manpower Boards – as a necessary obeisance to the principle of consultation and participation.

But he added in support of continued SCVO participation on behalf of the Scottish voluntary sector,

> SEMAG does, however, serve as a useful source of advance information about developments in Special Employment Measures and as an organisational focus for voluntary sector interests. (SCVO, 1985)

On the MSC's nine Area Manpower Boards in Scotland, the voluntary sector had one representative out of a prescribed membership of seventeen embracing the same interests represented on the Commission and on SEMAG. The remit of the AMBs was to advise on the local planning and delivery of MSC training and employment programmes, to approve local training plans within the Commission's guide-lines and to be responsible for the approval, within agreed budgets and policies, of local projects, and to give advice, on request, to the Commission.

Like the SEMAG representative, the voluntary sector representative on the AMB was selected by the Commission from a list of nominees provided by SCVO after consultation. About half the selected voluntary sector representatives were employees or committee members of organizations which were CP agencies. In some areas, the Manpower Boards played an active part in the approval and supervision of local projects and programmes. In others they were little more than rubber stamps for the decisions of the MSC officials. Their advisory role was little more than honorary. They could, of course, proffer advice on the programmes they supervised at local levels but their remit made it clear that the Commission would seek its advice as and when it wanted it.

Only a minority of the voluntary sector representatives on the AMB's succeeded in establishing regular procedures for reporting back to their local voluntary sector constituencies. Although they provided a useful contact point for voluntary sector agents and sponsors acting on their own account, they faced major handicaps in representing wider voluntary sector interests.

## THE SCOTTISH OFFICE

Given the ineffectiveness of the official channels of representation within the MSC structure, the voluntary sector came increasingly to use channels outwith the MSC. Although the Scottish Secretary was co-responsible with the Employment Secretary for the operations of the MSC in Scotland, the Scottish Office was not active in the development of policy in the MSC's Special Employment Measure training. By virtue of its responsibilities for further education, the Scottish Education Department had a 'territorial' incentive to monitor the development of MSC training initiatives in Scotland. But neither the Industry Department, where departmental responsibility for MSC operations in Scotland resided, nor the Social Work Services Group (SWSG) in the Education Department, which had responsibility for policy for the voluntary sector, had the expertise to make a significant contribution to the development of policy on Special Employment Measures. Until 1987 only one Social Work Adviser had responsibility for the MSC issues included in his listed remit. The characteristic response of the Industry Department to voluntary sector representation about the effects of the transition from CP to ET was to explain that policy issues were the province of the Department of Employment. The formal response of the SWSG to voluntary sector warnings about the impact of the change on social care projects was to pass on the official reassurances of the Department of Employment that ET was able to accommodate social care projects.

## MSC SCOTLAND

By contrast, officials of the MSC's Office for Scotland were far more sensitive to voluntary sector needs. Although they stressed that the Office for Scotland had no policy discretion voluntary sector representatives came away from meetings with senior officials feeling that their views had been taken seriously and that they would be faithfully represented to the MSC's Sheffield headquarters. It was through the good offices of the MSC's Office for Scotland that two leading Glasgow voluntary CP agencies facing political problems over the transition to ET were given repeated extensions to their deadlines for decision.

The most disappointing of all the official channels of representation was the Manpower Services Committee for Scotland. Excluded from membership of the Committee as from the Commission itself, the voluntary sector's access was limited to contacts with the individual members drawn from Scottish business, trade unions and local authorities. At meetings with the voluntary sector between 1986 and 1988, the Committee Chairman Sir James Munn acknowledged that the Committee for Scotland, like the Office for Scotland, had no specific policy remit. But the Committee made no attempt to elicit the views of the voluntary sector, nor did it circulate its minutes or issue public statements. Its formal advice on major issues remained unknown to the voluntary sector.

The most persistent – and perhaps the most effective – form of voluntary sector liaison with the MSC took place at the level of the local MSC office where local voluntary sector agencies lobbied and negotiated with the local MSC official responsible for the CP. Although meetings of voluntary sector representatives were rife with complaints about the inconsistencies in local officials' interpretation of CP rules, a voluntary organization with good relations with local officials could expect to benefit from local discretion. In some cases there was tacit collusion between officials and managing agencies in manipulating the MSC's rules.

## DEPENDENCE

While the voluntary sector's relationship with the MSC's Community Programme was one of mutual convenience, there was never any doubt that the voluntary sector with its hunger for funds was the dependent partner. For the voluntary sector the uncomfortable aspect of its dependence was the rate at which the MSC imposed changes in the CP. The pace of change became particularly hectic after 1984. The eligibility rates were changed in November 1984 to exclude married women not in receipt of benefit. In the spring of 1985 the size of the CP was increased by 70 per cent to 230 000. In the budget of 1986 the target was raised again to 255 000. Following the report *Value for Money in the Community Programme* (Department of Employment, 1986), a host of changes were proposed in a follow-up Action Plan. Towards the end of 1986 an announcement was made that expenditure limits required a cut of 10 000 places. The New Job Training Scheme was introduced in early 1987. Throughout the period, National Initiatives, Charities Initiatives, Enterprise elements, new monitoring requirements, new financial reporting systems, new guidance on training requirements, new eligibility rules followed each other without relief. Such constant change stretched the adaptive capacities and the tolerance of voluntary organizations to their limits.

The direction of the changes was also considered disadvantageous by most voluntary sector agents and sponsors. But in the first eight months of 1986, the announcement that the target had been raised to 255 000 and the publication of *Value for Money* did seem to offer the prospect of stability and consolidation. The voluntary sector welcomed the report's main conclusion that, in its drive for an increased number of places, the MSC had sacrificed quality to quantity. The SCVO's formal response welcomed the report's recommendations that more attention needed to be given to training, its acknowledgement that restrictions on the average-wage ceiling deterred older people with family responsibilities from joining the Community Programme and its call for greater professionalism in the voluntary sector management of CP schemes and for funding for development work.

But the 'window of opportunity' opened by *Value for Money* was firmly closed by the end of the year. In October 1986 the Employment Secretary Lord Young announced the new Job Training Scheme (JTS), a job based training scheme paying its trainees their benefit entitlement and aimed at 18–24-year-olds who had been unemployed for six months or more.

The launch of the new JTS was widely interpreted by the voluntary sector as a sign that the government had begun to seek an alternative to the CP which would have more direct effect on the flexibility and adaptability of the unemployed labour force than the CP could claim to have.

With a haste that was the hallmark of Employment Department initiatives, the new JTS pilots had been extended into a national programme by February 1987 with a target of 110 000 places. Combined with a Treasury-imposed cut of 10 000 places in the CP, the introduction of a new system of allocating places, a £15 million cut in the modest budget for Training linked to the Community Programme and the growing element of compulsion in recruitment to CP, Lord Young's initiative persuaded many in the voluntary sector that the days of a voluntary CP were numbered.

## ALTERNATIVE FUTURES

In May 1987 the Standing Forum published *A Future for the Community Programme* (SCVO, 1987), which expressed the voluntary sector's fears about the implications of the JTS and offered a radically different vision of the CP. It pointed out that the diversion of any significant portion of the 18–24-year unemployed population from the CP to JTS would undermine the voluntary sector's work in many of Scotland's most deprived communities. The document went on to call for, *inter alia*, an increase in the average CP wage to £77 to return it to its 1982 level, for extra financial incentives for 'heads of families' to join the scheme, the restoration of eligibility to married women, a supplement to the management fee for managing agencies willing to devise programmes for the very-long-term unemployed, a special per capita training allowance and an enhanced role for voluntary sector agents in the generation of 'permanent jobs' through the allocation of a share of the Enterprise Allowance Scheme budget to CP managing agencies.

But the government's thinking moved at an accelerating pace away from this voluntary sector vision of an upgraded CP. The Conservative manifesto for the June 1987 Election contained a commitment to merge the CP with JTS in a new employer-led training scheme for long-term unemployed who would be paid 'benefit plus premium' for an average six months on the scheme. The criterion for projects under the new scheme was to be their effectiveness in increasing the skills, qualifications and job prospects of the participants rather than the 'community benefit' which had underpinned voluntary sector support for the CP.

The announcement of what became known as the Employment Training scheme forced the voluntary sector to abandon its policy of separate lobbying on Special Employment issues in favour of seeking a wider political alliance. Many voluntary organizations had established contacts with trade unions at local levels and through the Area Manpower Boards. In most cases their dealings had been limited to consideration of projects which encountered problems gaining trade union approval. In relation to the CP as a whole, voluntary organizations and trade unions shared an approach of uneasy pragmatism. The voluntary sector's relations with local authorities had been on much the same basis. As we have seen, Scottish local authorities in spite of political misgivings had given wide support to CP. Rivalry in some areas between voluntary organizations and local authorities in bidding for CP schemes was limited by the voluntary sector's awareness of its wider dependence on local authority support.

THE TRIPLE ALLIANCE

Through the Standing Forum the voluntary sector took the initiative in proposing joint meetings of the voluntary sector, the STUC and COSLA to discuss the government's proposal. Between August 1987 and the start of Employment Training in September 1988, this Triple Alliance lobbied Ministers and campaigned through the media to secure changes in the government's proposals.

The Alliance represented an important step towards a more political stance by a sector which had traditionally preferred to put its case in terms specific to the voluntary sector. The higher political profile was justified on three grounds. First, the voluntary sector had always insisted that its support for the CP was dependent on the CP having the support of trade unions and local authorities. By abandoning the principle of 'the rate for the job' the new proposals threatened that consensus. By allying with the STUC and COSLA, the voluntary sector was simply defending the 'consensual' basis of its own participation in government employment and training measures. Second, the new proposals assumed a tightening labour market which simply did not exist in

Scotland. Third, the voluntary sector saw its alliance with the STUC and COSLA as a way of adding weight to its case that among the chief victims of the change from CP to ET would be the 'mainstream' voluntary sector provision of social care projects.

Meetings which the Alliance held with, variously, the new Employment Secretary Norman Fowler, Scottish Office Minister Ian Lang, acting MSC Chairman Sir James Munn and others yielded some concessions, notably on financial guarantees (of special interest to the voluntary sector) and on 'topping-up' of participants' incomes. But they fell far short of the Alliance's joint demand for 'the rate for the job', a guarantee against compulsion for the lifetime of the new Parliament, an increase in the training costs, exemption for local authorities from 'claw-back' penalties and special provision for social care schemes.

As the STUC and COSLA moved, rather unexpectedly, in the summer of 1988 from a campaign of lobbying to a campaign of boycott, the weakness of the voluntary sector's position became clearer. While Scottish voluntary organizations had been more vehement than their English counterparts in their denunciation of the new scheme, their dependence on MSC funding meant that they were able to consider boycotting the scheme only if the boycott offered good prospects of forcing the government to replace its election proposals with alternatives more acceptable to the voluntary sector. At a British level no such boycott was ever on the agenda.

In any case, the precarious financial base from which voluntary sector agents operated meant that the voluntary sector would have needed a firm decision on a boycott well ahead of the September start of the new scheme. Neither COSLA nor the STUC were capable of making such a commitment. As a result voluntary agencies were forced to enter negotiations with their local MSC offices to ensure that if ET started as anticipated they would secure their share of the places. By the beginning of September all but two voluntary sector agents had committed themselves to ET. As it built up in late August and early September, the trade union and local authority boycott proved to be sufficiently wide to embarrass the MSC in Scotland but insufficient to force further concessions from the government.

## CONCLUSION

Through the CP voluntary organizations provided temporary jobs for 60–70 000 unemployed Scots. As the majority has been composed of single under-twenty-five-year-olds the participants received a significantly higher income than their benefit entitlement, with knock-on effects on the economies of their local communities. The content of the work done by the CP brought significant, if highly variable, benefit to some of Scotland's most deprived communities. The CP also funded a major expansion of the voluntary sector itself, both the established voluntary sector of local development agencies and national specialist organizations, and the new sector of agencies created specifically to utilize the CP. Through both sectors it boosted the 'third sector', the 'not for profit' economic development agencies.

But there is another side to the voluntary sector support of the CP. The gains in temporary jobs have to be set against the displacement of 'permanent jobs'. The short-term basis of the projects and the constant changes in rules meant that social care provision was sometimes withdrawn after only one or two years, leaving vulnerable clients confused and resentful. Although, by the nature of the case, hard evidence is not available, many local voluntary activists in Scotland as elsewhere believe that the introduction of paid CP workers weakened their base of local volunteer support.

MSC funding of the voluntary sector also played its part in changing the voluntary sector's relationship with the state. It sponsored the sector's expansion at a time when government policy is encouraging the sector to play a greater role in social provision. Through the MSC large sections of the voluntary sector were educated in the new norms of state funding, including the more competitive 'contract culture'. As the voluntary sector reluctantly transfers its support from CP to ET, it may be haunted by an unanswered question: by supporting these government measures aimed at making the low-income groups in the labour force compete against each other more strenuously, how far is the voluntary sector helping to impoverish those it is dedicated to defending? One thing is clear. Through the CP the voluntary sector finally lost its innocence.

REFERENCES

Age Concern Scotland (1984). 'The Use of Short-Term Funding for Longer-Term Services or Service Development of Benefit to Older People', discussion paper, 5 November.

Cowl Ltd. (1985). 'What is COWL?', Annual Report.

Crossroads (Scotland) Care Attendant Scheme (1988). Minutes of Annual General Meeting.

Department of Employment (1986). 'Value for Money in the Community Programme'.

SCVO (1985). 'Manpower Services Commission: What Role for SCVO?', discussion paper.

SCVO (1987). 'A Future for the Community Programme', Standing Forum on Special Employment Measures.

SCVO (1988). 'Third Sector', Focus on Fact No. 5.

# CHAPTER 8. EDITORS' INTRODUCTION

The MSC's job creation schemes allowed the Church to become more involved in responding to the needs of the unemployed. The Church of Scotland directly sponsored a large number of projects, mostly under the Community Programme (CP), for unemployed adults. The MSC valued this participation very highly, and some Church-based schemes came to be regarded as innovative and exemplary CP projects.

The projects sponsored by the Church varied considerably. They gave rise to a wide range of experiences which affected the Church, particularly in its attitudes to unemployment. This impact was felt throughout the Church, from the level of local involvement with the MSC, to the national discussion at the General Assembly.

# 8

## THE MANPOWER SERVICES COMMISSION AND THE CHURCH

### THE REVEREND DONALD ROSS

The Churches in Scotland have been involved with the Manpower Services Commission almost from its very beginning. The story has been patchy, however, with in some places a whole community transformed by the close co-operation of the Church and the MSC, and, in others, very small projects of a simple pastoral and supportive nature.

The schemes that the Church became involved with were largely those which would be categorized under the heading of anti-unemployment initiatives. They were motivated by the need to do something to alleviate the worst effects of unemployment and to provide useful activity. There were reservations about specific programmes, but in general, as one churchman said, 'We have developed a pragmatic attitude to the question of the value of the programmes, recognising that you can always find fault with them, but in the end, for the vast majority of the unemployed these were the only opportunities on offer.' There were those in the Church who distanced themselves from the programmes, not out of apathy or lethargy, but on principle, believing that they were government measures which did not go to the heart of the economic and employment realities. This was not, however, a widely held view. In addition to those in the Church who became actively involved in the initiation and sponsoring and running of schemes, there were many more who gave careful and serious consideration to the possibilities and spent many hours discussing appropriate steps, and yet who were unable to bring into fruition a suitable project. The reasons for this varied from problems of accommodation, supervision, identification of a project suitable to the area, and the amount of time and effort essential for success.

### A GROWING INFLUENCE ON THE CHURCH

If there had been no such thing as the Manpower Services Commission, it is hoped that the Church would somehow or other have measured up to the needs of the day and the changing economic realities, but certainly the role and the influence of the MSC upon the Church has been considerable. All of the main Churches in Scotland participated in the various programmes, and were encouraged so to do by their Assemblies and Hierarchies. In the Roman Catholic Church, however, there was, according to Father William Slaven, 'no policy response through Bishops' Synod and little local involvement'.

One of the problems in making some kind of assessment of the role and influence of the Commission in relation to the work of the Church is the sheer difficulty of adequate records and statistics. There was no mechanism for ensuring that schemes operated in presbyteries and parishes throughout the country were recorded centrally by any Church. Attempts were made on a number of occasions, but at no point was it ever possible to say that a complete list of all projects had been compiled.

It would be useful if we could measure the role and influence of the MSC against a number of key factors: the time consumption by ministers and office bearers of the Church; the numbers of people employed within projects over the years; the number and type of project undertaken; the amount of MSC funds applied; the benefits experienced by the community which each Church sought to serve; the impact upon congregational life and activity; or perhaps most importantly the effect on the lives of the people employed within the various projects. Sad to say, there is no effective measure of most of those. It could rightly be said that the people involved from the Churches and the MSC were so busy getting on with the job, along with their multifarious other activities of Church and community, that they had no time or inclination to maintain an adequate historical record and analysis.

In 1976 the Reverend Roger Clark, a full-time industrial chaplain for the city of Dundee, along with others, initiated the Dundee Council of Churches Training Workshop. This was not the first training workshop in Scotland, but it was the first developed in partnership with the MSC, and this initial project of the Churches was highly commended by officials of the MSC. It was regarded as a model because not only did it provide jobs, it pointed to socially useful work which would be needed in the community, and which could supply young people and others with skills for wider application in later life.

A very rough measure of the growth of Church involvement with the MSC is provided by occasional listings of Church projects. In November 1983, for example, following a 'market place', during which Church-related projects were demonstrated, some 57 Church-based projects were briefly described. These were both YTS and Community Programme Schemes. There were YTS placements in Church Eventide Homes, at St Ninian's Youth Training Centre and in staffing of playgroups, toy libraries, community care and information sharing. Through the Community Programme there was the provision of advice and counselling, alternative employment initiatives, age care, disabled care, community odd jobs, furniture removal, afternoon centres for the unemployed and a resource centre. In 1986 the General Assembly of the Church of Scotland received an updated list and called for the Church to increase its involvement. Many of these schemes were small in size but dealt with pockets of local need and provided servi es which otherwise would have been absent from the local scene.

Two projects, which for different reasons are not characteristic deserve and have had elsewhere a fuller analysis. They are the projects at Buckhaven in Fife and in Gilmerton in Edinburgh. The Revd Donald Skinner, the Parish Minister of Gilmerton, first used church resources and buildings, and later along with MSC funds, to develop the potential of disadvantaged youngsters. Existing before MSC, this project had an important and sometimes profound influence on the 600 young people trained during the years of the MSC. Donald Skinner used his own engineering background to create a unique training workshop, and under the guidance of highly motivated supervisors, the youngsters developed skills and qualifications in woodwork, metalwork, knitwear, art, design, pottery and ceramics. Many became equipped to find work based on those skills.

It is impossible in the space of a few lines to summarize in any adequate way the interaction of the MSC and the community of Buckhaven in Fife. The whole town of Buckhaven and its surrounding communities have been physically and spiritually transformed by the vision of the Revd Dane Sherrard and his Kirk Session and Parish Church and by co-operation with the MSC.

In all, an astonishing total of 1 745 men, women and youngsters had their working lives changed for good, through this project. Whereas local employers had not been attracted by YTS, the local minister and his Kirk Session were invited by the MSC to consider the Community Programme. Beginning with the renovation of a church as a Craft and Youth Centre, a team began which was to surprise everyone in the community and indeed in the MSC. Youngsters became hopeful, marriages were stabilized; morale improved; 900 people found permanent employment; there was a transfusion of funds to the community from a £40 000-per-week pay roll, and finally the successful inauguration of an enterprise company marketing tapestry, furniture, and goods produced from silk-screen printing, leather tooling, bookbinding and other products. The *Economist*'s report on job creation said 'Buckhaven is held up as a model of how to apply the Community Programme and the Youth Training Scheme to best effect. There are many such schemes, but few where the impact upon the community has been so marked.'

### THE MSC AND THE CHURCH'S OBJECTIVES

The question has been asked as to how, working with the MSC might have helped the church better to meet its own objectives. There are people in the community and some in the Church who believe that the prime objective of the Church is the proclamation of the gospel for the salvation of individual souls. Many in the Church, however, interpret the gospel as meaning not only that, but involving also a commitment to the Kingdom of Christ, which includes working for peace and justice in society. To that end, any measures which alleviate distress, make constructive use of skills, encourage individuals to the development of their own abilities and serve the community, are objects worth pursuing and reflect the core of the Christian Gospel.

Throughout the Church there was a genuine appreciation for the MSC's help in fulfilling its task in relation to the community. More specifically, this appreciation was focused upon local area managers and MSC officers. Contact and dialogue and discussion with them in many cases brought benefit both to understanding and to discovering the appropriate path of action for the Churches.

Many congregations did 'go it alone', and quite successfully in certain cases, but others found that the objectives of serving the community were fulfilled more effectively when under the aegis of the MSC, or in early discussion about an MSC programme, wider discussions took place either with other local Churches, or indeed at times with organizations outwith the Church. These alliances have been found beneficial and have borne fruit for the Church's task in other areas of life. Where local congregations had been immersed in congregational activity affecting primarily their own members, involvement in the MSC programmes brought a wider grasp of community issues to their understanding. Church members gained a better understanding of social conditions affecting people in their parish and community, and this had its effect upon the worship and prayers of the Church.

One area of the Church's concern quite naturally has had to be the care of the distressed, the elderly and the disadvantaged, and over these years of the MSC there is little doubt that many excellent projects were initiated to serve people within those categories, which would never have taken place without the stimulus of the MSC and the funding placed at the disposal of such projects.

## PROBLEMS

The Revd Dane Sherrard has said that 'Our relationship with the MSC was not one in which "Problem" was an appropriate word. We both thought of each other as partners.' Others, however, did find certain difficulties, which might be expected since the aims and objectives of the Church and the MSC were never imagined to be identical. The MSC frequently made powerful and effective use of the concept of a partnership with other agencies, such as the Church and voluntary organizations, but there were obvious differences between the objectives of the MSC and the unemployment-orientated objectives of the Churches. The distinctive nature and the aims of Churches and the voluntary sector have been inadequately understood by many MSC staff, and the mechanisms for representation on issues of concern have rarely worked to the satisfaction of the Commission's operational partners. In the early days of the Churches' involvement there was a spirit of willingness by the MSC and its officers to listen to the concerns of the Churches and other operating partners. This was very much the philosophy of Sir Richard O'Brien's aim to achieve consensus when he was Chairman of the MSC. Then increasingly over the years the operating partners were excluded from matters of policy. Decisions and changes were made about the programmes with little effective consultation. There was no attempt to check out in advance the shifts of policy, and the operating partners were only brought in after the event. Local advisory Boards and Area Manpower Boards occasionally, and almost by accident, included representatives of the Churches and the voluntary organizations. This really was inadequate representation, when it is recognized that something like one-third of the total placements of community-programme activity in Scotland were mooted in the Church and voluntary sector. There was no appropriate representative voice percolating through to the Commission in a systematic way. Indeed in Scotland there was no specific Church representative on any national advisory body, and increasingly the operating partners' concerns were apparently unheeded. It is one thing for the government to decree a policy change, and for the Manpower Services Commission to decree a new set of guide-lines which the civil servants of the department are obliged to implement. It is a totally different thing for the people involved in Churches and voluntary organizations to understand the suddenness with which some of those changes were made and even if they could understand them, to arrange for the less enthusiastic partners in their organizations to accept. In the West of Scotland a frequent complaint was the rapidity of the shifting of the MSC goal posts. In the East the complaint differed only in that they became rugby posts.

Large organizations such as the MSC inevitably must make changes in their staff at local level, but this often had an adverse effect upon the local participants. The discontinuities caused by staff turnover; the difficulty of gaining confidence; the lack of knowledge of the newly arrived officer of local conditions; all these caused quite understandable but definite difficulties. In discussions with many Church participants, the word inflexibility was frequently used about the operational requirements of the MSC. In some areas where there was a particularly good relationship with an MSC official, this inflexibility could be overcome. Indeed it must be said that in some areas the local official was most co-operative in not only interpreting, but perhaps bending the rules, in order to make it possible for schemes to develop which were within the spirit if not the letter of the Act. Such mature and understanding servants of the Commission were much respected, and the aims of the Commission were as fully implemented under their guidance as under the guidance of their less flexible colleagues.

The one constant complaint inevitably was in relation to the annual turnover of Community Programme staff, which resulted from the fifty-two-week rule. This was of course well understood in the broad terms of overall policy, but at the local level it caused unending difficulties for projects. As the Revd Hugh Wylie, of Hamilton Old said of Community Programme staff, 'They were unsure of themselves for a month or two, then they were fine, then they were realizing the end was in sight, they slumped in efficiency and their time keeping and enthusiasm simply dropped away'.

This was an inevitable tension therefore between the purposes of local projects which of course had been approved by MSC, and the purposes of the MSC in ensuring a throughput of individuals. When project organizers had to get rid of employees who were beginning at that time to be experienced, of course there was regret and recrimination and complaint, but the rules required that these individuals had to be sacked. Many project organizers would say that this fifty-two-week rule was in part responsible for the deliberate misuse that many made of sickness leave and for poor performance.

Projects suffered frequently also in the way in which numbers of places allocated to them were suddenly altered. If there was a sudden increase, expansion and problems were grave. If there was a sudden reduction from, say, 30 placements to 20, this required a complete reorganization of the whole programme.

The monitoring process was something which did irritate Church based project leaders. In one West Coast Presbytery, the Church Elder appointed to sponsor MSC schemes on behalf of his Church, himself a professional engineer, said 'MSC officials were very helpful at the beginning of a scheme, but the monitoring process drove you skatty.' The Revd Donald Skinner will wax eloquent on this specific subject: 'In the early days the MSC training officers were all tradesmen. I respected them. But what credentials do some of those pen pushers have, on our ability to deliver?'

There was also the mixed blessing of operating within another agency. It will be remembered that instead of large numbers of individual sponsors establishing separate schemes, the MSC identified agencies under whose umbrella many of the smaller schemes would be co-ordinated. The Revd Iain Matheson of Hamilton Trinity says 'It was the MSC who 'suggested' that we come under an agency two years ago. It freed us certainly from administrative burdens, but produced a superfluity of bosses and resulting confusion to staff and supervisors.'

A number of schemes found the difficulty of gaining trade union approval. This was another case of perfectly legitimate but different interests coming into conflict. The trade union concern, understandably, was to avoid job substitution. For instance, one project initiated by the Church and housed within local authority premises, which had been successfully operating for a number of years, passing through the annual consideration of NALGO and being reluctantly allowed to proceed, came to an end, partly on the ground that the trade union pressed for the project and the staff employed to be taken into the mainline funding of the authority. In some cases there was a lack of understanding on the part of some Church people about the role and function of trade unions, and impatience developed over what they saw as unnecessary delay in the granting of permission for what would otherwise have appeared as valuable local projects.

But on the whole in Scotland, with the exception of one or two unions, the experience of the Church in Scotland was good in this respect. A number of projects were delayed for up to a year till trade union approval was given. This, however, was beyond the control of the MSC, as is well understood.

Some Church groups described the long periods of uncertainty during the development stage of programmes. Trying to arrange premises and local funding and to create the physical conditions on which the scheme might be based had to go on, while there was no guarantee at all of the project going ahead. This relates to the amount of time it took to undertake projects. Hard-pressed parish ministers and elders and office bearers of the Church, most of whom had full-time occupations, found the frustrations of form filling and monitoring a considerable impediment. Indeed one presbytery created a small committee out of which among many other useful things, was the proposal that there should be a glossary encompassing a brief description of what they so aptly described as 'those damned initials'.

In spite of those difficulties and many other smaller ones, the people involved from the Church have generally described themselves as being satisfied with their relationship with the MSC, and regarded the problems simply as part of the process of a changing society, and attempts by government to relate to a fundamentally difficult economic situation.

## WHAT DID THE CHURCH LEARN?

As might be expected, a lengthy history of interaction between MSC and the Church had effects upon the Church itself. Where a middle-class congregation, for example that of the Revd Keith Campbell in Broughty Ferry, takes the risk of venturing out into a project in which Church premises will be adapted in order to provide day-centre provisions for disabled teenagers, they engaged simultaneously in a learning experience. The Kirk Session of that congregation took the initiative of setting the project up, and the monthly reports made about the development, problems, and progress of the project, made them sensitive to areas of life of which they otherwise might have been ignorant.

Those Presbyteries, congregations and Churches whose representatives struggled through the laborious process of discussion, form filling, experimentation, sponsorship and supervision to create a viable and useful project had a satisfaction and indeed a pride in themselves for contributing something which their Church might otherwise not have achieved.

For many people in the Church, the Christian gospel was well understood in its 'spiritual' aspect. They could agree that the gospel's message must be applied in the concrete situations of the world, and they applauded the work of the Church in its overseas mission, in healing, in teaching and building, and they could applaud the work of the Church's Boards of Social Responsibility in their provision for disadvantaged groups in society. The prospect however of having to place their own resources of time and effort and property at the service of community needs, right on their own doorstep, was an eye opener for many. This became more than a theoretical lesson and something of practical experience whereby the difficulties of community Christian action were discovered.

There were, of course, some outstanding examples of the use of Church premises for MSC schemes. In Anderston in Glasgow, in St Aidan's Dundee, in Hamilton Old, in Provanmill, Paisley St Ninian's, and many other places, naturally including Buckhaven and Gilmerton, this was certainly the case. Whole congregations and whole parishes became aware of the impact of the programmes, and with various levels of enthusiasm were willing to accept the inconvenience of this new use of their premises.

In 1986 the body of the Church and Nation Report of the General Assembly of the Church of Scotland contained a whole section of some two and a half pages on the Youth Training Scheme and the proposal for a two-year training scheme. It recognized the deficiencies which had been experienced by some young people in the scheme, but welcomed the introduction of the two-year scheme and urged the government to improve the quality of the training offered, to consider a substantial improvement in the level of payment, and to encourage employers wherever possible to appoint trainees to permanent positions at the end of the training period in preference to replacing them with new trainees. In addition, the Assembly of that year instructed all presbyteries and congregations to consider actively undertaking projects to create new employment and drew attention to the opportunities for establishing such projects through the MSC funding of Community Programmes. At the same time, and in conjunction with this Assembly decision, every congregation in the Church of Scotland received a leaflet simply called 'The unemployed – is there something we can do?' designed to encourage congregations to involve themselves in appropriate schemes. It listed a great variety of projects which had already been undertaken by congregations in different parts of the country, mentioned the hundreds of jobs being provided through Church-based schemes throughout the length and breadth of Scotland, and gave a step-by-step guide on how congregations might, in consultation with the MSC, make a useful contribution to many individuals and to the community at large.

Sad to say, far fewer congregations than the Church had hoped, or who could have made contributions, stirred themselves into any adequate activity. Those in the Church who had gained experience of establishing projects were frequently telephoned or received written requests for guidance on how this or that local congregation might go about things. A lot of time was spent on this, but again and again, the story was that the ideas never resulted in action. In considering how the MSC affected the life of the Church, an even sadder commentary arises from the declared unwillingness of some congregations even to consider putting their resources at the disposal of the community. Some, indeed, with attractive leisure and sports facilities used by members of the congregation largely in the evenings or at the weekend, and which would have been ideal for unemployed young people as an adjunct to other MSC activities, were simply made unavailable through fear of damage or overuse.

On the other hand, many individuals and groupings within the Churches experienced a new way of working with their community. Skills available within the congregational life of Churches were placed at the disposal of others. New skills were developed in relating to the projects and the people involved, levels of pastoral care and support were discovered which would not have developed apart from MSC schemes. The relationships were particularly fruitful for particular aspects of the Church.

Industrial Mission is a specialized activity of the Scottish Churches relating to industrial people and issues. Its full-time and part-time staff throughout Scotland had over the years developed close working contact with many people within industry and industrial organizations. This knowledge and mutual confidence enabled Industrial Mission participants to see the opportunities of using some of the best features of the MSC programmes to aid people of all ages, and Industrial Mission was largely instrumental throughout the years of the MSC in encouraging the Church to play an effective role in MSC programmes. This did not however in any way inhibit Industrial Mission from making critical comment to government and the MSC.

Over the years a number of Church representatives found themselves serving on Area Manpower Boards, one Industrial Chaplain, indeed serving as Chairman of one AMB. Another writes, 'Membership of the Board was useful, it enabled us to keep abreast of the debate about changes in the programmes, as well as sharing in the monitoring of work at local level. It would be easy to exaggerate the influence we may have had over the work of the MSC, but I am sure that in a number of instances it was possible to shape the delivery of programmes at local level as well as making a contribution to the debate about new programmes.'

This particular Church representative, again an Industrial Chaplain was also a member of a voluntary representatives group at national level, and here he states that they were able to make firm recommendations to the MSC about the programmes in theory and practice, and able to modify some of the proposals that were made.

## DID THE CHURCH INFLUENCE THE MSC?

In the decade and a half during which the MSC poured large sums of money into explanatory brochures describing successive special programmes and during which same period, highly articulate representatives of the Church extended millions of words in attempts to understand and apply those programmes, it might be expected that the Church was able to influence the MSC in a number of ways. Sadly it was not, at least in any major way. There are certainly many Church people who would laugh at the very suggestion that the Church influenced the MSC. If one word could summarize the impression left upon the Church by working with the MSC, that word is 'inflexibility'.

This impression of the MSC's rigidity and apparent unwillingness to be influenced, may not be totally justified. In larger schemes certainly there had to be some give and take, in order to tailor resources to the potential. In Buckhaven certainly Dane Sherrard's experience was of mutual adaptation and flexibility to ensure delivery of the most effective projects, but other senior ministers of the Church with considerable experience of operating schemes have complained of the difficulty of finding an opportunity of meeting senior MSC officials face to face to discuss relevant questions.

## CHARITIES' INITIATIVE

In the summer of 1985 a Scottish Church representative joined others from British Churches at a meeting convened in London by the Department of Employment. The purpose of this meeting was to introduce a new churches element to the 'charities' initiative'. The existing Community Programme would continue operating in its normal role, but charities, voluntary organizations and Churches would be offered the opportunity to establish separate projects outwith the normal regulations of the CP. They would be able to distribute posts flexibly within their own structures in individual placements or small groups. The assumption behind this was that Churches, along with other bodies, were already in their ordinary and normal work providing benefit to the community. If they wished therefore, to play a part in helping the unemployed, but were not wishing to sponsor self-contained projects, then this scheme would be available. Funding would be by a flat-rate block grant per person employed per week, with no lump sum, and the national insurance contributions to be met from the £75 grant to cover each individual.

Careful consideration was given to this by representatives of the Scottish Churches involved in running MSC programmes, and there was at that time a universal rejection by the Churches in Scotland of this proposal. The main reasons were that though the CP arrangements were not perfect, they did allow for more normal and regular employment conditions and monitoring than might be the case within the charities' initiative.

This rejection might be interpreted therefore as a kind of negative influence upon the MSC and its programmes.

It must be said however, that the Baptist Church and to some extent the Methodist Church in Scotland did make some use of the charities' initiative, and found it workable and acceptable. It enabled Churches to employ individuals without the wider involvement applied by the CP, and on the whole they declared it to have been successful. Churches, they found, could provide the necessary supervision and learn quickly to be good employers.

TWELVE YEARS OF CHURCH STATEMENTS

The life and work of the Church of Scotland is organized through a Hierarchy of ecclesiastical courts. The highest of these is the General Assembly, which meets annually in Edinburgh. Decisions taken there are the decisions of the Church, and these can be decisions to instruct or guide the Church in its relationships to other organizations and in social and community matters. In addition the General Assembly may address the government or any other national institution as thought appropriate. Indirectly in the year 1975, and specifically from 1976 to 1988, direct reference was made to the special programmes of the Manpower Services Commission. Typical would be the reference in 1978:

> The General Assembly notes with approval the steps now being taken by Her Majesty's Government to implement the Holland Report proposals and urges local communities to make full use of the available finance for the relief of both youth and adult unemployment.

In 1981 the General Assembly

> reiterated the view that resources allocated for the alleviation of unemployment should be concentrated upon the young unemployed and the longer term unemployed, and commended the work of the MSC and welcomed the Government's decision to increase the resources made available to it.

In 1982 the General Assembly

> urged Her Majesty's Government to accept the unanimous recommendations of the Commission with regard to the proposed

level of trainee allowances and continued eligibility by those not participating in the scheme to supplementary benefit in their own right.

It referred in that same year to the 'low level of training allowances for young people in YOP and authorised a direct request to the Secretary of State for Employment to reconsider this low level of training allowance'.

Mention has already been made of the 1986 Assembly discussion (see Section 4). As recent as 1988 the General Assembly

viewed with great concern the Government's plan to end the Community Programme under which many thousands of jobs involved with care and support of the community had been created, which jobs will in general be lost in September when the programme comes to an end, and it viewed with concern the morality of the Government's new Employment Training Scheme and instructed the Church and Nation Committee to communicate with the relevant Government departments with a view to having the provisions of the scheme reconsidered.

The mere fact that the Assembly gave such time to the special programmes of the MSC indicated that the Churches in Scotland have regarded these schemes as vitally important, but the repeated inability to alter the proposals or the programmes in any significant way might be the very source of experiencing 'the triumph of hope over experience'.

CONCLUSION

The story of the partnership of the Church and the MSC has been described often as a love–hate relationship. The Church shared the Commission's concern to be agents of help to the unemployed but it had real cause to be sceptical about the inadequacy of some of the programmes proposed by government ministers. The Church with others was concerned about the quality of the provisions and the need for more adequate funding and more operational stability. Too often unnecessary frustration has been experienced by willing Church participants because of the changing whim of Ministers and the alterations of programmes. Church-sponsored projects fared badly in the transition from YOP to YTS and more recently from CP to ET.

The spirit of this story of some fifteen years might best be summarized in the words of the Revd Hugh Wylie of Hamilton Old Parish Church:

Had I known the time it would have taken and the amount of supervision it required of me, I might not have started the projects. But again, I would have done so. It is, in perspective, a small price to pay to be able to give people a start again. That is what matters.

# CHAPTER 9. EDITORS' INTRODUCTION

Local authorities were particularly important to MSC programmes and policies. Local-authority-run schools and colleges were responsible for the delivery of some of MSC's larger programmes, and were vital to the rapid development of these. Further education colleges were particularly important as providers of off-the-job training under the adult Training Opportunities Scheme (TOPS), and under the Youth Opportunities Programme (YOP) and the Youth Training Scheme (YTS). (Chapter 4 discusses the experiences of one FE college located in Fife, while Chapter 2 outlines some of the broader aspects of the FE role in TOPS.) The MSC's Technical and Vocational Education Initiative (TVEI) was a schools-based programme. (The TVEI is discussed in detail in Chapters 3 and 6.)

Local authorities were also important to MSC outwith their role as education providers. In many parts of Scotland, local authorities were the largest employers of labour and the most significant actors in the local labour market. As MSC schemes were mostly work-experience-based and employer-led, local authorities were to be found participating in MSC schemes for their own employees and trainees, and as sponsors of schemes for the local unemployed. They also participated in MSC initiatives designed to improve information about the local labour market (see Chapters 2 and 16).

In many areas local authorities were anxious to respond in some way to the problems of unemployment. A wide range of community-based projects was sponsored under the MSC's youth and adult programmes. These included YOP Training Workshops (see Chapters 2 and 15), Information Technology Centres (ITECS) under the YTS, and various CP schemes. Some of these were developed in partnership with voluntary agencies, and some were developed alongside forms of 'special needs' provision (see Chapters 13 and 14). Some authorities also used MSC funding to promote economic development in their areas.

Local authorities were included in MSC's formal, tripartite advisory structures from the level of the Commission itself down to the local Area Manpower Boards. They were an important part of the consensus which sustained the MSC and its programmes until 1987/8. The criticisms and opposition of local authorities to subsequent changes, particularly in MSC's adult programmes, were important factors in the ending of the consensus in 1988.

Despite the importance of their role, very little has been written on local government's interaction with the MSC. Indeed there is very little in the way of readily available information. The wide variety *within* local government – in size, population, budgets, powers and geographical area – present additional difficulties to any attempts at an 'overview' of local government and the MSC. Nevertheless, some common experiences and themes did emerge from the diversity of local government in Scotland.

# 9

## LOCAL AUTHORITIES AND THE MANPOWER SERVICES COMMISSION

ARCHIE FAIRLEY

INTRODUCTION

This chapter deals with the interaction between the Manpower Services Commission and Scotland's local authorities during the period 1974–88. Such a survey requires some understanding of the key features of the agencies concerned, the environment within which they operated during the period in question and the way they shaped and responded to that environment. Chapter 2 examines the MSC in that context, and this chapter begins with a brief review of the main features of the local-authority scene. The reorganization of local government is examined together with the factors that influence local-authority attitudes to the MSC and the significance of the financial regime under which local authorities have operated for most of the period in question. The motivation for and scale of local authority involvement is assessed, and the network of relationships which was established with the MSC is then examined in terms of its impact on councillors, council structures and council employees. An overview of the general local authority experience of the MSC is followed by an assessment of both the adult employment and youth training projects. Finally, some general conclusions on the overall experience are developed.

STRUCTURAL FEATURES OF LOCAL GOVERNMENT IN SCOTLAND

The birth of the MSC in 1974 coincided with a major reform of Scotland's local government system. The new system was defined in the 1973 Local Government (Scotland) Act and came into operation in May 1975. The old system had more than 400 local authorities based on cities, counties, large burghs, small burghs and districts. The new regime consisted of three all-purpose Islands Councils and, on the mainland, nine Regional Councils and fifty-three District Councils.

The functions allocated to the Districts and the Regions played a major part in determining the nature of their dealings with the MSC. The Regions were given responsibility for strategic planning, education, social work, police, fire services, industrial development, transportation and roads. Housing was the major function allocated to the Districts, along with local planning, environmental health, refuse collection, parks and recreation and building control. The single tier authorities on Orkney, Shetland and the Western Isles had responsibility for the whole range of local authority services.

Within this basic structure, local authorities vary substantially in terms of size, politicization, ambitions and policies. All these factors condition their dealings with the MSC.

In terms of size, the range is enormous. At one extreme, Strathclyde Region is the largest local authority in Europe with a population of 2.3 million and an annual revenue budget of around £2 billion. Its budget and resources would be the envy of many of the world's nation states. At the other end of the spectrum, seven of Scotland's District Councils, in Highland and Borders Regions, each have a population of less than 20 000. The size of the authority is obviously one factor which determines its importance for the MSC in terms of delivering schemes. It also influences the weight which the local authority can bring to bear in negotiations with the MSC.

The effect to which an authority is 'politicized' may also affect its attitude to the MSC and its schemes. In the central belt of Scotland and in the major cities, councils tend to be run on disciplined party-political lines, while in many rural areas, councillors stand as independents and councils are run without fixed party groupings. The extension of party politics into areas where local government had been the preserve of independent councillors has been a feature of the period under review.

These examples give a flavour of the diversity of local government. This diversity reflects the social and cultural diversity of Scotland itself, and should be borne in mind when considering general statements about local authority interaction with the MSC.

Another important and distinctive feature of the local government scene is the Convention of Scottish Local Authorities (COSLA). COSLA was established as part of the local government reorganization in 1975. Among its other functions, it represents local government in consultations and negotiations with central government on a whole range of issues including education, employment and training policies. It also deals with the MSC on issues which affect local government.

All 65 local authorities are members of COSLA, which can therefore speak for all of local government in Scotland. The position in England and Wales is very different. In these countries, local authorities belong to a number of different local authority associations, which often fail to reach agreement on a common local authority position.

The lack of a directly elected parliament in Scotland means that there has been no natural body to articulate Scottish opinion on a whole range of issues, including education and training issues. Perhaps for that reason, COSLA, like the Scottish Trades Union Congress (STUC) and the

Scottish Council of Churches, has taken more than a merely sectional interest in the affairs of Scotland. In the context of the MSC, this means that COSLA has moved beyond commenting on education, employment and training policies as they affect local government to a position where it takes a view of these policies as they affect the economic and social health and wellbeing of the nation.

## FINANCIAL RESTRICTIONS

The political and financial regime under which local authorities operate has also been a factor in their attitude to MSC schemes. From the mid-1970s, this has become increasingly difficult.

The Rate Support Grant (RSG) is provided to local authorities by central government as its contribution to the provision of local services. The RSG peaked at 75 per cent of relevant local government spending in 1975/6. By 1979, this percentage had been reduced to 68.5 per cent largely as a pragmatic response to external economic pressures. Since 1979, the curtailment of local authority expenditure has been a policy objective in its own right, and by 1988/9, the RSG had fallen to 55 per cent of relevant expenditure.

This policy in relation to the RSG has been accompanied by a series of Acts of Parliament which have restricted the rights of local authorities to raise money through their other major source of income, the rates.

From the mid-1970s, there have been a series of disagreements between central and local government about the desirability of curbing local government expenditure. The local government view has been that they have been starved of resources by reductions in the RSG and restrictions on their own local finance-raising powers.

This financial background has encouraged an ambivalent attitude towards the MSC. On the one hand, it has been a source of funds when resources were scarce. On the other hand, it has been viewed as an agent of a central government that was basically hostile to local government.

## FRAMEWORK FOR INVOLVEMENT

Local authorities approached their dealings with the MSC with an economic and social remit which distinguished them from both the private and voluntary sectors.

While many private companies also have a commitment to the community, the community interest is the starting point for local authority involvement. Councillors are elected by the community and are there to serve the community. The commitment to alleviate unemployment, to carry out work of value to the community and to provide training for young people and the unemployed is central to a local authority, while at best it is liable to be an 'extra' for a private company.

Over the period in question, the local authority commitment to economic development has also grown. This has influenced attitudes to MSC

schemes, both of the training and job-creation varieties. The scale of
local authority involvement is partly conditioned by their social concern,
their economic development remit and their role as providers of education and training. It is also influenced by the sheer scale of local
authorities as employers. Local authorities in Scotland employ almost
300 000 people across the whole range of skilled, unskilled, professional,
clerical, craft, manual and technical employments. In many areas of the
country, the local authority is the major employer. This, allied to the
factors mentioned above, illustrates their obvious importance in any
significant employment and training schemes. In fact, in most areas of
Scotland local authorities were often the single most important agency as
far as the MSC was concerned.

Local authorities are unusual in the variety of their dealings with the
MSC and the variety of the issues on which they have a joint involvement.
These range through adult employment, youth training, TVEI and off-
the-job college training.

Although the impact of the MSC on schools and colleges is dealt with in
other chapters of this book, it has a place here too in that education is the
major function of Regional and Islands Councils. While this chapter is
concerned with the Community Programme and the Youth Training
Scheme and their predecessors, some councillors and officers in education authorities have an overview of their authority's relationship with
the MSC which includes not just these particular schemes but all the
school and college related issues as well.

### COUNCILLORS, COUNCIL STRUCTURES AND EMPLOYEES

In local government, councillors make policy decisions which it is the
responsibility of officers to implement. The functions of policy making
and policy implementation cannot always be neatly separated, and
clearly, there is an interaction between the two; nevertheless this broad
principle holds true. As a result, councillors, officers and groups of
council employees often have different experiences of and perceptions of
the MSC.

At councillor level, one of the nine places on the MSC itself was
reserved for a Scottish councillor; so clearly there was an opportunity to
exercise some power and influence at that level. While COSLA was
allowed to make nominations for this position, it was the Secretary of
State for Employment who made the appointment and it was not always
in accordance with COSLA's recommendation.

Councillors served on the MSC's Area Manpower Boards (AMBs), and a
number of authorities found their position useful in information gathering and in lobbying for the council's view to be accepted on particular
projects and applications. However, there was also a general recognition
of the token nature of participation on the AMBs, which were there
essentially to implement MSC policy, which was decided either in Shef-

field or London. There was no real opportunity to influence policy through the AMBs, and any AMB whose decisions were at variance with MSC policy was simply overruled.

Throughout most of this period, councillors made policy decisions about whether, and to what extent, to get involved in MSC schemes against a background of high levels of unemployment. They often felt themselves under pressure to participate in schemes concerned with school leavers and the adult unemployed in spite of obvious defects in the schemes, because failure to participate would mean passing up an opportunity to 'do something' about unemployment. Areas of particular concern were the allowances payable to YTS trainees and the eligibility criteria and part-time employment built into the CP.

Council officers, once the political decisions had been made, were responsible for preparing schemes for approval, negotiating over the contents with MSC officials and implementing and monitoring schemes.

A wide variety of structures was developed to carry out these tasks. Centralized units were set up in some authorities, while in others the functions were carried out within different departments, sometimes within existing structures. There was probably no 'correct' structure as the circumstances of each authority varied so considerably as did the extent to which they became involved in different schemes.

Local authority employees had varied experiences of MSC schemes. With the major exception of some professional groups, most employees had experience of YTS trainees in their place of work. What was at first a novelty and, in some cases, a cause for concern, became commonplace as the years went by.

Some local authority employees became involved full-time with MSC schemes as authorities set up Special Programme Units or their equivalents and Community Programme Agencies. For many of these local government employees, it was a step outside the local government mainstream. The premises they worked in were often physically remote from the traditional council offices and work-places. And even if these employees themselves were in permanent full-time jobs on local authority pay and conditions, the same could certainly not be said for YTS supervisors or CP workers with whom they were in daily contact. The temporary status of these employees was a major deviation from the security of employment which was the norm in local government. For these CP workers and YTS supervisors there was a sense of remoteness from the council and this extended, on many occasions, to full-time permanent staff working in these areas.

Local authority involvement with the MSC also extended to indirect involvement through the newly created economic development initiatives and through the voluntary and community business sectors. Projects, such as the Landwise and Heatwise programmes in Glasgow, depended, wholly or partly, on council contracts, while a number of 'caring' functions which came broadly within the local authority remit were carried out by voluntary organizations using CP funding.

## THE GENERAL EXPERIENCE

A number of general points can be made about the relationship between local authorities and the MSC.

Firstly, they were important to each other. The MSC would have found difficulty in delivering many of its major schemes without local authority involvement, while MSC funding allowed local authorities to implement socially valuable projects. It can be argued that local authorities could have spent the money just as effectively, possibly more effectively, if it had been mainstream RSG funding, but the fact is that the RSG was being restrained or cut during most of this period.

Most local authorities take the view that the MSC failed to consult them adequately either individually or through COSLA about its policies and their development. Even when relations between central and local government are not good and when central government is imposing legislation which is not popular with local government, it is customary for government departments to consult with COSLA and the English and Welsh local authority associations, if only on the practicality of their proposals. It may be that the MSC's failure to follow precedent is due to the fact that it was not a government department but rather an agency concerned with delivering and implementing a policy established elsewhere. Its base in Sheffield also made it less likely that it would take on board any specifically Scottish considerations which might apply.

The fact that MSC schemes, in particular major ones like the YTS and the CP, were subject to regular changes in their conditions created major headaches for local authorities. There were many complaints that by the time a scheme had been tried and tested and was running smoothly, the MSC moved the goal-posts and it was back to square one.

Apart from the administrative inconvenience involved, some of these changes, for example in CP eligibility conditions, were unpalatable to many authorities. However, it was often felt that even if the scheme was not wholly satisfactory and was getting worse, total withdrawal was not a serious option. Having got involved in the scheme in the first place, there was no alternative but to continue.

Local authorities tend to be proud of the quality of their MSC schemes. This is particularly true when they draw comparisons between the quality of their YTS training with some of the private-sector schemes. While there was undoubtedly an element of job substitution (see Introduction) in local authority YTS schemes for example, there was a more serious commitment to training because of its social value and less of a tendency to use the trainees as cheap labour than in some of the 'shelf filling' schemes in the retail sector.

### ADULT UNEMPLOYMENT

Local authorities were keen to alleviate the effects of unemployment in their area and to ensure that work of benefit to the community was carried out. Local authorities and the voluntary sector provided virtually all the places on MSC schemes of this nature. In October 1987, local authorities were providing 20 100 CP places: some 57 per cent of the Scottish total. Interestingly, the corresponding figure in England was 39 per cent.

Sizeable Community Programme Agencies were established by a number of authorities although this was not the only mechanism used to administer CP schemes. These Community Programme Agencies or their equivalents were major employers in many areas of high unemployment.

There are differing views of the value to the community of the work carried out using CP schemes. Some schemes appear to have been poorly designed, offering repetitive manual work with little benefit to the community. However, most schemes did provide tangible community benefits. Environmental improvements were the focus for many District Council schemes. Care of the gardens of elderly and disabled people was another common CP application. The work done by many of the successful schemes was of such a nature that it would not have been carried out had the Council received a straightforward increase in the RSG. Such an increase in the RSG would have resulted in expenditure on the Council's own priorities, which would not necessarily have corresponded with the kind of project which attracted MSC funding.

### YOUTH TRAINING

Local authorities believe that they were the providers of many of the better YTS schemes. This is because they had the commitment and the resources to provide high-quality training. YTS has had an effect on local authority recruitment policies. Traditional craft apprenticeships have been replaced by the two-year YTS and an abbreviated apprenticeship. Recruitment to many white-collar and technical grades is now often through YTS. In some cases the YTS trainee is effectively on a two-year traineeship which may lead to a permanent job.

Local authorities were the main providers of mode B YTS places and take pride in the level of commitment shown by supervisors on the scheme.

As well as the training content of YTS, local authorities have been concerned about the low level of YTS allowances and the trainees' other conditions and in many areas ways have been found to improve conditions and top up allowances.

CONCLUSION

The overall interaction between the MSC and Scotland's local authorities is conditioned by the ambivalence of the MSC's remit. On the one hand it was to provide high-quality training, on the other stop-gap measures to alleviate unemployment. This made the MSC's task difficult and complicates any overall assessment.

Major criticisms voiced by local authorities concern the lack of consultation, and the constant changing of the criteria as far as the conditions of the schemes were concerned.

The period under review was a period of financial stringency for local authorities and money from any source to provide training, employment and projects of community benefit was welcome. Councils would have preferred the funds to come through mainstream funding to be spent in accordance with local priorities, but that was not an option and the MSC could not be refused in the circumstances. In the event, every attempt was made to utilize the available funds and to overcome the inherent weaknesses in the schemes for the benefit of the community.

# CHAPTER 10. EDITORS' INTRODUCTION

The trade union movement in Scotland has had an uneasy relationship with the MSC. The establishment of a body such as the MSC was something which the trade unions had campaigned for (see Chapter 1), but the initial responses to the Labour government's training proposals in the early 1970s was hostile. Further, when the Conservative government took office in 1979 on a radical economic programme of disengagement from Keynesian demand management in favour of policies to control inflation, the role of the MSC came under scrutiny. On the one hand most trade unions opposed the government's economic strategy, but on the other they did not want to be excluded from discussions and negotiations on the future training needs of the work-force.

In spite of reservations expressed over different aspects of training schemes, including the level of payment to trainees, the quality of training and trade union involvement and the opposition of some key individuals within the trade union movement, a relatively high degree of consensus existed about the involvement of trade unions in the planning and delivery of the schemes. For example, jobs of many trade union members in schools and colleges (see Chapters 2 and 3) were increasingly dependent on trade union co-operation with the MSC.

As circumstances changed, however, and as the government shifted from a policy of including the views and experiences of trade unions to one of excluding them, the consensus on which delivery had existed became more fragile until its eventual breakdown in 1988.

This chapter outlines the involvement of the STUC in training policy and its relationship with the MSC and charts the uneasy relationship through Congress debates, and the words of many of those involved. In conclusion, it argues for a training strategy which is relevant to Scottish needs.

# 10

## THE MANPOWER SERVICES COMMISSION IN SCOTLAND: THE VIEW OF THE STUC

BILL SPEIRS

For the trade union movement in Scotland, dealing with the Manpower Services Commission has been like chasing some supernatural animal lifted straight out of Celtic mythology. No sooner do you get hold of one leg than it is shed, and two others (and probably a new head and another arm as well) are grown in its place. Since the establishment of the MSC in the early 1970s, the myriad of schemes, structures, titles and terminology has on occasion become so baffling that people have actually been able to make a living out of advising on how to deal with the MSC.

The situation has of course been complicated by the major changes in the Scottish economy and labour market that have taken place since the 1973 Employment and Training Act established the MSC, by the massive increase in unemployment and by the altered political climate after 1979. The trade union movement, including the Scottish TUC, has had to decide how far to co-operate with the MSC and its operations in circumstances where it increasingly seemed that it was being used to implement government labour market policies with which the movement was in fundamental disagreement. It would often have been simpler to walk away than to continue to compromise, and it is perhaps surprising that the break – over the new Job Training Scheme, and then over Employment Training – took so long to come about. Yet there was always the argument (backed up to some extent by experience) that the interests of young people, the unemployed and union members were best served by using influence on the inside rather than shouting from the outside.

There have been a number of inter-related aspects to the trade unions' dealings with the MSC in Scotland. They include the relationship with the MSC's structures; training needs of young people; training needs of the adult unemployed; training needs of adults in employment; and the impact of the MSC's special employment-creating measures. It has not always been easy to separate these factors, and in some instances (such as Employment Training) they appear to have been deliberately confused by the MSC (or the government).

When the discussion document 'Training for the Future' was issued in February 1972, the overall response of the trade union movement in Scotland was hostile, particularly to the proposed phasing out of the levy grant system operated by the Industrial Training Boards (ITBS). It was this issue, and the level of funding (£35 million) proposed for administration costs of the ITBS and for grants in key training areas that attracted the most adverse comment. The suggested establishment of the Manpower Services Commission attracted little attention: when it was mentioned, it was generally welcomed.

At the 1973 STUC Congress, a motion was adopted which 'deplored the Government's proposals on industrial training' which it argued would 'lead to a worsening of industrial training in Britain'. After making a number of other specific criticisms of the government's proposals, the motion put forward three demands, all of which were to feature again and again in the training policies put forward by the STUC in subsequent years.

These demands were:

(a) Immediate steps to be taken to increase the number of persons participating in industrial training and, therefore, legislative action be taken to provide compulsory day release for all employed persons up to the age of 21;

(b) Action be taken to ensure the full participation of women in training programmes;

(c) The General Council, along with affiliated unions, should as an interim measure campaign for increased day release participation by young workers.

The mover of the motion, Tom Taylor of the National Union of Vehicle Builders (now part of the Transport and General Workers' Union) deployed arguments which covered specific aspects of the government's proposals, but also questioned the commitment of employers to voluntarily provide training in terms which are still being used today. He said that if training were restricted to the narrower requirements of the employer, then those involved in the training process would not get comprehensive training. There would be no comprehensive training available for his members and that would present problems not only for them but for industry as a whole. Past experiences clearly proved this was a danger, and it seemed to him that the proposed legislation would worsen the existing situation.

The question of the exemption of smaller firms also gave rise to concern. Conditions would certainly vary from industry to industry but his own experience in vehicle building told him that in the past, before the introduction in 1964 of the Industrial Training Act, some firms were prepared to accept their commitment to train while others avoided the responsibility or provided inadequate training. The ones who had not trained then pinched skilled workers from the firms who had trained. He argued that this situation would fast apply again if the government modifications to the Industrial Training Act went unchallenged (STUC Annual Report, 1973, p. 450).

Following on from the Congress debate, the STUC General Council held further discussions around the Employment and Training Bill, including discussions with the Scottish CBI. Following these deliberations, a submission was made to the Secretary of State for Employment which continued the criticisms outlined above, but which said that

the General Council broadly welcome the establishment of a Manpower Services Commission. They feel, however, that Scottish trade union opinion should be directly represented on the Commission and representation to this effect has been made to Government. The General Council feel there should be a specific obligation on the Manpower Services Commission to establish both local and regional advisory machinery. (STUC General Council Report, 1974, p. 204)

The question of a Scottish input to the MSC's operations and the nature of the Commission's sub-structures were to continue to trouble the trade union movement in Scotland right up until the abolition of the MSC itself, and the proposals for the establishment of 'Enterprise Scotland'.

## MSC STRUCTURES

Throughout the lifetime of the MSC, the Scottish TUC participated in its various consultative and advisory structures. STUC nominees served on the District Manpower Committees which were established in 1974; on the Special Programmes Area Boards established a few years later; and on the Area Manpower Boards (AMBS) which succeeded both the District Manpower Committees and the Special Programmes Area Boards in 1983.

Throughout the period when Congress nominees were serving on these various bodies, both the TUC and the STUC convened regular meetings to get reports from the nominees on how effective they felt the MSC structures were, and to brief them on up-to-date positions of the TUC and STUC on training and employment matters. Throughout the period, there were complaints about the various AMBS lack of any real authority, and of difficulties in coping with the volume of paperwork and the continual changes in the operation of MSC schemes. It was nevertheless felt that participation on the AMBS provided a considerable amount of useful information, and helped to keep the pressure on within the MSC to improve the quality of all schemes.

The round of appointments to the Special Programmes Boards, AMBS etc. always produced a considerable volume of good-quality nominations from STUC-affiliated unions and Trades Councils, who were keen to see their members serving on the AMBS. The process of selecting the final five STUC nominees for each AMB was not an easy one. In general, an effort was made to ensure that there was at least one educational trade unionist on each AMB; that in areas with specific industrial or commercial interests, a nominee from an appropriate union would be appointed; and in general, that there was a 'spread' of trade unions across the country. One particular problem that was continually encountered was that of obtaining women nominees to serve on the AMBS. The difficulty appeared to be related to the fact that it was largely full-time officials who were being nominated by the unions, and unfortunately the proportion of full-time union officials who are female is not large.

Following the establishment of the MSC, the STUC General Council (among others) pressed for the establishment of a Scottish Committee of the MSC. This was eventually established in 1977. The Committee mirrored the pattern of appointments of the UK Commission, with three nominees being sought from the STUC and CBI Scotland. The STUC General Council always gave a great deal of importance to this Committee, and the General Secretary (first the late James Milne, followed by Campbell Christie) served on the Committee throughout its existence. Despite the importance attached to it, the STUC nominees found their role on the Committee a frustrating one, since they – like everyone else involved with the MSC – continually ran up against its highly centralized nature, in which the overwhelming majority of decisions were taken at the Sheffield headquarters, and local initiatives had to be fitted to a template shaped in Sheffield. This problem reached its sharpest form when Scottish voluntary organizations, local authorities and trade unions all agreed that Employment Training was unsuitable for Scottish needs, but neither the Scottish Committee nor the MSC staff in Scotland were able to make alterations to the UK structure, with the result that in 1988 there was a large scale boycott of ET in Scotland.

TRAINING FOR YOUNG PEOPLE

At the time when the establishment of the MSC was under discussion, the STUC approach to training for young people was still largely related to the craft apprenticeship and the need to improve the use of day- and block-release for off-the-job training.

At the 1973 Congress, however, in the same debate as the government's consultative document 'Training for the Future' was discussed (referred to above), there was a motion from the Educational Institute of Scotland (EIS), which called for 'legislation providing for compulsory attendance at further education colleges of all young people up to the age of 18', with the compulsory release taking the form of day-release or its equivalent, without loss of pay, for young people in employment. The motion was remitted to the General Council because it was felt that it might conflict with the position adopted a few moments earlier in the

Table 19. Under-18-year-olds in Scotland receiving further education,
1967–1971 (per cent)

|          | Boys  | Girls |
|----------|-------|-------|
| 1967/68  | 28.67 | 6.33  |
| 1968/69  | 32.34 | 7.7   |
| 1969/70  | 33.66 | 7.86  |
| 1970/71  | 34.27 | 7.04  |

*Note*: Figures exclude students in higher education.

*Source*: Scottish Office educational statistics, quoted by Fred Forrester at STUC Congress, 1973.

debate which called for a legislative right to day-release for all those up to the age of 21. Before that decision was taken, however, the mover of the motion, Fred Forrester of the EIS, drew attention to the problem of the low percentage of young people participating in further education. He quoted Scottish Office statistics for 1971, which indicated the percentage of the population under the age of 18 receiving some form of further education: see Table 19.

The issue of the high percentage of young people in Scotland who were in employment but who received no off-the-job training was to acquire greater significance as the decade progressed, and as the various schemes leading up to the Youth Training Scheme (YTS) were introduced. The position was also complicated by the growth in youth unemployment. The motion from the EIS already referred to talked of 1973 being 'a time of high unemployment among young people', but it was 1976 before a motion specifically on youth unemployment appeared on the STUC Congress agenda.

At the 1976 Congress, John Reidford of the Glasgow Trades Council moved a motion which 'viewed with alarm' the level of youth unemployment and demanded immediate government action including 'a crash programme of youth vocational and professional training, covering all industries' with remuneration at 'trade union negotiated trainee and apprenticeship rates', and statutory day release for further education for young workers to the age of 21 years. Interestingly, the motion also called on local authorities to take advantage of job-creation schemes sponsored by the government for young people, indicating that the movement was prepared to co-operate with such schemes.

A few months before the 1976 Congress at which the motion on youth unemployment was carried, the STUC General Council had responded to a discussion paper produced by the Training Services Agency on vocational preparation for young people. In the response, the General Council pointed out that 'trade unions had argued that the major responsibility for training rested with the employer and that it was up to the employer to see that there were adequate training opportunities available for their young workers, but accepted that the implications of training were so important that government had a responsibility to ensure that training and educational facilities met the requirements of industry and commerce'. The submission went on to argue that a voluntarist approach would not work. It stated that the consultative paper was correct to 'draw attention to the large number of young people entering employment who receive little or no training' and went on to state that

> we believe that this situation will not be altered unless there is direct Government intervention. There is a growing weight of opinion in favour of legislation which would give all young people, at least up to the age of 18, the right to day release to pursue vocational orientated courses. The Scottish TUC goes even further in demanding day release or block release equivalent for all young people up to the age of 21 to pursue any recognised course, whether it be vocationally based or not.

At the same time as consultations around the Training Services Agency document were taking place, the STUC was participating in a working party examining the question of mandatory day release. Other participants in the working party were the EIS, the Association of Principals of Technical Institutions and the Scottish Business Education Council, with a representative of the Scottish Technical Education Council attending as an observer. Arising from the deliberations of the working party, a document was submitted to the government, the MSC and the Training Services Agency. The document drew attention to the provision in the Education (Scotland) Act 1945 'for the compulsory part-time attendance of young persons at junior colleges for either one whole day or two half days each week or for one continuous period of eight weeks, or two continuous periods of four weeks each and every year'. This provision had been meant to come into operation on a day appointed by the Secretary of State, but 30 years had passed and the day had yet to be appointed. The document from the working party went on to call on the MSC and the appropriate government departments to initiate as soon as possible the drafting of legislation to provide young people of 16 to 18 inclusive with the right to day-release or block-release.

Similar concerns about the inadequacy of training for many young people *who were entering employment* were expressed in STUC submissions to government on pilot schemes of unified vocational preparation. In the last days of the 1974–9 Labour government, a consultative paper entitled 'A Better Start In Working Life' was published which contained a number of proposals on improving vocational preparation for employed young people in Great Britain. The incoming Conservative government stated that they would welcome comments on the document. The document again drew attention to the problems of inadequate training for young people in employment. It pointed out that

> at present, over 200,000 young people leave school each year at 16

and take jobs where no further education or planned training is available . . . In 1976/77, 60% of boys and over 85% of girls aged 16 who were in work received no day time further education.

The STUC, in its response to the consultative document, again emphasized strongly the need for an expansion of provision of off-the-job training for young people in employment as part of an overall expansion of training in Scotland. By this time, however, the issue of meeting the training needs of young people in order to improve the level of skills available in the economy was becoming inextricably linked with the need to tackle rapidly growing youth unemployment. The position of the MSC as the agency delivering both youth training and special measures to combat unemployment led to a great deal of confusion and suspicion on the part of many trade unionists – particularly at work-place level – as to the objective of the various 'training' schemes which were coming forward.

IT WOULD MAKE YOU WEEP

When the Youth Opportunities Programme was introduced in 1978, it prompted a resolution to the 1978 Annual Congress of the STUC which stated that

> Congress welcomes the measures contained in the Manpower Services Commission Youth Opportunities Programme and believes that they will make a substantial contribution towards improving the conditions and prospects of unemployed youth.

The rationale behind this welcome was that the trades union movement had recognized that there was a real problem with a group of young school-leavers who were unable to obtain employment because they had no work experience, and were unable to obtain work experience because they could not get employment. The six-month YOP, and particularly the Work Experience on Employers' Premises (WEEP) version of it, was seen as a step forward in tackling this problem, and indeed for a period this form of YOP had a good success rate in placing young people in work. At the 1979 Congress in the debate on youth unemployment YOP was not mentioned, either positively or negatively. By 1980, there was a motion on the agenda which stated that 'Congress views with alarm the level of youth unemployment and the Government attacks on the Youth Opportunities Programme.'

The mover of the motion, from Greenock and District Trades Council, actually called for 'an expansion of the Youth Opportunities Programme', which may seem odd in view of later criticism of YOP as an exploiter of young people which did not provide any real training. In fact, however, the motion from Greenock and District Trades Council actually went on to call for a different type of Youth Opportunities Programme which would cover all industries and provide real training, with remuneration at trade-union-negotiated trainee and apprentice rates. The seconder of the motion, Stewart McIntosh from the General and Municipal Workers' Union, did give an indication that the role of YOP was coming under question. He said that

> This is a scheme which is sometimes controversial amongst trades unionists. There are many who make the accusation it is not a real job you are sending these young people out to. We are sending them into the field, into the factories, out on projects, but it is not really work . . . I'll say to you we don't pretend that it is a job. The Youth Opportunities Scheme is not as good as a job, and we do persuade the young people that it is a second best and they must always consider it second best to a real job.

It is noteworthy that Stewart McIntosh had served as a STUC nominee on the Strathclyde Special Programmes Area Board, and had in fact been its Vice Chairman.

By the 1981 Annual Congress in Rothesay, opposition to the work experience element of YOP had greatly increased. A motion appeared on the Congress agenda which called for the establishment of a Youth Development Programme of integrated education, training and work experience, but for the existing WEEP element of YOP to be replaced because 'in many cases it is being exploited as substitution and cheap labour'. The mover of the motion, David Kelso of the Scottish Further Education Association, concentrated on the positive gains which a Youth Development Programme could bring, but criticized some aspects of YOP, including its lack of flexibility, pointing out that 'the same schemes are expected to operate in industrial Lanarkshire and in the butt of Lewis alike.' This problem of inflexibility was a constant factor in all of the MSC schemes over the years. The author of this chapter well recalls lengthy discussions on the Strathclyde Special Programmes Area Board, in which the Board unanimously pressed officials to allow the managers of a YOP scheme in Argyll to purchase bicycles for use by trainees going to and from work, as a more efficient (and cheaper) alternative to providing them with money to use a totally inadequate public transport system. But there was no provision for such a development in the scheme, so it could not be done.

Returning to the 1981 Congress debate: it was the seconder of the motion on the Youth Development Programme who made the more serious attack on what was happening with the WEEP element of the Youth Opportunities Programme. Campbell Christie (later to become General Secretary of the Scottish TUC) spoke on behalf of the Society of Civil and Public Servants, who represented many of the MSC staff charged with implementing the scheme. The following are among the key points which he made in his speech:

> What my union is concerned about is the work experience side of the Programme. We welcome the concept of work experience relating to training for new skills, or training for skills in the first place,

we welcome the concept of work experience related to further education: but what we are concerned about is the present Work Experience Programme which has nothing at the end of it, which is designed only as a short term expedient to keep kids off the street, and perhaps more cynically, to keep the numbers of unemployed down for presentational purposes.

We are concerned about the work experience which simply provides a pool of cheap labour for some employers who are not prepared to pay the rate for the job . . . we support work experience only in the context of a comprehensive programme involving training and further education for our young people.

There is no doubt that there is great concern amongst trade unions who have been involved in the Work Experience Programme about the use of these youngsters as a substitution for people who should be in full time employment. It is no good saying we can monitor these schemes. There are many spheres where the schemes are operating in non-trades union areas. Trades union resources are not always available to monitor the schemes.

As far as the Manpower Services Commission is concerned, my members are involved in monitoring the schemes, and we are finding it impossible to get sufficient details from the Government because of public expenditure cuts to ensure the Work Experience Schemes are properly monitored. We want to see the end of the Work Experience Scheme because we have very grave doubts about it.

These comments encapsulated many of the worries which trade unionists, even those prepared to continue support for YOP, had about the Work Experience on Employers' Premises. These concerns were greatly heightened by an increasing number of newspaper stories about accidents involving young people on the WEEP Programme, some of them resulting in fatalities.

Nevertheless, when the 'New Training Initiative' consultative document was produced, and the Youth Training Scheme was announced, the STUC and trade unions generally were still prepared to take a constructive attitude towards it.

### THE YOUTH TRAINING SCHEME

When the consultative paper 'A New Training Initiative' was published in May 1981, the STUC gave it a generally positive response. The document outlined three objectives, the first of which dealt with apprenticeship training and skills standards, and the third objective dealt with the training of adults. It was the second objective that covered the area which subsequently led to the Youth Training Scheme. This objective stated that

we must move towards a position where all young people under the

age of 18 have the opportunity either of continuing in full time
education or of entering training or a period of planned work experience combining work related training and education.

This objective was fully endorsed by the STUC in its response, but with a
number of qualifications. These included the need for greatly increased
resources to be allocated to schemes covering the 16–18 age-group; for an
allowance that was sufficient to encourage participation and certainly
considerably higher in real terms than the existing level of YOP grant; and
the need for a scheme to replace the existing WEEP element of YOP, 'which
in many cases is being exploited as substitution and cheap labour'.

The STUC General Council's response also emphasized that

if the planned work experience and training envisaged in objective
two is not just to be a temporary measure to mask youth unemployment figures, then it should not be narrowly job specific.
Instead, it should take a broad educational approach, aiming to
provide a 'package' of skills, including life and social skills. Given
the general support for 'modular' systems of training, efforts should
be made at an early stage to devise modules which can bring
together those in full time education, in employment and in the new
work related training and education schemes. This would have
considerable educational and social benefits, and would demonstrate in a practical way the commitment of society to the full
education and training of all young people in the 16 to 18 age group.

The STUC response also emphasized that the scheme should last for a
two-year period, and that the work-experience element within it had to
be carefully planned and monitored, and should involve trade union
education.

### THE GOVERNMENTS PROGRAMME FOR ACTION

In December 1981, the government published a White Paper entitled 'A
New Training Initiative: A Programme For Action'. In relation to youth
training, it proposed a Youth Training Scheme guaranteeing one year's
'foundation training' for all leaving school at the minimum age. A
hundred thousand places were to be provided in 1982/3 in the UK, and
300 000 when the YTS became fully operational in 1983. A training allowance was to be paid of 'around £750 per annum'. Minimum-age school
leavers would, in general, cease to be eligible for supplementary benefit
in their own right until 1 September in the year after they left school.

In March 1982, the STUC met Norman Tebbit, then the Secretary of
State for Employment, together with Alex Fletcher MP, who was Minister
for Industry and Education at the Scottish Office, to discuss the White
Paper and the MSC document, 'A New Training Initiative: An Agenda for
Action', which had been published at the same time.

The discussion was a wide-ranging one, but, specifically in relation to
the proposed YTS, the STUC made a number of points to the Minister.

These included reservations about the level of resources being provided, including resources for the MSC for staff and for the further education service; they also included reservations about the likelihood of obtaining a sufficient number of high quality one-year placements for work experience.

It was pointed out that, for example, the vice president of the National Farmers' Union had stated in a letter to the *Times* that 'the temptation for employers to take on young persons at no cost, albeit that they will have to be released for a proposed minimum of 25 per cent training input, and replace them with another at the end of a year rather than face a bill of around £3 000 will prove irresistible in many cases' – the STUC General Council rejected the White Paper's statement that trainees 'should receive allowances that reflect their learning role' within a training scheme. A scheme involving the amount of work experience envisaged in the White Paper would contain a considerable element of involvement in the productive process, with consequent benefit to the employer. This was one of the reasons why many young people in the YOP found the level of remuneration provided inadequate. The situation would be far worse under the provisions envisaged for the new Youth Training Scheme. The allowance of £750 per annum was completely inadequate. (This question of the level of remuneration reflecting the amount of real work carried out during the work experience element of training schemes was to become a major factor in trade-union opposition to the new Job Training Scheme and to Employment Training in 1987/8.) It was argued that many of the trainees would be in a situation where they would be going on to a scheme virtually identical to those in which older brothers, sisters and friends had participated under YOP, but they would be receiving an allowance of £10 a week less. Similarly, the government's proposal to make school leavers ineligible for supplementary benefit until 1 September in the year after leaving school was completely unacceptable. It was an attack on the rights of young people as young adults and in the case of some Scots summer leavers, it would be 15 months after leaving school, when they were perhaps only two months short of their eighteenth birthday, before they would be eligible for benefit.

It was also pointed out that in Scotland 16 year olds were treated legally as independent adults, and that the responsibility of parents and local authorities to have concern for their welfare ended at age 16, rather than 18 as in England and Wales (this point came as something of a surprise to the Secretary of State, who had to have it confirmed to him by his Scottish Minister and by the civil servants).

Although the government subsequently moved on the question of the allowance and the withdrawal of entitlement to benefits, the increase in allowance from £15 to £25 a week which was introduced had to be funded out of the total resources made available to the programme, and was taken from the element intended for provision of off-the-job training. In other words, the young people on the scheme paid for their own allowances by foregoing an extra period of time at college.

With the increase in the allowances, and a number of other improvements, the trade union movement in the UK, including in Scotland, agreed to co-operate with and support the Youth Training Scheme. This did not, of course, mean that it could be introduced at every work place. Individual unions such as the National Graphical Association took a position of opposition to the scheme in principle. In other cases, shop stewards and full-time officials were not prepared to sanction schemes in individual work-places because it was feared that they would threaten existing apprenticeship schemes, or be used to substitute for full-time workers. Nevertheless, the YTS was supported by the broader trade union movement through the period when it was changed from a one- to a two-year scheme, and even after the re-introduction by government of legislation to withdraw entitlement to benefits of 16–18-year-olds.

## TRAINING AND SPECIAL MEASURES FOR ADULTS

Throughout the life-time of the MSC, provision of training for adults (whether employed or unemployed) tended to attract less attention and controversy than provision for young people: yet many developments in the field of adult training brought out sharply the divergence of views between the STUC and the MSC (with the government standing at their shoulder) on what role training should play in the re-generation of the Scottish economy.

Essentially, between 1973 and 1988 there was a steady shift of adult training provision away from 'training for stock' to 'training for employers' needs' (often very short-term needs). Two examples illustrate this.

The first was the run-down of the Training Opportunities Programme (TOPS) which provided a range of courses for unemployed adults, mainly in Colleges of Further Education and Skillcentres. TOPS was particularly helpful to adult women seeing to re-enter the labour market, either directly or through a move to other forms of further and higher education. The government decided that TOPS was insufficiently tailored to employers' needs, and complained about the number of TOPS trainees who went on to other forms of further and higher education. TOPS provision was accordingly slashed, despite widespread opposition from the trade unions, among others.

The second example was the shift of the Skillcentres onto a self-financing basis within the Skillcentre Training Agency. This resulted in the closure of Skillcentres such as Dumbarton and Port Glasgow on the grounds that there was insufficient demand for their services. The STUC, among others, argued bitterly that such an approach was tantamount to saying to the Vale of Leven and Inverclyde that they had been written off for the foreseeable future.

SPECIAL PROGRAMMES

At the same time as MSC provision of adult training was being increasingly tied to the short-term demands of employers (especially in the
private sector), the Commission was playing its part in governmental
efforts to overcome (or hide, depending on your point of view) the free
market's inability to provide jobs for Scotland's people. In typical MSC
style, one acronym succeeded another – STEP, CEP, CP – as schemes of
temporary work were introduced with various formulations of rules and
regulations. The longest lasting was the Community Programme (CP),
which was used to provide long-term unemployed people with up to one
year's work of community benefit.

The trade unions in Scotland largely supported the CP, although there
was sharp criticism of some aspects, particularly the fact that it became
overwhelmingly a part-time scheme when the rules were changed to
require an average wage of £65 per person on each scheme. A number of
reasons for this support can be identified. First, the vast majority of CP
schemes were run by local authorities and voluntary organizations that
were known to the unions, and with which they could work: indeed,
through the use of CP funding by Unemployed Workers' Centres, many
union activists were directly involved themselves in the management of
CP schemes. Second, the CP allowed the unions a specific and constructive role. Not only did CP schemes require the approval of the appropriate trade union before they could go ahead, the unions could recruit
those taking part in the scheme and provide a real service to them,
including ensuring that they were being paid the correct rate for the job
they were doing. These points are worth bearing in mind when considering the hostile reaction of the STUC to the 'New' Job Training Scheme
and its successor, Employment Training.

THE 'NEW' JOB TRAINING SCHEME

At the Tory Party Conference in 1986, the government announced that it
was launching a new training scheme for adults. This was called the New
Job Training Scheme (confusingly, since there was already a very different Job Training Scheme in existence). It quickly became known as the
NJTS, and at the STUC Congress in Perth in April 1987 it provoked an
intense debate which resulted in the STUC, for the first time, withdrawing
co-operation from a MSC scheme. NJTS involved young workers (the
target group was 18–25 year olds) undertaking an individually tailored
programme of off-the-job training and work experience on employers'
premises in return for their social security benefit plus some (very limited) expenses. The off-the-job training was very limited; in many ways
the scheme was an inferior YTS for adults. Because each 'scheme' was to
fit an individual, prior approval by trade unions was not judged to be
appropriate. For the same reason, AMBS would not be approving
schemes.

When the STUC Congress met in April it found itself, not for the first time, having to make a decision which would set the tone for similar debates at union conferences for the rest of the year. The STUC would be the first major trade union gathering to come to a decision on the NJTS. It can be argued convincingly that the debate which took place in Perth set in train the events which led to the government questioning the whole future of the MSC as a tripartite body. The debate began with a motion moved by the Society of Civil and Public Servants (SCPS) and seconded by the National Association of Local Government Officers (NALGO). The motion called for a coherent Scottish employment and training strategy and rejected the NJTS. A number of features of NJTS were identified as particularly objectionable, including:

1. the principle of working for benefit
2. the bulk of the scheme being spent on employers' premises with the likelihood of widespread job substitution and exploitation
3. the lack of effective trade union and AMB involvement in approving and monitoring the scheme.

In the debate around the motion, those in support of it referred repeatedly to the three main aspects. They emphasized opposition to the principle of working for benefit; they also criticized the inability of unions to negotiate a 'top up' of allowances within the rules and the use of the scheme to fiddle the unemployment figures. Those in opposition to the motion argued that to oppose the scheme would be to abandon the unemployed; that they would be driven into non-union workplaces; and that opposition would affect the employment of college lecturers and Skillcentre instructors. Some flavour of the argument is given by the following extracts from the verbatim transcript of the Congress:

> We have gone along with all sorts of MSC schemes designed to bring down unemployment because there was some positive aspect to them, but there is no positive aspect to the Job Training Scheme. It is simply a device for making the long-term unemployed work for their dole. (NALGO speaker)

> Unions can negotiate top-up allowances in YTS schemes, but there is no such facility on the Job Training Scheme . . . Some of us are worried that we are heading for American style ethics. (Glasgow Trades Council)

> It is clear the Tories have two distinct objectives: one is to massage the unemployment figures and the second is to lower wage rates to those already on low pay . . . the vast majority of the JTS trainees will not go into high wage areas of employment but into the low paid service industries such as retailing. (Union of Shop, Distributive and Allied Workers)

> I oppose the motion, for the following reason: where is the alternative for young people for jobs? . . . We should be looking at the

schemes and using them to our best advantage. (General, Municipal and Boilermakers)

There are three reasons why my union believes that total non-cooperation with the New Job Training Scheme would be wrong. Firstly, it would mean the loss of 150 instructors' jobs . . . Secondly, it will simply operate in non-unionized workplaces . . . Thirdly, there are those in government who I am sure are looking for excuses to end the whole process of trade union approval of MSC schemes. (Civil Service Union)

The JTS is a totally fraudulent scheme, designed to reduce the unemployment statistics in the run-up to the election. It is totally exploitative. It is of no educational value . . . but it is with great regret we feel we have to oppose this motion (or) the scheme will go ahead (and) private profiteers will benefit from it. (Educational Institute of Scotland)

Before I came here I had a discussion with people from the Edinburgh Unemployed Workers' Centre. You will not find anyone in any Unemployed Centre, or any unemployed organisation, in favour of JTS. (Edinburgh Trades Council)

The STUC Deputy General Secretary John Henry spoke on behalf of the General Council. There had been a lengthy debate on the General Council, but in the end a substantial majority came down in opposition to JTS, and so John Henry urged support for the motion. It was carried, and the STUC subsequently wrote to all affiliated unions asking them not to co-operate with JTS although lecturers and instructors were not asked to refuse to teach JTS trainees (the boycott was applied to work experience placements, not to off-the-job training).

By the time of the TUC Congress in September, a number of unions who had supported JTS had altered their position, and the scheme was rejected.

THE FINAL DAYS

The trade union movement in Scotland never had an easy relationship with the MSC, but it was really by the mid-1980s that the relationship began to deteriorate rapidly – largely as a result of initiatives originating in Sheffield (or Whitehall). Relations with the Scottish structures of the MSC were always perfectly amicable: it was just that they were tied hand and foot by rules made and enforced outwith Scotland.

By the time the STUC document 'Scotland: A Land Fit for People' was published in April 1987, the trade union movement had come to the conclusion that the MSC as currently structured could not meet Scottish needs, and sometimes actually worked against Scottish interests. In the course of a substantial section on the labour market and training in Scotland, the document had this to say:

The situation has now reached the point where the MSC and its operations are viewed with suspicion (and not just by the trade union movement) partly because it is seen as unaccountable; partly because it is seen as interfering in areas where it has limited expertise (for example, the secondary school system); partly because it has failed to effectively promote equal opportunities in its training and employment services; but most of all because it is being asked to carry out a government policy which is clearly damaging to the economy and damaging to training and re-training.

Nevertheless, there are advantages in the existence of an Agency which has a clear responsibility for devising, co-ordinating and delivering training programmes, especially when there is such a training crisis to overcome and when the response of the majority of employers training and re-training is so flabby.

We therefore propose:

(i) The establishment of a Scottish MSC, operated on a tripartite basis, accountable to the appropriate Ministry of a Scottish Assembly.

(ii) Greater autonomy within the MSC structure for Area Manpower Boards to provide more effective matching of local provision with local needs ('Scotland: A Land Fit for People', pp. 77–8).

Even in the context of the government's most recent proposals for a free market, employer-led initiative (Scottish Enterprise), as Campbell Christie stated, the trade union movement will continue to be 'in there working with the rest of the community . . . to influence the direction of change.' (*Scotland on Sunday*, 13 August 1989).

# CHAPTER 11. EDITORS' INTRODUCTION

Employers in Britain have traditionally had the lead role in relation to industrial training. Their efforts were central to the successes or otherwise of ITB and MSC initiatives in skill training.

As MSC programmes were developed to respond to youth unemployment, employers were called upon to provide the lion's share of training places under the YOP and the YTS. Employers were also called upon to assist community-based and education-led schemes by providing placements, participating in management boards and helping with premises, equipment etc.

Through the CBI, employers were represented on MSC's tripartite structures and were a key element in the consensus which sustained the MSC and its programmes. Towards the end of the MSC's reign, employers were called upon not only to deliver training places and programmes, but also to take responsibility for advisory boards and structures.

In this Chapter, Jim Wright reflects on his experiences of working with the MSC as training manager of one of Scotland's leading hi-tech companies, Ferranti.

# 11

## THE MANPOWER SERVICES COMMISSION: AS SEEN BY AN INDUSTRIAL TRAINING MANAGER

JIM WRIGHT

### INTRODUCTION

The activities of the MSC in Scotland included so many changes and innovations that I doubt if even those with nothing else to do were able to keep abreast of developments. Change has been a dominant characteristic of my working environment, but I question whether it would have been adequate preparation for employment by the MSC. I have been an interested participator, usually representing Ferranti or CBI (Scotland).

You may well ask 'How do you represent a company with 8 000 employees in Scotland and 21 000 in the UK?' or, even more difficult, 'How do you represent the members of an employers organization with about 1 000 members in Scotland across the whole range of commerce and industry?'. My answer was to listen carefully to the more influential voices, keep them as well informed as possible, and then do what I thought was best, taking comfort from the knowledge that a nominated representative is not a delegate. It is for these reasons that the views expressed in this chapter can only be ascribed to me.

My objective is to relate how I saw the activities of the MSC in Scotland affecting the job I was employed to do for the whole of this period: training manager for the Scottish Group of Ferranti Ltd.

My position therefore covers a matrix of organizations: the Engineering Industry Training Board, the Scottish Engineering Employers Association, CBI Scotland, the Scottish Education Department as well as Ferranti Ltd, and a substantial though not complete range of MSC programmes and services that led to the involvement of employers in TOPS, YTS, DMCS, AMBS, ATOS, TVEI, ITECS and LENS. My experience starts before 1974 and enables me to offer some opinions on possible development after 1988.

### BACKGROUND

In 1964 I was in charge of a Ferranti drawing office in Edinburgh. We had been faced with an acute shortage of engineering draughtsmen, and decided the best solution was to train our own. My involvement in setting up that one-year training programme aroused my curiosity to know more about the motivation to learn, the learning process itself and how it might be improved. I decided that my future career would be more satisfying if it had a strong element of education and training.

Two other events took place in 1964 which were to prove decisive in my job. The first was that our training officer retired, and I immediately indicated my interest in being considered as his replacement. The second was the Industrial Training Act, which was seen as a turning point by a majority of employers, particularly the larger ones in the industries (like engineering or construction) which traditionally had long periods of training for the majority of employees. They resented the costs of training being 'stolen' by employers who did no training, and poached from those who did. There was also strong criticism of the quantity and quality of training being done in the UK when compared with overseas competitors. It seemed obvious to me that the establishment of the Engineering Industry Training Board in 1964 would mark a period of renewed interest in the training function, and improved career opportunities for trainers.

I persuaded the general manager to appoint me in the position of training officer, and, as a result of this appointment, I attended an intensive course sponsored by the Department of Employment and organized by the British Association for Commercial and Industrial Education (BACIE) aimed at providing a nucleus of professional training staff capable of handling the post Industrial Training Act situation. It was a six-week residential course with most of the days lasting twelve hours, and only one weekend off. It covered all the topical aspects of training, including identification of training needs, skills analysis, cost benefits, learning theory, assessment, T-groups as well as a detailed analysis of the 1964 Act. A principal contributor was James Stewart, who had been responsible for piloting the Bill through Parliament. It was probably the most effective training I have had and it gave me improved credibility in the company as an authority on the training function.

My new responsibilities were to run a well-established central department to provide a training service for the line managers in an organization with 5 500 employees, with an unusually high proportion of technically qualified staff.

The first Ferranti factory in Edinburgh was built in 1943 to manufacture gyro gunsights, and after a difficult period when the war ended, a few highly talented engineers struggled successfully to get contracts from the Ministry of Defence to design and make radar systems. This new technology, which revolutionized navigation for aircraft and provided a whole new order of accuracy for firing weapons from them, was the basis of a new industry in Edinburgh. It was clear from the very early stages of development that the people with technical skills would not be available in the area, and the numbers required would have to be trained by the company. A very far-sighted policy was adopted and led to recruitment of school leavers to train as craftsmen and technicians, and engineering graduates to train as design, development and production engineers. Growth has been almost continuous and the company now employs over 8 000 in Scotland, including 1 200 graduates, 2 000 technicians and 800 craftsmen. Current recruitment, over the last five years is about 120 school leavers, 80 graduates and 35 diplomates each year. The manpower plan and its implementation have a significant impact on employment and training, not only in Edinburgh, but throughout Scotland.

I quickly learned that my new job required a sound knowledge of what goes on in schools, FE Colleges and universities and, hopefully, the opportunity to influence policies. As a major customer, I quickly became involved with Schools/Industry links, the Scottish Technician Education Council (SCOTEC) and recruitment from Scottish Universities.

The newcomer to this scene was the Engineering Industry Training Board set up with well publicized objectives:

(a) To ensure a skilled work force in the industry;
(b) To improve the general standards of training;
(c) To spread the costs of training more equitably.

The mechanisms used to achieve these objectives, a tripartite board (employers, trade unions and education) with powers to call for statutory returns on manpower, training plans and costs, and impose a levy/grant system, were the most radical interventions in the industrial scene for decades.

I believe the impact of an organization with powers to reward companies doing acceptable training, and impose financial penalties on those who did not, was underestimated. In the following ten years many engineering employers developed a hostile attitude to the EITB based on the feeling that their essential rights to determine their own training budgets were being eroded by interfering bureaucrats, using an iniquitous financial system.

The training levy was held at 2.5 per cent of total emoluments each year up to 1972 when it was reduced to 2 per cent, to 1.5 per cent the following year and then in 1974 to 1 per cent. Payment of the levy, followed by completion of grant claims, which had to be justified by inspection, and then waiting to get back what was clearly seen as 'our own money' was a constant source of irritation. A summary of the Ferranti in Scotland position for that period shows the annual levy as between £140 000 and £183 000 and grants from £148 000 to £240 000 with annual training costs about £2 million. It is significant that in 1988–9 the EITB is reducing the non-returnable levy to 0.05 per cent.

In the early years the levy/grant scheme favoured the traditional type of training for craftsmen, technicians and technologists, and companies like ours, which had well-established apprenticeship schemes, were able to achieve a fairly modest subsidy to training costs.

A further effect of the new interest in training costs was to reinforce arguments for long-term training, particularly for school leavers and new graduates, to be funded by the state rather than by individual employers.

In support of these arguments it was pointed out that employers were being forced to train in a wider range of skills, applicable to the whole industry, rather than for their own needs. A case was also being made for differential funding which recognized that training engineers is considerably more expensive than training shop assistants or typists.

In 1972, with the publication of the consultative document 'Training for the Future', the changing role of Training Boards from inspectors with considerable financial muscle to advisers charging fees for the service was given a new impetus.

The personal relationships between training staff in the industry and Board officers during this period were quite interesting. In some respects they had a common aim: persuading company managers to spend more money on training. Many of the Board's Staff had been recruited from a fairly restricted pool of existing training officers in the larger engineering companies. In some cases there were suggestions of unholy alliances; I am sure these were completely unjustified!

## THE MANPOWER SERVICES COMMISSION: THE NEW PARTNERSHIP

It was against this background that the MSC began operating in 1974 as a co-ordinating partnership of employers, trade unions, education and government with the task of changing attitudes to vocational training while responding to rapidly increasing unemployment.

Larger employers came under considerable pressure to provide representatives at both national and local level, and I was nominated as an employer representative by CBI Scotland. When I was invited to join the local Board covering Lothians, Borders and Fife, the company's view was that, while we may not have direct involvement with many of the MSC schemes we could not afford to be out of touch with such a significant influence on employment and training. There was also a strong feeling that these MSC civil servants were dabbling in something which they knew very little about, and if we did not help to control the situation they might soon be controlling us. At the very least we might slow up the rate at which they were throwing our money at crazy schemes!

So started a period in which I got to know more of the local full-time trade union officials, some senior members of the education system and the civil servants charged with implementing the programme. I remember most clearly the increasing size and cost of schemes that we were asked to approve, and the interminable discussions about how we measured 'success'. Statistics inevitably became over simplified, and implied that the best programmes were those from which the largest percentage found 'permanent' employment. It could equally be argued that some programmes were so bad that the trainees found something else to do out of desperation! Most members of the board were frustrated by being able to fund training programmes while lacking the ability to influence the number of jobs available to those being trained.

A more positive outcome for me was a growing respect for some very hard-working officials and an improved appreciation of the sincere motivation of the 'part-timers' who ploughed their way through never ending forms and papers, to meet once a month and give their views on the allocation of very substantial sums of tax-payers money.

In spite of obvious differences and political objectives of the Board members my lasting impression is one of decisions reached in the best interests of the trainees. It is also significant that I can only remember two situations in which the chairman had to call for a vote of the members. I believe consensus of this kind results from a combination of desperate situations and plain speaking.

After a few meetings of the Area Manpower Boards, it became clear that those members nominated by CBI Scotland could benefit by meeting occasionally to review progress, avoid situations which seemed to indicate absence of any policy and consider possible future developments. Thereafter one or two meetings a year were arranged by the CBI executive in Glasgow. I found these meetings very helpful. They were generally well attended, represented every AMB in Scotland, and conducted in a way which allowed the sharing of knowledge with no suggestion of imposing opinions or policies.

In May 1981 the MSC published their consultative document 'A New Training Initiative', with the full support of the CBI for the main objectives. It would be churlish to be critical of proposals to reform and modernize youth training, and also improve opportunities for adults to be retrained at any point in their careers. The means of achieving the objectives, however, had no shortage of critics, and the proposed funding was regarded as clearly inadequate.

This document laid the foundations of the new Youth Training Scheme (YTS), which offered 12 months work experience, including a minimum period of 13 weeks off-the-job training and education. From our point of view in Ferrantis this seemed to offer an opportunity for us to get more directly involved with the MSC and perhaps achieve some savings on our training costs. It was agreed that we would support the initiative by considering reasonable modifications to our Training Plan.

The basis of our Training Plan is the 1-year and 3-year business plans. The manpower budget is established and monitored by a committee representing the departmental managers. Each category of employees from labourers to managers is examined in turn to determine changes in numbers employed in the next twelve months. Consideration is given to projected work load, labour turnover and recruitment patterns. When these figures have been agreed they form part of the consultation process with all employees and trade union representatives.

When the MSC announced their 1-year YTS programme it included what came to be known as the Additionality Clause. This said that financial incentives would only be paid to employers who trained young people in addition to their planned programme of recruitment. We had already informed our trade union representatives of our intention to recruit 100 school leavers to apprenticeship. We proposed that we should recruit 120, employ them all on the YTS programme and thereby have financial assistance for the additional 20. At the end of the year we would select the top 100 to progress to second year and do our best to employ some of the remaining 20 in less skilled occupations, or assist them to find places in other companies. The trade union rejected this proposal on the grounds that it would dilute our apprenticeship training.

Eventually we ran a scheme for 12 young people, quite separately from the apprentices. Although this provided good basic engineering training and all but one trainee moved on to related jobs with us or other companies, the YTS trainees were always regarded by their peers as being second-class citizens, and they were certainly paid less! We decided not to repeat the experiment, but our training staff had acquired very useful experience in dealing with MSC staff and establishing the essential administrative tasks, including filling in the forms correctly, which can be irritating and counter-productive unless you accept that the disbursement of tax-payers money calls for full documentation, and carefully monitored progress.

We also believed that in the course of implementation we had made good contacts with MSC staff, who now understood how we worked, and could be relied upon for effective communications. Our expectations, in this respect, were not realized, because as a result of very rapid expansion of the MSC we found ourselves dealing with a very transient population.

A further advantage derived from the experiment was to demonstrate to our local trade union representatives our genuine concern to provide high quality training to as many young people as possible, within the limits of our manpower requirements. We were still faced with opposition, on principle, from full-time trade union officials who regarded YTS as a cheap labour scheme aimed at massaging the unemployment figures. While this was disappointing, and probably resulted in the loss of YTS places in the engineering industry, it was clearly a matter for persuasion rather than confrontation.

We continued to criticize the additionality clause, pointing out that the MSC were paying new training organizations which were largely unproved in the delivery of skilled training programmes, while refusing any assistance to well-established training departments well known for producing highly skilled craftsmen and technicians.

Eventually this argument was accepted by the MSC, and, when 2-year YTS was introduced in 1985, it covered all young people in the first 2 years after leaving school at the statutory leaving date. The elimination of the additionality clause allowed us to propose a new scheme in which we applied and were accepted by the MSC as an Approved Training Organisation, including endorsement by our trade union representatives. We have operated our apprenticeship schemes combined with 2-year YTS since the intake of August 1986.

This means that all school leavers recruited to our craft and technician training schemes are offered four years of training and related education as well as joining our 2-year YTS. They are employees from the day they join the company and continuation of training to successful qualification as a craftsman or technician is only dependent on satisfactory progress and behaviour. The company has operated schemes of this kind for more than forty years, training over 3000 craftsmen and technicians. Apart from forming the core of technical employees below graduate level, many of them occupy management positions.

The MSC and the EITB have both had significant influences on our training department and our individual training programmes. These recognize and reflect the differences between training to meet the needs of a large organization, and the perceived needs of industry and society. Both organizations present themselves as advisers and act as inspectors, while insisting that they can only be effective with our co-operation.

We therefore, have two external auditors, the MSC and the EITB, looking at the quantity and quality of training which we provide. We are confident of our ability to meet these requirements, but from time to time we ask:

(a) why approval by one organization could not simply be accepted by the other;

(b) why such a small contribution to industrial training costs should buy a disproportionate amount of influence on training provision;

(c) do watchdogs serve any purpose in companies where training is essential to survival?

FURTHER EDUCATION

I have mentioned Further Education as an essential part of building an effective industrial community. This was recognized in 1984 when considerable funding (about 20 per cent of the total) was transferred from LEAS' rate-supported grants to the MSC giving them significant responsibility for work-related non-advanced further education in England and Wales.

The Scottish Education Department had launched its Action Plan, and the Scottish Vocational Education Council was rapidly building up a catalogue of modules to replace Ordinary National Certificate courses. We welcomed this development because we recognized an answer to our criticism of an inflexible syllabus, an inability to update courses to take account of new technology and overdependence on terminal examinations after two years of study. Perhaps the timing was coincidental, but I was not the only one to be relieved when it was decided that FE in Scotland would continue to be administered by people who knew the business, and did not have to start learning about it, before assuming responsibility for the allocation of funds.

This did not mean that the MSC had no influence on schools and FE Colleges in Scotland. In 1983 the Technical and Vocational Education Initiative (TVEI) was introduced in England and Wales and in spite of considerable suspicion that this was a back-door method to move control form educational to commercial and industrial interests, most Regional Education Departments submitted proposals. Pilot projects started in Strathclyde, Fife, Borders and Dumfries and Galloway. Lothian Region Education Department submitted proposals that were not given approval, but the following year a scheme involving Forrester High, St Augustines, Tynecastle, Wester Hailes Education Centre and Stevenson College was approved to start in August 1985 with funding to cover a 4-year period.

I had been involved in the discussions which led to submission of both proposals, and accepted an invitation to join the TVEI Steering Group, which was aimed at providing advisory support, reviewing progress and suggesting how it should develop.

In Ferranti we saw this activity as an essential part of our campaign to spread awareness of the career prospects offered by our industry, as well as the more general need to strengthen links between schools and industry. We were able to offer work experience in various forms, and in particular we introduced a programme for a simulated working day. Groups of about 30 pupils are briefed by our training staff in school. They are allocated to teams which spend a day in our training centre, designing and making a fairly simple device, for example an alarm system which they offer for sale at the end of the day to senior engineers in the company. Points are awarded on the basis of value for money. Each team has the services of a final-year apprentice as a technical adviser provided they pay his fee, and include it in the cost of the product.

We see considerable benefits in this work by forming new relationships between our engineering and training staff and the pupils and staff of local schools. Perhaps even more significantly it has given an added motivation to some pupils who have found a new interest in school as a result of seeing the relevance to the world of work. Our evidence applies to pupils across the whole range of ability. In addition to the four schools directly involved we have had many participants from other schools, including some in the private sector. Parties of teachers have made consistently favourable comments, and encouraged similar projects with other companies. If we have any lingering doubts it is about our ability to provide such facilities on the scale required to meet the spread of TVEI to all schools in Lothian. A further side-effect of TVEI has been a very rapid growth in the number of schools and the number of pupils who have SCOTVEC modules as a part of the curriculum for S4, S5 and S6.

I have been associated with SCOTVEC since its establishment in 1985, and the development of the National Certificate, with its modular structure, its criterion-based assessment and the provision of access for industry, commerce, education and professional and trade associations, is a model which is attracting attention from many countries, not only in the UK and Europe.

I am concerned, however, that a programme which was initially created for delivery in further education, but with a natural extension to schools, has become a significant part of the school curriculum. My concern is not that the very wide range of modules may be unsuitable for pupils, but I wonder whether all schools can provide the ambience which is an essential element of delivering vocational education. TVEI Related In-Service Training (TRIST) has been very helpful, but there are differences between schools and FE Colleges, for which we should be grateful, and ignore at our peril. In particular, the staff have quite different backgrounds, and the vocational content of the syllabus reflects the increasing awareness of the students towards career prospects.

In the period from 1979 to 1986 FE colleges were significant public-sector contractors on behalf of the MSC over a very wide, and sometimes confusing, range of programmes. During the same period the tripartite structure of MSC became increasingly unpopular in government circles, and moves to give employers majority representation became the central thrust of policy. Employers' organizations continued to express doubts about the validity of such moves, and particularly the proposals to make participation in YTS compulsory, but the government's intentions were obvious, and the end of the Commission, in its tripartite form, could be clearly seen.

THE COMMUNITY PROGRAMME

A parallel development in the 1980s was a huge expansion of adult training provision in the Community Programme. Community Programme was run by the Department of Employment but the MSC acted as agent, and, as an AMB member, I was aware of its growth although it had very little direct effect on the engineering industry. It represented, for me, the need to provide useful (though not profitable) employment as a social need, and which could not reasonably be funded by an industry which was constantly being exhorted to be more efficient, leaner, and cost effective.

Now that the MSC has been dismantled and the Community Programme is being phased out, the ever-present dichotomy of providing effective training and experience for people without jobs by using the resources of employers who are trying to reduce labour costs is being highlighted once again.

The most recent attempt to tackle this problem is the setting up of Local Employer Networks (LENS) to encourage groups of employers to become more involved in vocational education and training. In the current industrial and commercial scene, with heavy emphasis on professional management and tight financial control, it becomes necessary to identify training and human resource development as an investment. This assumes that there is clear evidence that increased expenditure on training results in increased benefits to the training employer, preferably in financial terms. I have heard many opinions which indicate that the benefits of raising the level of training are so self-evident, that attempts to measure them are unnecessary. I believe that more work needs to be done in this field if we are to achieve the breakthrough which will see training costs directly associated with next year's profits. Until that is achieved there will be a reluctance for employers to become involved in, as opposed to being an active critic of, our education system.

CONCLUSION

For 14 years the Manpower Services Commission in Scotland has implemented a large number of programmes in support of the government's policy on employment and training. The annual budget has exceeded £300 million pounds, with a staff of 750 in 1988.

In retrospect, it is surprising that one of the largest employers in the engineering industry, with a very substantial training organization, should have been directly involved in only two main programmes: TVEI and the 2-year YTS.

An assessment of the value of that involvement falls far short of being an accurate measurement. Has TVEI resulted in more school leavers being interested in and better prepared for a career in industry? How many teachers are better informed, and more comfortable discussing with pupils the essential role of industry and commerce in the national economy? How many more craftsmen and technicians are now employed in the engineering industry as a result of YTS?

I am confident that attitudes towards training in particular, and industry in general, have changed to the benefit of the whole community, but I would be hard-pressed to produce credible figures to support how much of that change can be attributed to MSC.

Perhaps obscurity is the fate of institutions which operate at national level to meet the needs of local organizations and individuals, particularly when results are measurable only in the longer term.

# PART IV

# Scottish People and the MSC

# CHAPTER 12. EDITORS' INTRODUCTION

Increasing the opportunities for the employment and training of women was stated to be an important objective for the MSC. Many aspects of training in the past, especially the apprenticeship system in specific industries, were criticized for reinforcing sex stereotyping and occupational segregation in the labour market.

This chapter looks at the impact of MSC policies on women in Scotland. This is an enormous task, given the other factors affecting employment and training opportunities for women in the past fifteen years and the lack of available comprehensive data. The results from the MSC's own data are disappointing. The few figures which do exist show a decrease in female participation in MSC-sponsored training. (Chapter 15 also illustrates how gender differences can be reinforced by training schemes themselves.) Current pressure for employers to become more involved in training is not encouraging, given past and present evidence of employers' discriminatory recruitment policies. Nevertheless, the MSC has played a role in putting the employment and training of women on the agenda and in providing resources for special training programmes and research to inform the debate.

# 12

## WOMEN AND MANPOWER: THE EMBRACE OF THE MANPOWER SERVICES COMMISSION IN SCOTLAND

ELISABETH GERVER

### INTRODUCTION

Assessing the impact of the Manpower Services Commission on women in Scotland is an almost impossible task.

In the first place, of the factors which have changed women's lives in Scotland between 1974 and 1988, it is not possible to isolate those elements which have been directly or indirectly caused or affected by the policy and operations of the MSC. Oglesby (1988) and Breitenbach (1989) have noted the extent to which social and economic factors interact in complex ways with education, training and employment patterns for women. In relation to the MSC itself, as Cockburn (1987) has noted, there are many inter-relating factors involved in patterns whereby females appear to be disadvantaged by sex stereotyping.

Secondly, even if the disentangling of social and economic factors from the effect of the MSC were possible, there is insufficient information on which to found a case. 'There is a marked paucity of literature about women and employment in Scotland during this century . . . and . . . the . . . current role of women in Scottish education is not well documented' (Women in Scotland Bibliography Group, 1988; see also Bamford, 1988). Statistics about male and female participation in training in Scotland are sparse, and the MSC's publicly available statistics are rarely broken down by sex.

Thirdly, the frequent changes in the basis on which employment statistics are collected, mean that one cannot reliably assess trends over the period 1974 to 1988. Moreover, even before more recent changes, official UK figures were believed to underestimate the numbers of jobless women by 50 per cent (Breitenbach, 1989). Finally, as the editors have noted in their Introduction, the MSC's own constantly changing programmes mean that trends over more than a year or so are difficult, if not impossible, to quantify or to assess.

Bearing these constraints in mind, I shall explore various indicators of the interaction between women and the MSC in Scotland. I shall set my discussion in the context of the general pattern of the employment and training of women in Scotland during the 1970s and 1980s; my main emphasis will lie on the period since 1977, when the MSC Committee for Scotland was first established. Working primarily from published MSC reports, I shall then consider how far MSC policy and practice in Scotland was or was not addressed to issues in women's training and employment in Scotland. Finally, I shall hazard a few conclusions.

If more comprehensive and reliable evidence had been available, what criteria might be used to assess the impact of the MSC on women in Scotland? Given the MSC's own remit for training and for employment, one might compare trends in women's participation in these areas with MSC policies and programmes. One might also compare the rates at which women have participated in specific MSC programmes, as compared with their overall share in unemployment. One might also consider how far the MSC has been publicly aware of gender as an issue in training and employment. Finally, one might consider how far the MSC has attempted to overcome the well-known barriers which tend to limit female participation in training and employment, such as the care of dependents, relative lack of geographical mobility, employers' and trade unions' practices, and the under-representation of women in decision-making.

In what follows I shall touch on all of these criteria in varying degrees. But the lack of comprehensive, reliable information – about both women's training and employment in Scotland and their participation in MSC programmes – means that I shall often focus on tiny points of light. It is not that these points of light are the most significant. It is simply that the rest lies in darkness.

RECENT TRENDS IN WOMEN'S EMPLOYMENT AND TRAINING IN SCOTLAND

The most striking characteristic of women's participation in vocational education and training and in employment in Scotland is that of enterprise: despite barriers greater than those their sisters face in the rest of Britain, women in Scotland tend to participate in larger numbers in education and employment than in England and Wales (EOC, 1985; Breitenbach, 1982). Against women's participation in employment are ranged the formidable obstacles of low pay (the earnings gap between the sexes is greater in Scotland than in the rest of Britain) and lack of child-care (there is less government-provided child-care in Scotland than in the rest of Britain) (Breitenbach, 1989).

Women's employment in Scotland is characterized by low-paid low-grade semi-skilled or unskilled jobs in the secondary sector of the economy, heavily concentrated in the service sector and predominantly part time. As in the rest of the United Kingdom, women's work tends to be concentrated in a few areas of the economy: in the 1970s, over half of all women in paid employment were located in only four types of work: clerks, typists/secretaries, cleaners and shop assistants (MSC, 1980). It appears that little has changed since that time. In 1988 the same pattern of sex stereotyping continued in the Youth Training Scheme: 'the vast majority of female YTS trainees are concentrated in three occupational areas, . . . the traditional ones of retailing, caring and clerical work' (Johnson, 1988).

The general trend from 1975 to 1987 has been for the number of women working to increase: the census of 1981 showed an increase from 54.3 per cent in 1971 to 61.7 per cent in the number of women between 16 and 59 either in work or seeking it. Women's share of the labour-force has also been increasing, from 42.6 per cent in 1979 to 46.6 per cent in 1987. There is also a notable trend towards increasing part-time work. In 1981 63 per cent of working women worked full-time with 37 per cent working part-time. By 1987 the proportion of women working part-time had increased to 43.6 per cent, with a corresponding decrease in full-time women workers to 56.4 per cent (Breitenbach, 1989).

The crucial value of education and training in improving both the quality of individuals' lives and their employment prospects is well known; amongst many others, Nelson (1989) illustrates clearly the positive link between educational qualifications and employment status. Hart (1988) has found, therefore, that women in Scotland are determined to undertake education and training, despite the problems created by their domestic responsibilities, and the lack of adequate guidance provision, flexible learning opportunities and child-care.

In education, the proportion of women achieving formal qualifications continues to increase. In 1983, at a point when they formed 48.8 per cent of their age group, girls gained 52.7 per cent of all O grade passes and 51.8 per cent of all Higher grade passes (EOC, 1985). Of those adults studying for formal qualifications in school classes in Scotland, the great majority are female (Bannister, 1989). Women also form the majority of enrolments in non-advanced further education: in 1983 they formed 54.2 per cent of such enrolments (Bamford, 1988), while the percentage of modules achieved by women under the National Certificate continues to increase (Johnson, 1989). In higher education women are taking a growing share of the places available (Bamford, 1988); this trend is expected to strengthen with the current increase in access courses and in part-time opportunities for mature students.

But these levels of women's achievement are overshadowed by their much lower participation rates in employer-sponsored training. It appears as if employers are more prepared to invest in the education and training of their male rather than of their female staff. Far more men than women get day-release in all areas of employment except distribution, business services and banking, insurance and finance (EOC, 1985). In Scotland in 1988, half of all male returners but only 16 per cent of female returners to education and training reported that their fees had been paid by their employers (Bamford, 1988). Three times as many males as females have sought advice from their employer about education and training (Nelson, 1989). Women in full-time employment are less likely to get paid educational leave than their male counterparts (Munn and MacDonald, 1988).

In decision making in education and employment, as in almost all other areas, women in Scotland are under-represented. There are no female heads of tertiary education institutions or of local authority departments of education in Scotland, while only 3 per cent of head teachers in secondary schools and 12 per cent of the Inspectorate are women (Bamford, 1988). Detailed figures about the representation of women at senior levels in other forms of employment in Scotland are generally lacking. It appears, however, that there are relatively few women at senior levels in Scotland in the occupational grouping 'managerial', where only 22 per cent are women; in science, engineering and technology professions and related occupations only 8 per cent are female (SCDI, 1988).

Many of the common characteristics of women's employment in Scotland are shared with others in Europe, as Oglesby (1988) suggests. She notes that throughout Europe:

(a) more women of child-bearing years are remaining in the labour market with fewer and shorter interruptions for childbirth;

(b) more middle-aged women with grown-up children are returning to the labour market;

(c) the labour market in each country sex-stereotypes its jobs into those held by men and those by women;

(d) the major part of women's employment tends to be concentrated in low-status occupational sectors, carrying low rates of pay and often part-time; women occupy 90 per cent of part-time jobs in Europe;

(e) there are serious deficiencies in vocational guidance, education and training for women;

(f) women are having to balance the demands of their working day between their jobs and their domestic commitments.

Given, then, that many of the characteristics of female employment and training in Scotland are widespread throughout Europe, is it realistic to expect the MSC to have had any significant impact on these patterns? Has it tried to do so?

## MSC POLICY IN WOMEN'S TRAINING AND EMPLOYMENT

It appears that, from its inception, the founders of the MSC considered the employment and training of women as an important issue. The Employment and Training Act 1973 included the following duties amongst the functions of the Commission and Agencies:

It shall be the duty of the Commission to make such arrangements as it considers appropriate for the purpose of assisting persons to select, train for, obtain and retain employment suitable for their ages and capacities and to obtain suitable employees .... Arrangements in pursuance of this section may ... include arrangements for encouraging increases in the opportunities available to women and girls for employment and training.

In 1975 the Training Division of the MSC made the training of women a special priority. Recognizing that 'despite women's increased activity rate in the work-force, they experience particular difficulties in entering, planning and developing certain careers' (MSC, n.d.), the MSC reported that it had initiated a programme of positive action for women, including experimental training schemes, action-research projects and a wide range of awareness raising activities. The MSC's programme aims:

(a) to expand the opportunities for women and girls to train, across a wide range of occupations, across a wider range of industries and service sectors and across a wider range of skills and levels of responsibility.

(b) to improve the training provided for women and girls in occupations and industries in which they at present predominate and the development of better opportunities for career development.

(c) to provide training to meet the special and additional needs of women and girls designed to compensate for the past lack of educational opportunities, the effects of discriminatory attitudes and social factors and the problems experienced on returning to employment after a period of absence.

(d) to influence institutions and individuals who are similarly interested and involved in improving the employment and training opportunities of women and girls.

The MSC has evolved the following strategy to achieve these aims:

(a) exploring means of ensuring that women take more advantage of the existing mainstream training provision.

(b) offering continued opportunities for single-sex training where this is appropriate to the needs identified, and where the general aims above can be met.

(c) helping women to manage the career break and to re-enter employment in a manner that ensures the continued full use of vital skills and experiences.

(d) ensuring that women in employment have access to training which can assist their upward mobility and outward mobility into a broader range of occupations, particularly into areas of new technology (MSC, n.d.).

Oglesby (1988) has noted that, within Europe as a whole, 'de jure declarations of intent ... are not automatically followed by de facto states of equality.' How far might this assessment be applied to the way in which the MSC in Scotland has attempted to realize the aims of its parent body?

## MSC PRACTICE IN WOMEN'S TRAINING AND EMPLOYMENT

The MSC's annual report for 1977/8, the year in which the Committee for Scotland was formed, refers to women only in connection with their contribution to unemployment rates. Figures for participation in MSC programmes are not broken down by sex. On the whole, the pattern set by this report was to be followed for most subsequent years. As the more detailed account below illustrates, until recently and with the partial exception of figures for Training Opportunities Programmes (TOPS), MSC reports and plans in Scotland have shown little emphasis on, or even awareness of, women in training. The MSC has, however, placed a consistent emphasis on tracing the different patterns in female and male unemployment.

In the annual report for 1978/9, TOPS completions are broken down by sex, showing that women formed 50.8 per cent of TOPS completions. Women were, however, very unevenly distributed across the range of training provision. Female participation was particularly pronounced in further education colleges, where 79 per cent of TOPS completers were female. In employers' establishments, only 7 per cent of completers were female, in Skillscentres only 1 per cent and in heavy-goods-vehicle driving only 0.6 per cent. The statistics also report that completions at colleges of further education had decreased by 927 since the previous year. However, there is no breakdown by sex for the other programmes provided by the MSC, such as direct training services, grants and awards and training for unemployed young people. Figures for placing individuals in employment are not broken down by sex. There is no discussion of gender as an issue in training provision or in employment placing.

In 1979/80, the annual report shows that women overall represented 49 per cent of TOPS completions. As in the previous year, the female completions are almost entirely in further education colleges, and women are massively under-represented in employers' establishments, skills centres and in heavy-goods vehicles. The report notes the establishment of the first experimental Wider Opportunities for Women (WOW) course, but gives no reason for it. Other than for TOPS completions, no figures for programmes are broken down by sex. Gender is referred to only in the contrast between rising female employment and falling male employment.

In the following year, the annual report for 1980/1 notes, without comment, the appointment of Elizabeth Carnegy as Chairman, the first female to occupy the post in Scotland. TOPS completions included 44 per cent females in this year, again very unevenly distributed amongst the different kinds of providers. The report also notes the expansion of WOW to four courses at the University of Edinburgh and one at Stevenson

College. It states that the evaluation of the former 'has shown the course
to be of value in assisting participants to decide on the broad areas of
employment training or further education they would wish to pursue',
while the course at Stevenson was 'designed for women interested in
seeking employment in areas of new technology'. There is no breakdown by sex for any other programmes.

In 1981/2, the annual report provides provisional figures for TOPS
completions, showing that 34 per cent of those who completed were
female. Other than for TOPS completions, no figures are broken down by
sex. There is a reference to an experimental scheme at Bellshill Skillcentre
' to help women assess their aptitudes in practical skills, particularly in
areas such as engineering and construction, where few have so far been
employed', but substantially more space is devoted to help for the
disabled than to help for women. Subsequent annual reports do not
contain any breakdown of any figures by sex, although the annual report
for 1983/4 records that Elizabeth Carnegy ended her term as Chairman in
November, 1983.

The MSC also publishes four-year plans for Scotland which include
reports on the preceding year's activities. The only reference to women
in the plan for 1983–7 merely notes that the labour force in Scotland may
not increase in line with the growth in the population of working age
partly because, when jobs are hard to find, 'some people, especially
women, may withdraw from looking for work or may be discouraged
from re-entering the labour force.' No figures are broken down by sex.
There is a substantial discussion of help for special groups, including the
long-term unemployed, disabled people and ethnic minorities, but no
discussion of help for women.

Much the same pattern is found in the plan for 1984–8. There is,
however, a reference to the fact that the new benefit based count of
unemployment figures excludes many married women who had previously registered as available for work. Women are again mentioned in
the discussion of the trend towards part-time employment in services.

For 1985–9, the plan of the MSC in Scotland notes the increasing
proportion of women in the labour force in Scotland, where they have
risen from forming 42.6 per cent of the labour-force in 1979 to forming
45.5 per cent in 1984. The plan reports that in the year 1984/5, women
formed 32.7 per cent of TOPS trainees. It also notes, without comment,
that entrants to the Community Programme in Scotland comprised only
20.7 per cent females as compared with 22.6 per cent in Britain as a
whole. No other figures are broken down by sex.

The plan for 1986–90 contains the first formal statement from the MSC
in Scotland of equal opportunities in relation to the Youth Training
Scheme:

> all eligible young people regardless of religion, race, sex or disability
> will have the choice of participating in two year YTS. All ATOS will be

expected to declare a commitment to provide equal opportunities for trainees and will have to demonstrate this, not only in their recruitment procedures but also in their subsequent dealings with trainees in the course of their training.

The remainder of the discussion on equal opportunities, however, deals only with provision for ethnic minorities.

The same plan also acknowledges for the first time that employers may be engaging in illegal sex discrimination and proposes actively to work against such discrimination:

Jobcentres play an important role in the Commission's policy of equal opportunities in the provision of all its services by advising employers who appear to be discriminating on grounds of sex about the provisions of the Sex Discrimination Act 1975, and reporting to the Equal Opportunities Commission (EOC) those employers who continue to discriminate unlawfully on grounds of sex. A staff training video package has been produced, with EOC help, which should ensure that jobcentre staff are fully aware of their obligations under the Sex Discrimination Act and are more effective in educating employers on the subject.

The plan also implies that the MSC's understanding of the role that can be played by WOW courses has deepened. WOW courses, which then included just over 400 entrants in Scotland, were designed, it reports, 'to provide women returning to the labour market, after a break in their careers, with the confidence and basic work skills they require'.

Finally, the plan for 1987–91 contains a number of important indicators of increasing awareness of gender as an issue in MSC policies and programmes. It notes that the Wider Opportunities Training programme would have a major role for those not in the priority client group for the new Job Training Scheme or Restart, particularly married women wishing to return to the labour market. Within the account of YTS, there is reference to:

a package of measures designed to encourage more young women to consider occupational areas not traditional to their sex. One of these measures encourages YTS providers to set up single-sex schemes and reserved places on schemes for young women. A small number of reserved place schemes have been arranged in Scotland with a total of 80 places on offer. A wide range of industrial sectors are covered and the Commission in Scotland will be looking to improve both providers' and young women's participation in these schemes.

The document also notes the expansion of WOW courses to 900 in 1987/88. Despite this increasing awareness, however, there is no breakdown of participation in MSC programmes by sex, although figures for employment continue to be broken down into males and females.

So, over the period from 1977 to 1987, the MSC in Scotland has demon-

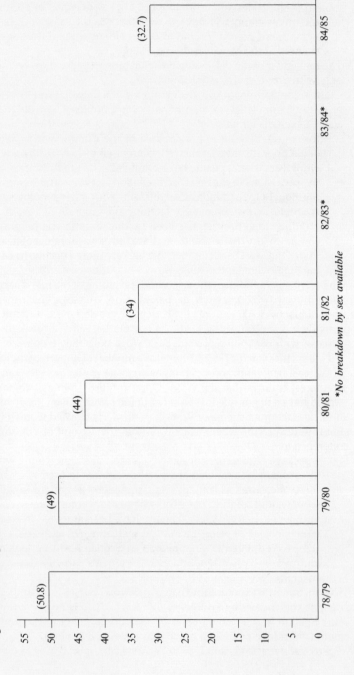

Figure 4   Percentage of Women in TOPS Completions

*No breakdown by sex available

strated a gradually developing awareness of gender as an issue in training and employment and has attempted to a limited extent to tackle some of the issues involved. Its measures have included the provision of courses designed to help women regain their self-confidence; the reporting of employers who discriminate illegally; the training of its own staff to recognize illegal sex discrimination; and the provision of single-sex courses. How far its intentions have been realized in practice may be examined through the few statistics which do exist for female participation in MSC programmes during this period and in the MSC's own practice as an employer.

The evidence is so scanty that it is impossible to draw any firm conclusions. Nevertheless, it does appear that, at least on the few programmes for which I have been able to obtain male/female breakdowns, women are significantly under-represented. Amongst TOPS completions in 1977/8, women formed about 53 per cent (Fairley, 1982). This proportion declined steadily until, as Figure 4 shows, in 1984/5 they formed under one-third of those completing.

It might be argued that this decline in female participation in TOPS was off-set by the growth in WOW courses, which began at about the same time as the decline in TOPS completions by women. Valuable though WOW courses appear to have been for their participants, such an argument would not be comparing like with like. TOPS courses were directly vocational, whereas WOW courses were pre-vocational, with a lower level of skill training but a broader range of possible outcomes.

Figures provided by the MSC in Scotland show that, amongst entrants to Community Programmes in Scotland, female participation in 1985 ranged between 17 per cent and 31 per cent, with apparently seasonal variations; in 1987 the variation ranged between 20 per cent and 28 per cent. In the period ending March 1986, females formed 34 per cent of those starting on the old Job Training Scheme, a proportion which fell to 26 per cent by the end of March 1988. In 1987 the new Job Training Scheme was only 14 per cent female. Of those on the Enterprise Allowance Scheme at July 1988, 30 per cent were female.

In 1986/7 (the only year for which a breakdown into male/female is available), in Scotland as a whole, females formed 41 per cent of YTS trainees, a figure which ranged from 35 per cent in Lothian to 43 per cent in three other areas. Although I have not been able to obtain specific figures for Scotland, in the UK as a whole in 1988, figures which illustrate the extent to which sex-stereotyping occurs on YTS represent, in the view of the MSC, a 'rather appalling and disappointing set of statistics' (Fairley, 1988).

Official statistics during the 1980s show that female unemployment rates have been considerably below those of men. In June 1985, for example, females formed only 30 per cent of those registered as unemployed in Scotland, while in October 1987, they formed only 29 per cent of those registered as unemployed. Since the MSC has tended to focus primarily on those who are unemployed, the case might be argued that females – in most areas for which figures are available – actually take a fair share of MSC provision.

But in reality one cannot compare levels of unemployment with levels of participation in MSC programmes: very few figures for male/female participation on MSC programmes are available and official unemployment figures do not reflect the full extent of female unemployment. There is thus an overwhelming lack of evidence, a fact which in itself leads to suspicions about the extent of MSC commitment to women's training.

A further indication of MSC practice towards women may perhaps be glimpsed from its own practices as an employer. Merely counting male/female heads at senior levels of organizations rarely enables one to say much about the policy of that organization towards men and women as a whole. Nevertheless, together with the MSC's apparently increasing awareness of gender as an issue in training and employment in Scotland, there has been an interesting shift in male/female appointments within the Commission itself over the past few years. I have not been able to obtain a breakdown of gender distribution in the top posts before 1983. In that year, the MSC Committee for Scotland was composed of seven men, chaired by a woman. All of the senior staff (the director, employment manager, area managers of training and employment divisions and the operations manager of the Skillcentre Training Agency) were men. By 1987, the Committee, chaired by a man, comprised seven men and one women. Of the total of 20 senior staff, two were female, and one out of the eight Chairmen of the Area Manpower Boards was female.

CONCLUSION

The sad truth is that 'no one regularly collates and publishes data on women in Scotland that would allow us to fully monitor the position of women in Scotland' (Breitenbach, 1989). Nor, as Hamilton (1988) has shown, are we able to make any detailed assessment of MSC spending on its programmes for either men or women in adult training in Scotland. Much more substantial research and monitoring in the field is essential; indeed, this is a field in which support from the proposed agency, Scottish Enterprise, would be particularly valuable. Meanwhile, some tentative conclusions can be hazarded.

In the first place, there is considerable uncertainty about how far MSC policies of supporting women in training and employment have actually had very much impact in practice in Scotland. The few areas for which figures are available tend to show decreased rather than increased female participation in MSC-sponsored training, with the important exception of enrolment in single-sex training.

Secondly, one may wonder why the MSC appeared for so long to be unconcerned about employers' neglect of the training needs of their female staff. The Commission's policy that 'the primary responsibility for looking after women over the age of 18 who are in employment, rests with them and with their employer' (Johnston, 1988) sits uneasily beside evidence that employers take the training of their female staff much less seriously than that of their male staff. Through the Scottish Institute of Adult and Continuing Education and other agencies, the Training Agency funded in 1988/9 a local collaborative project, 'Training Women for Management in Strathclyde Region'. Like other MSC programmes and projects, this work is short-term, and much of the impact of the project is expected to take place through its dissemination of good practice. However, the Scottish Council Development and Industry has concluded that 'government policy to promote adult training and education by employers by means of exhortation will not succeed' (SCDI, 1988).

Thirdly, the very fact that so much speculation has to rest on so little evidence raises doubts about how seriously the MSC in Scotland has taken its responsibilities towards women under the 1973 Employment and Training Act. To some extent, in failing to provide adequate statistics and other information about male/female participation in its programmes, the Commission has merely been following what still remains accepted bad practice in Scotland: as Bamford (1988) shows, gender has rarely been recognized as a variable in information about Scottish education and training. Nevertheless, there is an unacceptable hiatus between the Commission's responsibilities towards women under the 1973 Act and the fact that lack of information means that we cannot hold it accountable for its practices in women's employment and training.

But there are some hopeful, if perhaps slight, indicators for the future. The MSC, under its various titles, has for several years supported fully the work of the Women and Education Steering Group of SIACE through sponsoring conferences and seminars, helping to meet the cost of publications, funding research, and sponsoring a series of educational guidance events throughout Scotland for women who are considering education and training. Symbolically, eliminating the term 'manpower' from more recent names for what had been the MSC points to the possibility of a future of equal partnership for men and women in Scotland. All of us now need to find ways in which Scottish Enterprise can promote more substantial long-term gains for women in employment and training.

REFERENCES

Bamford, C. (1988). *Gender and Education in Scotland: A Review of Research* (Edinburgh: Scottish Institute of Adult and Continuing Education).

Bannister, S. (1989). Adults in school classes (Edinburgh: Scottish Institute of Adult and Continuing Education).

Breitenbach, E. (1982). *Women Workers in Scotland: A Study of Women's Employment and Trade Unionism* (Glasgow: Pressgang).

Breitenbach, E. (1989). The impact of Thatcherism on women in Scotland. In *Scottish Government Yearbook*.

Cockburn, C. (1987). *Two Track Training: Sex Inequalities and the YTS* (London: Macmillan Education).

EOC (1985). *Women and Men in Scotland: A Statistical Profile* (Manchester: Equal Opportunities Commission).

Fairley, J. (1988). Industrial Training in Scotland, *The Scottish Government Yearbook, 1982.*

Hamilton, R. (1988). Budgets for adult education (Edinburgh: Scottish Insitute of Adult and Continuing Education).

Hart, L. (1988). Women's perceived education and training needs (Edinburgh: Scottish Institute of Adult and Continuing Education).

Johnson, I. (1988). Address to Women and New Technology Conference (Edinburgh, May).

Johnston, J. (1989). Modules for all: overcoming barriers to the National Certificate for adult learning (Edinburgh: Scottish Institute of Adult and Continuing Education).

MSC (1978). Report on Scotland. In Annual Report 1977–78 (Sheffield).

MSC (1979). Report on Scotland. In Annual Report 1978–79 (Sheffield).

MSC (1980). Report on Scotland. In Annual Report 1979–80 (Sheffield).

MSC (1981). Report on Scotland. In Annual Report 1980–81 (Sheffield).

MSC (1982). Report on Scotland. In Annual Report 1981–82 (Sheffield).

MSC (1983). The Commission's work in Scotland. In Annual Report 1982–83 (Sheffield).

MSC (1984). The Commission's work in Scotland. In Annual Report 1983–84 (Sheffield).

MSC (1985). The Commission's work in Scotland. In Annual Report 1984–85 (Sheffield).

MSC (1983). The Commission's work in Scotland. In Annual Report 1982–83 (Sheffield).

MSC (1983). Plan for Scotland 1983–1987 (Edinburgh).

MSC (1984). Plan for Scotland 1984–1988 (Edinburgh).

MSC (1985). Corporate Plan 1985–1989 Scotland (Edinburgh).

MSC (1986). Corporate Plan Scotland 1986–1990 (Edinburgh).

MSC (1987). Corporate Plan Scotland 1987–1991 (Edinburgh).

MSC Training Division (undated). Training for Women (Sheffield).

Munn, P., and MacDonald, C. (1988). *Adult Participation in Education and Training* (Edinburgh: Scottish Council for Research in Education).

Nelson, P. (1989). Advice and guidance to adults in Scotland: training and vocational education (Edinburgh: Scottish Institute of Adult and Continuing Education).

Oglesby, L. (1988). Vocational education for women in Europe: facts, issues and future directions. In, C. Bamford (ed.), *Women's Vocational Education and Training: European Perspectives*

(Edinburgh: Scottish Institute of Adult and Continuing Education).

SCDI (1988). Tomorrow's jobs in Scotland (Edinburgh: Scottish Council Development and Industry).

Women in Scotland Bibliography Group (1988). *Women in Scotland: An Annotated Bibliography* (Edinburgh: Open University in Scotland).

# CHAPTER 13. EDITORS' INTRODUCTION

Disabled people are widely held to suffer the greatest disadvantages in education, training and employment. The MSC, as the agency responsible for employment and training was particularly important to disabled people. However, discussion of this aspect of the MSC is seriously hampered by the lack of reliable data, a problem which the MSC itself did little to remedy.

Disabled people were catered for in the MSC's general programmes, like TOPS, YTS, CP etc., and were also offered a variety of special forms of provision. Each of the various operating Departments of the MSC, from the youth training section to the Jobcentres, was involved in trying to meet the needs of disabled people.

This chapter assembles the available information on a wide variety of MSC schemes and assesses their impact on disabled people in Scotland.

# 13

## WHO COUNTS? WHO CARES?
## THE INFLUENCE OF THE MSC ON EDUCATION,
## TRAINING AND EMPLOYMENT OPPORTUNITIES FOR
## DISABLED PEOPLE

LIZ SUTHERLAND

INTRODUCTION

This chapter sketches out an overview of the impact of the MSC on the education, training and employment of disabled people in Scotland. Arguably, these areas involve some of the most complex issues to be found in any study of education and the labour market. Unfortunately it is probably also the case that these issues are the least discussed and least well understood of all.

The major problem confronting those who wish to examine the issues is the woeful lack of data. As recently as October 1987, Sir Michael Quinlan, KCB, then Permanent Secretary at the Department of Employment, had to admit to the House of Commons Public Accounts Committee that 'the absence of reliable information on the numbers and location of the disabled and the unemployed disabled is a matter of concern: it prevents the proper setting of targets and objectives.' This problem makes it extremely difficult to discuss experience at either the Scottish or the British level.

A further problem is raised by the unreliable nature of much of the data which is available. This problem is discussed in more detail below. However, at the simplest level, the fact that disabled people (quite rightly) do not have to make their disability known means that there are no reliable figures for participation rates in major schemes, like the Community Programme.

Within these major constraints this chapter attempts to provide an indication of the main issues and experiences in Scotland. Given that it is necessary to examine both the special provisions made by the MSC for disabled people and the experiences of disabled people in the MSC's general programmes, it is clear that even a substantial chapter cannot hope to deal adequately with the many very important questions to which policy-makers, providers and consumers should address themselves. Nor is it possible to discuss in comprehensive detail the numerous schemes and programmes open to disabled people during the years between 1974 and 1988. This chapter focuses on the period from 1982, largely because the major policy review of employment-related provision for disabled people which took place in that year provides a convenient and appropriate point of entry to the discussion. However, before proceeding to a discussion of the impact of the MSC on disabled people, it is necessary further to consider the concept of disability itself.

## WHAT IS DISABILITY?

There are two basic models of disability: the first is the 'deficit' model which sees disabled people as not quite whole. The second sees disability as a distinctly social phenomenon. These two models and the tensions between them are well described by Jim Elder-Woodward (1988), Development Officer for the Forums on Disability in Strathclyde. Beginning with the social model, he states that the social definition of disability is:

> The disadvantage or restriction of activity caused by a contemporary social organisation which takes no or little account of people who have physical impairment and thus excludes them in the mainstream of social activities. The medical definition (of disability) first promoted by one of the most powerful lobbies in British society – doctors – insists on the disabled person coming to terms with his/her lot and adjusting to the status quo of society. Whereas the social definition, first developed by the least powerful lobby in British society – disabled people – but now gathering more recognition, calls for social change and egalitarianism.

Central government has defined disability differently for particular purposes. For the purposes of employment and training legislation, its definition is set out in the Disabled Persons (Employment) Act 1944, which states that a disabled person is

> a person who, on account of injury, disease or congenital deformity, is substantially handicapped in obtaining or keeping employment, or in undertaking work on his own account, of a kind which apart from the injury, disease or deformity, would be best suited to his age, experience and qualifications.

This definition contains a confusing mix of the medical (deficit) and the social models. The Act proposes the two separate criteria of medical condition and employability and attempts to establish some causal link between them: it must be shown that it is the medical condition which causes the employment disadvantage. This muddled thinking has run through many of the provisions made for disabled people by the MSC and other agencies.

In providing separate services for 'the disabled' central government clearly sees them as a separate group; but the term 'the disabled' is both misleading and dangerous. To refer to disabled people as 'the disabled' is to ignore their individuality and, more significantly, to fail to understand the nature of disability.

Generally, official thinking has failed to take on board the single most important fact about disability, namely that it is always a relative state. One is disabled not in or of oneself, but in relation to the environment one finds oneself in. In turn this implies a uniqueness to each individual disabled person which demands a high degree of flexibility if policies and programmes are effectively to meet needs.

## THE 1944 ACT AND THE QUOTA SYSTEM

The Disabled Persons (Employment) Act was a product of a war-time environment and was primarily concerned to provide for those who had become disabled. It established a voluntary register. Those who were capable of open employment could join Section 1 of the register. Section 2 registration (necessary to secure access to sheltered employment and to one or two other programmes) was for those capable of sheltered employment and those capable only of 'diversionary activity'. Disablement Resettlement Officers (DROS) were given the tasks of deciding whether people were disabled within the meaning of the Act, and into which category they should be placed. While the MSC was required to operate the rather rigid 1944 definitions, it must be said that generally the DROS interpreted these in a very practical and flexible way.

The Act established a range of provision for disabled people including funding for special aids to employment, employment training and rehabilitation facilities and financial support for sheltered workshops. The Act also established the quota system. All employers with 20 or more staff had to ensure that at least 3 per cent of their employees were registered disabled people. Employers who were 'under quota' could only take on new employees who were not disabled with specific permission. The quota scheme was designed with the needs of the transition from a full-employment war economy to a full-employment peace economy uppermost.

By the time the MSC assumed responsibility for operating the legislation in 1974, there were clear difficulties with both the register and the quota. Registration was voluntary and to disabled people often seemed to bring insufficient benefits to outweigh the considerable perceived stigma of being registered disabled. A situation emerged where there were insufficient registered disabled people to allow employers to meet their quota even if they wanted to. Large numbers of employers were given permits to recruit labour even though they were under quota, and the quota itself was not enforced. Between 1944 and 1986 there were only ten prosecutions of employers for breaking quota requirements. The last prosecution was in 1974, and the fine remained at £100 throughout the period. In their study, Mair, Mackintosh and Fraser (1981) found that DROS in Scotland had become 'uniformly negative' in their attitude to the quota. Later in the decade, as concerns for short-term cost-effectiveness came to dominate whole areas of labour market policy, the quota system came under fire for being expensive to operate, unproductive and bureaucratic.

The MSC's major review of the quota scheme in July 1981, found it to be ineffective and recommended its replacement 'by new legislation, linked to a code of Good Practice'. The Code of Good Practice was issued (with the support of the CBI and the TUC) in 1984, but it was not given the basis in law which the MSC had felt was necessary to ensure its effectiveness. The MSC's own Equal Opportunities code states that 'it is an offence to discriminate against an individual on the grounds of disability' but there exists no legislation under which cases of discrimination on such grounds can be brought. Since 1979 there have been three separate attempts to introduce such legislation (the last one initiated by Donald Stewart when he was Scottish Nationalist MP for the Western isles). All these attempts have failed.

## THE RISE OF THE MSC

In 1974, the MSC took over responsibility for the central employment and training responsibilities of the Department of Employment (DE) in relation to disabled people. In 1976 the MSC also became responsible for providing sheltered employment and for monitoring the quota scheme. By 1982 the MSC had grown considerably as unemployment continued to rise. It was the rise in unemployment which had the most significant effect on the lives of disabled people.

There is an overwhelming body of evidence to support the view that in times of unemployment and recession, people with disabilities are hit much harder than the rest of the labour force. It has long been recognized that people with disabilities often have a lower general level of skill and attainment than the rest of the work-force. In their study (1981) of Employment Rehabilitation Centre (ERC) entrants in Scotland Mair *et al*. found that the entrants not only suffered from disablement but 'from multiple employment disadvantages in terms of occupational level and level of marketable skill, previous employment record, length of unemployment and depression anxiety'. In other words it is not the disability *itself* which is the major barrier to employment, but the multiple and complex disadvantages the individual has already been subject to *because* of the disability. Depressed expectations (of themselves or by others of them), missed or interrupted schooling, lack of easy access to flexible opportunities for catching up on learning or relearning later in life, all contribute to the diminishing of a disabled person's chances of employment in an employment market which it itself diminishing.

The available data on unemployment is unreliable. Figures can be considered accurate only in relation to those who chose to register as disabled *and* who registered as unemployed The real level of unemployment amongst disabled people is generally agreed to be understated by the official figures, particularly since the introduction of voluntary unemployment registration in 1981. Since that time, only those disabled people who choose to register at a Jobcentre *and* who make their disability known are included in the count of unemployed disabled people. Those who are unemployed but choose not to register at a Jobcentre, those who register at a Jobcentre but do not declare their disability, and all those who are out of work but living on benefits other than unemployment benefit are now excluded from any statistics relating to the numbers of disabled people registering for employment. In 1980/1 the 196 000 disabled people registering for work in Britain constituted 2.8 per cent of all unemployed people. In 1983/4 the 91 000 disabled people registering for work made up 5.8 per cent of all those unemployed. It is at this point that official figures of the disabled unemployed become completely unreliable.

Voluntary registration for employment meant that many disabled people who were unemployed chose not to register at a Jobcentre. At that point the employment services lost touch with a whole swathe of people who had special needs in relation to employment. The MSC Employment Division Internal Report to the National Advisory Council on the Employment of Disabled People for 1982/3 showed that between April and September of that year the numbers of disabled people registering at Jobcentres had fallen by 41.2 per cent. It is particularly ironic, then, that the review of services to disabled people in 1982 took place at a time when the major policy change of the review, the move of large numbers of disabled people into mainstream employment service provision, could have been backed up by the additional staff time resulting from the 70 per cent drop in Jobcentre registers. In fact, the drop in registers was followed almost immediately by severe cuts in Jobcentre services.

THE REVIEW OF ASSISTANCE TO DISABLED PEOPLE

There is no doubt that the main reason behind the review was growing concern about the rise in unemployment and an awareness that in times of high unemployment it was difficult to justify spending significant amounts of money on one particular group of disadvantaged unemployed people. 'Specialist services should be provided when, but only when, they meet identified needs which are different in kind to those of other job seekers' (MSC, 1982). The review acknowledged the difficulties faced by DROs who were carrying increasingly heavy caseloads while at the same time having to find time to do more positive marketing to employers: it suggested a reorganization of services which resulted in the setting up of small teams of specialist staff, to be known as the Disablement Advisory Service (DAS), whose primary role was to take over responsibility for influencing and educating employers to pursue positive personnel policies and practices. DROs who remained as the primary client contact were asked to re-examine their case loads, retaining responsibility only for those who were hard to place, who were newly disabled, who needed advice, guidance and advocacy, and all others on their case load were to be passed over to mainstream Jobcentre staff on the grounds that for these individuals the primary problem was not their disability but their unemployment. It was anticipated that DROs' case loads (on average 250–300) would go down to around 50 people. (By 1987, Scotland had 39 DROs, 32 of whom were full-time with 7 employed part-time.) The MSC recognized that 'the effectiveness of placing services for disabled people will depend crucially on the state of the labour market' but it also recognized that it depended on 'the commitment on the part of the general placing service to make special efforts for its disabled clients' (MSC, 1982).

At first sight, the thinking behind this reallocation of tasks and priorities seemed sound. It encouraged DROs to use their skills with those who needed them most, recognizing that for many unemployment and not disability was the major problem. It moved towards integrated rather than separate provision, acknowledging the need for small numbers of staff specifically trained in marketing skills, but it failed for two major reasons, both to do with staffing. The implementation of the review, despite its stated commitment to the general placing service making special efforts on behalf of its disabled clients, coincided with cuts in mainstream Jobcentre staffing (cut by 25 per cent between 1979 and 1984) which resulted in a diminishing and deteriorating service to *all* the unemployed. Subsequent low morale among Jobcentre staff meant they were far less likely to respond positively to the additional responsibility of working with disabled people and, in practice, there was simply not enough time to provide Jobcentre staff with the support and training they needed in order to be able to work effectively with individuals whom they had never considered as part of their client group. Knowing this, DROs were often reluctant to cut their case load as they had been instructed, and at the same time the post of assistant DRO more or less disappeared; many DROs, though they found themselves dealing with fewer numbers, no longer had the services of an assistant DRO to call on but had to rely for administrative help on the limited support available from mainstream Jobcentre clerical staff, who knew virtually nothing about services to disabled people.

The target for implementation of the review was 1983/4 and in July 1983 eight Disablement Advisory Teams were set up in Scotland to work alongside the existing DROs. By 1987 these eight teams had a combined total of 24 staff. Their remit was to encourage and persuade employers to adopt more progressive employment practices towards the disabled not only in terms of recruitment but also in the retention of those who became disabled at work and in the career development of their disabled employees. The teams were encouraged to make special efforts to increase the number of Sheltered Industrial Groups particularly in the more remote areas of Scotland. Overall, the nature and quality of the service to disabled job seekers changed radically in 1982 as a result of the review.

However, within a few years it became clear that the radical restructuring which followed the 1982 review had run into difficulties. In particular the very large cuts in Jobcentre staffing and services made it extremely difficult to deal with the needs of disabled people through mainstream (rather than special) provision. By 1987 both the MSC and the Jobcentre staff recognized that the new system was not working. In Scotland, it was reported that 39–45 per cent of Jobcentre staff felt that the service to disabled people had deteriorated since the 1982 review. The perceived problems in the quality of Jobcentre services meant that many DROS became reluctant to pass their clients over to mainstream services.

During the 1980s, the schemes offering disabled people specialized aids to employment continued, but the strategic objective of the MSC was to bring about a shift towards meeting special needs through mainstream provision. The numbers of disabled people in Scotland who benefited from these services in 1987/8 were as follows (figures for Britain in brackets): special aids to employment, 301 (3 041); Job Introduction Scheme, 176 (1 629); Fares to Work, 68 (553); adaptations to premises and equipment 12 (151). Only in the last of these did Scotland's share seem disproportionately low. However, on the more positive side a large proportion of Fit for Work awards (26 out of 100) came to Scotland, indicating that the DROS and the DAS teams were making some progress in the task of changing employers' attitudes to disability.

TEMPORARY EMPLOYMENT PROGRAMMES

Coinciding with the shift of large numbers of disabled people into mainstream employment services came a growing awareness that the various temporary employment programmes for unemployed adults could provide useful work experience for disabled people, as well as for other unemployed adults. In 1983/4, for the first time after several years of falls in placing figures for disabled people in Scotland, the MSC's Annual Report for Scotland showed 5 045 disabled people 'placed in work'. Included in this figure, however, were 1 377 entrants to the Community Programme, which cannot be considered to be work in the usual sense. But CP did provide disabled people with opportunities to get access to work experience that would otherwise have not existed for them. It has been noted that disabled people are much more likely to have difficulty getting into employment and building up a useful employment record. The CP came to be an even more valuable route into potential employment for disabled people than it was for other long-term unemployed people. The MSC looked very definitely towards local authorities and voluntary bodies to take the lead in encouraging disabled people to take up CP places. It especially looked to voluntary bodies already involved with the disabled to become sponsors of CP schemes. It became acceptable for CP money to fund 'work that would not otherwise be done in the next two years'. In the case of voluntary bodies struggling just to keep going, never mind to develop, CP presented a particularly attractive source of funding.

In Scotland, both local authorities and voluntary bodies used the CP as a way of creating new forms of provision for disabled people and, sometimes simultaneously, as a way of giving employment experience to disabled people. Much was achieved in the Borders Region in particular. In large part, this success was due to the understanding and commitment of the Region's training manager, who also chaired the local Committee on the Employment of Disabled People (CEDP). From the beginning he insisted that work based schemes in the Borders should aim to take on disabled people in at least 10 per cent of their programme places. The region has been able to meet and maintain this target over the years and has supported several schemes providing services to the disabled: the Community Gardens Project at St Aidans, Gattonside, which supported and employed disabled people; the Borders Directory of Amenities for Disabled People compiled solely by people with disabilities and sponsored by the Ettrick and Lauderdale Association of Voluntary Service; and the Regional Council's district environmental teams made up of ten workers each, of whom at least two are workers with disabilities. Even though the training manager fully acknowledged the short-term nature of CP provision, he felt it was successful in providing disabled people with opportunities to prove their value as workers (and as people) that they would not otherwise have had.

Certainly there is no doubt that, in the absence of accessible employment rehabilitation provision for *many* disabled people in Scotland, the CP proved a highly accessible and acceptable method of gaining work experience. Geoffrey Holland himself said in his evidence to the House of Commons Public Accounts Committee in 1987 that

> when it comes to training itself, work readiness, the Committee may be interested to know that last year more people who are disabled had up to twelve months of temporary work and associated training in the Community Programmes than through the whole of the employment rehabilitation programme.

He saw CP as an integral part of a widespread and diverse range of opportunities for assessment, training and work experience and certainly as early as 1984/5 in Scotland the numbers of disabled people entering the CP (1 900) were higher than the numbers attending Employment Rehabilitation Centres (1 650).

There have been difficulties for disabled people with CP, however. To be eligible for the CP one had to be registered as unemployed. Many disabled people, although unemployed, chose not to register as such. Some were unemployed but derived their income from benefits other than unemployment benefit, for example invalidity benefit (IVB). In order to be eligible for the CP, someone on IVB had to come off that benefit and make a claim for unemployment benefit. The stay on IVB was counted towards the qualifying period of unemployment (which was reduced for disabled CP entrants) but they still had to be unemployed for at least one day and counted as such in order to take up CP. Once their time on the CP was over, if they were still unemployed, they often experienced difficulties re-establishing their right to IVB, which is essentially a benefit paid to those 'who are not fit for employment'. While on the CP, disabled people were regarded by the DHSS as being in employment, and as a result those who qualified normally for the higher rate of attendance allowance (the 24-hour-rate) generally had their attendance allowance reduced to the lower day rate, the (false) assumption being that if you were disabled and in work you could not possibly need as much attendant care as when out of work. There is no doubt that these anomalies prevented many more disabled people participating in CP.

The MSC, when approving proposals for CP schemes, aimed at providing services to disadvantaged groups, appeared not to take into account whether the services involved were already being provided. For example, at any one time in Scotland, there were several CP schemes with the common aim of building up a database of services to the disabled. These schemes were not necessarily aware of each other's existence. To the MSC, this was clearly not a major problem, as their main priority was to remove people from the unemployment register. Ensuring the rational development of community-based services to disadvantaged groups was not their concern. To workers already active in the field, however, there were times when the proliferation of CP-supported database schemes created tension, cynicism and frustration at the lack of any apparent co-ordination of effort.

Where CP was most valuable to disabled people collectively was when it produced or provided a product or a service which had a life beyond the limited time of the programme itself. For example, the Edinburgh and East of Scotland Society for the Deaf applied for CP funding late in 1984 to take on staff to produce 'a sign language book relevant to the needs of the people in Scotland who want to learn the sign language of the deaf'. This book was to be accompanied by training videos. The application was successful, and the goods produced are still available. The first group of CP employees all had hearing impairments themselves. It would have been quite impossible, the Society say, to have done this work (which clearly had a value beyond the life of the project) without MSC funding.

In 1985 the West Lothian Council of Voluntary Organisations, in co-operation with the West Lothian Council of Social Service, set up a CP scheme which employed disabled people as researchers to conduct a thorough survey of the needs of the disabled in their area (particularly the needs of those people not known to service providers). The preliminary results of the survey subsequently informed joint planning in the area between the health, social work, employment services and the voluntary sector. Strathclyde Region Social Work Department conducted a similar survey, also using CP funds, in order to establish what had previously been an unknown quantity, the nature and extent of the needs of the disabled in the Region. Schemes like these had a potential lasting value well beyond the life of the project itself.

Assessing the value of the CP to individual disabled people is more difficult. MSC data for Britain (July 1986) showed that eight months after leaving the CP, 25 per cent of registered disabled people who had been on the CP were in work, 5 per cent were in training, 3 per cent were back on the CP and 59 per cent were still unemployed. (Figures for unregistered disabled people are not available and figures for the total CP population are 31 per cent, 3 per cent, 3 per cent and 54 per cent respectively.) Certainly the placing rate into work was better than the ERC figures (14 per cent in 1980/1) but nevertheless a large proportion (59 per cent) remained unemployed and disabled people did less well than the population as a whole.

Many voluntary organizations used the CP as a calculated gamble, a way of establishing a need which had not previously been met or recognized, in the hope of attracting more stable and permanent sources of funding in the longer term. In Scotland, many of the Crossroads Care Schemes (designed to provide regular breaks to carers of disabled people through a pool of relief care attendants) got off the ground with CP funding and were ultimately successful in securing more permanent sources of funding. But some became victims of the transition from the CP to Employment Training and, in 1988, 10 of the 24 Crossroads Care schemes faced closure. It was estimated that over 2 500 families in Scotland caring long-term for someone with a disability would directly be affected by the closures. It was those CP schemes whose original aim was to provide training and rehabilitation opportunities for disabled people which seemed likely to make the most successful transition to Employment Training.

The available data for CP participation by disabled people in Scotland in 1986 show that 4.2 per cent of all CP entrants were unregistered disabled people (compared to 2.7 per cent in GB) and 2.4 per cent were registered disabled (compared to 2.2 per cent in GB). In 1987/8, 3 134 disabled people were placed on the CP in Scotland compared to a GB figure of 19 100. The percentage placed on CP in Scotland (approximately 15 per cent of all CP placings of disabled people) is of interest: the data appear to indicate a greater (and increasing) readiness by CP schemes in Scotland to take on disabled people.

## SKILL TRAINING FOR ADULTS

Disabled people were also able to make use of government-funded training schemes for unemployed adults. The MSC took over the Training Opportunities Programme (TOPS) in 1974. TOPS was the MSC's most significant mainstream training programme at that time. From the early years the programme was fairly accessible to many disabled people, in part, no doubt, because the pre-TOPS Government Training Centres had always given priority to the needs of disabled ex-servicemen.

The greater part of TOPS took place in FE colleges. They were asked to earmark for disabled people a number of places on each TOPS course. Some colleges, for example, Stevenson College in Edinburgh, also ran pre-TOPS courses in communication skills. These were particularly valuable to disabled people who had often missed out on parts of their statutory schooling. Applications for places from people with disabilities were given priority, and disabled people were permitted to go straight onto another TOPS course if necessary, thereby avoiding the usual minimum three-month waiting period between courses.

As TOPS began to be cut back in the late 1970s and early 1980s, steps were taken to make courses even more accessible to people with disabilities. Disabled people were permitted to start on TOPS at 16 (rather than the usual minimum age of 18) and were allowed a longer stay on courses. There were some TOPS courses specifically for disabled people only; for example, the Royal Blind School in Edinburgh ran clerical and commercial courses, and a telephonists course for people with visual impairment. In the main though, provision was integrated. TOPS clerical and commercial courses proved particularly popular with disabled men. As these courses were cut (by some 15 per cent between 1979 and 1982) a gap in training provision was created which was never to be adequately filled thereafter during the life of the MSC. From the late 1970s, the value of TOPS had been increasingly assessed by the MSC on the very simple and crude yardstick of short-term placement of trainees in work that used their main training skill. This type of evaluation led to severe cuts in TOPS as the recession reduced demand in the labour market. It also created difficulties in justifying the value of TOPS provision for disabled people as their placement rates were significantly lower than the average figure for all trainees. In 1980/1, 35 per cent of the disabled people completing TOPS in Britain were in employment three months later, compared with a figure of 53 per cent for all trainees. These figures have much more to do with the bigger problem of employers' attitudes to disabled people than with any shortcomings in TOPS or in disabled TOPS trainees.

TOPS was generally regarded as a relatively good MSC scheme from the point of view of disabled people, offering in the main integrated training provision. Scotland has, however, always suffered from a total lack of residential training provision. Some disabled adults who could make much of training would find the physical effort involved in daily travel to an attendance at a college or centre so demanding that their training needs could only be met by a residential facility. Scotland has no MSC/DE funded residential training colleges, and in 1987 of the 970 trainees who attended the four RTCS in England, only 59 were from Scotland.

## YOUTH OPPORTUNITIES PROGRAMME AND YOUTH TRAINING SCHEME

The MSC's involvement in provision for the school leaving age group has been of more evident lasting benefit than the CP. It also taught the MSC a great deal about the problems of devising schemes sufficiently flexible and imaginative to meet the needs of the individual. The publication of the Warnock Report in 1978 had a profound and lasting influence on the way in which education responded to children and young people who had disabilities which affected their learning. It moved the emphasis away from 'special educational treatment' towards a client-centred approach based on the 'special educational needs' of each young person. ('Special educational need' is a broader concept than disability. In education the broader concept is more commonly the basis for policy and provision.)

The Warnock Report, along with other major reports on education services for this group, established quite clearly that 'young people with all forms of handicap typically achieved less than they were capable of doing by the time of leaving school, and that they could thus benefit from continuing education' (Zaklukiewicz and Corrie, 1984). In Scotland, after the Warnock Report, there was a marked expansion in a number of regions (notably Fife and Lothian to begin with) in provision within further education for young people with special needs. Such expansion took the form of school–college link courses, bridging and extension courses. In regions which were slow to expand into this area, the Youth Opportunities Programme acted as a catalyst. Further education colleges found themselves becoming involved in running 13-week Work Introduction Courses (WICS) and 13 week Short Training Courses (STCS) under the YOP. These were particularly taken up by young disabled people as well as providing off-the-job life and social skills to young people on other forms of YOP provision. Crucially, the YOP helped to create a pool of expertise among college staff, which later helped in the development of the Youth Training Scheme (YTS) and other programmes.

The interplay between education and the MSC was clearly seen in Fife. In 1984 provision for students with special needs at Lauder College in Fife was organized by the Department of Industrial Studies and Special Programmes, which had a remit to administer all MSC funded courses.

Fife was unusual at that time in that it used wics to provide continuing education for young people with learning difficulties. Most other Regions who were making continuing educational provision for this group were doing so through full-time one-year local-authority-funded extension courses. msc regulations allowed students with special needs an extension on wics from 13 to 26 weeks, and the region was able to vary the content of the wic so that for example Lauder College concentrated on electrical work while Glenrothes focused on basic electronic skills. However, when yts succeeded yop, at first the maximum period which could be spent in college was 13 weeks. At this point, colleges successfully sought funding for a full-time extension course, which had not been regarded as viable by the region earlier. Both yop and yts had a direct influence on local-authority-funded educational provision for young people with special needs, enabling educationists to establish need and argue successfully for additional local-authority resourcing.

Initially, the yts was intended by government to be predominantly an employer-led scheme. Little thought was given to special provision for disabled school-leavers. Effective lobbying changed this, however. The Institute of Careers Officers and the National Bureau for Handicapped Students argued for changes, as did some trade unions.

As a result of these pressures, the upper age-limit for participating in the yts was raised to 21, and the length of stay was extended by six months for disabled youngsters. Employers offering suitable places were able to claim an additional allowance known as Premium Assisted Funding for the Disabled (pafd), although take up of this was disappointing. The various msc programmes which had applied only to disabled individuals in or about to take up employment (e.g. grants for adaptations to premises, purchase of special aids, personal reader services for the blind, and a communication service for the deaf) became part of the overall yts provision for young disabled people, creating a much more comprehensive package than had originally been envisaged. This extension of practice from the msc's employment measures to its training schemes was a major and particularly significant innovation. As a result of these changes young people who were capable of benefiting from the yts with some additional support were able to obtain any special assistance which they required to take up a suitable yts place.

Local authorities, voluntary bodies and colleges of further education were particularly crucial in their provision of Mode B yts opportunities for young people, and it was on this type of yts provision that young people with special needs (who were not staying on at school or moving into bridging or extension courses) were often placed. In 1983/4 there were 9 915 approved yts Mode B places in Scotland out of a total of 45 868 places. Government policy, however, favoured Mode A employer-based schemes (they were slightly cheaper, and they gave power and responsibility to employers rather than to local authorities and the voluntary sector), and by the following year there were only 7 861 approved YTS Mode B places in Scotland while Mode A places remained constant at around 32 200. In particular Mode B2 (college-based schemes which dealt almost exclusively with young people with special needs) was heavily cut back from 2 302 places to 1 119 places. Mode B provision was particularly suited to young people with special needs because it was trainee-centred and it took account of the fact that many of these young people needed a well-supported transition from school to life beyond school. To place them immediately into an employer-based setting would not have been productive.

Cutbacks in Mode B provision presented some young people with special needs with a real deterioration in the range of YTS opportunities available to them. It was also well recognized that Mode A provision, which could well have suited some young people with special needs, had a poor record in this respect. The MSC's own surveys found that 'a quarter of Mode A Schemes did not accept either those with handicaps or disabilities, or ex-offenders – and a third did not accept people with learning difficulties' (Finn, 1986). A survey conducted by the Institute of Careers Officers and RADAR (Royal Association for Disability and Rehabilitation) in 1984 showed that only 18 per cent of those YTS entrants with multiple disabilities were employer-based, and amongst YTS entrants with learning difficulties only 13 per cent were on Mode A schemes. In other words the prejudices that mitigate against disabled adults seeking employment mitigate also against young people with special needs seeking YTS places.

Lothian Regional Council surveys point to similar difficulties. In April 1987 a survey showed that by the previous Christmas, 40 of the 216 school leavers with special needs were unemployed while 19 had sampled YTS and left. It would seem there were insufficient YTS and educational opportunities which were appropriate to the special needs of these school leavers. The Regional Careers Service analysis of the first destinations of school leavers seemed to bear out this possibility. Some 21 per cent of leavers from the Region's special and residential schools were unemployed.

Data from YTS application forms (an unreliable source because of the widespread reluctance to declare disabilities) show that in Britain in 1987/8, 2.9 per cent (11 513) of young people on the scheme were disabled. A comparable statistic for Scotland is not readily available. However, an indication of the possible level of need is given by the MSC's anticipated provision of over 10 000 grants of Premium Assisted Funding for the Disabled (PAFD) in Scotland in 1987/8.

Just as the MSC was prepared, under pressure from educationists, to change its perspective it in turn had an influence on education, particularly special education. One of the most positive results of the report

'From YOP to YTS Meeting Special Needs of the Disabled' (1983) was that it highlighted the fact that 'special schools evidenced a limited understanding of post school options and furthermore indicated a virtual absence of follow up procedures'. Special schools (at least those included in the survey) simply had not known where their school leavers were going once they had left school. The Technical and Vocational Education Initiative has similar potential to act as a catalyst for change.

## THE ADVENT OF TVEI

From its introduction, the MSC's Technical and Vocational Education Initiative was intended to be 'available to all students across the ability range' (MSC, 1983). Despite this assurance, in Scotland very few special needs students were included in the first five pilots.

A notable exception was the TVEI pilot in Renfrew Division of Strathclyde. From the beginning special schools in the Renfrew area were involved and early on the special needs staff could see the need to do more to meet TVEI demands to make appropriate use of new technology and build links with the world of work and the community. They have used TVEI to enhance their programmes in these areas in particular. TVEI funding permitted the appointment of technical and home-economics teachers to work in the special schools. Teachers began to build up more links with the community outwith school, creating opportunities for work experience for pupils and leading, for example, to the establishment of a café lunch-club for older people run by the youngsters.

In Ayr, TVEI was used to initiate a programme of partial integration into mainstream schooling for pupils from special schools. Similarly in Argyll and Bute and the Western Isles, pupils with special needs were offered the opportunity to integrate with mainstream pupils on TVEI programmes. This use of TVEI brought benefits to both groups of pupils. The introduction under TVEI of short courses to S3 and S4 pupils was viewed as particularly helpful to pupils with special needs (just as the introduction of SCOTVEC modules has been to disabled students in further education) because it offered easier access on a fully integrated basis to flexible courses which are manageable in terms of time commitment.

In Lothian, special schools were not included in the original TVEI pilot. As TVEI expanded in the region, however, the authority recognized the need to bring special schools into the project and, in doing so, has encouraged much closer collaboration and co-operation between special schools and mainstream schools in their local neighbourhood group. TVEI could well blow some fresh air through the world of separate special-education provision.

## SHELTERED EMPLOYMENT

As well as having access to mainstream employment and training programmes some disabled people also have access to provision specifically for them alone.

When the DAS teams were set up in Scotland in 1983/4 they were 'encouraged to make extra efforts to increase the number of Sheltered Industrial Groups (SIGS) particularly in the more remote areas of Scotland' (1984, MSC) This was in keeping with the recommendation in the 1982 MSC review that 'sheltered employment could probably be considerably expanded'. It is quite clear that considerations of cost drove the MSC to a re-examination of sheltered-employment provision. In this case the changes in policy away from sheltered-workshop provision and towards placement in open employment have been generally beneficial rather than damaging, as SIGS and their successor, the Sheltered Placement Scheme (SPS) enabled disabled people to take up work opportunities in an integrated setting.

Under SPS, a sponsor (a local authority, a voluntary body or Remploy) employed a Section 2 disabled person and contracted the worker to a host company, who paid the sponsor for the work done. The payment made by the host firm was based on the disabled person's output, so that if the disabled person's output was 50 per cent of the output of a fit person, the host firm paid 50 per cent of the costs of employing a fit person to do the work. The costs to the sponsor were offset by the payment from the host firm for the work and by a contribution from the MSC. The MSC contributed 75 per cent of the costs (net of host firm's contribution) of a local authority sponsor and 100 per cent of the net cost of a voluntary body sponsor.

There were 29 SIGS in operation in Scotland in 1983 offering 67 individuals work opportunities. By 1984 there were 83 openings and by March 1985 there were 96. In that year SIGS developed into Sheltered Placement Schemes in recognition of the fact that the term Sheltered Industrial Group was a misnomer as only individuals were placed and often, too, the environment was not 'industrial'. The MSC maintained its commitment to expanding this particular type of sheltered employment provision, and in 1987 there were 247 disabled people in SPS in Scotland compared to 2 684 in Great Britain as a whole. 175 of these were placed in local authorities and 72 were working in the voluntary sector. SPS took off particularly well in certain regions of Scotland. Highland and Grampian Regions were the first regional authorities to make a real commitment to the development of SPS, giving responsibility for its development to specifically appointed members of staff. Fife was quick to catch up and became the biggest sponsor of SPS in Scotland with 107 places in November 1988 (out of 460 places). Fife's policy as an SPS sponsor was to take on half its total number of SPS workers itself (i.e. be their host as well as their sponsor) and to find other hosts for the remaining 50 per cent. Two members of staff were employed to work solely on SPS development.

The SPS was widely viewed as a progressive step in terms of meeting the needs of disabled people. However, the scheme had its difficulties.

Some disabled people objected to sps on the grounds that it perpetuates the deficit model of disability. The scheme was not sufficiently flexible to accommodate the disabled individual whose physical condition fluctuated significantly and unpredictably. The sps was restricted to Section 2 disabled people despite the evident needs of some people registered according to Section 1. For some disabled people sps also carried the same financial disadvantages met with under CP. It does, however, represent a positive move towards integration, it erodes stereotyped perceptions of disabled people's employment capacities and it is an attempt to meet individual needs. It is also cheaper to provide than traditional sheltered employment.

In January 1987 there were 2 108 people working in sheltered workshops in Scotland: 1 045 were employed by Remploy, 609 by local authorities and 454 by the voluntary sector. (These figures compare to a total of 14 716 in Great Britain: 8 934 in Remploy, 4 495 in local authorities and 1 287 in the voluntary sector.) From these figures it will be evident that Remploy was the major provider of sheltered workshop places throughout Britain. But the voluntary sector in Scotland did have a significant involvement compared to the voluntary sector in England and Wales. This can largely be explained by the existence of two major centres of sheltered workshop provision in Scotland: Camphill at Newton Dee (112 places) and the Scottish Council for Spastics New Trinity Centre (72 places).

EMPLOYMENT REHABILITATION CENTRES

In 1988, Scotland had four Employment Rehabilitation Centres (ERCs), catering for over 1 600 people, and a residential rehabilitation centre for the blind run by the RNIB at Ceres in Fife. MSC spending on employment rehabilitation in Scotland during the last five years of the MSC's existence remained fairly constant at around £2 million. During the 1980s, the role played by the ERCs was increasingly called into question. Uncertainties over the ERCs emerge fairly clearly from MSC documents published during these years. In the mid-1980s, the MSC began to support alternative approaches to employment rehabilitation on a pilot basis.

One of these was successful, if only in demonstrating that employment rehabilitation could be achieved through a well-thought-out and well-supported Community Programme. This scheme was located in Edinburgh and was known as Sprout. The Scottish Association for Mental Health sponsored this scheme (with some support from the City Council) to reclaim derelict land for use as a market garden. Sprout provided employment for people who had had psychiatric problems. This development was in keeping with the last recommendation of MSC's 1981 review of employment rehabilitation that voluntary bodies be encouraged to mount projects under CP to assess their rehabilitative value.

A radical shake up in the management and direction of ERCs was announced by the MSC in October 1987. Granton ERC in Lothian was chosen as the first ERC to be reorganized around a mobile team of assessment staff. All four ERCs now have mobile teams. Scotland recently gained its first ACT team (Assessment and Counselling Team), based in Aberdeen, to cover an area not previously served by an ERC. ACT teams were set up to make use of employers' premises and facilities in order to provide assessments. Mobile assessment teams provided briefer on the spot assessments. Both developments represented a move away from the 'bricks and mortar' facilities of ERCs, which in 1984/5 were costing £1 071 per entrant, and towards flexible provision to meet individual needs. It is, however, too early to comment on the effectiveness of these changes.

## CONCLUSIONS

The 1987/8 Annual Report of the MSC stated that the Labour Force Survey estimated that the unemployment rate for 'people with a work limiting disability' was 23 per cent, or two and a half times the rate for non-disabled people. There is much evidence to show that disabled people suffer multiple employment disadvantage because of the social and psychological effects of disability.

The lack of comprehensive and reliable data, together with the failure to secure a firm basis in statute for the Code of Good Practice, suggest that overall the MSC failed to move the needs of disabled people to the centre of the policy stage. Arguably substantial progress across a broad front will not be made until there is legislation which is comparable to the laws which prohibit discrimination on grounds of race or sex. Indeed the MSC itself argued that such legislation was necessary. Equally it can be argued that until good information systems are in place, the proper planning of programmes and policy is impossible.

On the other hand, the fragments of information and data which are available suggest that within its budgetary and programme constraints the MSC did pursue a broad range of programmes within which it attempted to meet the needs of disabled people. The MSC made attempts to evaluate its programmes and tried to develop new strategies. It encouraged innovation and listened to those with expertise in related fields like further education. Although there is still undoubtedly a long way to go, there is clearly much to build on in these experiences.

## ACKNOWLEDGEMENTS

I would like to acknowledge the special help of Julie Bowen, TVEI Adviser; Dermot Dick, Senior Education Officer (Careers), Lothian Region; Sue Leckie, Local Programme Manager, Training Agency, Lothian and Borders; Elaine Stewart, Development Officer, Scottish Council on Disability; Douglas Watson, Assistant Resettlement Adviser for Scotland for the Department of Employment; Ian Watson, Disablement Advisory Service Manager (Lothian and Borders); Jim Elder-Woodward, Development Officer, Strathclyde Forum on Disability.

## REFERENCES

Dick, D. (1987). YTS: ladder to progress or merely a maze? In *British Journal of Special Education*, 14. 4.

Disability Alliance and MPIS (1974). *Fundamental Principles of Disability*.

Elder-Woodward, J. (1988). *What is Disability Awareness?*

Finn, D. (1986). YTS: the jewel in the MSC's crown. In, C. Benn and J. Fairley (eds.), *Challenging the MSC*, Pluto Press London.

Greater London Council (1985). *Employment and Training for People with Disabilities*.

HMSO (1942). Report of the Interdepartmental Committee on the Rehabilitation and Resettlement of Disabled Persons (Cmnd. 6415).

HMSO (1944). Disabled Persons (Employment) Act.

HMSO (1978). Special Educational Needs: Report of the Committee of Enquiry into the Education of Handicapped Children and Young People (Cmnd. 7212).

HMSO (1986). Disabled Persons (Services, Consultation and Representation) Act.

House of Commons Public Accounts Committee (Report 144 Session 1987/8). Employment Advice to Disabled People (Department of Employment and Manpower Services Commission).

Lothian Regional Council Education Committee (1987). New Training Initiative (4 April).

Mair, Mackintosh and Fraser (1981). *Work, Personal and Social Difficulties of Handicapped Persons Seeking Employment*.

MSC (1978). *Developing Employment and Training Services for Disabled People: An MSC Programme*.

MSC (1981). Review of Services for the Unemployed (Sheffield).

MSC (1982). Review of Assistance to Disabled People (Sheffield).

MSC (1983). From YOP to YTS: Meeting Special Needs of the Disabled (Sheffield).

MSC (1983). MSC Programmes and Disabled People: Annual Report (Sheffield).

MSC (1984). *A Code of Good Practice on the Employment of Disabled People*.

MSC (1986). Job Centre Staff Perception of their Services to Disabled People (Sheffield).

MSC (1987). Employment Rehabilitation (Sheffield).

MSC (1987). Review of Disablement Advisory Service (Sheffield).

MSC (1988). YTS Special Training Needs: A Code of Good Practice (Sheffield).

MSC (undated). Training Opportunities for Disabled People (Sheffield).

MSC (various years). Annual Reports and Corporate Plans for Scotland (Sheffield and Edinburgh).

National Audit Office (1987). *Employment Advice to Disabled People*

(Department of Employment and Manpower Services Commission).

National Advisory Council for the Employment of Disabled People (1986). Annual Report.

National Advisory Council for the Employment of Disabled People (1985). The Additional Employment Problems of Young People.

National Council of Voluntary Organisations (1986). Conference Report on Adult Education, Training and Employment of Disabled People.

Oliver, M. (1983). *Social Work With Disabled People.*

OPCS Study (1986). Disabled Job Seekers.

Raffe and Courtenay (1988). *Both Sides of the Border* (Centre for Educational Sociology, Edinburgh University, pp. 16–18).

University of York (undated). *Job Centre Services for Disabled People.*

Woodward, J. (1988). *What is Disability Awareness?*

Zaklukiewicz, S., and Corrie, M. (1984). Further Education and Special Needs. Project Paper 4, Scottish Council for Research in Education.

A more detailed account of the MSC's influence on the lives of disabled people, written by Liz Sutherland, is available from SKILL, The National Bureau for Students with Disabilities, 336 Brixton Road, London.

# CHAPTER 14. EDITORS' INTRODUCTION

It is often argued that racism is not a problem in Scotland. This chapter reminds us that it is and refers specifically to the effect on the training and employment opportunities of the Black/Minority Ethnic community in Scotland. As with other chapters (especially Chapters 12 and 13), data on the involvement of the Black/Minority Ethnic community in Scotland is seriously inadequate and makes an overall assessment difficult. This chapter examines the experience of one voluntary organization's relationship (the Roundabout Centre) with the MSC and its attempt to implement MSC programmes.

The author challenges the MSC's stated policy of open access and equal opportunity for minority groups, pointing out the difficulty of implementing such a policy within a racist and discrimatory structure.

The chapter examines the experience of the Roundabout Centre in various projects and highlights the increasing problems of meeting MSC criteria, the discriminatory nature of eligibility criteria and the present lack of attention given by the MSC to the employment and training needs of Black/Minority Ethnic communities. Although the MSC did provide resources for important development work, the relationship between the MSC and the Roundabout Centre finally broke down with the arrival of Employment Training, when the Centre no longer felt that it could reconcile the gap between its own objectives and criteria and those set by the MSC.

# 14

## THE MANPOWER SERVICES COMMISSION AND THE BLACK/MINORITY ETHNIC COMMUNITIES IN SCOTLAND: THE EXPERIENCE OF ONE VOLUNTARY ORGANIZATION

### KALIANI LYLE

This chapter is not a comprehensive overview of the relationship between the MSC and the Black/Minority Ethnic community in Scotland. Instead it records the experience of one voluntary organization in its relationship with the MSC and tries to draw out any implications which this may have.

Before discussing this experience, it is, however, necessary first of all to examine the nature of racism in Scotland and the effects of racism on employment and training. Secondly it is important to discuss the problems which arise from the almost complete absence of data pertaining to Black/Minority Ethnic participation in the labour market.

### RACISM IN SCOTLAND

The demographic survey conducted by the Scottish Ethnic Minority Research Unit estimated that 10 000 of the 710 000 of the Lothian population were of Black/Minority Ethnic origin, that is around 1.6 per cent. The minority ethnic population consists predominantly of three groups, those of Indian, Pakistani and Chinese origin with a smaller but significant number of African/Afro-Caribbean and Bangladeshi origin. The fact that the Black/Minority Ethnic numbers are small has given rise to the perception that racism does not exist in Scotland. This is a function of a crude empiricist logic, whereby the problem, i.e. racism, is equated with the presence or absence of Black/Minority-Ethnic people. As well as this, the belief that Scotland is a relatively egalitarian and tolerant society summed up in the phrase 'we're all Jock Tamson's bairns' has contributed to the myth that racism does not happen here. The complacency and tendency to sweep racism out of sight has led to the charge that Scotland is fast becoming a racist society by default.

This is despite the fact that according to the BBC, 80 per cent of the Pakistani and Indian Scots interviewed in Glasgow experienced racial harassment from abuse to physical attack. There is very little acknowledgement of this and even less done about it. The 1985 report from

the Department of Education's Working Group on Multicultural Provision illustrates the point with regard to Lothian Region:

> Overt racism which manifests itself in racial attack or open discrimi-
> nation is fortunately not conspicuous in Lothian educational
> establishments.

This was revised following consultation, and a procedure for logging
incidents of a racialist nature instituted.

The question as to who defines 'racial' harassment still exists. Too
often the racialist element in these acts of harassment is denied and the
victim is blamed. Such explanations as 'they don't mix' or 'there are
others of minority ethnic origin who are not being harassed' or 'there is
no racism here – you're creating a problem where none exists' are
commonly offered. The effect of this denial is that the situation is allowed
to continue. There are some measures being taken especially in the field
of education to counter racism. However, with limited resources, cutbacks and the general moves by central government towards the privatization of education, these are constantly being undermined.

Overt racism is a symptom of a much deeper structural racism that is
endemic to most institutions in Britain. In employment this is evidenced
by the fact that of a total of 1 194 staff employed by Lothian Social Work
Department in 1987, only one person was from the Black/Minority
Ethnic communities. This, I suggest, in the absence of ethnic monitoring, is fairly representative of the employment pattern of most institutions in Lothian (save those specialist agencies whose main concern is
the eradication of racism). This seems also to be the case in the voluntary
sector, where a recent survey showed that, out of 246 organizations who
responded, 231 had no paid staff from the Black/Minority Ethnic communities. The reasons for this include discrimination in recruitment and
selection practices, the lack of access to training for Black/Minority
Ethnic people and a disregard for their language and other skills.

The situation in service delivery to Black/Minority Ethnic people in
Lothian and in Scotland tells much the same story. Only 1 in 7 of the
voluntary organizations providing a direct service were able to claim a
measurable client group of Black/Minority Ethnic origin. It is clear from
this that in the main the white voluntary sector is not providing a service
to members of these communities. The support structures, facilities and
resources that are part of the social welfare of this society are, therefore,
not available to this section of Scottish society.

The MSC inherited this situation. As the national training agency it
could have opened up and exposed assumptions, prejudices and discriminatory practices and effected real change. But it did not. As will be
shown later, the fact that it was operating within racist structures, and
employing racist criteria meant that it could not. Following pressure
from the Commission for Racial Equality (CRE), and from research findings and reports that made public the high level of discrimination oper-

ating in its schemes, the MSC produced policies and guide-lines on equal opportunities and appointed 13 Development Officers for the whole of Britain (with one of the officers assigned to Scotland as the Youth Training Scheme Development Officer).

## THE PROBLEM OF DATA

The main problem involved in assessing the extent of racism in Scotland is the almost complete absence of reliable data. The only figures from the Training Agency office in Edinburgh on Black/minority ethnic participation in the Community Programme in Scotland are derived from a question on a form used to gather information for other purposes, namely the availability-for-work tests. On 31 August 1988 people starting the programme described themselves as is shown in Table 20. There were 28 635 people on the CP at this time.

Table 20. Participants in the
Community Programme in
Scotland, August 1988, by Ethnic
Origin (per cent)

| | |
|---|---|
| White | 93.3 |
| Black/Afro-Caribbean | 0.16 |
| Indian | 0.21 |
| Non-White | 1.34 |
| Prefer not to say | 4.98 |

The categories used in this method of classification by ethnic origin are questionable and raise doubts as to the validity of the information so derived. In particular, it is unclear what precisely is meant by the term 'non-white' and which minority-ethnic groups in Scotland it encompasses.

This classification bears little relation to the composition of the Black/Minority Ethnic communities in Scotland. The estimate accepted by the CRE in 1988 of the relative sizes of the different minority ethnic groups is given in Table 21. Comparison of the tables reveals that the disaggregation of all beginners to the CP on the 31 August 1988 makes no reference to the largest minority ethnic community in Scotland, whilst

Table 21. Relative Sizes of Minority Ethnic Groups in Scotland, 1988
(per cent of Minority Ethnic Population)

| | |
|---|---|
| Pakistani | 40 |
| Indian | 25 |
| Bangladeshi | 5 |
| Chinese (including Vietnamese) | 25 |
| Afro-Caribbean/African | 5 |

containing information on one of the smallest. Reliance on data produced in this way is problematic. The experience of London boroughs like Haringey, that have attempted ethnic minority monitoring has shown that the formulation and presentation of questions on ethnic origin affects the accuracy of the response gained.

There are no exact figures available for the nature and the size of the Black/Minority Ethnic population, since the 1981 census did not include a question on ethnic origin. An estimate of the total Black/Minority Ethnic population accepted by the CRE is in the order of 55 000 to 60 000 (roughly between 1 and 1.5 per cent of the total Scottish population).

The aggregation of the three categories that the MSC have used (Black/Afro-Caribbean, Indian and Non-White) to represent the Black/Minority Ethnic communities in Scotland puts their participation in CP at 1.7 per cent; this is exactly proportional to the estimated total Black/Minority Ethnic population in Scotland. If the above figures are to be believed, the MSC would have succeeded where almost every institution in Scotland has failed. A remarkable achievement (unclaimed by the MSC) and one which is flatly contradicted by other research into the employment of Black/Minority Ethnic people in Scotland. For example, out of 4 185 people employed by those Scottish voluntary organizations responding to a survey on voluntary organizations and minority ethnic groups in Scotland, only 28 are of minority ethnic origin.

Finally, it is worth pointing out that the Training Agency office in Edinburgh could not provide any data on CP projects which had a Black/Minority Ethnic focus.

The absence of reliable quantitative data as indicated above, on both the employment of and services to Black/Minority Ethnic people on CP projects has, therefore, necessitated this project-centred approach. However, the experiences of projects at the sharp end of dealing with racism, like the YWCA Roundabout Centre, need to be listened to by those responsible for education and training. The experiences of these projects may shed light on the impact of the MSC on Black/Minority Ethnic communities in Scotland and on the MSC's failure to deal with institutional racism and the limitation of its equal opportunities policy.

## MSC POLICY: 'OPEN ACCESS' AND 'SPECIAL NEEDS'

The MSC's equal opportunities policy states that:

It is the Manpower Services Commission's policy that its programmes including the Community Programme should be open to all people within the relevant eligible group regardless of race, religion, sex, married status or disability. Where the need arises and legislation permits MSC also provides programmes specifically for particular groups such as people with disabilities, people from ethnic minorities and women returning to work after periods of absence or wanting training in non-traditional skills.

This implies that past inequalities in the employment sphere could be remedied by open access and special needs. However, the Training Agency office knew of no CP projects in 1987/8 with an ethnic minority focus, at a time when £30 million was being spent on CPs by the MSC. One of the main reasons for the MSC's lack of knowledge can be explained by its lack of contact with Black/Minority Ethnic communities.

The MSC did not actually go out to seek projects, but took a reactive stance. This lack of outreach work meant that only those already 'in the know' were in the position to apply to the MSC for funding. Since the Black/Minority Ethnic communities knew very little about the MSC, and the MSC was not very interested in them, they were effectively excluded from the CP.

Such efforts as were made to inform the Black/Minority Ethnic communities about the MSC were fairly ineffectual. The Roundabout Centre discovered, when enquiring for information, that leaflets translated into the main community languages lay undistributed on the shelves in the Jobcentre, and that the staff there were at a loss to know what to do with the leaflets.

Despite the advice to sponsors and agents on recruitment, selection criteria and interviewing procedures contained in the guide-lines for the implementation of the equal opportunities policy the experience of the YWCA Roundabout Centre and the research findings of the Scottish Council of Voluntary Organisations (SCVO) survey point to extensive discrimination in these areas. The fact that an effective equal opportunities policy was one of the 'quality indicators by which a project's value was to be judged' by the Area Manpower Boards (AMBS) appears to have made little difference to the translation of this advice into practice. According to a member of the Lothian and Borders AMB, the ability of the AMBS to evaluate this indicator was severely curtailed by the lack of assessment criteria and by the constant changeover in the staff servicing the Board. The ineffectiveness of this sanction exposes the declaration in the MSC Corporate Plan for Scotland 1987–91 that 'Area Manpower Boards following guidance issued after the AMB review have co-opted representatives of ethnic minorities in Scotland to serve as Board members' for the tokenist gesture it was.

The MSC was, of course, operating as I have noted in a racist society and labour market. These structures imposed limitations on the MSC's freedom of action. Not only did they operate against the effectiveness of equal opportunities policies, but they also undermined the viability of equal-access and special-needs policies.

The whole area of special needs is one that is fraught with problems for the Black/Minority Ethnic communities, and requires some examination. The special-needs syndrome entails an overemphasis on ethnicity and pathologizes black people as having deficit cultures that require special measures. An example of this is the spate of referrals from Restart in 1987 and 1988 to the YWCA Roundabout Centre for lessons in English as a second language, whether the person wished or needed it. The ability to speak only Black/Minority Ethnic languages is seen as a problem that requires corrective treatment in order to increase employability. The blame for the lack of jobs as with the explanation of racism once again centres on the oppressed and exploited.

In focusing on 'race' in terms of open access and special needs the issue of racism is divorced from other political processes and the articulation of racism with other social relations disappears. In this way racism becomes as excrescence readily extractable from everything else: what Paul Gilroy calls the coat-of-paint theory. The implication is that by tinkering with the system, for example through proper dissemination of information, translation into other languages, and the rigorous implementation of an equal opportunities policy, inequality and disadvantage would dissolve, and the benefits of the MSC's training strategy would be enjoyed equally by black and white communities. But racism, as with other forms of inequality, is not marginal but rather is central to the problem.

This is most clearly seen in the way that successive immigration laws enacted by Tory and Labour governments alike both control and racialize migrant labour. Phrases such as 'the alien presence' and the connection made between immigration control and good race relations testify to this racialization process. The extension of immigration control into social-welfare provision, linking eligibility for welfare benefits (as well as access to free health-care and education) to immigration status augments this process, by creating a national identity from which Black/Minority Ethnic people are excluded. Black/Minority Ethnic people wishing to claim benefit have to prove their Britishness. This has direct implications for MSC schemes. Many Black/Minority Ethnic people who are unemployed, but are unable to claim benefit, are simply excluded from MSC schemes. A large proportion of Black/Minority Ethnic Scots eligible for benefit do not claim, either because of the complexity of the system, lack of information, or because of fear of the connection between the Home Office and the DHSS. They cannot, therefore, participate in CP projects. This link between the MSC and immigration status structures inequality and disadvantage so that equal opportunities can never be anything more than rhetoric.

The attempt by the MSC to ride two horses at the same time is apparent. On the one hand, to avoid the charge of being racist it employs the language of equal opportunities, open access and special needs. On the other, it operates racist criteria and within a racist structure. It is clear that policies of equal opportunity cannot work when they are confronted with endemic structural inequalities.

It is within the above context that the experience of the Roundabout Centre should be assessed.

THE YWCA ROUNDABOUT CENTRE

In September 1967 the Church of Scotland, aware of an increasing problem of isolation amongst Black/Minority Ethnic women, asked the YWCA to release a member of its staff to work among black women in Edinburgh. This became an ecumenical project with support also given by the Roman Catholic, Episcopalian and other Churches.

The Women's International Centre was thus set up to provide a meeting place for women. Since 1967 the Women's International Centre has moved twice, with accompanying changes in name and emphasis of work. Initially the approach of the centre gave priority to assisting individual women to assimilate to their Scottish society. This has changed, however. The current work of the Roundabout Centre, as it is known today, whilst focusing on anti-racism is concerned with the articulation of race, class and gender. The change has come about because centre workers, dealing with a mass of individual cases, have repeatedly found themselves coming up against the same structural inequalities in society.

The centre provides a range of services, including case-work, community development work, counselling, a women's group, a youth forum, training in anti-racist perspectives with a variety of professional groups and agencies, a multi-lingual and multi-cultural crèche and volunteer and home-tutoring schemes. The centre has attracted funding from a wide variety of sources. The making of a claimants' guide to supplementary benefit, which explains the link between immigration status and eligibility for benefit and stresses the rights of Black/Minority Ethnic people to benefits, is an example of their work. The home based teaching of English as a second language, which is person-centred, and which stresses the importance of the first language is another. The community development principle is also evident in the Chinese Elderly Support Project which the centre initiated and supports.

The Roundabout Centre was the first agency in Edinburgh to work with Black/Minority Ethnic Scottish communities. (The Lothian Community Relations Council was set up in 1972.) The Centre has developed its own perspective over 21 years, both on the concerns and experiences of the Black/Minority Ethnic communities in Lothian as well as on the effects that changes in the political and economic climate have wrought.

THE ROUNDABOUT CENTRE'S PROJECTS AND THE MSC

The Roundabout Centre's projects which were funded by the MSC included English as a second language classes; crèches; the Interpreting Pilot Project; and the Volunteer Tutor Organization (VTO). These projects are detailed and discussed below.

The first project that the Roundabout Centre set up was concerned with the provision of classes to teach English as a second language to

Black/Minority Ethnic Women in Edinburgh. Unable to obtain main-stream local authority funding, they turned in 1976 to the MSC. A project for aid workers was funded first of all under the Job Creation Programme (JCP) and then under its successor the Special Temporary Employment Project (STEP). It should be stressed that the initial approach to the MSC met with a lack of understanding of the disadvantages arising from discrimination faced by people of minority ethnic origin.

The centre wished to set up a multi-lingual/multi-cultural crèche to assist adult minority ethnic women who were re-entering employment or training. These crèche facilities were staffed by young people from the Youth Opportunities Programme (YOP). It is clear that these early MSC schemes did allow the Roundabout Centre to get new projects estab-lished that were unavailable in mainstream service provision because of the low priority accorded to child-care provision and because of institutional racism. There were, however, major problems with these schemes as far as the centre was concerned. The YOP, which was charac-terized by extremely low pay and very poor training, was an exploitative scheme. The JCP and STEP brought with them uncertainty because of their short-term funding and were also characterized by low pay. In comparison with the succeeding schemes, however, the criteria for entry were less restrictive and therefore made it easier to recruit Black/Minority Ethnic workers. This was extremely important. Given that the project was seeking to provide fairly specialized services to Black/Minority Ethnic women, it was vital that the workers fully under-stood the experiences of Black/Minority Ethnic women and children in Scotland.

The next stage of the Roundabout Centre's involvement with the MSC was the Interpreting Pilot Project, which grew out of a concern that the right to be understood was a fundamental one and affected access to social services and health-care. Once again with local authorities facing severe cutbacks and under attack from central government the issue of numbers as an indicator of need, raised its head and long-term statutory funding was impossible to secure. The Roundabout Centre looked to the now flourishing and expanding MSC which had devised another scheme with yet another name: the Community Enterprise Programme (CEP). This had an emphasis on community benefit. The CEP showed little interest in this project, having scant local knowledge and complete ignorance of the hidden unemployment within the Black/Minority Ethnic Communities.

Several applications were submitted by Roundabout, only to be turned down by the MSC, which demonstrated a real lack of understand-ing of the needs which the centre was trying to meet. Funding was only secured after very lengthy negotiations, so long in fact that by this time the CEP had become the CP. The pilot project began in 1983 with one full-time and four part-time workers.

The CP was a more restrictive scheme than its predecessors. In particular, only claimants were eligible to participate. This quickly threw up a major problem for the Interpreting Project, because many of those with the required language skills were unemployed but were not registered for a variety of reasons. Under the new scheme, it proved impossible to persuade the MSC to waive the usual eligibility rule. (It had been possible to get such waivers under JCP and STEP.)

The Interpreting Project produced an extensive statistical report which was used to argue for the long-term statutory funded interpreting service that exists in Lothian Region today. In April 1987, after protracted negotiations, the Lothian Interpreting and Translation Trust was set up by a consortium of the Lothian Health Board, Lothian Regional Council and Edinburgh District Council. Paradoxically even a restrictive scheme like the CP, with racist eligibility criteria, nevertheless helped the centre to establish need and to convince the statutory authorities to provide resources.

As with all MSC schemes the CEP and CP made little attempt to research and obtain an accurate profile of the employment/training needs of the Black/Minority Ethnic communities. The prevailing view that unemployment is insignificant amongst these communities because of their involvement in small family businesses masks both the wide variation within the aggregated figures presented in the 1981 census and the considerable degree of hidden unemployment, which had been exacerbated by the economic recession and widespread discrimination in the job market. This hidden unemployment is not reflected in the unemployment register for a variety of reasons, including lack of information, communication difficulties, racist notions concerning the rights and the presence of Black/Minority Ethnic people and difficulties for anyone whose family has a business to prove 'the availability-for-work rule'. A case in which reluctance concerning college-based classes and the request for a job within the Punjabi-speaking community had been construed by Restart as 'being obstructive' and as 'deliberately making oneself unavailable for work' indicates the link between the MSC and the DHSS and sheds light on a more sinister aspect of the MSC.

The last two Roundabout Centre projects to be funded by the MSC were the VTO and the crèche for children of minority ethnic women. The experience of working with the MSC on these two projects shows up the contradiction between the fine intentions expressed in the equal opportunities policy and the guide-lines to sponsors and what happened in practice. The project workers felt that the workers involved in these projects must be from minority ethnic backgrounds in order to gain the confidence of women attending the centre and also to be able to provide the right services. Exemptions from the usual eligibility were applied for on these grounds and initially they were granted. However, as the implementation of the rules was further tightened, it became increasingly difficult to get waivers. The Roundabout Centre was trying to employ people who were not on the unemployment register, and this was contrary to the government's aim of only employing claimants and thus reducing the unemployment statistics. The effect of this inflexibility was that the Roundabout Centre was compelled to fit people to the MSC criteria rather than the requirements of the job.

The centre wished to include in the advertisements for its jobs the conditions that:

(a) individuals must be willing to undertake anti-racist training;

(b) knowledge of community languages was desirable;

(c) experience of working in a multi-ethnic setting was desirable. However, the Roundabout Centre was advised strongly by the MSC through the link officer against this. The Centre, therefore, removed the statements as they wished to secure funding.

The other main difficulty was the short-term nature of employment contracts. This prevented continuity in projects that depend upon a high level of staff skill and building up the clients' trust and confidence in the staff. Frequent staff turnover, which was built into and required by MSC schemes, prevented projects of this kind from being successful.

CONCLUSIONS

Throughout its involvement with the MSC the YWCA Roundabout Centre was plagued with doubt. The new economic realism of the government, with its philosophy of self-reliance, was at odds with state welfare provision. The role of the voluntary sector was consequently increasing as the state sector was cut and the scramble for money made the funding provided by the MSC more and more essential. The dilemma of using the MSC as a pump primer to secure funding elsewhere, in the knowledge that this was an instrument to cut wages both in real and social terms and which, whilst professing equal opportunities built and structured disadvantage and inequalities, was real. The compromises in going for short-term expediency against long-term considerations came to an end in 1988 with the advent of Employment Training (ET). For centre workers the bottom line had been reached, because firstly it was unacceptable to have people working simply for their benefit entitlement; and secondly the centre was not a training agency and could not meet ET requirements.

However, despite the validity of these doubts, and the objections to ET, it is important to stress that the Roundabout Centre and its workers did benefit from its involvement in MSC's programmes. No matter how bad these programmes seemed to be at the time, some important, if limited, advance was made.

It would have been unrealistic to have expected an agency such as the MSC, to succeed in combating racism, which has deep roots throughout society. On the other hand, the MSC could and should have done more to consult with Black/Minority Ethnic communities in the planning and resourcing of an employment and training strategy.

If the MSC had done this, MSC schemes would have been addressed to the real concerns of those communities, and thus the agenda would have been set for real and meaningful change.

# CHAPTER 15. EDITORS' INTRODUCTION

Of all the groups affected by MSC programmes, young people have received most attention from researchers. The focus of much of this research has been on the relationship between education and training; the placement rates of young trainees; and payment rates and conditions of work for those involved. This chapter approaches the topic from a different perspective, that is through the words and actions of the young people themselves, and illustrates how the official objectives of the MSC were experienced by the boys and girls on the scheme and the staff involved in providing their training.

The author of this chapter observed boys and girls in one Training Workshop in the YOP programme in Scotland, participating herself for five months on the training scheme. She outlines the way in which boys and girls worked out the new conditions of their lives (conditions out-with their control) in relation to the workshop. She highlights the differential experiences of the boys and girls involved and the limitations of equal opportunities policies in breaking down gender stereotypes. Finally she draws on the specific experience of the scheme in making recommendations for the future.

# 15
## YOUNG PEOPLE AND THE MSC

ANNE STAFFORD

INTRODUCTION

The effect of the Manpower Services Commission has been to alter radically the way people think about unemployment, employment, training and education. The impact of this change in thinking on young people has been particularly marked. The changes, however, have concerned more than simply attitudes. Lives have also been transformed.

Where over ten years ago, early school-leavers, with very little careers advice, tended to manœuvre their own way into the labour market (Finn, 1984), for subsequent generations of young people, MSC schemes have increasingly mediated the transition from school into (or not into) work. In its first year in Scotland, 23 000 young people passed through the Youth Opportunities Programme (YOP). (There were 162 000 in Britain.) This figure had doubled by the end of the first year. In the five years from 1978 YOP catered for 247 600 young people in Scotland. This chapter examines the complexities and implications (some of them unintended) of this.

Chapter 1 outlined how the 1970s were characterized by economic recession, a declining manufacturing base, a retreat from Keynsian economic and social policies and high levels of unemployment. Within the problem of unemployment as a whole, youth unemployment came to be seen as a matter of separate and overriding concern.

In July 1974, there were 80 000 unemployed under-20-year-olds in Britain. By July 1976 there were 390 000 (Loney, 1983, p. 27). In the five years from 1972, the number of unemployed 16- and 17-year-olds had risen by 120 per cent. Between 1966 and 1976 youth unemployment as a percentage of all unemployment had increased from 19 to 30 per cent for boys and for girls from 40 to 60 per cent (Finn, 1984, p. 5). In Scotland, in 1982 there were 50 000 16- to 18-year-olds unemployed, with a further 30 000 participating in YOP (MSC, 1983).

By the late 1970s jobs for young people were scarce. The kind of jobs available was also changing. Young workers have always been seen as recalcitrant, casual and temporary (Frith, 1980), and employers were now in a position not to employ them. From an employer's point of view, young people did not embody qualities which fitted them to current industrial needs. The Holland Report (1977) included a survey of employers' attitudes to young workers, and Simon Frith (1980) claims that about half of the employers interviewed referred to the declining calibre of new recruits. Youth unemployment continued to escalate.

Historically, young single men have always been seen as posing a potential threat to social order (Mungham, 1982). Even when employment has been high, there has been concern that the transition from school to work should be smooth. At this point it was perhaps the unprecedented number of young people making the transition from school, with only the dole to go to, that partly fuelled and partly legitimated the meteoric rise of the MSC as the main agency attempting to alleviate the problem.

In 1978, YOP, the MSC's first mass programme was introduced as a quick response to the scale and potential implications of youth unemployment, embodying, from the outset, notions about containing and disciplining young people and fitting them to employers' needs.

## THE TRAINING WORKSHOP

The problem of 'youth' was in many ways the problem of the 1980s. And, if it was a problem for policy-makers and the public, it also provided a major topic of concern for academics. It is no accident that youth schemes are the most-studied part of the MSC's work. (See Raffe, 1985, 1988; Finn, 1984, 1987, 1988; Cockburn, 1988.) These studies provide valuable insights; there are, however, some gaps. This book examines one of them. Few books have dealt comprehensively with the particular ways in which the MSC operated in Scotland. This chapter discusses the work of the MSC not at the level of policy, in a top-down approach, but from the bottom up, from the perspective of young people themselves. Rather than provide yet another comprehensive overview of all the schemes provided by the MSC for 16- and 17-year-olds, this study is concerned with what young people actually experienced.

Studies like these are important for a number of reasons. This one provides insights into what it was like to be young, unemployed and to participate in a down-market part of MSC programmes in 1980/1. And while it is impossible to generalize from one scheme to the MSC as a whole, I think this approach can afford important insights for policy-makers. My study involved mapping out the ways in which the official objectives of the MSC were experienced. I looked at the different impact of the schemes on boys and girls, at the extent to which the ideal of equal opportunity was a reality. I tried to gauge the extent to which trainees were offered real training for real jobs and how far their YOP workshop was able to facilitate their transition into the labour market.

By far the major component of YOP was Work Experience on Employers Premises (WEEP). This constituted 60 per cent of places in 1980 and 1981. The rest did some form of Project Based Work Experience (PBWE) or participated in Training Workshops.

In Britain Training Workshops made up only a very small part of YOP (3 per cent). In Scotland, however, 7 per cent of YOP trainees were in Training Workshops, with over 4 000 young people participating in such schemes in 1980/1. There were 54 Training Workshops in Scotland, and 17 000 young people went through Training Workshops in Scotland during the life of YOP (MSC, 1983). The scheme I studied, which I will call Seafield, was a Training Workshop. In general, boys learned painting and decorating skills and girls learned to knit on small knitting machines. It was a model scheme and something of an MSC showpiece. Training Workshops generally had an unofficial reputation amongst young people and employers of falling somewhere near the bottom of a hierarchy of provision. (Though some educationalists considered them good from the perspectives of 'trainee-centred learning' and 'special needs'.) The negative image of Training Workshops in general was somewhat mitigated in the case of Seafield. At least in the initial stages of its existence, it had the reputation of being able to place large numbers of its graduates in jobs. This meant that Seafield was able to attract 'quality' trainees.

In the course of my study of Seafield, I spent two and a half months with girls in their workshop and two and a half months with boys in theirs, and in each case I tried as far as possible to participate as one of them. I kept a daily diary which formed the basis of most of what has been subsequently written. To trainees I appeared as someone who was young and without authority. Most felt little urge to modify their behaviour while I was around. They also thought I was dowdy, old fashioned and naïve, but they liked me. I was seen as someone who was kind, straightforward and thoughtful.

## THE BOYS' WORKSHOP AT SEAFIELD

In Seafield there was a rigid division of labour. Girls were concentrated in one workshop, where they learned to knit. Boys learned painting and decorating skills either in the other workshop or in the local community: in local halls, schools or churches, in private homes and wherever community need existed. The decorating workshop was set up to resemble as closely as possible a commercial paintshop. It was cold, bare and filled with ladders, paint and scaffolding. On starting, boys were issued with a pair of white overalls and a scraper, the tools of the trade. They clocked in in the morning and out in the evening, and a hooter marked the beginning and the end of breaks. Most mornings a group of boys would load up the van with tools and paint and head out on a job.

One of the first things to strike a visitor to Seafield was the taken-for-granted assumption that the place worked. If it was successful, it was the paintshop that gave it its good reputation. As a visitor myself, I was shown round and was indeed impressed at boys' achievements, I saw church halls beautifully painted with high and ornate ceilings. Everywhere, boys seemed to be working on their own initiative, being productive and capable. There were many reasons for this.

## Tam's Regime

The attitude that you had to be strict to be kind pervaded the boys' workshop. It justified a regime that was at times tough and harsh and at times authoritarian. This operated in each workshop in different ways. It was in the paintshop that it was at its most stark. Order here was partly based on fear.

> *Chavvy*: Ye want tae huv' seen Tam this mornin'. We wiz a' skivvin' an' in he walks. He went completely berserk – effin' an' blindin' a' owr the place. Ah thought he wid burst an' his eyes jump oot.

Tam was head supervisor, a man in his fifties, a working-class tradesman. He had in the past trained large numbers of apprentices. He took a pride in his work and took the ideals of the MSC seriously. And out of a sense of responsibility to trainees he attempted to replicate workplace discipline here. In a world where few young people were going to be employed, he wanted to give his boys a head start. And for his own satisfaction he tried to keep the job manual and male. All of this justified a tough regime and a masculine setting for work. Apart from Tam's bad temper, which scared even the toughest of boys, he had several other means of keeping the boys in order.

Whenever new trainees arrived, they were subject to 'punishment' exercises. They were not allowed near a paintbrush for weeks. For example, when I worked in the decorating workshop, my one female companion and I spent our first few days with steel wool and scrapers, removing the paint from hundreds of doorhandles around the building. Initially, we worked furiously. Proudly, we went to tell Tam we had finished. He next suggested that we clean the paint off every window in the building. This took three days. We did not rush this job. Like boys before us, we were learning about the world of work in its formal as well as its informal aspects. Being a good worker meant looking busy, keeping out of the way and behaving as if you were skilled at the job.

If someone was caught misbehaving, they would often be sent to the 'garden' to 'pick flowers'. This was not what it seemed. The 'garden' was an overrun patch of ground at the side of the building, and the task was a euphemism too. The first task would be to pick all the 'purple flowers' (rose bay willow herb). Someone new would set about the task with a vengeance and report back.

> *Kenny*: We've picked a' the purple flowers Tam.

*Tam*: Ye've picked them? Well whit aboot the yella' yins [dandelions]? If they came back again, Tam would send them off to pick the 'green stuff' (grass).

This was a punishment exercise, a task without end; the boys hated it. Some boys had been known to spend as much as a whole week in the 'garden', looking productive but achieving nothing.

Indeed, it is difficult to think about discipline in the paintshop without thinking about analogies with the army. Order was kept in a regime partly based on fear. New recruits received the harshest of treatment and then it eased off. It was partly Tam's discipline that wrung good behaviour out of boys and which played its part in creating Seafield's image as a model scheme. It was, however, only a small part.

Somewhat surprisingly, perhaps, for all of Tam's harsh ways and boys' genuine fear of him, he was at the same time respected.

*Frankie*: Ah like Seafield. Ah've learned a lot fae Tam. He's really scarey when he's mad. An' sometimes ah think he'll land somebody wan o' these days. But if ye' dae yer work, he's fair. He makes ye' feel that yer' no' jist pissin' aboot. It's real.

Only a short time previously, these boys had been aimless schoolboys. At school they had learned subjects that were irrelevant to them, in an atmosphere that defined them as children. What they most wanted on leaving school was a real job and an adult identity. Where schools had failed, and in the absence of real jobs, working-class tradesmen in the workshop created an approximation to work which was real enough to win their good behaviour. Boys identified with the atmosphere and culture of the workshop. They clocked in and clocked out, hooters marked the beginning and end of breaks, they wore overalls and carried tools. The image of themselves they were given was one they could live with and of which they could be proud.

They took real pleasure in knowing and explaining to newcomers how to clean brushes properly, what chemicals to use, the amount of water needed to mix putty. They took enormous satisfaction from undercoating and glossing doors and windows in the right way, from decorating a room from top to bottom.

'Jobs out' were the pinnacle of achievement for boys. Loading up the van with scaffolding, paint and tools, driving off to decorate a local hall or church was the activity most liked by boys. Only a few boys went to each new job, disappointment followed for those that were left behind. And, too young to go to the pub at the end of a hard week, the boys would, on occasion, celebrate the end of the week and 'payday' by buying enormous cream cakes at the nearest baker's shop.

The success of the paintshop was about a lot more than the harshness of Tam's regime. Boys wholeheartedly grasped the work they were given, the context in which it was given and the image of themselves that resulted from this. It was the whole cultural experience of the workshop that they liked and which won their good behaviour. Boys worked hard in a formal sense but also put a lot into creating a lively and complicated culture of their own. Life in the paintshop was never dull. It is in this context that boys' real enjoyment of their work, of the skills they were learning, can be understood. Here, for Tam, the boys' good behaviour and acceptance of the scheme had not been hard to win. The importance of the provision of real and relevant skill training cannot be overestimated.

Disruption, when it happened in the paintshop, was within well-defined limits. What characterized it was that it was always hidden, separated off from supervisors and never directly confrontational. Boys could be wildly hurling putty at each other one minute and quietly painting a door the next. Walking past scaffolding was always a hazard. Someone, for example, could drop a dustsheet on you. If Tam walked in, everyone concerned would be busily trying to fold it up. Scenes of disruption transformed themselves from chaos into industry in seconds. Tam knew this went on, but it was disruption within his acceptable limits and he tolerated it.

*Jobs at the End*

The paintshop had one more thing to offer boys which ensured their acceptance of the scheme; a job at the end.

> *Tam*: Right you guys, o'er here, ah want tae talk tae ye's. Ah've jist heard that Keith [an ex-trainee] has been taken oan wi' D. . . [a local decorating firm]. He wiz started intae the second year o' his apprenticeship – no' the first year – dae ye's hear – the second year. An' ah jist want tae impress wan thing oan you guys, the reason Keith got ta'en oan wiz because o' his reference. Noo ah jist hope you guys are listenin' – it pays tae muck in – ah'm tellin' ye'.

In the first year of YOP, an estimated 80 per cent of trainees moved in to jobs. By 1981/2, this had fallen to 39 per cent. My involvement in Seafield occurred at the time when many of the boys had been able to move out of the workshop and into jobs with local firms.

When a 'good boy' neared the end of his year, typically Tam or Robbie (the supervisors) started asking around their friends and contacts in the decorating trade about vacancies. A large number of boys had found openings in this way. There were, however, increasingly fewer of them.

> *Robbie (to me)*: See that laddie there, he's an' exceptionally good laddie. Last year he'd have walked into a job. Now, there's nae jobs. But ah'll get that laddie a job if ah've tae get in the van an' take him roon' every firm masel'.

Personal contacts from the past ensured that supervisors here, heard of vacancies as soon as anyone. Boys too were familiar with local job possibilities. They knew the local firms by name, the number of trainees/apprentices they took on and when they hired them.

Ironically, Seafield's good reputation for placing boys with firms owed very little to the presence of an in-house training and personnel officer. Neither did the expanded and modernized careers service seem to be having much effect at this time. Trainees got jobs because working-class tradesmen were well placed to get them for them. What had been in the past an informal arrangement, with older men facilitating the entry of boys into the labour market, here, formed the basis of a whole new way of organizing and disciplining young people.

Male supervisors were tradesmen and working-class. They were without qualifications and sophistication. They were rough, ready and unpolished, hired on the basis of trade skills.

Boys' acceptance of the workshop was based on learning skills that were culturally relevant in a setting that was acceptable. Where genuine employment was denied them, a close approximation was set up in Seafield. It gave boys the opportunity to build an image of themselves as real men with real jobs.

### Girls in a Boys' Workplace

> Since 1975 the MSC has considered the training of women and girls to be a special priority of national importance. (MSC Youth Training Board, 1983)

*Me*: Do girls do painting too?

*Lynn (the Training Officer)*: Not really. Well actually, we do have a girl starting in the paintshop. It's our first and none of us is very keen. To tell you the truth I'm always suspicious of girls who claim they want to paint. They usually only want to do it for really flightly reasons. Anyway, there are so many boys desperate for apprenticeships that that has to be my priority. We just don't have places for girls. But this girl was so determined to paint, we decided to let her.

I started 'work' at Seafield on the same day as Jaci; we were the first two 'girls' in the paintshop. To us, as 'girls', the surroundings felt alien and offputting. And (at least initially) it was more than the surroundings that put us off. Our acceptance in the workshop passed through a number of phases. After the first day, I wanted to leave and not go back. We faced stony silence and silent hostility. The few comments that were addressed to us (by boys and staff alike) were sexist.

*Tam*: Bring yer' stuff – handbags tae fur them that has them.

Jaci had her own strategy for getting herself accepted in the workshop. She set about making herself useful in ways which were feminine.

*Jaci*: Ah'll jist finish ma tea, Tam, an' then ah'll make you wan.

Jaci swept up, made paste and slowly became indispensable, bringing to a very male environment a woman's touch. But Jaci's aspirations for herself were more than was originally apparent. Once accepted, she quickly demonstrated that she was not there for flighty reasons. She worked hard at the painting jobs she was given and did them well and meticulously. Her work was eventually recognized.

*Tam (to me)*: She's daein' well, the wee lassie. An' she can paint. Wan day she'll hae a hoose o' her ain, an' by God she'll kin dae it up.

Before long, Tam's expectations of Jaci were changing again. This time he began to see her as one of the first female apprentices to be taken on by a local decorating firm. Partly he was impressed by Jaci's hard work. He also had one eye on publicity for the workshop.

Jaci was eventually successfully integrated into the workshop. As so often happens when women try to break into male areas of work, she was seen as exceptional rather than typical. Far from really challenging gender stereotypes, the workshop was no more amenable to a girl than would have been a real workplace. But it is in this context that it becomes possible to understand why female trainees were met with hostility. The presence of girls diluted the image of the work place as male and the boys' image of themselves as real men with real jobs.

## The Boys and Sexuality

In terms of providing 'real' and 'quality' training that was relevant to trainees, Seafield went a long way towards meeting the criteria for boys. But equal opportunities criteria were not met. The workshop reinforced traditional workplace gender relations, the implications of which run very deep.

Typically, men are defined in the world as workers. If you cannot be a real worker, it seems, you cannot be a real man (Willis, 1977). Since real work was denied to the boys, they had only a tenuous hold on a masculine identity through work, and so the workshop sometimes bore less of a resemblance to a real workplace than a caricature of one. Some of the less savoury aspects of men-only workplaces were heightened, not lessened.

Male workplaces are renowned as places where women are objectified, discussed and ridiculed. And everyday chat in this one turned with monotonous regularity to discussing women as objects of sex to be used and abused. I never heard a girl referred to, except in comments about her anatomy.

Russell was in awful form one morning. It was easy to tell: he spent the morning staring at the bench, swinging back and forward in his chair, hands in pockets. He rose only to give the locker door a periodic smash. Chavvy homed immediately in on the root of the problem.

*Chavvy*: Ye' didnae score last night did ye'?

*Russell*: Na, she wiz feart her auntie wid come in.

The night before had been Russell's big night. It was widely known. Failure meant that he had to cope, not only with his own disappointment but also with the humiliation and embarrassment of facing his pals.

He did, though, manage to engender a fair amount of support, sym-

pathy and advice from his friends, who obviously identified strongly
with his predicament. Practical help took the form of finding him a
replacement. (His girlfriend had seemingly been dropped for her cow-
ardice.) Chavvy confides that his own 'burd' has a 'nice looking pal'.

*Russell*: Whit's she like?

*Chavvy*: She's dead nice lookin'.

*Russell*: Ah bit, wid you go oot wi' hur?

*Chavvy*: Aye, ah'm tellin' ye'

*Douggie*: Dinnae listen tae him, ah ken hur, she's gobbin'

*Chavvy*: Naw, she's really nice lookin'.

*Russell*: Well, tell me exactly whit she's like.

*Chavvy*: Well, she's wee, goat a nice bum.

*Russell*: Is she thin?

*Chavvy*: Aye

*Russell*: Huz she goat big tits?

*Chavvy*: Well she's goat tits. Ah'm tellin' ye, ah'd go oot wi' hur
    masel'.

*John*: Ah've been gaun' up tae S. . . . Ma' burd stays there. It's crawlin'
    wi' nice lookin' burds. Ye' kin come up there wi' me if ye' want.

In a world where there were so many hardships for these boys, the way
they lived and laughed through their difficulties was admirable. More
difficult to take was the fact that so many of the tactics they used to divert
themselves away from their difficulties and boredom were undermining,
humiliating and degrading for girls. Boys here, learned real skills and
bad gender relations.

### THE GIRLS' WORKSHOP AT SEAFIELD

If boys learned skills that were traditionally male, girls were offered a
skill that was distinctly and traditionally feminine. They learned to knit
on small knitting machines.

In this workshop too, my aim was to analyse the extent to which girls
received real skills training. I was also interested in the gender relations
of their workshop and in whether or not they were able to move on to
jobs at the end.

### Cath's Regime

*Cath (a supervisor)*: In this place, the skills they learn are more or less
    redundant. All we can give them is work discipline. If we can send
    them out of here with a reference saying they've been punctual and
    hardworking, then it's a lot. It'll help them get a job.

The girls' supervisors, like the boys', were hired on the basis of their
skill. Knitting, however, was a skill of a different type: a handicraft rather
than a male craft skill, and this had implications for the different way
girls related to their workshop.

Girls' supervisors also cared about trainees. Here, though, discipline
took on a form that was slightly different. Cath, the head supervisor in

the knitting workshop, also believed that for their own good it was important to be strict.

This is probably best illustrated. It was Cath who first told me about Tina (one of the trainees). Cath was obviously concerned about her. A lot of people did not like Tina. She was loud, noisy, aggressive and at times uncontrollable. She was from a big family and was the eldest of a lot of siblings. Her father was a drinker and the family lived in fear of him. Eventually Tina's mother had thrown him out. He still tyrannized the family and would return home periodically and beat them up.

Tina's mother was very ill. Cath had tried to persuade Tina to go with her mother to the doctor. Eventualy she did and took a morning off work to accompany her. This resulted in a long discussion between supervisors about whether or not Tina should lose a morning's 'wages'. It was decided in the end that she should. Tina was furious, feeling that the decision was not only unfair but unbelievable. She was uncontrollable in the workshop for the rest of the week.

Cath's caring attitude was mediated by the aims of the scheme. For their own good, and in the interests of their future employability, to be kind, you had first of all to be strict.

*Cath*: When I first came here I used to get really upset when girls came in and told me they were late because they'd been up all night because their mother had been getting hit or something. I used to get really upset for their mothers and be really soft. Now I'm really hard. I put trainees first and I tell them to put their jobs first. No employer would take that as an excuse for being late and I don't see how we can do it here. I make them come in here, no matter what's happening at home.

*Formal Work and Girls' Disruption*

*Tam*: Tha' lassies are really outrageous, ah'm no kiddin' ye'. Ye' walk in there an' they're cursin' an' swearin' at supervisors. Ah've heard folk swear but ah'm tellin' ye', ah never ken't women could swear like that till ah came here.

*Robbie*: Ken whit tha' lassies are up tae noo? They've spent the whole day leanin' owr the balcony spittin' oan boys.

Generally in the workshop, the girls' behaviour was held in low regard. In sharp contrast to the boys, who seemed mature and productive, girls were locked into continuous battles with supervisors. Far from resembling a real workplace, 'knitwear' most resembled a sewing class at school.

*Louise (to me)*: Dae ye' no' think this place is jist like school? Ah dae! They're oan yer backs here the whole time.

*Ally*: Ah hate this place, it's jist like school. It's too strict. An' everybody, ma uncle, ma ma, everybody gets mad when ah tell them whit ah've tae dae here fur twenty-three pounds.

Given that Cath operated a discipline structure as tight as Tam's, how are we to explain the differences between boys and girls? I introduce the discussion of girl's disruption at an early stage for good reason. It is difficult to discuss the nature of work in knitwear without discussing it in relation to the continual battle over work which raged between supervisors and girls. Where boys' disruption was separated off, girls' disruption was an integral part of most of their day.

All of the girls learned to knit on the machine, use the sewing machine to sew seams, finish garments and press them. First they knitted simple garments and then proceeded to more complex ones. Four of each type of garment had to be completed before trainees were allowed to proceed to the next. They knitted first scarves, then hats, socks and jumpers all in stripes. Then they learned to punch pattern cards and to knit patterned garments. Goods were then sold as seconds in local shops or at local craft fairs.

Confrontation with supervisors occurred throughout this process. And supervisors used many mechanisms and techniques to win the consent of girls.

Trainees were allowed to buy the first of every new garment they knitted for the price of the wool (their first scarf, their first hat and so on). As an added incentive, on this garment they were allowed to put together the choice of colours and patterns they wanted. In many ways, allowing the trainees to keep the first of everything they knitted was no loss. No matter how hard trainees tried, first garments were rarely perfect. And indeed, trainees often put a lot into learning how to knit a new type of garment when they knew it was for themselves. Without this incentive, trainees might never have learned to knit at all!

For example, when Ally came to knit her first patterned jumper, rather than knit a traditional Fair Isle, she persuaded Cath to let her knit a 'Siouxie' jumper. (She was an avid fan of Siouxie and the Banshees.) Cath spent a lot of time transferring the pattern from an album sleeve onto graph paper and then helping Ally to punch the pattern onto cards for the machine. Ally eventually knitted an impressive jumper of which she was proud. She was also a better knitter because of it. It did not always work out this way.

When Joyce knitted her first scarf for herself, she was not interested in producing a scarf that she liked, she wanted an easy life. She chose two colours (red and white) and wanted to knit broad, evenly spaced stripes (meaning fewer changes of wool). Cath objected.

*Cath*: You don't really want a red and white scarf, do you?

*Joyce*: Ah dae, honest ah dae. Ma brother supports Hearts.

*Cath*: Look Joyce, you won't learn anything like that.

There was a gap between what supervisors wanted girls to knit and what girls themselves wanted to do. Supervisors pushed girls to knit complicated garments, girls aimed to knit nothing at all.

*Margaret (a supervisor)*: Ruby, you've done one hat and scarf since last
week, it's really outrageous. Yvonne's nearly finished four jerseys.

*Ruby*: Ah huv' nut. Ah've did much mair than that. Ah jist forgot tae
pit it oan ma sheet.

*Margaret*: That's a lie. Where are they? Show me?

Supervisors struggled as much as possible to keep girls on the machines,
girls tried to make space to get off them. Machines were noisy and
solitary, they preferred to get together in collective fun. They tried to
minimize the amount of time spent on machines, to maximize the
amount of time they spent 'finishing off'. They much preferred pressing
and sewing up. Invariably girls spent more time off the machines than on
them.

Forced to work, the girls knitted jumpers with the backs at different
lengths to the fronts, the neck too small, one sleeve bigger than the
other. They walked around with half-finished jumpers on their heads,
round their waists and pulled along behind them by the arm.

*Jen*: Ah hate stripes, stripes make me dizzy.

Girls disrupted and avoided work in any way that they could. Sometimes they used tactics which were specifically feminine. Headaches,
sore stomachs and bad periods were continually used by girls to try to
win time for themselves away from knitting. Supervisors tried to prevent
this and could seem harsh in the process.

*Margaret*: I've just handed out ten aspirin this morning. It's a piece of
nonsense.

After this aspirin were sold to trainees at ten pence each! Trainees went
to incredible lengths to demonstrate they were ill. Most were expert.
They would, for example, spend time in the toilet, pressing their stom-
ach and holding their breaths, returning to the workshop looking white
and ill. Linda had looked ill all day. Cath would not believe her and
would not let her go home.

*Margaret*: I think Cath was wrong this time. I followed Linda into the
toilet at break. I saw her throw up. She didn't have time to put her
fingers down her throat or anything.

Where boys were productive and happy to produce the kind of work
supervisors wanted, girls produced very little that was usable. Where
boys had wholeheartedly grasped the work they were offered, girls
hated it. Anything they did do, had to be coaxed, cajoled and threatened
out of them.

There are then stark differences between the two workshops; it is
perhaps slightly counter-intuitive that in this setting, boys were well
behaved and girls were confrontational.

I tried to explain boys' relationship to their workshop in terms of their
desire for adult status through manual work. For girls too, the work they
were offered touched at the very heart of their image of themselves.

When boys thought of jobs, they thought of overalls, tools and manual work. Girls thought of glamour (Sherratt, 1983). What they most wanted was jobs in offices, in shops and in hairdressers. They organized their lives around images of glamour and glamorous lives. They did not find this in the formal content of work in the workshop. Girls hated what they were offered. Where machine-knitted garments can in some circumstances take on an image that is creative and fashionable, here, they represented something completely different. Knitting symbolized old women, women whose lives were over, women with boring lives stuck at home. Girls' definitions of work were utterly at odds with supervisors.

> *Ruby*: God, if any o' ma pals saw me daein' this, ah'd die. It's whit auld grannies dae.

> *Jen*: Ma da' widnae even wear wan o' these.

## No Jobs at the End of the Scheme

The total inappropriateness to girls of their training and of the skills they were offered to a large extent explained their behaviour. The worst effects of this could perhaps have been mitigated had supervisors been successful in securing them jobs at the end. However, in contrast with boys at the time, the vast majority of girls were leaving the scheme and returning to the dole. At the very least, this contributed to girls' feelings of futility and apathy in relation to the workshop. The Careers Service seemed able to do little to place girls. And supervisors had no trade contacts that were useful.

This raises questions about how working-class supervisors, with experience of work in local knitting factories would have fared in creating an atmosphere that was more relevant to girls. Since all the local knitting factories had long since closed down, it would not, however, have increased girls employability. In all the time I was in the workshop there was only one girl who moved on to a full-time place elsewhere. Ironically, that girl was Tina. Her aunt had found her a job in the local whisky bond. This also had nothing to do with the new formal structures created by the MSC, neither did it have anything to do with supervisors. It had everything to do with the informal contacts Tina had herself.

The similar cultural backgrounds of boys and their supervisors meant that boys learned relevant skills. They were well behaved and integrated. In knitwear, supervisors came from backgrounds that were culturally different. For girls, the practical skills they learned were largely irrelevant and useless in terms of local labour market requirements. Their relationship with supervisors was confrontational.

## Informal Culture and Space to relate to Boys

If girls rejected work, they did not reject the workshop completely. That they came to the workshop at all was for reasons other than work. Girls were preoccupied by the way they looked. The workshop did provide them with their major social outlet for looking glamorous. Girls organized their lives around how they looked. Many of them washed and styled their hair, often elaborately, every morning, getting up at 6.30 a.m. to do so.

Another positive feature of Seafield for girls was simply that in contrast to what were often appalling conditions at home, the workshop offered them somewhere else to go. The reality of life for most of the girls outside the workshop was at best boring. Too young yet and too poor to spend much time in pubs or discos, many of the girls spent their evenings watching television or preparing themselves and their clothes for work next morning. At worst, girls lives were depressing and often subject to violence. And where boys could often escape into some kind of street culture, apart from the workshop, girls had very little diversion from homes where there was stress, where adults were not coping, from housework, child-care and family rows.

Even if the workshop was not the kind of job they wanted, it was a 'job'. Girls aready brought to the workshop, little expectation that jobs would be anything other than boring, irrelevant and without a future. Many of them saw Seafield as a job like any other, to be put up with and tolerated. Tina, for example, had three paid jobs: two cleaning jobs and a job in the workshop. She worked fifty hours a week and earned forty pounds. Her wages went largely to her mother to help her keep house and to keep the family together.

Indeed, for a lot trainees, their 'wages' represented a lot more than pocket money. It is very difficult to view the YOP allowance as 'pin money' when, week after week, mothers would wait outside the gate on a Thursday to collect money from trainees to buy food for the family meal that evening.

For boys, the central focus of life in the workshop was work. But for girls, if work in the workshop was meaningless, they created instead a social environment away from the machines. This was perhaps the major motivation for girls being in the workshop at all. They used the space they had created to think about, talk about and relate to boys. And where boys' culture seemed harsh and brutal in relation to girls, and concerned with sex and scoring, girls fantasies were romantic. Overwhelmingly they wanted boyfriends and long-term relationships. They wanted someone to take them out, to hold hands with them in the street. They wanted to feel like they had a real boyfriend.

*Netta*: He's comin' up for me the night.

*Ruby*: He's meetin' me after work tae go roon' the shops. He's gaunnae buy me a jaiket.

Throwaway remarks like these represented, in fact, the pinnacle of achievement for girls and masked a whole hidden culture of longing and private failure. And the desperation girls felt about boys was not so much revealed in what they said about boys as in how they behaved.

*Netta*: Lena's gaun' oot wi' Gavin noo!

*Linda*: Aw naw, here we go again! He'll make mincemeat oot o' her.

*Netta*: Naw, no' Lena. She's as hard as nails.

*Linda*: She better watch hersel', he's a'ready fancied everybody here.

*Netta*: Lena's awffy, she'd gaun' oot wi' onybody.

Lena's behaviour was painfully hard to watch. Her actions seemed to arise out of desperation. In the few months I had been in the workshop, Lena had been picked up and dropped by almost all of the boys. My presence in the boys' workshop was good news for Lena.

Trish and several of the boys and I were sitting downstairs outside the paintshop waiting for the van. Lena sauntered over. Girls rarely came downstairs. I was her excuse to make the trip. She strolled past and draped herself around a pole near me. The ensuing conversation, her mannerisms and gestures were constructed for the benefit of the boys. Her neck was covered with 'lovebites'.

*Lena*: Are tha' marks still oan ma neck, Anne?

*Me*: Aye

*Lena*: That wiz some pairty. It went oan till three in the morning. Then me an' these guys drove through tae . . . It wiz barry.

*Lena*: I bagged off wi' Phil at Joyce's pairty last night.

*Me*: Phil? I thought you were after Steve?

*Lena*: So ah wiz, bit, Steve couldnae make up his mind, so ah jist bagged off wi' Phil.

Lena wanted a boyfriend. But she used dangerous tactics to get one. The way she was behaving now would certainly have implications for the rest of her life. With every new disastrous attempt to create what she desperately wanted, the possibility of getting it became ever more remote. Already she was stuck with an image of herself and a reputation she did not want. She hated herself but could see no way out of her predicament. And behind her funny, flighty manner, lurked nightmares with which she was forced to live.

*Lena*: Anne, huv' ye' ever wanted tae be deed?

*Me*: Naw, no' really.

*Lena*: Ah huv'. Ah wish a' the time ah wiz back at school.

Almost all of the girls in the workshop had suffered violence of some kind or another: from fathers, brothers, boyfriends.

*Jaci*: We wiz at this pairty last night. Ken' how ma brother's gaun' oot wi' Yvonne. Well, he calls her owr, right, an' when she went, he jist stuck oot his fist an' punched her – fur nae reason! Honest! An' she's still gaun' oot wi' him.

In their separate workshops, where boys were integrated in trying to appear like real workers, girls were irrepressible. They won space for themselves away from the constraints of formal work. But for girls, freedom was paid for at a price. They were frantic not about jobs, but about boys. In the absence of real work and of the creation of a meaningful alternative in the workshop, girls organized the space and time they won for themselves to manœuvre into situations where they could be with and find out about boys. In a world where there has been little enough alternative to marriage for women in the past, it seems that, at this point, these girls were deciding that there was almost none. Here, it seemed they were exempting themselves from the job market altogether and looking for a way out of their difficulties through boys.

Where teenage relationships have always been fraught and difficult, the prevailing conditions of life for these girls cannot have made it easier. The implications are not minor. Their increasing dependence on parents, their lack of freedom, lack of money, lack of any alternative way to leave home apart from marriage, leave girls vulnerable. It left many of these young women behaving in degrading and submissive ways in the hope of improving their lives through men. It left the reality of the relationships they were forming, less than romantic. It seems likely, that in relationships with boys, at the very least, girls will be prepared to accept less and to stay longer in relationships which are bad. These girls were often picked up, beaten up and expected to have sex, often with men a lot older than themselves. Sex was often brutal, and often ended in a physical struggle. The early sexual experience of many of these young women tended to be not only humiliating and painful but dangerous as well.

CONCLUSION

## YOP to YTS

As my study was coming to an end, YOP was being replaced by YTS. YTS was intended to be a long-term training strategy. No longer simply a short-term measure introduced to deal with the numbers of unemployed young people, it became the mechanism for delivering training and managing the transition from school to work for all 16- and 17-year-olds. YTS was introduced partly to deal with criticism of YOP. Had it been successful in solving some of the problems, its implications might have had a bearing on this study. Somewhat ironically, though, the move to YTS in the workshop could have jeopardized the basis upon which the success of the workshop was built.

As Seafield moved to fulfil the new conditions of YTS, there was a push to streamline the workshop. A trainee contract and tighter assessment were introduced and productivity sheets were brought in. A new manager was appointed whose ideas were more in line with the new vocational ideals of the MSC. Where the old manager had allowed Tam to create the feel and atmosphere of a real workplace, Frank wanted supervisors to be more like teachers, boys like students. He tried to introduce formal lessons in numeracy and literacy and was more interested in effecting a change in attitudes than in providing them with trade skills.

Frank, without understanding the basis of boys' acceptance of the workshop, tried to change it. Whether or not this would have worked with trainees or not is open to speculation. In the first instance, the changes met with resistance from supervisors.

> *Tam*: Ah've been a tradesman a' ma life. Ah've been dealin' wi' apprentices for God knows how many years, an' he thinks he can come an' tell me whit tae dae wi' ma laddies. Ah've been here longer than anybody. It'll be owr ma dead body.

Frank did in the end understand the difficulties of involving himself too much in the day to day running of the workshop and (this time) he withdrew. The paintshop was relevant to boys because of who supervisors were and what they did. It is not difficult to predict the likely effect of a move to YTS and the introduction of the ideals of the new vocationalism, with its emphasis more on changing attitudes than on the passing on of real skills. The effects may not be the ones intended.

## Implications for Change

I do not intend to spell out in a detailed way the implications for change which result from the experience in this particular workshop. For one thing, this is not straightforward. For example, from an appreciation of the culture and background of the girls, it is easy to understand their attitude towards knitting. It would be another easy step to allow girls to knit what they wanted. To do this would undoubtedly make the substance of girls' everyday existence in Seafield more meaningful. At the same time, the knitting workshop raises questions about introducing such a traditional woman's skill into their training, and a skill which would have little place in the local labour market. There are also questions which could be asked about mixed workshops, where boys and girls would have access to all the skills. The advantages and disadvantages of this are complex. A mixed workshop would have fundamental implications for the organization of the workshop and for its relevance to staff and trainees.

It is also important not to lose sight of some of the positive (if perhaps unintended) consequences of the scheme. For example, we saw how the early sexual experiences of girls was far from ideal. This has undoubtedly been true for generations of working-class girls. Here however, these new institutional arrangements meant, if nothing else, that girls' first relationships were more likely to take place in a sheltered context. Before the development of such schemes, girls were dropped into an adult world at sixteen, taking such vulnerabilities as we have seen here into the world of work. At the very least, in the workshop, girls' early sexual experiences (bad as they were) tended to be with boys their own age and not with adult men.

More generally, I would argue that for any future developments in youth training, staff training has to be a key consideration. And by staff training, I do not simply mean 'trainer training'. If equal opportunities is to be taken seriously there needs to be training here too. I would also argue that any improvement also requires that those involved in service provision receive training in and have access to information about teen-agers and about youth culture.

With regard to equal opportunities, I would argue that attempts to break down gender stereotypes by the MSC are important. Introducing a note of caution, I would also argue that too much should not be expected from such attempts. Because of the very nature of schemes like these, attempts inevitably only scratch the surface. There are a number of reasons for this. First, while schemes exist to give young people a taste of the world of work and while gender stereotypes remain unchallenged in the world of work, nothing much will change. Also, this age-group is in the process of forming gender identities which are fragile. What they most want is an adult identity and adult status. The world of work holds the promise of this, gender relations and all. At this point in their lives, asking them to reject and challenge traditional roles and relations of work is perhaps asking too much. It may be more important simply that they are given training which is relevant to them and which may afford them a point of entry into the world of work. If nothing else, this chapter re-emphasizes the importance of women's financial independence.

For a number of reasons, it is important to understand and respect youth culture. Cohen (1984, p. 126) has outlined assumptions on which YOP and YTS were based. Young people are

> ignorant of their rights and weakly motivated to defend them. They lack any kind of work experience. They have no access to useful information and advice other than that provided by official and professional experts. They have difficulty in organising their lives in a rational or satisfactory way.

This assessment belies the fact that when it came to the local job market, both boys and girls had a good knowledge of it. They were sometimes better informed about what was possible for them and had better means to achieve it than could be offered by the local careers service.

And far from being irresponsible, by the age of 16 many of the trainees, particularly the girls, already carried huge burdens of responsibility. Many had already faced poverty, homelessness, joblessness, difficult relationships, sexual abuse and domestic violence. Many were at the time playing vital and pivotal roles within their families, holding parents together, mediating (and often physically intervening) between them, caring for younger family members, cooking and cleaning and making a

valuable financial contribution. I agree with Dan Finn when he says of
young people:

> essentially they are not really in need of many of the social and life
> skills on offer from the MSC and its training programmes – of 'cop-
> ing', 'resisting provocation', 'taking orders', 'getting on with fellow
> workers' and so on – because they have already had so many of
> these experiences and learned how to cope with them competently
> and realistically. (Finn, 1984, p. 54)

They are already familiar with such things. And the new formal arrangements can undermine their competence and skills, and can negate the
knowledge which informs decisions they make about which aspects of
schemes are valid and relevant and which are not.

For anything to change means taking into account and respecting their
culture. It means taking into account the different culture and needs of
girls and boys. It means bearing closely in mind the conditions of the
local labour market and building something on the basis of that.

## The wider Social Context of Teenage Life

In this chapter I have looked at how boys and girls worked out the new
conditions of their lives in relation to the workshop. It must also be borne
in mind that the changes described here have developed hand in hand
with much wider changes in their lives. Taken together, these have
meant a declining standard of living and have affected every aspect of
their lives. There have also been declining material standards for their
families. Many of their parents were unable to provide a safety net into
which young people could fall.

In addition, the 1988 Social Security Act has effectively left 16- and
17-year-olds with no independent status at all. For those not on YTS it
leaves most of them with no entitlement to benefit. For those on YTS it
leaves them without the financial means to support themselves outside
their families. An increasing number are

> cut off from an anticipated future of leaving home, material con-
> sumption and marriage. In place of . . . a traditional passage to
> adulthood there is now a period of extended dependence on the
> state and on a sometimes unwilling family. (Finn, 1988)

Poverty and declining material standards must be the worst position of
all from which to build good quality youth training.

REFERENCES

Bates, I., et al. (1984). *Schooling for the Dole* (Macmillan).
Brown, S. (ed.). *Education in Transition* (Edinburgh: SCRE).
Cockburn, C. (1987). *Two Track Training: Sex Inequalities and the YTS*
   (Macmillan).

Cohen, P. (1984). Against the new vocationalism. In, Bates *et al.* (1984), *Schooling For the Dole*.

Cole, M., and Skelton, R. (eds.) (1980). *Blind Alley*.

Fiddy, R. (ed.) (1983). *In Place of Work: Policy and Provision for the Young Unemployed* (Falmer Press).

Finn, D. (1984). Leaving school and growing up: work experience in the juvenile labour market. In Bates *et al.* (1984), *Schooling For the Dole*.

Finn, D. (1987). *Training Without Jobs: New Deals and Broken Promises* (Macmillan).

Finn, D. (1988). Why train school leavers? In *Unemployment Bulletin* (autumn).

Frith, S. (1980). Education, training and the labour process. In, Cole and Skelton (eds.) (1980), *Blind Alley*.

Holland Report (1977). *Young people and work* (Sheffield: MSC).

Loney, M. (1983). The Youth Opportunities Programme: requiem and rebirth. In Fiddy (ed.) (1983), *In Place of Work*.

MSC (1983). Plan for Scotland 1983–87. (Sheffield).

MSC Youth Training Board (1983). Equal Opportunities for girls in the Youth Training Scheme (Sheffield).

Mungham, G. (1982). Workless youth as a moral panic. In, Rees and Atkinson (eds.) (1982), *Youth Unemployment and State Intervention*.

Raffe, D. (1985). Youth unemployment in the UK, 1979–84. Paper commissioned by the International Labour Office.

Raffe, D. (1988). Going with the grain. In, Sally Brown (ed.) (1988), *Education in Transition*.

Rees, T., and Atkinson, P. (1982). *Youth Unemployment and State Intervention* (Routledge and Kegan Paul).

Sherratt, N. (1983). Girls, jobs and glamour (*Feminist Review*, 15).

Willis, P. (1977). *Learning to Labour: How Working Class Kids get Working Class Jobs* (Saxon House).

# CHAPTER 16. EDITORS' INTRODUCTION

Most of the recent writing on the MSC concentrates on its large youth programmes and on its impact on the youth labour market. By comparison, the MSC's impact on adult unemployment and training is under-researched and little discussed. Yet arguably these aspects of the MSC were at least as important. Indeed it was the changes in MSC adult provision put forward in 1988 which ended the tripartite consensus which had sustained the MSC since 1974.

The MSC had a wide-ranging impact on adults in Scotland. Through TOPS and its successor programmes, the MSC tried to address the skill-training needs of unemployed and employed adults. The Enterprise Allowance Scheme promoted self-employment and small-business formation. The Community Programme and its predecessors provided temporary 'jobs' for the long-term unemployed. (These schemes are also discussed in Chapter 2.) Alongside the job-creation and training schemes, the MSC was also responsible, for most of its life, for the Jobcentres and the Employment Services.

This chapter summarizes and discusses the diversity of MSC provision for adults in Scotland. It should be read in conjunction with Chapters 7, 8, 12, 13 and 14.

# 16

## THE IMPACT OF THE MSC ON ADULTS IN SCOTLAND

ANGUS ERSKINE

### INTRODUCTION

This chapter examines the impact of the Manpower Services Commission on adults in Scotland. As a result of its rapid growth the MSC came to affect adults in Scotland through a wide variety of programmes. By 1986/87, provision for adults accounted for 68 per cent of the MSC's expenditure in Scotland: £21.4 million was spent on Adult Training for 42 005 adults; £4.5 million was spent on the Restart Programme, interviewing 147 564 long-term unemployed people; £133.8 million was spent providing 36 725 Community Programme places; and £16.2 million was spent on the Jobcentre Service (Manpower Services Commission, 1987). Surprisingly, the adult programmes have been the least discussed of all the MSC's activities, receiving much less attention than, for example, the Youth Training Scheme and the Technical and Vocational Education Initiative. It clearly is not possible to examine all the MSC's activities in Scotland. This chapter examines the MSC's operations in four areas: as a training agency, as a deliverer of employment services, as a response to high unemployment and finally as an organization with a strategic role in the labour market.

### THE MSC AND TRAINING

Between 1974 and 1988 Scotland and Great Britain saw unparalleled change both in the structure of the labour market and in the provision of training. For instance, in 1979, 603 900 people were employed in manufacturing in Scotland compared with 395 500 in 1987. In engineering there were 237 900 in 1979 and 156 500 in 1985 (Hansard, 1988a).

The changes meant two things. First, training in traditional skills for manufacturing industry became less needed in the short-term. Second, new skill-training needs emerged where there was employment growth. In electronics there was a net gain of 2 400 jobs between 1979 and 1987, which gave rise to new training needs. Similarly, construction and development in the North Sea created a demand for training.

The MSC, as a body charged with a remit which covered Great Britain as a whole, and with a highly centralized policy-making structure, was by and large unable to adapt its national training programmes to the great variety of needs in different regions, although there are some exceptions.

The conventional wisdom of the brand of market economics which increasingly influenced the MSC thinking after 1979 suggested that the establishment of an effective training market would ensure the satisfaction of local training needs. Local Collaborative Projects (LCPs) and Local Employer Networks were programme examples. In pursuing this analysis the MSC influenced the institutional structure of training, the Skillcentres, the further education colleges, the Industrial Training Boards (ITBs) and the Group Training Centres (GTCs). Courses had to be able to meet efficiency and quality criteria based almost solely on demand. The nature and content of training was market-determined. The result was that the weaknesses which stem from meeting the short-term needs of employers have been magnified. It was questionable whether, at a time of rapid change in the industrial structure, the sum total of short-term needs equalled the long-term needs of the economy as a whole.

The involvement of the MSC in training has been characterized by a consistent movement. Initially the MSC played a role in conjunction with the ITBs in encouraging the development of a strategic training policy. The abolition of 16 ITBs in 1982, the sharp reduction in the surviving ITB's levy powers, the decline of the Skillcentre network and the elimination of Exchequer funding for the ITBs in 1982/3 meant that training became more and more determined by immediate market needs. Those Group Training Centres and Skillcentres left operating in Scotland came to receive MSC funds on a contractor–consumer basis rather than as joint partners in a strategic plan. In 1977/8 there were 2 334 grants/awards taken up in the ITB sector as opposed to 646 in the non-ITB sector. By 1980/1, the last year in which the MSC's Annual Report makes a distinction between the two sectors, the number of grants had halved, with 1 160 grants in the ITB sector and 305 in the non-ITB sector, in part as a result of the recession.

The MSC underwent a transition to short-term training for immediate market needs. To quote the MSC's Annual Report of 1977/8: 'The training strategy during the year [1977/8], after the rapid expansion of 1973/76, was one of consolidation and adjustment to bring TOPS provision more closely in line with labour market needs' (Manpower Services Commission, 1978).

An inevitable result of this withdrawal of grants was the impact upon the training capacity, both of industry, through Group Training Centres, but also of the Skillcentres.

GTCs, which had been well stocked with advanced equipment and skilled trainers, found that relying upon short courses and the recruitment of YTS trainees to maintain their training capacity produced a deterioration in the performance of their centre.

In 1978 there were 9 Skillcentres and 3 annexes in Scotland. By 1987, there were 6 Skillcentres. The Skillcentres were reorganized in 1983 when the Skillcentre Training Agency was established as a commercial agency, operating at arm's length from the MSC and working towards full cost-recovery for its services. By 1987 operations in Scotland were expected not only to make a return on capital employed of 5 per cent, but also to make a contribution to the running of Regional and Head Office operations of 21 per cent of sales turnover.

As part of the drive for self-funding, the Skillcentres changed the nature of their courses. Traditional courses were broken down into self standing modules to allow the customer to purchase the elements required. Additionally the Mobile Instructor Service sending instructions out to employer's premises was expanded.

Consistent with government philosophy, the MSC was instrumental in an institutional shift which reduced training provision and imposed short-term market forces on a deregulated training market. But it moved even further. By 1984, following the publication of the discussion paper 'Towards an Adult Training Strategy' (ATS) in 1983, the MSC saw its role as acting 'as a catalyst for action by others'. The MSC's part had gradually changed from providing training, to responding to a training market and ultimately to marketing training.

This did not preclude the MSC's direct involvement in training. TOPS courses continued, but with a heavy emphasis on the provision of courses which met the immediate needs of the local and regional labour market. The MSC measured the success of TOPS by whether it quickly led to employment using the skills acquired during training. However, there was no attempt to measure whether the acquisition of the skill had led to employment even where the skill itself was not used nor whether or not the skill acquired was subsequently used in employment. The launching of the ATS in 1984 meant a move away from TOPS provision. Expenditure on normal provision was decreased in 1984/5 in favour of the development of pilot schemes. In the following year there was a further decrease. In 1983/4 8 250 adults completed TOPS training courses, and in 1984/5 7 900. In 1985/6, the Job Training Scheme, the successor to TOPS, had 5 112 entrants.

The MSC through the ATS began to prioritize the important role of extolling the benefits of training to industry, while shifting away from illustrating well organized quality training provision. The ATS also gave rise to a plethora of schemes, pilots and experiments. There were over 30 different schemes by 1987. Local Collaborative Projects (LCPS) were designed to bring together employers and training providers to identify and meet training needs. This programme was jointly funded by the Scottish Education Department. It offered financial support for projects initiated by groups of employers and training providers to come together at a local level. By 1986 there were eighteen small-scale LCPs in Scotland, mainly geographically based and covering a wide range of industries. The Agricultural Training Board promoted an industry wide project, and there were three large-scale projects in Dundee, Inverclyde and Glasgow.

Training Access Points (TAPS), launched in 1986, illustrated the weakness of the MSC's post-ATS approach to training. In itself the idea behind TAPS was excellent. The TAP initiative aimed to promote the take-up of education and training by improving access to information about training. Computerized information points were established where members of the public could get direct access to information about local and national education and training opportunities. However, at a time when the training infrastructure was being reduced and the sources of training for individuals and companies were drying up, TAPS' major weakness was the likelihood that users would become discouraged by the lack of suitable training opportunities displayed on the screen, opt out of the market and no longer express a demand. TAPs and LCPs presupposed the existence of a healthy range of adaptable training-providers and demand from a range of customers with money to spend on training.

Within this overall shift away from strategic training there were two exceptions which stand out: enterprise training and work preparation. In 1977/8 two courses were set up in Scotland to assist entrepreneurs to start up in business. Over the following years these courses expanded. Self-Employment Courses ran for three weeks, Small Business Courses for 8 weeks and New Enterprise Courses for 16 weeks. In 1984/5 there were 550 entrants in Scotland to these courses. In addition a Graduate Enterprise Scheme was piloted at Stirling University to encourage final year students to consider setting up their own small business.

These courses and to a small extent, the Wider Opportunities for Women (WOW) Courses, represented the only vestiges of strategic training left in the MSC's repertoire. They were strategic in the sense that they were aimed at providing training which was not just a response to a skill shortage or the need for reskilling in a particular industry. However, WOW courses, being pre-vocational, were a poor substitute for the reduction in TOPS training. The numbers involved were also very small: 400 in Scotland in 1986/7.

The development of small businesses was promoted by the government as a response to the growth in unemployment throughout the United Kingdom. The weakness of this approach, leaving aside any assessment of its merits, was that, as the only strategic training, it was severely deficient in that the economic setting for the development of small businesses clearly was extremely variable in different parts of the UK. This again demonstrates the problem of an overcentralized strategy which could not answer to local needs.

In Scotland, industrial policy was based on efforts to create a stock of modern factory buildings, through the Scottish Development Agency, and efforts to attract foreign capital to occupy them. In 1987 overseas-owned manufacturing plants represented 19 per cent of all manufacturing employment and 25 per cent of all employment in plants of 500 or more. In the Highlands and Islands the proportion reached 27 per cent (Industry Department of Scotland, 1988). At the same time, policy was moving to encourage the development of jobs, many of them low paid, part-time and low skilled in tourism and services.

1984/5 saw two other developments of significance. First, the establishment of new courses aimed at self-employment for the unemployed linked to the Enterprise Allowance Scheme, and second, pilot projects linking work preparation and training to the Community Programme. These two developments were precursors to the linking of training to the employment services, which, following Restart and the New Job Training Scheme, saw their culmination in the Employment Training scheme. This is discussed below.

The impact of MSC training policies and programmes was arguably greater on the training institutions – the direct providers, the co-ordinators and companies with training needs – than on those seeking training. The policies have been directed at the structure of training provision, imposing short-term market forces and encouraging marketing techniques rather than addressing the long-term training needs either as expressed by individuals, or as determined by analysis of the weaknesses in the labour market in Scotland. Perhaps it could be argued that the MSC helped to 'deconstruct' Scotland's vocational education infrastructure.

EMPLOYMENT SERVICES

The growth of mass unemployment was a significant feature of the changing labour market, particularly in certain areas of the country. Accompanying these high levels of unemployment was an associated growth in levels of long-term employment. High unemployment accompanied by long-term unemployment and geographical concentrations of the unemployed meant that the employment service of the MSC was operating in a very different environment from that for which it was intended. At the same time, as a British organization with consistent policies throughout Great Britain, the MSC implemented the same programmes in areas with very high unemployment as in those with low unemployment.

The forerunners of Jobcentres, Labour Exchanges, were first established in 1909 with the intention of matching vacancies to the unemployed. This essentially passive role, assisting in providing information to improve the working of the labour market, changed dramatically over the century with the linking of the payment of benefits to the condition of registration. Under the MSC's control from 1974, the employment services went through a shift in purpose.

A fundamental change for the Jobcentres came in 1982 with the ending of the condition that the unemployed register at a Jobcentre as unemployed as a condition of receiving benefit, mirroring the decision in 1914 not to insist on registration of the unemployed as a condition of benefit at Labour Exchanges because of the large numbers involved. From October 1982 registration became voluntary.

A major review during 1984/5 proposed that the service improved self-help methods for job seekers, centralized specialist services and made greater use of new technology. Both of these moves represented an attempt to cut costs and staffing at a time of rising demand for the Jobcentre services.

If the aim of the employment service was to iron out distortions in the labour market, the task was almost impossible in a labour market that simply contained too many unemployed. Between 1977 and 1983, the number of vacancies notified to the MSC employment service only increased slightly from 230 300 in 1977 to 253 099 in 1983.

Staffing reductions combined with increasing unemployment meant that the employment service had difficulty coping with their role of regulating benefits through registering the unemployed. Providing employers with an access point to advertise vacancies presupposed that at times of high unemployment, employers recruit in an open market. The evidence suggested that employers were more likely to recruit through informal networks.

There was one consistent feature of the Employment Services. It played an active role in the encouragement of the long-term unemployed back to work, first through positive help and latterly through threat to benefit. This fitted well with a range of government policies that impacted on the labour market. A succession of Employment and Social Security Acts weakened Wages Council protection, curtailed the power of the trade unions, and reduced entitlement to social security. All of which put downward pressure on wages, encouraging workers to take lower-paid jobs at a time of high unemployment.

As early as 1978, programmes were developed for the long-term unemployed. The Special Employment Needs programme was an experiment providing intensive counselling and help to the long-term unemployed. By March 1980, the Special Employment Needs experiment was dropped. The demands of registration at a time of rapidly increasing unemployment meant pressure on existing staffing and expenditure. The programme could not be accommodated, and in any case its philosophy no longer fitted the new policies coming from central government.

The Restart Programme first established on a pilot basis in 1986, linked together, in a different way, the employment services and benefits administration, and included an emphasis on 'counselling'. The threads of benefit policing, job placement and employment counselling came together with the Restart Programme. Designed in the belief that those who were long-term unemployed required special help to re-enter the labour market, the programme was flawed by a lack of suitable vacancies in the labour market. There was an over reliance on public presentation of the scheme instead of focusing resources on staff training. Restart created a direct link between the employment service and the policing of benefits through the change in the definition of availability for work. In the autumn of 1987 the Restart Programme along with the Job Centre Service and the Enterprise Allowance Scheme was transferred from the MSC to the Department of Employment; £33.5 million was removed from the MSC in Scotland's budget.

Between June 1986 and May 1988, 428 787 people in Scotland were interviewed under the Restart Programme. Of these 10 per cent were placed on the Community Programme, 10 per cent in Jobclubs, 3 per cent on the Enterprise Allowance Scheme, 12 per cent in training which included the New Job Training Scheme, 9 per cent on a Restart Course, 1 per cent in Voluntary Work and 11 per cent in jobs (Hansard, 1988c). The numbers of unemployed alone meant that even with vacancies in the labour market and trained staff implementing the programme, it could not have counselled the long-term unemployed in any really helpful way. Between April and September 1987 the MSC interviewed 128 495 people on Restart while between April and October of the same year there were only 115 112 vacancies notified (Manpower Services Commission, 1987).

The function of the Employment Service changed over the years of the MSC's existence. At first, it primarily provided information and guidance to the unemployed while policing benefit entitlement. More recently it has played an important role in disciplining the unemployed and particularly the long-term unemployed through the Restart Programme, the New Job Training Scheme and Employment Training.

SPECIAL EMPLOYMENT MEASURES

The roots of much of the MSC's operations derived from its foundation as an agency operating to counteract cyclical fluctuations in the training and labour market. Yet since 1974, the exposure of structural weaknesses in the Scottish economy tended to make counter-cyclical responses increasingly irrelevant. Temporary employment programmes or the encouragement of the filling of gaps in training provision made sense in a healthy economy faced with short-term problems. In the Scottish context, however, this approach fails to come to grips with the longer term structural problems of an economy overly dependent upon, on the one hand, declining industries, and on the other, externally controlled investment in new industries.

Special Measures to respond to unemployment grew in size late in the

MSC's development, paralleling the rise in unemployment. In the early years of the MSC, the rising levels of unemployment presented a political problem of symbolic significance for the Labour government and one which the MSC's counter-cyclical policies seemed to meet.

Labour's problem before 1979 was how to indicate a commitment to reducing unemployment at the same time as pursuing the deflationary policies that were generating unemployment. The response was largely symbolic of a will to do something. Given its different electoral base and economic interests, the high levels of unemployment during the Conservative government presented a different challenge: how to maximize the benefits of high unemployment in a process of economic restructuring. This was achieved by using high levels of unemployment to exert new disciplines on those in work, while, at the same time, minimizing the potential political consequences of these very high levels of unemployment.

The Job Creation Project was as small scale as was its successor, the Special Temporary Employment Programme (STEP). In 1979/80 4000 unemployed adults took up places on STEP in Scotland. In June 1979, there were 166 986 unemployed claimants in Scotland (2 per cent on STEP) (Manpower Services Commission, 1980; Hansard, 1988b). By December 1987 there were 30 147 filled places on the Community Programme (CP) at a time when there were 324 007 unemployed claimants (9 per cent). Even at its peak the CP catered for less than 10 per cent of its client group.

By 1988, the major role of the MSC was the administration of the CP on behalf of the Department of Employment. In Great Britain, the CP alone, in October 1987, involved more people than the combined personnel of the Army, Navy and Royal Marines and the expenditure on the programme in 1986/7 exceeded the total expenditure of the whole of the Department of Energy. In 1987/8 the estimated expenditure on the CP in Scotland was £134.9 million out of a total MSC budget in Scotland of £295.3 million.

As the MSC developed, the conditions for those on Special Measures Programmes deteriorated. STEP was designed as a small-scale scheme where work was provided for those who were unemployed. It paid "the going rate" for the job. The CP on the other hand provided largely part-time work because of the condition that was imposed on the average level of pay within a scheme, linked to the "rate for the job". Projects had to provide part-time work to keep the weekly average pay down. Over the years of the CP, the reliance on part-time work was increased because the average wage was not increased in line with inflation. Additionally the small per capita grant to schemes to provide for equipment and training meant that many projects had to seek additional funding from other sources unless they were to restrict themselves to activities where there were few capital overheads required. Given the part-time nature of the work and the low level of wages, CP schemes overall tended to recruit only those with very low levels of benefit. In Great Britain as a whole during October 1987 12 per cent of those on the CP were full-time and 41 per cent were over 25 (Hansard, 1987).

Some of the weaknesses of the CP were pointed out in a Cabinet Office paper, 'Value for Money on the Community Programme in 1985'. The paper highlighted the need to improve the quality of the programme. As with many of the MSC's programmes, however, exhortation was taken as a substitute for policy. Training linked to the CP over the years of its operations were reduced. Quality for the participants would have been produced only by a relaxation of regulations and an improvement of conditions.

Another concern reflected in the Cabinet Office paper was the lack of involvement of the private sector in the CP. The criteria of community benefit meant that projects could not be in the direct interest of a private company. In 1986, the MSC launched a controversial pilot project of private sector sponsored CP projects. The per capita fee for Managing Agencies was increased for these projects. However, the community-benefit criteria could not be easily be mixed with private-sector needs.

In part as a consequence of demographic changes, the MSC looked to a successor for CP, taking the experience of YTS into account. The fragile coalition, of, at times, conflicting interests eventually broke up with the introduction of the New Job Training Scheme (NJTS) and ultimately Employment Training (ET).

The NJTS was piloted in Dundee in 1985 and extended throughout the country in 1986. It marked a move away from what had previously been public or voluntary sector dominance in the field of special measures. It provided work experience for the long-term unemployed on employer's premises, although participants' conditions were worse than on the CP. The NJTS provided participants with their benefit plus a small top-up. Less eligibility has become the rule with the benefits of encouraging the unemployed to take low paid jobs.

The long-term unemployed provided a potentially large reserve army of very cheap labour for the private sector. The NJTS and Employment Training were attempts by the government to encourage the private sector to mobilize this potential. However, as with the case of YTS, there was a problem which illustrated a contradiction within the overall ideological direction of government policy. The long-term unemployed were portrayed as unemployed because of their personal characteristics. The message, through Ministers' statements and TV advertising was that there were jobs if the unemployed would only look for them. This message was made concrete in programmes like the Job Clubs. But if this was the case, then, not surprisingly, private employers don't want to employ them, however cheaply. Many employers indeed believed that people were unemployed because of their personal characteristics. Action for the long-term unemployed then became an adjunct to the

major commercial activities of industry, as a philanthropic activity separate from the normal recruitment and training process. I would suggest
this goes some way to explaining the reluctance of the private sector to
fulfil the government's expectations of the NJTS. The benefits of long-
term unemployment to the private sector are not in the direct recruitment of the long-term unemployed through state programmes, but
through the effect of the numbers of unemployed and the experience of
special measures on the general climate within the labour market and on
wage levels.

Special-measures programmes illustrated the government's belief that
those who were most disadvantaged in the labour market needed the
incentive of lower pay and less eligible benefit conditions. A more
effective approach to special measures would have had to tie together a
specific remit of providing individuals with experiences which sub-
stituted for work and improved employment prospects, while overall
alleviating the worst consequences of unemployment through ensuring
that training and other measures worked towards the creation of new
employment. This the MSC failed to do, although, in fairness, it would
have brought the MSC into conflict with government policy.

### THE MSC IN THE LABOUR MARKET

In Scotland the role of the MSC in relation to labour market strategy was
always somewhat confused given the, at times, conflicting responsi-
bilites of the Scottish Development Agency, Highlands and Islands
Development Board and Industry Department for Scotland in these
fields. After 1979, public policy moved sharply away from active policies
to plan industrial development. If the sum total of training and special
measures programmes indicated any strategy in relation to the labour
market, it was the expansion of the supply of a cheap, flexible, low-
skilled work force.

Alongside this there was a coherent attempt to create small businesses
and encourage self-employment. During the 1980s, the different parts of
the MSC developed programmes aimed at the creation of small businesses. In the field of training, there was the development of Enterprise
Training ranging from training on YTS through to postgraduate courses.
Amongst the Special Measures was the Enterprise Allowance Scheme
(EAS). The Employment Services played an active part in the encouragement of the unemployed in the direction of self-employment.

By and large the commitment to developing new small businesses
derived more from ideology than from any long-term assessment of
structural weaknesses. The modernization of industry and new investment in up-to-date plants, machinery and training required more than
an army of the self-employed, particularly when many of them were
driven there by necessity. No strategic attempt was made to direct small
business formation. EAS applications were not subject to any rigorous

tests of business viability. An early survey found that over one in ten of all EAS businesses were associated with car repairs or dealing and almost one in ten with general house repairs. Sixty-five per cent were in the service sector (Allen and Hunn, 1985). In May 1986 less than 4 per cent of those applying to the Enterprise Allowance Scheme in Great Britain were turned down (Finn, 1986).

Expenditure on the EAS in 1986/7 was £12.8 million in Scotland. In that year there were 8 312 entrants. Assessing the net cost of the EAS is difficult. The gross expenditure per person was relatively low: an allowance of £2 080 for the year in which they participated in the scheme. There were other hidden costs and savings associated with the scheme. There were anticipated tax revenues generated by new businesses and savings in social security payments. But there were hidden costs in the displacement effects of creating new, marginal businesses. A survey by the Small Business Research Trust (Gray and Stanworth, 1986) found that 40 per cent of participants were sure that their own business had either completely or partially displaced competitors and more than 60 per cent employed a business strategy aimed at taking away customers from their rivals.

The entrant to EAS had to be receiving benefit as unemployed for at least eight weeks and be able to invest in the form of savings or a loan guarantee in the business. These conditions meant that as a form of directed support for the establishment of new small businesses, the EAS was crude. However, from the start, it was clear that the scheme embodied two elements, an ideological belief in the virtue of small businesses and a desire to reduce the unemployment count.

In 1986 the MSC decided to encourage enterprise development through the CP and allowed applications for pilot schemes in the North-East of England and in parts of Strathclyde. The Enterprise Projects Experiment allowed projects to trade and to retain any surplus generated over the last six months of their operation with the aim of establishing a self-sustaining business enterprise. However, the rules adopted for the schemes were neither applied to local conditions, nor sufficiently flexible to allow for the easy establishment of new businesses.

Over the years the MSC's enterprise development policies have had an effect. Self-employment reached its highest level for many years following a steady growth. In June 1987 there were 174 000 self-employed people in Scotland representing 7.1 per cent of the total civilian labour force, compared with 5.3 per cent in 1979 (Hansard, 1987).

Further research is required to assess how far this growing army of the self-employed overlapped with the unemployed. Has the rise in self-employment been a product of recession or government policy? It is likely that government policies have created two types of small business. The first, the conventional small business with prospects of long-term growth given the right market conditions, and the other a new form of small business severely undercapitalized and unstable requiring few skills and providing another shade of grey in the transition from the black economy.

## THE IMPACT ON THE MSC OF UNEMPLOYED ADULTS

The final question to be answered in this chapter is what impact adults who were affected by MSC programmes had upon the MSC. And the answer is probably very little or none. As a highly centralized body, with ultimate responsibility through the Secretary of State to Parliament participants in the programmes had no formal mechanisms of representation. While individual projects may have allowed for participant input in planning and management the overall policies remained geared towards the delivery of services to a passive client group through a highly centralized bureaucratic structure. Any flexibility at local level depended on the creativity and sympathy of MSC field staff.

The MSC did operate programmes in selected areas but these were either programmes, like STEP, where eligibility was restricted to assisted areas or experiments like the piloting of Restart and the EAS. In neither case were these programmes developed in local areas in response to local needs. In the first case, it was an administrative form of rationing resources, without recognizing the different local needs in the assisted areas, and in the second case of experimentation in local areas where the MSC had the co-operation of agencies on the ground. There are also examples of programmes which were restricted to geographical areas, but which were never launched nationally. The Enterprise Projects Experiment in the CP was an example.

This inability of the MSC to develop rules for projects sensitive to local needs was symptomatic of its centralized nature. Local Area Manpower Boards had little effective influence: their role was confined to prioritizing and rationing resources. They were not given the powers to develop their own local programmes.

The MSC did co-ordinate, promote, initiate and experiment in the field of industrial training, but with its centralized structures it was unable to do so in a way which took sufficient account of local contexts except for the narrow range of variations which find some short-term market expression. National programmes were tapped into by local organizations to obtain funding. The intentions at a local level were adapted to the strictures of national policies rather than national policies creating the structure for the meeting of local needs.

## CONCLUSION

A brief overview of the MSC's operations for adults in Scotland cannot have the depth to examine practice on the ground. Consequently this overview does not discuss the best in MSC practice during the time of its existence. Nor does it deny that individual projects have achieved something over the years. Rather the focus of this chapter is on the overall policies and direction of the MSC as a major institution of Scottish government, with wide-ranging implications for Scottish society and economy. As such the conclusions are largely negative. The sum of the MSC's activities represented a major intervention in the labour market in Scotland. An intervention which reinforced rather than resolved weaknesses that already existed.

The legacy of the MSC in the field of industrial training was the imposition of short-term market forces on training institutions, forcing a change in their mode of operation and encouraging flexibility. However, this flexibility has meant a weakening in the ability of the training institutions to respond to future industrial change. Changes that could be anticipated and planned for do not express market pressures today.

Under the MSC the Employment Service became closely attached to the disciplining of the unemployed through the Restart Programme. Some of the advances made with the development of modern, shop front, accessible Jobcentres have been eroded as the unemployed were put under pressure to accept low paid work, inappropriate training or courses in motivation.

Special employment measures designed initially to ameliorate unemployment were unable to cope with the sheer size of their potential client group. A tension between quality and cost meant that for many the experience of special measures was not useful. In the last years of the MSC's operation, a belief in the virtues of small business came to dominate a great deal of its operations. This response to the changes taking place in the Scottish economy meant directing resources towards encouraging the development of small businesses and 'enterprise skills'.

The MSC was first and foremost an important instrument in national policy-making. As such it has been a very effective instrument. Each of its main areas of operations has achieved results that would have been possible only for a nationally organized agency: creating in Scotland the conditions for inward investment in manufacturing based on a source of low-skilled, flexible, cheap labour and a growing number of small businesses operating on the margins of profit in the service sector.

REFERENCES

Unless otherwise stated all statistics are from the relevant Annual Report of the MSC.

Allen, D., and Hunn, A. (1985). An evaluation of the EAS, *Employment Gazette*, August.

Finn, D. (1986). Free enterprise *Unemployment Bulletin*, 22.

Gray, C., and Stanworth, J. (1986). *Allowing for enterprise*. (Small Business Research Trust).

Hansard (1987), 4 December (c770w).

Hansard (1988a). 25 February (c283w).

Hansard (1988*b*). 25 February (c280w).
Hansard (1988*c*), 18 May (c508w).
Industry Department of Scotland (1988). *Statistical Bulletin*, A3.2 (November 1988).
MSC (1978). Annual Report 1977–8.
MSC (1980). Annual Report 1979–80.
MSC (1987). Corporate Plan for Scotland 1987–91.

# INDEX

*Note:* Page references in italics indicate tables and figures. Please refer to List of Abbreviations for abbreviations used in the index.